MILTON'S EDITORS AND COMMENTATORS FROM PATRICK HUME TO HENRY JOHN TODD (1695—1801)

A STUDY IN CRITICAL VIEWS AND METHODS

BY

ANTS ORAS

Revised Edition.

HASKELL HOUSE PUBLISHERS Ltd.
Publishers of Scarce Scholarly Books
NEW YORK, N. Y. 10012
1967

First Published 1931

HASKELL HOUSE PUBLISHERS Ltd.
Publishers of Scarce Scholarly Books
280 LAFAYETTE STREET
NEW YORK. N. Y. 10012

Library of Congress Catalog Card Number: 67-31494

Haskell House Catalogue Item # 604

New Material Copyrighted 1968 by
Haskell House Publishers, Ltd.,

Printed in the United States of America

CONTENTS.

In the present edition of this study—the third since 1931, when it first appeared—a "Postscript on Bentley's Milton" has been added, discussing some recent publications concerning the most sensational and controversial of eighteenth-century commentaries on Milton.

A POSTSCRIPT ON BENTLEY'S MILTON

Two items concerning Bentley's edition of Milton, published since 1931, when the present study originally appeared, need to be mentioned here: Miss Helen Darbishire's remarks in her paper *Milton's Paradise Lost* (Oxford, 1935) and William Empson's comments in *Some Versions of Pastoral* (London, 1935).

Miss Darbishire's observations, though excellent on Milton, and often taking Bentley for their point of departure, do not shed much new light on Bentley, except in one important respect. Her examination of Bentley's own copy of *Paradise Lost*, containing the notes he made for his edition, "reveals beyond doubt," she says, that he had seen the manuscript of Book I on which the text of Milton's own edition is based. He not only saw it "but collated it carefully . . . though he says *there was no manuscript.*" Hence, his theory concerning the meddling editor falls to the ground: Bentley was "a rogue." This, I admit, seems to settle the problem, and my own tentative arguments in favour of his having acted in good faith have, in spite of the tempting nature of the internal evidence, to be regarded as mistaken.

Miss Darbishire, the careful scholar, addresses herself to scholars. The most widely known discussion of Bentley's Milton, the chapter of Empson's book bearing the title "Milton and Bentley: The Pastoral of the Innocence of Man and Nature" (pp. 149-191), falls somewhat outside the field of scholarship, but it has attracted a good deal of attention even in scholarly circles and so must be briefly examined here for what it says in direct reference to Bentley. Empson's larger speculations concerning Milton's attitude towards the paradisial childhood of pre-Christian mankind hardly belong in the present context.

VII

Empson's remarks, considered "exceptionally suggestive" as a stylistic study by such a notable Miltonist as James Holly Hanford, still, for all their stimulating qualities, are often apt to lead the unwary reader astray. They are typically Empsonian in their combination of frequent imaginative insight with occasionally rather unbridled flights of fancy. Empson's interest in, and keen ear for, semantic overtones enable him to use Bentley as a guide to enlightening discoveries, but his impetuous ingenuity sometimes leads him close to, and even beyond, the point of absurdity. Much more imaginative than Bentley, Empson yet resembles him in the way he jumps to surprising but hardly convincing conclusions.

While admitting Bentley's blindness to many of Milton's essential qualities, Empson, not altogether unreasonably, grants him the virtue of vigorous if narrow commonsense and a flair for seizing upon problems not noticed by others. He finds him superior to his critics in the keenness with which he often spotted points of aesthetic importance, however unsatisfactory most of his answers may have been. Empson undertakes to find the right answers.

A number of these attempts seem successful, especially where Empson discovers webs of associations missed not only by Bentley but also by later commentators. Thus, when Satan's reference to his newly invented artillery as "pregnant with infernal flame" (P.L.VI.484) is bluntly ridiculed by Bentley as premature since Satan is still in heaven, Empson finds good reasons for approving it. "Infernal" is right not merely because hell has been mentioned before by the celestial combatants, as Pearce points out, but because the inflammable substance referred to actually comes "from below," in keeping with the Latin meaning of "infernus." "Pregnant" is likewise apposite, for, ironically, the weapons to secure victory for the rebels are "pregnant with more fire" than the Satanic party had planned—the flames of punishment awaiting them in hell. What to Bentley seemed inconsistency and mindless confusion is thus shown to abound in complex, apt suggestion (p.158). This is true also of Empson's explanation of the plural in "aires, vernal aires" (P.L.IV.264), attacked by Bentley as suggesting music rather than breezes. Empson's examination of the context makes clear that what is meant is both air and music—airy music (p.157).

Where Bentley finds double meanings but condemns them, Empson, as expected, sees good poetic sense in Milton's text. When Belial, wanting to avoid the risk of a new war, assures his fellow apostates that "This horror will grow milde, this darkness light" (*P.L.*II.220), Bentley takes objection to the pun in "light." Empson defends the ambiguity. The combination of two meanings here permits Belial "to suggest high hopes without obvious absurdity" (p.158).

These remarks of Empson's, along with a number of others, show him to be digging "pretty far below the surface" for half-concealed meanings, much in the manner recommended by the elder Richardson, but unmarred by Richardsonian eccentricity. His tools here are his imagination, his sensitive grasp of the complexities of language, and just about the right amount of critical caution. He is less successful where, in addition to imagination and intuition, some of the more workaday tools of scholarship would have been required for the unravelling of semantic tangles. The useful data accumulated by lexicographers, above all in the N.E.D., but also in Lockwood's Milton Lexicon, often do not seem to exist for Empson. The verb "to incarnate," for instance, according to the N.E.D., used to have several early meanings not associated with religion, one of these, "to despiritualize," recorded as late as 1684. Among the illustrations for this meaning in the N.E.D. are Satan's lines: "This essence to incarnate and imbrute, / That to the hight of Deitie aspired" (*P.L.* 166-167). Bentley, living in pre-N.E.D. days, had some excuse for his comment that Milton "would not use thus the word *Incarnate*: He knew a higher Essence, than Seraphical, was afterwards Incarnated." No such excuse holds good for Empson's somewhat too unqualified acceptance of the expression as suggesting a "curious parallel between Satan and the Christ" (p.165). A glance at the N.E.D. might have made him consider a less curious interpretation as, perhaps, more probable.

An area where Empson's usual alertness of imaginative sympathy sometimes fails him surprisingly is Milton's catalogues of proper names, both superb for their music and—nearly always—opening wide horizons of meaning to the understanding reader. He joins Bentley in his classification as "pedantry" of one of most imposing of these. On p.152 he approves of Bentley's facetious comment on the long geographical list of kingdoms in (*P.L.*XI.387-411). "Very useful," says Bentley, "if he was explaining to a young boy a Sheet-Map of the World," and Empson incautiously agrees. True, in this, one of the longest, and on the face of it barest, of his catalogues, Milton provides little help to the reader in the way of suggestive epithets or comment, but the manner in which the list moves from the far east to the extreme west, as one would imagine Adam's astonished eye to move as he is surveying the world of the future from the Top of Speculation, should have been enough to make the critic hesitate: there is dramatic value in this view of vastness and splendour, enhanced by the music of the names. But there is more in this than a mere view, however gorgeous: this view embodies an entire philosophy of history, as Robert A. Bryan's recent study "Adam's Tragic Vision in *Paradise Lost*" (*Studies in Philology*, LXII, 197-214) convincingly shows. A long tradition of the notions of *translatio imperii* and *translatio studii* is summed up in a tragically inverted form in this enumeration of great but cruel empires —a panorama of the might of evil moving from the rising sun towards sunset to engulf the world.

A greater taste for scholarly research of the conventional type would have helped Empson to discover more of the subtle complexities he loves, and in which Milton so satisfactorily abounds. Lacking this taste, he tends to create his own complications. When Milton describes Uriel as "gliding through the Eev'n / On a Sun beam," Bentley emends "Eev'n" to "Heaven" because, he says, evening is not "a Place to glide through." To Bentley's literalism "gliding through the Eev'n" is equivalent to "gliding through Six a clock." Empson does not find the passage preposterous but his justification of it is strange. Claiming to know "what was evidently in Milton's mind," he considers the angel to be choosing "a safe gradient, down a nearly even sunbeam." Such a concern for safety on an angel's part seems surprising. Besides, Milton says "through the Eev'n," not "on the Eev'n." Here Empson's ingenuity slips up as badly as Bentley's unimaginativeness (p.158).

The above example suggests a conception of Uriel, the angel, as inconveniently burdened with materiality. In other contexts, when it happens to suit him, Empson takes a different point of view. He forgets that sometimes, though not here, Milton makes his angels invest themselves with bodies not essentially differing from those of human beings. Both Bentley and Empson are dissatisfied with Milton's description of Eve's "Heavenly Forme / Angelic, but more soft and Feminine" (*P.L.*IX.-457-458). "If Eve had been more soft . . . than such were; she would have been no fit Mate for her Husband," says Bentley, thinking of the "soft etherial essence" of angels. Pearce, quite sensibly, explains the phrase as "spoken metaphorically." Empson, seconding Bentley, refuses to be "fobbed off when there are living metaphors just round the corner" (p.154). The fact that Milton's angels, when appearing to Adam and Eve, can assume sufficiently substantial bodies to partake of substantial human meals, ignored by Bentley, is quite as conveniently forgotten by Empson. The results in both cases are witticisms.

It would be useless and unfair to deny the liveliness, the stimulating quality of a good deal of Empson's discussion of Bentley, but there is little in it that could be safely accepted without very careful preliminary scrutiny. The somewhat self-consciously posturing wit in Empson too often keeps gaining the upper hand over the scholar and serious critic.

PREFATORY EXPLANATION.

Although the present study confines itself to annotated editions and independent collections of annotations on Milton's poetry, eliminating the investigation of the text, except inasmuch as seemed desirable for an examination of literary views and methods of literary criticism, the length of the work exceeds my original intentions. This is due partly to the amount of material to be dealt with, and partly to the miscellaneous character of this material, which had to be discussed in a number of sometimes almost independent subsections.

As much of the best material deals with very special points, this manner of treatment seemed advisable. Some of the commentators were mediocre theoretical thinkers but did good work in some narrow department of their own. The need of deviating into a study of these various branches of criticism has lessened the unity of the book but may have caused the discovery of some interesting matter, which I have endeavoured to relate to the general development. In certain cases, especially in the chapters on Hume, Pearce, the Richardsons and Peck, the unfamiliar nature of the matter induced me to dwell upon it at greater length and to quote more than would have been desirable in the case of less neglected writers.

I beg to acknowledge my debts of gratitude to Professor George Stuart Gordon, now President of Magdalen, Oxford, to whose advice and guidance I owe more than can be conveniently expressed here, as well as to the members of the Board of English in Oxford who instructed me in the principles and technique of literary scholarship. To the University of Tartu I am obliged for having been given the opportunity of browsing among the riches of English libraries. Mr. H. F. Brett-Smith very kindly communicated to me some unsuspected new material not otherwise accessible.

The abbreviations of the titles of Milton's poems here adopted are as follows: N. O. = "On the Morning of Christ's Nativity"; Ps. CXIV = "A Paraphrase on Psalm 114"; Ps. CXXXVI = "Psalm 136"; Pass. = "The Passion"; Time = "On Time"; Circ. = "Upon the Circumcision"; Sol. Mus. = "At a Solemn Music"; March. Win. = "An Epitaph on the Marchioness of Winchester"; M. M. = "Song on May Morning"; Shak. = "On Shakespeare"; U. C. = "On the University Carrier"; L'A. = "L'Allegro"; Il P. = "Il Penseroso"; Arc. = "Arcades"; Lyc. = "Lycidas"; Co. = "Comus"; D. F. I. = "On the Death of a Fair Infant"; Vac. Ex. = "At a Vacation Exercise"; Hor. V. = "The Fifth Ode of Horace. Lib. I."; Sonn. = "Sonnet"; El. = "Elegia"; Sylv. Lib. = "Sylvarum Liber"; In Prod. Bomb. = "In Proditionem Bombardicam"; Ob. Proc. = "In Obitum Procancellarii Medici"; V. Nov. = "In Quintum Novembris"; Praes. El. = "In Obitum Praesulis Eliensis"; Nat. n. p. sen. = "Naturam non Pati Senium"; Id. Plat. = "De Idea Platonica quemadmodum Aristoteles Intellexit"; Ad Pat. = "Ad Patrem"; Ad Sals. = "Ad Salsillum..."; Mans. = "Mansus"; Ep. Dam. = "Epitaphium Damonis"; Ad J. Rous. = "Ad Joannem Rousium..."; P. L. = "Paradise Lost"; P. R. = "Paradise Regained"; S. A. = "Samson Agonistes".

The "Dictionary of National Biography" is referred to as DNB., the "New English Dictionary" as NED.

1. INTRODUCTORY SURVEY OF THE SUBJECT.

Milton annotation is a considerable branch of English literary criticism. After the impressive start made by the first
commentary on "Paradise Lost" in 1695, and Bentley's impetuous
onslaught of 1732, the number of Milton commentators grew
continuously throughout the eighteenth century. Even if the
chance materials published in periodicals be left out of account
(and in the present inquiry they are dealt with only where special
reasons seem to make this desirable), the amount of printed
annotation on Milton's poetry is remarkably large, and more or
less faithfully reflects the general evolution of literary views and
methods. Much of the best criticism on Milton is contained in
these annotations, and the amount of valuable research to be found
in them has made them the indispensable basis of the work of
later Milton scholars. The student of Milton's literary models,
of obsolete allusions, of obscure passages and archaic expressions
in his works cannot afford to ignore the labours of Hume, Newton
and his collaborators, Warton, Todd and various others. Indeed,
the edition of the last-mentioned scholar, which includes most
of the better remarks of his predecessors, is, if used with discrimination, one of the most useful tools in the hands of the
Milton student.

The nineteenth century has been less fertile of elaborate independent annotation of Milton than the eighteenth, at any rate
if Todd be regarded as an eighteenth century commentator.
Much, or perhaps most, of his actual work was done before the
close of the century, and his variorum edition appeared almost
immediately after the new century had started, in 1801.

The rise of the idea of annotating English poets, in a manner
which had become traditional with classical scholars (who applied
it also to later Latin writers), and owing to the impulse of the
Renaissance also in the treatment of vernacular poets on the
Continent, seems to be mainly due to the endeavour to explain

obscurities of language, and especially archaic expressions. This
appears from E. K's notes on Spenser's "Shepheardes Calender" 1). This commentary is primarily a glossary, as E. K's
dedication to Gabriel Harvey emphasizes. Spenser's deliberately
archaic style had to be explained. However, the commentator
adds remarks on many other matters which he wishes to ex-
pound, sometimes stating his personal views on things without
much reference to his author, though generally keeping his text
in view. Mythological, historical, geographical and personal
allusions, literary models both classical and modern, English and
foreign, the leading ideas of the poems, points of style and even
of character are all discussed. The annotator's prefatory words
indicate that his commentary emulates the similar enterprises of
"the learned of other nations", though he does not specify which.
    Thomas Watson annotates his "Ἑκατομπαϑία" in a similar
learned fashion (1582). Thomas Speght's notes on Chaucer in
the Folio edition of 1598 2) confine themselves more rigidly, though
not exclusively, to the explanation of difficult words and phrases.
The title-page announces that they also verify Chaucer's quotations and explain other difficulties, but this is not done very
industriously. Mediæval habits, references of various kinds,
literary debts etc. are dealt with, but rather briefly and in a
primitive manner. Francis Thynne, the son of the editor of
Chaucer, William Thynne, whom Speght criticized, finds much
opportunity of expatiating on the latter's mistakes in his MS.
"Animaduersions" 3). Fr. Thynne's knowledge of philology,

---

1) The Shepheardes Calender Conteyning tvvelue Æglogues proportion-
able to the twelve monethes. Entitled TO THE NOBLE AND VERTV-
OUS Gentleman most worthy of all titles both of learning and cheualrie
M. Philip Sidney. [device] AT LONDON. Printed by Hugh Singleton,
dwelling in Creede Lane neere vnto Ludgate at the signe of the gylden
Tunne, and are there to be solde. 1579. [4°].
    2) The Workes of our Antient and Learned English Poet, GEFFREY
CHAVCER, newly Printed. In this Impression you shall find these Additions. 1 His Portraiture and Progenie shewed. 2 His Life collected. 3 Argu-
ments to euery Booke gathered. 4 Old and obscure words explaned. 5 Authors by him cited, declared. 6 Difficulties opened. 7 Two Bookes of his,
neuer before Printed. LONDON, Printed by Adam Islip, at the charges of
Bonham Norton. Anno 1598. [Motto].
    3) The title according to the edition of the Chaucer Society in 1876:
ANIMADUERSIONS vppon the Annotacions and Corrections of some

history and older poetry seems to surpass Speght's. He cites
Italian and old English writers to show that Speght had unnecessarily latinized certain forms which Chaucer seems to have
borrowed from later sources than the original classics [4]) and
explains some of the philological laws on which the Italian forms
depend. Textual criticism, the possibilities of misprinting
words [5]), metrical questions [6]) and various allusions are dealt
with. Speght was sufficiently impressed by this criticism to
renounce in his next edition (1602) all ambition of composing
a complete commentary on Chaucer, or, as he puts it, "a Coment
in our tongue, as the Italians haue *Petrarke* and others in their
language" [7]). This observation is valuable as indicating a possible source of the methods and aims of these first pioneers of
English literary annotation. Speght's own glossary in this
edition is more careful in philological matters than previously.
Etymological information is given, and supposed dialectal and
Anglo-Saxon forms are pointed out.

A different type of commentary is represented by Selden's
elaborate annotations on Drayton's "Polyolbion" [8]) (ed. 1613).
The poem itself is an encyclopædia of traditions and geographical
lore, and so, is the commentary, though literary remarks are to
be found incidentally. These notes fall outside the traditions of
orthodox literary comment, owing to the non-literary objects of
the work they deal with. The commentaries by E. K. and Francis
Speght and Francis Thynne's "Animaduersions" represent a more
normal line of development. Their main common feature is
probably the importance given to the explanation of difficulties
of vocabulary, but all three of them also deal with miscellaneous
allusions and literary parallels, classical, French, Italian and old
English poetry being taken into account. Speght and Thynne,

---

imperfections of impressiones of Chaucers workes (sett downe before tyme,
and nowe) reprinted in the yere of oure lorde 1598 sett downe by Francis
Thynne. Soortee pur bien ou ne sortee rien.

[4]) E. g. "Ca*m*paneus" according to Boccaccio, Gower and Lydgate,
instead of Speght's "Ca*p*aneus", cf. Chaucer Soc. ed. 1876, p. 43.

[5]) Ibid. p. 44.

[6]) Cf. p. 64.

[7]) Preface "To the Readers".

[8]) POLY-OLBION by Michaell Drayton Esqr: London printed for
{ M Lownes. I Browne. / I Helme. I Busbie. } Ingraûe by W. Hole. [Folio].

who, in contradistinction to E. K., treat of a poet of the past, show distinct indications of a historical point of view, studying the period of their author in order to explain him [9]).

The first commentary on Milton is far more ambitious than these attempts. Only Selden's voluminous notes may be said to resemble it in bulk. It is the collection of annotations written by "P. H. φιλοποιητής" (probably Patrick Hume) and published by Jacob Tonson in 1695. Its size shows that Milton was to be treated as a real classic, and the same intention appears from the motto on the title-page as well as from its contents [10]).

The aim of the commentary is, according to the title-page, to indicate Milton's scriptural and classical parallels, to give paraphrases of the obscurer passages and to explain difficult words, stating their etymology. The first and last objects agree with the aims of the commentators just discussed, whereas the second is apparently a concession made to the less educated part of the public. However, the annotator does much more than this. His notes on various references and allusions remind one of Selden's elaborate comments, though they hardly equal these in erudition. They are immeasurably inferior to them in information on national and modern subjects. Old English words and provincial forms are studied, but English poetry interests the commentator much less, and the author's time hardly at all. Milton's personal circumstances, the personal element in his work do not occupy the critic, but the traditional, academic aspects of his subject, its connections with classical antiquity and Scripture are minutely explored. This side of the matter is of such unusual importance, however, in Milton's case, as to make the commentary valuable in spite of its one-sided point of view.

Much of it is superfluous. It lacks discipline. But some of its critical judgements are stimulating and unconventional despite the annotator's moralistic and classicist bias. Notwithstanding its accumulation of unnecessary information, acute observation will sometimes be found combined with solid erudition. Later commentators are often greatly indebted to this work, particu-

---

[9]) As a further commentary on an English poet, Sir Francis Kinaston's notes on Chaucer's "Troilus" should be mentioned (1639), though they have not been published.

[10]) Cf. chap. 2.

larly to its collection of literary and biblical parallels. It must be added that these debts are generally insufficiently acknowledged.

Addison's Milton articles in the "Spectator" have been reprinted by many editors, sometimes (e. g. in Newton's edition) partly in the form of foot-notes to the passages to which they refer. They contain much material on individual passages and occasionally resemble a conglomeration of separate notes, but on the whole they constitute a coherent treatise, and cannot be separately discussed in the present dissertation. Their influence on Milton annotators might, however, be made the subject of a special study, and has indeed been touched upon in various parts of the present work. They seem to have encouraged the persistence of classicism in the treatment of Milton. Fenton's edition 11) contains a few notes which add little except the suggestion that the authenticity of Milton's texts is not always beyond doubt, — an idea which seems to have influenced Bentley.

The second regular commentary on Milton, that contained in Bentley's edition of "Paradise Lost" 12), published 37 years after the first collection of Milton notes, is quite different from the undisciplined, rambling, characteristically seventeenth century performance of Hume. It is very straightforward, matter-of-fact and narrow-minded, consistently keeping one definite object in view. Its aim is textual. A certain definite theory is pursued, and the explanatory matter is introduced almost exclusively for the purpose of proving the editor's freakish hypothesis that great parts of the poem are spurious or altered. The trained hand of the classical scholar is, however, almost everywhere to be felt, in spite of many crude faults of taste and pedantry.

Bentley's bold assumptions as to the spuriousness or authenticity of the various parts of Milton's text depend mainly on his literary views. He ascribes his own ideals to Milton and describes everything or nearly everything disagreeing with them

---

11) PARADISE LOST. A POEM, IN TWELVE BOOKS. THE AUTHOR JOHN MILTON. The TWELFTH EDITION. To which is prefix'd *An* ACCOUNT *of his* LIFE. [*motto*] LONDON. Printed for JACOB TONSON in the *Strand.* MDCCXXV. (12⁰: pp. XXVIII + [8] + 350 + [45]: with a portrait of Milton).

12) Cf. chap. 3.

as interpolated, or altered from the original text. To justify this, he is forced to formulate his views on many aspects of Milton's poetry, thus affording definite starting-points of discussion as well as opportunities to his opponents. Bentley's vigorous though one-sided logic and his methodical consistency stimulated Milton research, even though his classicism was pedantic and his sensitiveness to poetry severely limited. Knowing little of older English language and literature, he lacked the necessary perspective and judged Milton according to contemporary standards. By his energetic defence of the classicist standpoint he inaugurated the debate on the classicist features in Milton and those elements in him which partake of the freedom of the Elizabethan spirit and prefigure the Romantic Revival. Bentley's philological training caused him to devote particular attention to Milton's style, of course from his own peculiar point of view.

Of the indignant or facetious replies to this edition the best, because the most serious and restrained, was Pearce's ''Review of the Text of the Twelve Books of Paradise Lost'' (1732). It uses Bentley's methods of textual criticism against himself, showing that what he regarded as spurious must be genuine. Pearce's solid training in scholarship, his cautious, balanced manner, his greater familiarity with the style of older English poetry and evidently also of Milton's own works, his obvious recognition of the fact that an author has to be judged according to what he really is and that imposing one's own standards is a dangerous practice in textual criticism, enable him to refute most of Bentley's attacks and to achieve considerable positive results of his own. He is very conscientious in going through Milton's grammar, his vocabulary and phraseology, in looking for parallels to phenomena denounced by Bentley as non-Miltonic, and in investigating the poet's sources where his main object requires it. Owing to his understanding of the poetic mind and his awareness that Milton's time was rather different from the 18th century, he is able to do justice to many unnoticed features of the poet's art. His book establishes a fairly safe scholarly method of investigating the characteristics of Milton's poetry. Purely æsthetic judgements occur relatively seldom, but Pearce shows how honest, straightforward research may attain to very valuable results in removing the obstacles to a full understanding of Milton's text. Without his work, Bentley's prejudices might have taken a firmer hold of Milton criticism and research.

The two Richardsons, father and son, who are the next to appear upon the field, preferred a freer kind of procedure. Theirs is the point of view of the enthusiastic common reader, not that of the erudite scholar, though the younger Richardson supplies a number of classical parallels and references to classical subjects, and though they discuss questions of style, and try to elucidate obscure passages, allusions, etc. Their information is by no means always reliable. Yet a certain shrewdness and insight appear in many of their notes, and their thought, though undisciplined, is at times vigorous. Their main contribution to Milton annotation is their consciousness that things of the spirit have to be discerned spiritually. The elder Richardson's introductory matter deals at some length with Milton's personality and with the peculiarities of his literary manner, urging the reader to try to attain to the poet's level instead of cavilling at him because he does not descend to the standards of his public. The extravagant, unusual, ecstatic style of the father is in keeping with his appreciation of originality. "Irregularities" are often not merely acknowledged but even highly valued, so long as they add to the impressiveness of the work. The classicist narrowness which sometimes seemed to beset even Pearce disappears. The training as painters of both father and son enables them to study the visual qualities of Milton's descriptions, and a considerable sensitiveness to acoustic impressions helps the elder of the two to discern the phonetic character of some of Milton's spellings and to perceive the charm of the intricate texture of his blank verse. Many subtle features are noticed, though in terms sometimes rather vague and unguarded. The Richardsons are the impressionists among the commentators on Milton.

Bentley altered what he did not understand. The Richardsons, on the other hand, were more particularly attracted by what appeared to be out-of-the-way and quaint, thinking it a critic's duty to delve into the hidden quarries of his author's mind. Their main fault is their lack of method, which compels one to study their speculations and guesswork with considerable reserve.

Peck's "New Memoirs... of Milton" (1740) is likewise a work showing more enthusiasm, zeal and occasional insight than method. It is a medley which defies all definition, but it contains some valuable material and affords some new starting-points. Only a part of the volume is occupied by Peck's commentary on Miltonic passages; the rest is largely a collection of miscellaneous material on Milton, Shakespeare and others.

The origin of the work partly explains its character. It is essentially a selection of what Peck happened to collect while trying to prove Milton's authorship of an English version of George Buchanan's Latin play "Baptistes". To defend his case, he studied Milton and other authors, making notes on the principal works of the poet. This is apparently the reason why his comments deal also with "Paradise Regained", "Samson Agonistes", and some of the minor poems, instead of being confined to "Paradise Lost" as was then the fashion.

These notes lack solid method, but show a keen interest in many things, especially in the mediæval and modern background of Milton's poetry, and most of all in its national setting. Ballads, folklore, obsolete English writers, rabbinical lore, Spanish and Italian novels and pamphlets, popular customs, court life, all have their attractions for Peck, and are referred to repeatedly in order to illustrate Milton. His spirit is more democratic than that of any of his predecessors except the Richardsons. He studies the intimate life and views of the common people as well as of the gentlefolk of his own country, and likes to quote poetic sources, especially Shakespeare, in order to describe life in the times previous to, or coeval with, Milton. In this respect he is a precursor of those eager antiquaries who performed the task of studying in detail the setting of Milton's and Shakespeare's poetry. Thomas Warton's inquiries into the aspects of life and letters which influenced Milton in many ways follow the same method, though in a far more finished style.

There is a strong experimental vein in Peck. He ventures on various critical enterprises. Having seen the Cambridge MS. of Milton's early poems, he tries to analyse the corrections in his text. The schemes of tragedies in this MS. cause him to recast parts of "Paradise Lost" into the dramatic shape which he regards as their original form. The poetic parts in Milton's prose-works lead him to conclusions as to the poet's method of composition, conclusions which seem to be wrong, but which show some insight into the possibilities and processes of literary workmanship. The evidence of Milton's interest in music induces him to study the rhyming scheme of "Lycidas" from a purely musical point of view, and to explain its seeming anarchy on the analogy of musical composition with its distribution of bars and its admixture of discords.

Peck does a good deal of bibliographical and purely antiquarian work which does not concern us here. More important from our point of view is his chapter on Milton's style — an attempt, however imperfect, to systematize Milton's peculiarities of language. It is marred by his lack of grip in welding together the chance materials collected mainly from other critics. Nevertheless, the free character of Milton's style is recognized, and efforts are made to trace his phonetic devices. Peck, with all his weaknesses, at least gives some idea of the variety of problems to be dealt with.

His blunders of ignorance and the deficiencies of his taste led several critics, Newton among them, to treat him with contempt. But though he lacks the scholarly neatness of many of his contemporaries, his natural inquisitiveness and unconventionality enable him to notice new fields of research ignored by the more academic students of that period.

Philological pedantry is one of the principal characteristics of James Paterson's commentary (1744), a work explaining the simplest metaphors and at the same time indulging in elaborate and unpractical etymological inquiries. Paterson collects much superfluous miscellaneous material, his æsthetic remarks are trite and general, yet his study of the words which he believes Milton to have introduced seems to be based on careful observation, as a comparison with the "New English Dictionary" appears to show.

Another popularizing work which appeared a little later, the prose paraphrase of "Paradise Lost", "The State of Innocence" — which according to its title-page contains notes by the French academician Dupré de St. Maur, or "Raymond de St. Maur", — is apparently a work by the same pen. Most of the historical, geographical and other explanatory notes, except those of a preeminently philological kind, are retained. The typically English-looking matter of many of these remarks makes it doubtful whether there is much French influence in them, though this point wants some study in French libraries. These two commentaries contain more mediæval and national matter than the majority of their predecessors, with the signal exception of Peck's volume, though their notes rarely refer to literary problems. Both works suggest that the less educated public began to feel a serious need for help towards a better understanding of Milton. The comparatively numerous editions of the prose-adaptation indicate that it met a genuine demand.

The few notes in Hawkey's edition of "Paradise Lost" (1747) deal mainly with textual problems, but touch also on artistic questions. The poet's right to be original is recognized, and some care is shown in tracing his peculiarities of language where the textual problems make this necessary.

Bishop Newton's large variorum edition was the first attempt to collect all the valuable work done in Milton annotation for more than fifty years, and it remained the most conspicuous event in Milton scholarship for a long time. This was not because of any unusual originality or profoundness in the editor, but because he had collected a vast amount of solid material in a relatively neat and accessible form. It is a remarkable attempt to organize scholarship, as the numerous contributions to this edition by other critics prove.

Newton confesses in his preface his indebtedness to Pearce, whose conscientious scholarship seems to have influenced the character of the work. The commentary contains the majority of the better remarks of Newton's predecessors, either in full with their names, or in an abridged and adapted form in Newton's own notes. Extracts from various critical works, and a number of MS. contributions add to the bulk and often also to the value of the edition. Addison's essays are reprinted. A life of Milton is the main original performance of Newton included in the edition beside his notes. "Paradise Regained", "Samson Agonistes" and the minor poems are edited with less care and thoroughness, mainly, no doubt, because Newton's predecessors had chiefly confined themselves to „Paradise Lost", so that less preliminary work had been done on the rest of Milton's productions. But probably, also, the lyrical pieces corresponded less with Newton's taste and the character of his erudition, which were both of the traditional classicist stamp.

The work is mainly of a retrospective character. Newton hardly introduces any very new methods or does much pioneer-work, but is chiefly occupied in sifting what had been done before him. The preface to the edition of "Paradise Lost" states his main intentions: to ascertain the genuine text (the emphasis laid on this point seems to indicate Newton's honest endeavour to find out the truth about his subject), to explain Milton's meaning and artistic import, to study his language and verse, and to point out his imitations and allusions. None of these ideas are new, and in his handling of them, also, Newton remains more or less in the old track. This prefatory description does not, however, include all that Newton did. He tried to trace the personal elements in Milton's poetry, to identify his references to contemporary and ancient events and names, etc. Yet often he uses the material of other critics without making any acknowledgement, and in certain departments, in that of metrics, for example, his seemingly new views (e. g. his insistence on the importance of the varying distribution of Milton's pauses) are clearly borrowed, often without much skill. Newton's inability to distinguish between the principles of accentuated and quantitative verse seems to have been radical, and is responsible for worse blunders than any committed by Bentley [13]).

Newton's comparisons of passages from the different works of Milton are relatively numerous, and show an assiduous study of the poet. His knowledge of the "Gothic libraries", on the other hand, is not very considerable, as Warton emphasizes in the preface to his edition of the Minor Poems. Newton's treatment of Milton's language shows some diligence, but does not do justice to the archaic elements of his style, more particularly to those of national origin. Milton's art is interpreted in a one-sided manner, theological and classical prejudices preventing Newton from reaching a full appreciation. Even the "romantic" vocabulary of Milton is attacked. The inveteracy of Newton's preconceptions is illustrated by the fact that even the derivation of forms of words from the Italian and French is condemned. He substitutes Latin forms, because these have the right of seniority, whereas the later forms are "copies" [14]).

Purely formal matters are dealt with more successfully than those which require emotional sympathy. A notable exception

---

[13]) Cf. chap. 9, sec. J.
[14]) Cf. P. L. V. 399, "perfect" for "perfet".

is his treatment of "Samson Agonistes", where the echo of the author's personal experience impresses the editor so deeply that he for once abandons his formalistic attitude and even asks for a directer expression of feeling. As a rule, poetry with Newton is a means merely of pleasure and instruction.

Among Newton's contributors, Thyer and Warburton deserve particular attention. Warburton's study of Shakespeare and his time seems to have deepened his understanding of the imagination. Thyer's theoretical statements still remind one, sometimes, of the moralism and didacticism of the classicist school, but his knowledge of the Elizabethans and Italians appears to have sharpened his sensitiveness. He analyses subtle moods, and apparently holds that not adherence to the rules but the impression produced on the reader's mind is important. The garrulity of the Italians is condemned by him as deadening the imagination, yet for the very same reason extreme formalism and rigidity are also objected to. The irregularities of Milton's lyrical poetry find due appreciation from Thyer where they enhance the effect. His criticism of "Paradise Regained" shows the delight he takes in impulsive, spontaneous outpourings of beautiful imagery.

Newton's edition imitates the thorough manner of the variorum editions of *classical* authors, as his preface states at the very start. Its scope and careful execution seem to have silenced competition for a very considerable time, until Warton's edition of the Minor Poems appeared. Most of the commentaries published in the interim are of a popularizing character, and testify to the interest which the larger public took in the poet's works. Only Callander's edition of the first book of "Paradise Lost" (the only part published) is more ambitious. But despite the learning and culture displayed there, and the editor's knowledge of ancient and mediæval mythological lore, the work fails to be of much service because relatively little of all that erudition is applied to the elucidation of Milton's text. Callander's plagiarisms from Hume, which cannot be denied, are hardly worse than Newton's borrowings from other annotators and critics.

The popularizing edition of Marchant (1751) mainly reprints older notes, though some few items are added. Massey's and Dodd's commentaries are designed for an unpretentious public. The latter particularly is very primitive. Massey's knowledge

of the older language is very defective, and his literary principles
tend to the theories of classicism: but his instinctive judgements
clash with his theoretical views, as he himself confesses. Spenser is his favourite poet, and the splendours of the imagination
are his delight in literature. Of Buchanan's and Wesley's editions
little need be said. Buchanan's paraphrases and expositions of
linguistic difficulties are frankly pedagogic and meant for young
readers. Wesley's simplified and abridged edition of "Paradise
Lost" 15) contains only some very rudimentary notes, and keeps
the least fastidious literary public in view. The period from
1749 to 1785, which includes these commentaries, added few
scholarly annotations, and little of original value in criticism.

A great impulse was given to the scholarly study of Milton
by Thomas Warton, when he published in 1785 his edition of
Milton's Minor Poems. Both as a critical performance and as a
collection of material it stands supreme among the Milton commentaries of the century. Even Newton with all his collaborators,
and Todd in his edition of "Comus", together, added much less
that is really new. Warton also had some contributors, but his
commentary is no collection of *notæ variorum*. His erudition
and critical insight, combined with his literary skill, enable him
to open new prospects and to interest the reader.

Warton accomplishes, in fact, what Peck vaguely designed.
Milton's poetry is explored from many points of view. Warton's
historical sense helps him to understand the subtle influences of
Milton's time on his writings; his inquiries in this department
are of a very extensive and deliberate kind. His preface describes how he felt it to be his duty to exploit the black-letter libraries
which Newton avoided, and to indulge in "the idler tracks of
reading". He knows that Milton is "an old English poet" in his
earlier pieces, and accordingly treats him in connection with the
literature of his age. Obscure poets are carefully studied, obsolete documents examined, superstitions and popular tales collected, romances and fabulous narrations diligently perused. Milton's personal circumstances and the contemporary allusions in
his poems are traced with an unprecedented minuteness. His
peculiarities of language, imagery and thought (the last-mentioned,
however, least of the three) are studied throughout his poetry

15) Cf. chap. 10.

and prose, with abundant supplementary illustrations from other writers.

The literatures of the Latin countries and of the classical nations are familiar to Warton, as his notes on Milton's Latin and Italian poems prove. The life of the upper and the lower classes, the traditions, habits and linguistic peculiarities of town and country seem to be equally well known to him. His information is far wider and more many-sided than Peck's, who nevertheless is the only one among Warton's predecessors who in any considerable degree shares this variety of interests.

Yet Warton's designs are not merely those of a scholar. He is also a literary propagandist and a herald of definite poetical ideals. "To illustrate or vindicate his [= Milton's] beauties" (preface, p. XIX) is one of his main aims, and the very first page of his preface shows his antagonism to the artificial poetical atmosphere of his period. His remarkable sensitiveness to poetical impressions helps him to discern the fundamental mood of the poet as revealed in irregularities and abnormalities of style and structure, and induces him to look first of all for the mental basis of a work of art before judging of the right or wrong of the artistic devices found in it. He knows that artistic objects are valuable only so far as they impress the mind, thus explaining some important poetic effects, and proclaims the justification of the poetry of vague but effective suggestion. Moralism, theological preconceptions, and the dogma of the rules have almost entirely disappeared from his critical code.

Warton's edition realized in a remarkable degree for Milton what Shakespeare scholarship had already accomplished, and in some respects with more instinctive insight and literary skill. The minute inquiries into Elizabethan literature and lore found, for example, in Steevens's contributions to the First Variorum do not convey the same feeling of atmosphere, and deal less with distinctly artistic qualities than Warton's remarks. How much he impressed some of his contemporaries, is shown by the *Critical Review* of May 1785 (pp. 321—328) where a eulogy of Warton's edition is published. He is found to have "raised a durable monument, on which his name will appear, though in a different department, with a splendor little inferior to Milton's."

Of the subsequent commentaries on Milton, those by Dunster and Todd bear witness to Warton's influence. The slight attempt by Gillies and the notes by David Steele [16]) are one-sided and insignificant, and fall outside the scope of Warton's work. Capel Lofft's unfinished, or rather hardly begun, edition of "Paradise Lost" has its own quite special aims (1792). Lofft specializes in the phonetic aspect of poetry, partly under the influence of his uncle, the Shakespeare scholar Edward Capel, of various theorists like J. Walker, the author of the "Rhetorical Grammar" (1785), and probably also of the elder Richardson. Milton's spellings are analysed for their phonetic value; his rhythm and intonation are studied. But the editor seems to put too much of his own personal interpretation into the elaborate system of punctuation adopted by him to convey the refinements of Milton's verse.

Dunster's edition of "Paradise Regained" (1795), the first really careful edition of this poem, was designed to vindicate its beauties [17]), and succeeds in giving a far more adequate explanation of Milton's references to classical and biblical lore than is to be found in Newton. It contains numerous literary parallels, not infrequently from modern poets, but more often from the ancients, explains Milton's language, though not so copiously as Warton, traces parallel passages in his own works, expounds his artistic effects and sometimes also the relationship between his personal life and his poetry, and generally combines wide learning with a keen poetical sensibility. Dunster is a less eager student of romantic literature than Warton, but his classical and theological tendencies agree with the character of the poem edited by him.

His combinative logical faculty helps him to give some good analyses of structural features. Though his poetical theory still contains some traces of moralism and a somewhat one-sided intellectualism, this hardly affects his critical practice. Warton's influence seems to be observable in the numerous literary parallels, in the diligent study of the background of the poem, and possibly also in the distinct literary quality of the notes; but Dunster is somewhat less skilled in tracing Milton's personal moods. Dunster's preface intimates that he was conscious of performing a task which it would have been the duty of Warton to undertake, had he not died.

---

[16]) Cf. chap. 12 sec. A.
[17]) Cf. chap. 12 sec. C.

Most of the valuable work in Milton annotation done in the course of the century is included in Todd's edition of Milton's Poetical Works (I. ed. 1801). As a preliminary instalment, "Comus" was published in 1798. The preface to this first attempt emphasizes the importance of the scholarly care of Newton and particularly of Warton, and the attention which the latter especially gave to the study of seeming eccentricities of language and style in Milton. Todd finds these peculiarities venerable and significant, and devotes some space to the discussion of the spellings of Milton, in which, like Lofft, whom he names, he sees the author's peculiar phonetic intentions. He deals in the same preface with the influence of considerations of rhyme on Milton's orthography. It is evident that a scholar with a very considerable knowledge of older literature is taking up the work of Warton. The edition of "Comus" already aims at embodying the remarks of earlier annotators in the manner of Newton's edition, but it is mainly based on Warton's notes, which are fairly fully reprinted. The personal allusions, the history of the performance of the play, the personalities of its actors, its sources etc., are examined with a minuteness which often greatly exceeds that of Warton, though Warton's critical acuteness is looked for in vain. Detailed, careful research, supported by much erudition, is the principal feature of Todd's observations. His textual and bibliographical labours are painstaking.

All these qualities distinguish, also, his great edition of the Poetical Works. A large life, for long the standard work on its subject, contributions to the commentary by a number of collaborators (among whom Dunster is conspicuous), extracts from most of the more important critical works dealing with Milton, reprints of articles by Addison and others, textual and bibliographical appendices etc. make this edition a veritable Milton encyclopædia. Todd's own contributions towards the elucidation of allusions, literary, personal, historical, mythological, of Milton's language, his numerous Miltonic parallels, his illustrative quotations from miscellaneous publications of the author's time, show a zeal equal to that of Warton, and a care superior to his, but Warton's keen spirit is missing. Todd prefers quoting other critics to advancing views of his own. His possibly too numerous parallels and illustrations from classical, older English, rabbinical, Italian, French and other sources are relatively seldom accompanied by explanatory remarks. The work impresses one as pre-eminently a collection of rather carefully verified material. By the application of the old methods of research and by the preservation and systematic arrangement of the work of his predecessors Todd supplied the new century with a treasury of information, which the forthcoming generations might use according to their own methods. What his edition proves to have been the most fruitful object of his own labours as well as of the efforts of most of the leading commentators of the 18th century, is the establishment of a conscientious historical method of investigation.

2. PATRICK HUME'S COMMENTARY ON "PARADISE LOST"

Hume's commentary was published in 1695 in folio together with Jacob Tonson's folio edition of that year. The title-page is as follows:

> ANNOTATIONS ON MILTON's Paradise Lost. WHEREIN The Texts of Sacred Writ relating to the POEM, are Quoted; The Parallel Places and Imitations of the most Excellent *Homer* and *Virgil*, Cited and Compared; All the Obscure Parts render'd in Phrases more Familiar; The Old and Obsolete Words, with their Originals, Explain'd and made Easie to the *English* Reader. By *P. H.* φιλοποιήτης. *Uni, cedit* MILTONUS, *Homero Propter Mille annos.* Juv. VII. 38. LONDON, Printed for *Jacob Tonson,* at the *Judges Head* near the *Inner-Temple-Gate* in *Fleet-street,* MDCXCV.

The commentary contains a title-page and 321 pages of text. The title-page, as was pointed out in the introductory survey, shows the main objects of Hume's [18]) notes: 1) the study of Milton's biblical allusions; 2) the examination of his reminiscences of the classics; 3) the simpler rendering of difficult passages, and 4) an inquiry into the obsolete expressions in Milton.

The first object has been carried out with remarkable thoroughness and very considerable success. The later commentators had only to fill in, in this respect, the relatively slight gaps he left. Even such a systematic worker as Newton seems to have added here less than he has borrowed from Hume, in spite of his scanty and grudging acknowledgements [19]): Hume's knowledge

---

[18]) Though the DNB. and its sources ascribe the commentary to Patrick Hume, no definite evidence is given, nor is it made clear who he was.

[19]) A study of Hume's and Newton's notes to the first 500 lines of book I of P. L. would show that more than half the biblical references of Newton are already found in Hume's comments.

of Hebrew helps him to discover the reason of some of Milton's deviations from the established text of the Scriptures. He also adds a number of interesting illustrations from biblical lore and Scripture exegesis.

The treatment of Milton's relation to the classics shows wide reading and great industry. Although the additions which later commentators have made are perhaps a little more considerable in this department, Hume's commentary even in this field has been a valuable and usually unacknowledged treasury from which subsequent generations have borrowed freely. His title-page mentions only Homer and Virgil, but his notes are concerned with a great number of other classical authors, and, what is even more remarkable, with Tasso and Spenser. He analyses his parallels very briefly if at all, so that his work in this department is mainly to be valued as a collection of material.

This applies, indeed, to his whole study of allusions, which is not confined to the Bible and to literature proper, but extends over history, geography, astronomy, chemistry, alchemy etc. etc. Details are usually heaped on details without any close connection with the context in Milton. Hume seems to be pouring out the superabundance of his knowledge on the reader, and to be giving him a course in general education.

Hume's renderings of Milton's text are obviously meant for readers of very inconsiderable learning. Few lines escape paraphrase; it would at times be possible to get a continuous text merely by cancelling the intermediate paraphrastic comment. Hume no doubt was partly carried away by his enthusiasm, and could not resist the temptation to reshape Milton after his own fashion.

The last object named in the title-page, the explanation of obsolete words, bulks disproportionately, and becomes almost the main feature of the work. Many useful observations are made, but too often Hume becomes a copyist of lexicons or a linguistic theorist, and fails to remember that his original aim was to help the public towards a better understanding of Milton. The simplest words are etymologically dissected, sometimes successfully, sometimes not. Elucidations of Milton's ways of coining words or of contrasting them with the ordinary speech of the time are comparatively rare. Hume's knowledge of Greek and Latin, however, instinctively helps him to discover the meaning of many of Milton's more difficult Græcisms and Latinisms. Here and there he even notices some Hebraisms, etc.

In all these respects Hume became a quarry for future annotators of Milton. His accumulation of material was too vast to be neglected. What is too often absent in Hume is a direct interest in the poet himself. He gives no biographical information about Milton, but confines himself to a study of the work considered quite apart from the writer's personality. Milton is already a classic, and "Paradise Lost" an engine of edification and instruction. Hume especially dwells on the moral importance of Milton's epic, very much as a commentator on the Bible tries to bring home the rules of conduct deducible from the stories of Scripture.

From the mass of Hume's commentary a number of remarks may be extracted which illustrate his views on some of the most important problems of Milton criticism. The following is largely an attempt to summarize them, perhaps at greater length than would have been advisable if Hume had not been the first commentator of Milton, and the first person also who tried to deal with a great English poet in the thorough manner of classical philology.

A. GENERAL NOTES, RANGE OF GENERAL ERUDITION.

Hume's reading in the field of biblical exegesis seems to have been considerable. The fathers of the church, especially St. Augustine, are alluded to very frequently as in I. 46 *n.*, but Hume has also studied the Cabbala [20]) or some exposition of it. He explains the word "Manna" according to the Talmud [21]). Moses Barcephas is his authority on the question why Satan entered into the serpent [22]). Joh. Malala supplies him with the explanation of the origin of the name of Jehovah [23]), etc. etc. An enumeration of the books or even of the authors he seems to have consulted on biblical questions would lead too far. It may suffice to point out that I. 17 *n.*, dealing with the meaning of Gen. I. 12: "the spirit of God moved upon the waters", refers to the

---

[20]) Cf. I. 386 *n.*
[21]) II. 113 *n.*
[22]) I. 34 *n.*
[23]) I. 386 *n.*

teachings of St. Jerome, St. Basil, Theodoret, Athanasius, Tertullian, St. Chrysostom, Hermogenes, Cajetan, Zoroaster, Heraclitus, Orpheus, the Platonists and Pythagoreans, and Virgil. Theorizing seems to be indulged in for its own sake. Sometimes its application to Milton's text is more tangible. Hume notes [24]) Milton's deviation from the ordinary, literal interpretation of Gen. 10. 9 "A mighty hunter", and points out that in Milton it probably means a hunter of men as well as of animals, hunting of animals being understood only as a preparation for manslaughter. The next note (on XII. 34) continues the idea and explains Milton's conception of the words "before the Lord" (from the same passage of Genesis) in accordance with the opinion of those Bible commentators who regard the expression as a hint at Nimrod's objectionable ambition and haughtiness. Newton's notes on the same passage, which go a step further and study the possible political allusions implied in these lines, are entirely based on Hume's preliminary inferences, although Newton, as usual, makes no acknowledgement of his debt. This is a typical example of Hume's contributions to the study of hidden references in Milton, and of later indebtedness to his work.

Sometimes Hume's scientific and philosophic notes seem to anticipate even the achievements of recent research. Long before Dr. Liljegren [25]) and other scholars of to-day Hume saw the connection between Milton and Stoicism, relating Satan's belief in "the fixt Laws of Heaven" to "the Opinion of the Stoicks, well express'd by *Lucan:*

> *Sive Parens rerum —*
> *Fixit in æternum causas, qua cuncta coercet*
> *Se quoque lege tenens, & sæcula jussa ferentem,*
> *Fatorum immoto divisit limite Mundum.* Phar. 2."
> (P. L. II. 18 *n.*)

His industry in exploring out-of-the-way corners of knowledge is remarkable. A selection of names from the notes on the first books of Paradise Lost may show his versatility: Celsus and

---

[24]) XII. 30 *n.*
[25]) STUDIES IN MILTON BY S. B. LILJEGREN LUND C. W. K. GLEERUP [1918, 8⁰: pp. XLII + 160]. — Der andere Milton von Heinrich Mutschmann, M. A., Dr. phil. Kurt Schroeder, Verlag, Bonn und Leipzig 1920 [8⁰: pp. XII + 112]. Hume's anticipations are vague but interesting.

Paracelsus are referred to on questions of chemistry [26]), Farnaby on the architectural term "cornice" [27]), "Cook's Proemium to the 4 Justitiæ" on legal terminology [28]), Gassendi [29]), Galileo [30]) and others on astronomy, Suidas [31]), Eustathius [32]), Spelman [33]), Vossius [34]) on linguistic problems, Selden [35]), Helladius [36]), Sandys' Travels [37]), Pliny [38]), Aulus Gellius [39]) and others on mythology.

That Hume did not take this agglomeration of his too seriously, is shown by himself in note I. 438. He there quotes some opinions on Astoreth, and adds: "Who desires to heat his Head with more Quotations and to fill it with more Uncertainties, may consult the Learned *Selden*". His scepticism is justified by his not infrequent mistakes. In his note on IV. 986, for example, the base of the peak of Teneriffe is described as being "about 48 *Spanish* Leagues in compass, and its Summit about 15 miles high, to be seen about 120 English miles at Sea." Hume's weaknesses, however, were the weaknesses of his time, which was not yet sufficiently used to accuracy and careful, critical study.

B. HUME'S RENDERINGS OF MILTON'S TEXT.

Hume's paraphrases are one of the main features of his commentary. It is of some interest to see how far they succeed in reproducing Milton's tone and style. There can be no doubt of Hume's endeavour to give more in them than a mere sober account of the contents of Milton's text. Hume's enthusiasm is obvious, and often leads him beyond the limits of scholarly exactitude to over-emphasis and bombast.

[26]) Cf. I. 674 *n*.
[27]) I. 716 *n*.
[28]) II. 318 *n*.
[29]) II. 1052 *n*. & *c*.
[30]) I. 290 *n*.
[31]) I. 353 *n*.
[32]) II. 284 *n*. & *c*.
[33]) II. 90 *n*.
[34]) I. 375 *n*.
[35]) I. 438 *n*.
[36]) I. 462 *n*.
[37]) I. 479 *n*.
[38]) I. 576 *n*. & *c*.
[39]) II. 945 *n*.

Where Hume feels particularly elated and inspired, his renderings sometimes aim at keeping the blank-verse form. Lines I. 230—237, for example, are made to read as follows:

"And such for Colour shewed, as when the Strength
Of Wind pent under Ground, removes a Hill
Rent from *Pelorus,* or the ragged side
Of Roaring *Etna,* whose wide Womb well stor'd
With Matter fit to burn, thence catching Fire,
Heighten'd with Flaming Sulphur, Wing the Winds,
And leave a Boyling Bottom, Clouded o'er
With stinking Fumes."

Hume's first intention probably was to substitute simpler expressions than Milton's, as the first two lines seem to show: *Colour* for *hue, Wind pent under Ground* for *subterranean wind, removes* for *transports.* The same is partly true of the rest of the passage. But the third and fourth lines play independently with alliteration ("rent", "ragged", "roaring"), and "whose wide Womb well stor'd / With Matter fit to burn" is a somewhat pompous simplification of "whose combustible / And fewel'd entrals". Another paraphrase, that of I. 424—431, is even more pretentious and heavy:

            ... "these Heavenly Beings,
Not linkt to Limbs, or bound with Sinews up,
Or weakly underpropt with brittle Bones,
Like heavy Clods of Clay"...
            (See also on VI. 1 & c., VI. 58 etc.).

Even Hume's prose-style reads at times like disguised blank-verse, and alliterations and epithets abound in many notes. See e. g. III. 539 *n.*: "... the enraged Ocean's proud swelling Waves, whose Briny Billows rising much higher than the shelving Shore, cannot be imagined to be stopt by the yielding Sand." The notes on bk. III. ll. 329—342 are an instance of the accumulation of this kind of language. I am referring to expressions like "those many Mutations of Matter" (335), "their long and lazy Lethargy" (329), or somewhat further below, in III. 459 *n.*: "the Moon, the Mother of Moisture and Mutation."

A passage like the following in note IV. 700 shows how far Hume could go in this luxury of language: "Within each lovely

Flower, fair to the sight or fragrant to the smell, all-colour'd
Iris, and the blushing Rose, and snowy Jessemin advanc'd their
flowry Heads, mix'd and inwoven, chequer'd the beauteous Bo-
wers with the most charming variety of view."

Sometimes the commentary is facetious and grotesque on
some of the finest and most serious passages. Thus the giants,
the sons of Vesta, in note I. 198 "Rendezvousing in *Thessaly*,
piled the Mountains one upon another, till they gave *Jupiter*
a terrible Scalado at Heaven-Gates." The style is like that of
Milton's prose or some of the suppressed readings of "Comus".
The next note describes how the gods, attacked by Typhon, "finding such hot Work on't, ran shamefully away into *Egypt*, disguis-
ing themselves there, in the shapes of divers Beasts..." Galileo's telescope becomes "his Spectacles" in note V. 268. Even the
passage on Sin and Death does not subdue Hume's spirits; he
comments on it in the following manner [40]: "Sin, that is hatch'd
in the Imagination, is said to be brought forth out of Satan's
Brain-pan, as *Pallas* armed Cap-a-pied, (by which the Poets meant
Wisdom, & c.) was fabled to have been the Offspring of *Jove*'s
Noddle." It does not seem likely that Hume had any intention
of ridiculing the text, but he evidently had little tact and little
feeling for style. He is very reverent towards the Bible, but he
talks in the same breath of "Gods flaming Chariot loaden with
Almighty Vengeance" shaking "Heaven's everlasting Basis" and
of "*Juno* giving her self but a jogg on her Throne" [41].

He has better qualities, however. His analysis of rarer
literary effects is as a rule not good, but he appreciates fine
descriptive passages and is capable of rendering them. He loves
colours, and translates the language of "Paradise Lost" into
a style very near to that of Milton's early poetry. On P. L. IV.
702, for example, relating how "The blue Violet, and yellow Cro-
cus, with the purple Hyacinth, inlay'd the fragrant Floor with
soft and sweet Embroidery"; or describing the fish in VII. 406:
"*Their wav'd Coats;* Their Scales like little Waves, wrought over
one another, glistering in the Sun like Gold." He elaborates
Milton's brief reference to the nightingale in VIII. 518 into a long
passage, full of legendary atmosphere and emotion: "*The*

[40]) II. 757 *n.*
[41]) III. 394 *n.*

Amorous Bird of Night; Till the Nightingale began to tune the Bridal Song: She is called the *Amorous Bird of Night,* from her solitary mournful Song, seeming to bemoan her Misfortune that befell her by the wicked Amours of the Lascivious *Tereus,* related at large by *Ovid,* Met. 6. *Et virginem & unam vi superat, & c.* She is indeed well styl'd, *The Bird of Night,* from chearing Darkness with her Passionate Song, that seems to imitate the solitary Complaints of Languishing Lovers."

Sometimes he gives a glimpse of the dreamy and half-conscious: "In Sleep... Fancy, free from those many Avocations that draw us away when waking, exerts its utmost force, and represents its dark Masquerades and dumb Shews, with strange Advantage" [42]).

Thus Hume's style, though not subtle, ranges from a very crude kind of humour to a comparatively sensitive rendering of some of the less obvious sides of the mind, flagging, however, where it has to interpret any very many-sided and complicated *intellectual* experiences.

C. HUME'S LITERARY VIEWS.

Hume's two main authorities are the classics and the Bible; among the former mainly Homer and Virgil, but very frequently also most of the other prominent literary personalities of classical antiquity. Hume's scope is wide enough to include *e. g.* Callimachus, the hymns of Orpheus, Seneca, Euripides, Lucian, Plato, Aristotle, Cicero and Josephus, not to mention obscurer names, many of which are of a less distinctly literary character. Later poets hardly exist for him, except Tasso and Spenser, who are quoted quite frequently, and Milton himself, though of the works of Milton he concerns himself only with "Paradise Lost". References to mediæval and modern scholars and biblical commentators are found every now and then, as has already been remarked. He refers also to Sir Walter Raleigh's "History of the World" [43]).

Hume's respect for classical literature is that of the usual man of letters of his time. Virgil is "the sublime Virgil", by

---

[42]) V. 53 *n.*
[43]) Cf. *e. g.* I. 307 *n.*

whom the belief "that God was all in all, in all things" is "admirably exprest" in Geor. ⌄:

"Deum namque ire per omnes
Terras tractusque Maris, Coelumque profundum" 44).

He seems to take it for granted that in a general way nearly everything in the classics was excellent. This is the belief that induces Hume to justify questionable points in Milton by merely referring to similar cases in Greek or Latin literature, as if these parallels were sufficient evidence. The comparison of a "bearded grove of ears" 45) with "a vast number of armed Men ranged close together" is satisfactory because of "its familiar use and occurrence among the best Poets. *Homer* by it expresseth the power *Agamemnon's* Oration to the *Grecian* Army had on the affected Multitude... Virgil brings it nearer, calling a great number of Darts, *Telorum segetem ferream"* & c. The parallel between a lightning-scathed tree on a heath and the fallen angels 46) is defended because Virgil had used one resembling it: "And if this Simile was not too superlative for the *Cyclops* [referred to by Virgil], this cannot be so for the *Seraphim.*"

Yet the Bible comes first. It is not only the great basis of Christianity; it is also the ancestor of a considerable part of classical mythology. Hume has hardly any doubt as to the truth of the opinion of the rabbis that Elysium, "This happy Seat, and State, free from all Disturbance, had not its Foundation only from Fancy, but was borrowed from the Sacred Writings, and was Copied from Moses's Paradise; and accordingly the Rabbins tell us, that Elysium sounds in the holy Language אל אשר *the Grove of God"* 47). "Satan by his malicious cunning designing as much as in him lay, to undermine and invalidate the Credit of the Holy Text, promoted among the Heathen Poets many strange Fictions, that seem borrowed or imitated from the Sacred Writers, as their *Nectar* and *Ambrosia, Nepenthe* and the wonderful Herb *Moly*, by *Hesiod, Homer*, etc." 48). The note on I. 17 derives Zoroaster's, Heraclitus' and Orpheus' doctrines from the

---

44) I. 17 *n.*
45) IV. 982 *n.*
46) I. 614 *n.* & *seq.*
47) III. 359 *n.*
48) IV. 218 *n.*

Bible. In this matter Hume followed the model of Milton himself,
who represents the deities of the ancient world as fallen angels,
notably in the long infernal procession in book I of "Paradise
Lost".

That whatever is based on the Bible, is true and that the
rest is inferior fiction; is one of the doctrines repeatedly emphasized by Hume. Milton's description of the vegetation of
Paradise in V. 297 & seq. "if compared with *Virgil's Inter Odo-
ratum Lauri nemus*, Æn. 6. the best Grove in his *Elysian* Fields,
in which his happy Souls and the famous *Musæus* sat and sang,
will as far out-do it, as *Paradise* did all the *Poetic Fictions* imagi-
nable." The Bible has the right of seniority, the classics are
"neoterics". "Old Euphrates" [49]) is rightly called "old", "since
remembered so long ago in the History of the Creation by *Moses*,
Gen. 2. 14. compared with whom, these are *Neotericks* that speak
of him, as *Virg.*

> *Cæsar dum Magnus ad altum*
> *Fulminat Euphratem Bello.* Geor. 4. And *Ovid,*
> *Arsit & Euphrates Babylonicus.* Met. 2."

As the poet of the Bible and Christianity Milton, therefore,
surpasses the ancients. His subject is greater than the wars
and heroic deeds of the Greek and Roman writers. Hume emphasizes this in one of his first notes [50]): "*Things unattempted
yet*, so *Hora. Non usitata nec tenui ferar penna;* but not on so
sublime a Subject as this, not undertaken as yet by any Poet:
As in the beginning of the Ninth Book, he |*Milton*| says of him-
self, he was not sedulous by Nature to indite Wars, hitherto the
only Argument, Heroic deem'd — *trita vatibus orbita.* So *Virg.*
on a Subject much inferiour makes his Brags,

> *Sed me Parnassi deserta per ardua, dulcis*
> *Raptat amor: Juvat ire jugis, qua nulla priorum*
> *Castaliam molli divertitur orbita clivo.* Geor. 3."

A natural inference from all this is the superiority of Milton's "spiritual" heroes to those of Homer and Virgil [51]): "That
Lucifer, the Chief Leader and Champion of the laps'd Angelick

---

[49]) I. 420 *n.*
[50]) I. 16 *n.*
[51]) IV. 986 *n.*

Host, should, swoln with rage, be compared to Mountains of such
vast Immensity, will seem modest enough, when parallel'd with
the liking of *Æneas* by *Virgil* to some others, not so much inferior
to these, as his *Heroe* must be allowed to have been below any
one of those *Spiritual Beings*"... Satan's address to the spirits
of Hell [52]) is better than Sarpedon's speech to Glaucus, *IΛ*. M.
"Which will be found as much exalted in the Imitation, as a
Seraphim is superiour to. a Man even of Homeric make." Even
the somewhat long and incoherent description. of the future of
mankind in book XI, which is scarcely as successful as the best
parts of the previous books, is valued extraordinarily highly,
partly because of its chronicle form, (which in fact is a defect),
but also because it is "taken out of Sacred Story" [53]): "Most
admirable and excellent are those *Episodes,* which here begin,
and adorn our Author's *Poem* to the end, surpassing all those
tedious Stories, and the vainglorious Boastings of the *Homeric
Heroes,* and *Virgil's* artful Enumeration of the *Roman* Conquerors,
down to *Augustus Cæsar* and the bemoan'd *Marcellus, Æn.* 6. as
much as a Relation of what was to come to pass, from the beginning of the World, to *Adam* and all Mankind, to the end of it, and in
order to a better, (taken out of Sacred Story,) must excel any
particular or *Humane History* whatever."

Hume goes even further in this conventional direction,
accusing Homer and to a certain extent Virgil also of not observing the rules of religious decorum, of τὸ πρέπον. He commits
the anachronism of wishing Homer to write like a Stoic philosopher. Many of the Elizabethans were fundamentally anachronistic
in their views of classical antiquity, but Hume, though a man of
a later period, differs very little from them in this respect.
"Homer", he says, "instead of Treating the Deites of his Days,
with any tolerable Decency, makes them Quarrelsome, Vulnerable,
and of a Behaviour below that of a Stoic Philosopher, as is frequent through all his *Iliads:* His *Venus* stands with a Fly-flap in
her hand, to keep the corrupting Insects from infecting the Corps
of her Son's dead Favourite, *IΛ*. T. & c. *Virgil,* thô less blameable,
gives the same Goddess the weakness of Weeping:
Lacrymis oculos suffusa nitentes. Æn. 1.

---

[52]) II. 451 *n.*
[53]) XI. 433 *n.*

And the Character of his *Juno* is very angry and spiteful:

Nec dum enim causæ irarum, sævique dolores
Exciderant animo, manet alta mente repostum
Judicium Paridis, spretæque injuria formæ.

Æn. I.

And he styles her frequently *Sæva Jovis conjux;* and there is so bitter an Altercation between her and *Venus*, Æn. 10, that enraged *Jupiter* is forced to end it, by swearing he will take neither of their Parts. The Parallel therefore as to the τὸ Πρέπον of these Poems and our Authors, is infinitely to his advantage[54])." *Τὸ πρέπον* is also one of the main virtues of Adam and Eve, cf. note XII. 625: "Our Poet observes, the ὁ Πρεπὸν, the *Decorum* to the last degree, making our first Parents such perfect Patterns of Modesty, as to forbear their Endearments, though but in Words, at the Angels approach." He weighs the relative difficulties which the Ancients and Milton had in observing this principle. Milton's success in this respect becomes one of Hume's main reasons for praising him, and a word of enthusiastic approval of his "towering fancy" seems to slip in almost inadvertently [55]): "But when we reflect how shamefully the one [*i. e.* Homer] exposes all his Deities, though the other [*i. e.* Virgil] in that respect much better observes the τὸ πρέπον, it must be acknowledged a much harder Task to form a right *Idea* of that Eternal Being, which made the Universe; and to observe with all due Veneration, and Awful Respect, the great *Decorum* requisite in speaking of the True God; and to offend in nothing against the Revelations he has been pleased to make of himself; and yet to manage all this under the Heats and Heights of Towring Fancy; than either *Homer* and *Virgil* undertook, a Task, by none, but himself, attempted, (as he may justly boast) and impossible to be, by any Undertaker, better performed."

This *τὸ πρέπον*, as may be judged from the note on Adam and Eve's conduct, is no profound quality of the mind but rather the refraining from indecorous acts or words. It seems of some interest that the last-quoted remark on this characteristic seems to be echoed in the "Spectator" papers on "Paradise Lost" by

---

[54]) III. 342 *n.*
[55]) I. 25 *n.*

Addison, which, on the whole, do not appear to bear many traces of Hume's influence. The fact that "decorum" was a commonplace of criticism at that time induces one to avoid insisting on Addison's dependence upon Hume, but the coincidences are rather close, and the circumstance that both critics compare the same features in the same authors makes it an interesting task to compare their respective attitudes. The passage in question in the "Spectator" of Jan. 5. 1712 reads as follows: "It is possible that the Traditions on which the *Iliad* and *Æneid* were built, had more Circumstances in them than the History of *the Fall of Man*, as it is related in Scripture. Besides it was easier for *Homer* and *Virgil* to dash the Truth with Fiction, as they were in no danger of offending the Religion of their Country by it. But as for Milton, he had not only a very few Circumstances upon which to raise his Poem, but was also obliged to proceed with the greatest Caution in every thing that he added out of his own Invention. And, indeed, notwithstanding all the Restraint he was under, he has filled his Story in Analogy with what is delivered in Holy Writ, that it is capable of pleasing the most delicate Reader, without giving Offence to the most scrupulous." It is in the main the same idea, and Addison had most probably seen at least the first pages of Hume's commentary, which was without competitors at that time. The note in question is one of the very first by Hume that contains any coherent discussion of a leading principle, and it was therefore likely to attract any reader's attention. However, the difference between Hume and Addison is not insignificant, for the latter is not only more scholarly, precise and cultured but even more moderate and cautious than Hume. At least one expression, that about "the Heats and Heights of Towring Fancy", shows very clearly how much nearer Hume was to the time of Milton even if he may not have experienced all the poetic enthusiasm of the Jacobean period which influenced Milton's early work.

Hume's grounds for preferring Milton to the ancients are not merely moral and religious. Sometimes he applies artistic criteria, for example in his repeated dwelling on Milton's greater conciseness and expressiveness. After quoting Homer's description of the Garden of Alcinous and Virgil's passage on Calypso's grotto he observes that one "may without affectation affirm, that in half the Number of Verses, that they consist of, our Author

has outdone 'em" [56]). He compares Milton's lines on the
nightingale in III. 40 etc. with bk. I. 518 & seq. of the Odyssey
and with the verses "Qualis populea merens Philomela" etc. in
Virgil's fourth Georgic and finds that Milton's passage, "thô very
short, (consisting only of two Verses) is as expressive of the
Melodious Moan of this Night-Singer, as all those before recited."
Here he only forestalls the judgement of nearly all his successors.
Sometimes he is carried away by Milton's intense, restrained
passion and heaps parallel on parallel from the classics only to
prove Milton's superiority. Virgil, Lucan, Claudian, Silius
Italicus, and in addition to them Tasso, are quoted to show that
Milton's treatment of terror in II. 711 surpasses theirs: " I give
the judicious Reader his Option, out of the six Quotations to find
any one so expressive of the common Sentiments of Mankind, and
the fearful Effects they apprehend from the Appearance of
Comets, as is our Author's, *And from his horrid Hair shakes
Pestilence and War.*" Hume seems to feel the power of Milton's
address to light at the beginning of the third book of "Paradise
Lost" quite as keenly as any modern reader: *"Light,* and the
Blessings of it, were never drawn in more lively Colours, and
finer Stroaks, than by these [verses]; nor was the sad loss of it
and them ever so passionately and so patiently lamented. They
that will read the most excellent *Homer,* bemoaning the same
Misfortune, will find him far short of this" [57]). Here he shows
a real appreciation of Milton's greatest manner. Occasionally
his analysis does not reach far enough, emphasizing merely the
external, mathematical superiority of Milton's range of vision,
but Hume's way of expression seems to betray some traces of
a deeper admiration. In his note on I. 74 he quotes some classical
similes describing the distance between hell and earth and finds
them inferior to Milton's: "Our Author says, God, in his Justice,
had appointed the dark Infernal Dungeon for those Disobedient
Spirits, thrice as far from Heavens chearful Light, and his own
blest Abode, as is Earth's Center from the utmost Pole: Which
of 'em has measured the Distance most Mathematically, is hard
to determine; but *Milton's* Description of this Infernal Region,
far exceeds both the Τάρταρον ἠερόεντα, of the one, and the

---

[56]) IV. 151 *n.*
[57]) P. L. III. 54 *n.*

Pallentes umbræ Erebi, Noctemque profundam, of the other;
neither of 'em having ventured on so large a Survey of that sad
Seat. *Tasso's* Description is curt and inconsiderable:

> *Itene maladetti al vostro Regno,*
> *Regno di pene, é di perpetua morte.*

Cant. 9. St. 64."

Hume clearly had some feeling for the impressiveness of Milton's
vast cosmic background.

He is more speculative in his parallels from the classics than
elsewhere, probably because he had his fixed opinions about them
and felt more secure in comparing them with Milton than in
independent criticism. Yet some of his views on other literary
questions are clear enough, esp. those on romance. Though
capable himself of a very bizarre, irregular style, in which he
does not hesitate to compare the sun to a head covered by
a wig [58]), he dislikes the superfluities of romance. His main
objection to it seems to be that romance is necessarily fictitious.
Even the classics seemed inferior because of the element of
fiction in them, and there was nothing like the weight of classical
authority to support the feebler claims of romance. I. 580 &
586 *nn.* show his matter-of-factness in these things: *"Uther* and
Arthur and all their Descendants, though they gave Noble Subjects for the Histories of the Ages they lived in, yet by the gross
Ignorance that over-spread those times, there is nothing trans-
mitted to us but what is foolishly fabulous and fantastick."
"Milon, Count of *Angiers* his [*i. e.* Charlemain's] Brother-in-Law,
Rowland his Nephew, *Renaud* of *Montauban, Roger* the Dane,
Arnold of *Belland & c.* famous Warriours, Subjects of the *French*
fabulous Romances, who in that Illiterate Age, confounded their
Story, and cover'd it with much Confusion and Obscurity." In
these examples his refusal of romance almost equals Bentley's in
severity.

His own style was not free from some touches of romance
and Elizabethan richness, as was shown above. He likes to
describe old legendary events and mythological stories at greater
length than Milton's text requires, as very many of his notes on
Milton's fabulous allusions prove. Moreover, he has some feeling
for the "strange" and "curious", but only half-consciously, and

[58]) I. 596 *n.*

in practice, not in theory. He notices some subtler shades of expression that allude to the less conscious experiences of the mind and interprets them in a way which seems to show some pondering over this kind of experience. "As my Dream had in the Images of my Imagination represented it express and plain" is his manner of rendering the simple words of P. L. VIII. 311: "as the dream / Had lively shadow'd", and he dwells on the last expression: "*Shadow'd*, is an admirable word, setting forth the dark Resemblances of Dreams, those imperfect Nightpieces, dimly presented to our drowsie Senses." Both words, "night-piece" and "shadowy", come again into their rights in note V. 43: "*Shadowy sets off;* Our Poet has shaded his Night-piece excellently, *Silence* and *Shade* do make great Additions to the *Midnight Majesty* of the *Full-Orb'd Moon.*"

There is in these notes some sense of the combination of strangeness and beauty defined as romanticism by Pater, but it is undeveloped. Hume seems to appreciate balance and natural ease, but "Nature's charming Melody", as he calls it, is evidently not of the freer Elizabethan type [59]). His attitude towards the artificial style of cavalier love poetry is very contemptuous; he defines a serenade as "An evening Song, performed under the Window of some Lovely or beloved Mistress; ... a lamentable Ditty sung at some disdainful door, best rewarded with Disdain... From being exposed to the accidental injuries of the Weather, the sneaking humble Lover is stiled *starved*" [60]). Milton's text is not nearly as emphatic as this. Hume obviously disliked Italianate convention of this extreme type. His note on V. 151, on Adam and Eve's "unmeditated" morning prayers, "more tuneable then needed Lute or Harp", expresses his point of view quite distinctly: "*More tuneable, so melodious and musical, as not to stand in need either of Lute or Harp, to add more charming sweetness:* All Instruments of Musick, being but Imitations of Human Voice, made use of to assist, but incapable of exceeding it; invented to please those, who by some indisposition of their Organs or their Ears, deprived of Nature's charming Melody, are forc'd to divert themselves with artificial sounds, rack'd from strain'd Strings and Wyres, and hollow Wood, &c. as much inferiour to the former, as Art is to Nature."

[59]) V. 151 *n.*
[60]) IV. 769 *n.*

38

D. MILTON'S LANGUAGE AND STYLE.

Hume's main interest in this department is in the etymological analysis of Milton's vocabulary. Many of the commonest words of the language are studied from that point of view, whereas subtler grammatical questions are usually ignored. Almost the only advantage Hume gets from his philological attitude of mind is his susceptibility to the finer shades of meaning and the considerable skill he shows in dealing with the influence on their actual meaning of the origin of the words. However, he does not practise this skill very often. Difficult syntactic problems are mostly avoided; his terminology is monotonous, and only a small percentage of Hume's remarks are of any very particular interest.

His keen interest in etymological matters is probably partly to be explained by the great emphasis the earlier commentators of English poetry laid on the study of unfamiliar words. His title-page indicates that an inquiry into linguistic questions is intended to be one of the main characteristics of the commentary. This is especially understandable in the case of a poet like Milton who could not fail to stir the curiosity of his commentators by his elaborate, original vocabulary. Sometimes Hume really contributes to a better understanding of Milton in points of language, or at least leads the way to future students and teaches them new manners of approach. Fr. Thynne's Manuscript "Animaduersions" or E. K.'s glossary to "The Shepherd's Calendar" may have shown him the importance of *archaic* expressions. Notes III. 533, II. 704, VI. 86, & c. are instances of his treatment of these. Spenser, *even Chaucer* [61]), are his sources here. Certain forms are explained as *dialectal* (I. 334 n.: "rouse" = "a more Northern pronunciation of Rise, like the Dorick Dialect"; V. 35 n.: "irksome" = perhaps "the Lincolnshire *Werk* or *Wark*, Grief, *Irksom*, tedious, troublesome"). In certain cases where he deals with words felt by later critics as peculiar and obsolete, but does not mention the archaic shade in them, the explanation is that those expressions were not yet out of use at his time, e. g. V. 94 n.: *"Answer'd sad, concern'd; Sad* here, is no more than serious, considerative; for sinless *Adam* was incapable of *sadness,* sorrow." In IV. 50 n. Hume points out an Italianism

---

[61]) II. 704 n.

("sdein'd", Ital. "sdegnare") but usually he tends to trace Milton's words back to the French where the Italian and French forms happen to be similar, e. g. IV. 245 n.: "Imbround, made the Bow'rs that were convenient at Noon, look dark and brown. Embrunir, Fr. to darken, to make obscure." He could hardly have noticed that Milton had used the Italian form of the word in one of his sonnets, for he shows no traces of an acquaintance with Milton's early work: "Qual in colle aspro, al imbrunir di sera."

On a few occasions Hume registers some expressions as coined by Milton, (cf. 1. 756 Pandæmonium, VI. 169 servility, IV. 506 imparadized, IV. 264 attune, IX. 165 imbrute, IX. 289 misthought, even VI. 553 Enginry). Milton's language must have appeared individual and peculiar to him, as these observations show.

Blunders are not infrequent among Hume's linguistic remarks but they may be largely due to the times, e. g. fantastic etymologies like "Climbs... of Κλίμαξ, Gr. a Ladder" 62), or "Blossom, of which Bloom seems a Diminutive, of the Ger. Bluhen" 63). On the other hand, he has some knowledge of Anglo-Saxon, or at least has studied the authorities in Anglo-Saxon with some care, as is evident throughout the commentary.

The imitation of sounds heard in nature, the expressiveness of the phonetic side of words is often alluded to, though generally in a vague manner, without much explanation. Some sensitiveness is shown in his remark on the sombre sound of II. 287 n.: "With hoarse Cadence lull; Words not easie to be altered into others half so expressive, the Winds with their decreasing hoarsness hush and lay asleep the o'rewatch'd Seaman." In II. 951 n. he finds "the word Hubbub... coined of the confused Noise made by many low Voices at a distance", as it is "expounded in the following Verse, of Stunning Sounds and Voices all confused".

Several remarks deal with pleonasms, e. g. II. 58 n.: "Opprobrious Den of Shame; A Pleonasme, this dark disgraceful Den of Shame." I. 797 n.: "Frequent and full; Compleat and full, a Pleonasm." So on I. 495: "In Courts and Palaces; a Redundancy frequent with the Poets, Palatium Lat. for a Prince's Court."

---

62) IV. 191 n.
63) III. 43 n.

Hume seems in fact to have liked this figure, if we may judge by his own style, where it occurs so frequently.

On the other hand, he decidedly disliked what was to be condemned by most of the later commentators, — Milton's habit of "punning", of playing on words similar in sound but hardly or not at all connected in meaning. He calls it "jingling", taking notice of it comparatively frequently, and (in note I. 642) gives a definition of his dislike: ."Which tempted our Attempt;... Words, thô well chosen, and significative enough, yet of Gingling and Unpleasant Sound, and, like Marriages between Persons too near of Kin, to be avoided." This is well said. Hume did not see the better side of the habit, its occasional stimulating effect on the mind, later on pointed out by Richardson [64]), nor its roots in Milton's temperament traced by the late Sir Walter Raleigh in recent times. His analytic power does not reach as far as that.

He pays some attention to the formation of compound adjectives in Milton, attributing the habit wholly to classical influence and either not knowing of, or forgetting the frequent occurrence of such formations in Elizabethan literature, cf. note II. 425: "Here our Author, in imitation of the Greeks, who delighted in the significancy of Compound Words, useth Heaven-Warring Champions for Heavenly Warriours, Champions that waged War in Heaven." In one instance [65]) he even becomes too bold and assumes a compound where Milton probably meant to use two separate words, for the first edition has no hyphen between them, and even Hume writes them without one: "Blasting voly'd, a word seemed to be compounded in imitation of the significancy of those of that sort used by the Grecians, like Τερπικέραυνος and ῾Υψικέραυνος, Jove's Epithetes, OΔ. ς and IΛ. δ." Hume does not seem to have any objections to this violent way of forming compounds. He is not a follower of the smooth, neat ideals of style to be held later by most of the 18th century commentators.

Hume's observations on syntax are slight. He notices a way of using the present tense which is hardly typical of Milton [66]):

[64]) Rich. on the paranomasia (IX. 11 n.): "it has oftentimes Good Effects, it Awakens the Attention, and gives a Like Pleasure to the Ear as Rhyme."

[65]) IV. 928 n.

[66]) IV. 965 n.

"I drag thee; The present Tense used for the future, to signifie the immediate execution of the menace." Another observation on Milton's use of adjectives for nouns is more illuminating, but the parallels given are exclusively classical, and older or contemporary English usage seems to be totally neglected, as in note II. 278, on "the sensible of pain", or II. 407: *"Obscure* for Obscurity, an Adjective for a Substantive, as *Magnum per inane & per inane profundum:* Lucret. lib. I." Hume's study of syntax is confined to such stray remarks as these.

One aspect of Milton's style, the importance of learned associations in his vocabulary, the part the history of a word plays in its Miltonic meaning, has been analysed at some length and with considerable acuteness by Hume. Thus, he sees the possible double meaning of "edge" in VI. 108 — on the one hand the usual English meaning, on the other its interplay with another well-known Latin signification of the word: *"On the rough Edge of Battel;* On the bold brink of Battel. *Edge* is a word not to be exprest by any other in our Language; and in the Sense here meant it has a strange Relation to the Lat. *Acies*, that signifies both the sharp Edge of any Weapon; and also an Army in Battel Array ready for the Charge, in which it is expressive of this *rough edge of Battel.*

> *Haud aliter Trojanæ Acies, Aciesque Latinæ*
> *Concurrunt. — — — Æn. 10."*

He is capable of explaining unusual cases such as the epithet "marble" in "the pure Marble Air", P. L. III. 564: *"Marble Marmoreus...* of Μαϱμαίϱω, to shine, to glister, is often used to express clearness or whiteness, without any reflection on its hardness. So *Virg.*

> *Marmorea Caput à cervice revulsum.* Geo. 4."

He has a feeling for the ennobling influence of literary or biblical associations on common words, as in IX. 714: "The Phrase of *Putting on,* is not only familiar in Scripture, to denote the highest and most exalted Changes that can happen to Humanity, in Immortality, and glorious Eternity, as *This mortal must put on immortality, & c.* 1 *Cor.* 15. v. 53. where the Original word is Ἐνδύσαϑαι, signif. *Induere,* Lat. to put on. But *Virgil* uses it in his *Circean Metamorphoses:*

> *Quos hominum ex facie Dea sæva..."* etc.

In one case his analysis becomes rather minute. In note III. 364 he seems puzzled by the irregular use of the colour epithet "purple" in ancient poetry: "The Poets are much in love with this Colour:

> *Manibus date lilia plenis*
> *Purpureos spargam Flores.* Æn. 6."

"The Light it self must be tinged with it:

> *Et lumine vestit Purpureo.* Æn. 6.
> *Lumenque juventæ Purpureum.* Æn. 1.

But all this is outdone by a Neoteric, *Brachra* [*sic*] *Purpureâ candidiora nive;* daring to a Contradiction."

He seems to regard the last instance as a paradox and a mannerism. However, in note IV. 301 he reflects on the application of the adjective to human hair and concludes that its meaning must have been different in ancient literature. It is true that he does not seem to be quite at ease about the correctness of his inferences but his final conclusion shows some freedom from pedantry and, on the whole, is corroborated by poetic practice: "It is very observable, that such Epithets as this are not to be taken in too strict a sense; for Gold being the most excellent among Metals, Purple among Colours, the Rose, and anciently the Hyacinth, among Flowers; hence *Venus Aurea*, Æn. 10. *Rosea Cervix & lumenque juventæ Purpureum,* Æn. 1. and this *Hyacinthin* Hair." A further note (IV. 764, on Love's "purple wings") defines the word a little differently, giving what Hume thinks to be its exact meaning here as well as in ancient poetry: "*Purple* here signifies, as among other Poets, no more than shining, gawdy, glittering; as *Virgil:*

> — *Lumenque juventæ* Purpureum. And.
> *In mare* Purpureum *violentior influit amnis.* Geo. 4.

Horace gives the Swans (whose Whiteness is pass'd into a Proverb) the same epithete:

> *Purpureîs Ales coloribus.* Carm. lib. 4. Od. 1."

Hume's way of reconsidering his statements, of arriving at valuable general conclusions and of still weighing the problem over again until he has found the exact meaning of the word, shows his method in the making and proves the sensitiveness of his linguistic instinct. It is regrettable that he did not concentrate on interesting cases like this, instead of wasting his shrewdness on barren etymological investigation.

Some isolated observations deal with imitations of classical peculiarities of style. Hume points out what probably is a real "Homericism" as he calls it, in note V. 371: *"The Angelick Virtue: The Angelick Power; The Angel; An Homericism:* who used Πριάμοιο βίην, *the Strength of Priam,* for Priam himself, *IΛ. Γ.* & Έκτορος μένος, for *Hector, IΛ. Ξ.*

Αὐτὰρ ἐπεὶ τὸ γ᾿ ἄκουσ᾿ ἱερὸν μένος ᾿Αλκινόοιο.

After the sacred Strength of Alcinous heard that."

One of the few examples of Hume's adverse criticism of Milton deals with the latter's habit of repeating whole lines. In III. 405 & c. he finds fault with the repetition of the words "but much more to pitie encline[d]". But his taste is at fault, for Milton here is not lacking in invention, but evidently wishes to emphasize the words as sounding the keynote of the passage. Hume's view reminds one here of Bentley's blind hatred of repetition: "A Repetition affected after the Homeric manner, who often uses the same Verses and Words, in which Commands were given, or Messages sent, as supposing it not possible to change them for better."

In note I. 50 he studies the question of putting a certain for an uncertain number but gives only some of the possible historical causes in particular instances without trying to draw any general inference [67]).

Hume's simple way of seeing things helps him to reach the plain truth in certain places where more sophisticated annotators stumble. Richardson's commentary contains a whole theory about the apparently paradoxical expression "darkness visible" in I. 63; Bentley regards it as nonsense. Hume solves the problem in a straightforward way: *"Darkness visible,* seems nearer a Contradiction, than that *Egyptian* Darkness sent on *Pharaoh,* which was such as to be felt, Exod. 10. 21. But a Mist is often the cause of Darkness that may be palpable, though that in the text was preternatural: But our Poets meaning by this *Darkness visible,* is only, that from Hell's flaming Dungeon here issued no Light,

[67]) Cf. also I. 609 *n.*

but such a Darkness, as through it might be discovered those dismal Scenes and Seats of Everlasting Wo."

There is hardly much else of any considerable value to be found among Hume's notes on questions of style. A note on III. 364 where a number of classical parallels are quoted to justify Milton's treatment of nature as animate does not succeed in showing more than that nature smiles in ancient poetry as it does in Milton. Hume does not exercise his analytic gift in the field of style very industriously except in the directions already indicated.

E. MILTON'S CHARACTERS.

Hume's remarks on the characters of "Paradise Lost" are very few and casual, but they show his general attitude. His starting-point is mainly moral, although now and then there is a shade of artistic appreciation in his descriptions.

Satan is the character that impresses Hume more than any other, in spite of his usual preference for the decorous and lawful. Much of what he says is conventional, and his general condemnation of Satan as the spirit of Evil is that of the ordinary religious person of his time. Thus Satan's powerful speech at the beginning of the poem [68]) is dismissed very curtly as "A vain boast of the Father of Lyes, whom the Lord of Host had in derision." Hume is far from admiring Satan's pride, cf. note I. 111: "Another of *Satan's* blasphemous Boastings, and suiting well his cursed Character, which our Poet holds up to the heighth of *Luciferian* Pride" (he is alluding here to Satan's refusal "To bow and sue for grace", & c.). Even the lines "The mind is its own place" & c. [69]) only impress him as "Another vain-glorious Boast of the Father of Lyes". II. 34 *n.* represents Satan as the sly spirit of Hell who by magnifying the danger of his position tries to conceal his selfish and ambitious motives. This is probably more than Milton intended to say. Milton does not lose sight of the grandeur of Satan's character, even where, as at the beginning of this book, he is slightly ironical in describing him as "insatiate to pursue Vain Warr with Heav'n" and as displaying

[68]) Cf. I. 97 *n.*
[69]) I. 254 & seq.

"His proud imagination", "by success untaught." Hume certainly adds a somewhat crude popular touch to this irony and exaggerates it in I. 667 *n.*, while commenting on the defiant rage of the fallen angels: "And bold with Armed Hand, [they] bray'd on their Sounding Shields War's dreadful Din, daring outrageous Heaven's Almighty Arm: A Graphick Description of the Foolish Defiance given by these Damned Spirits, in their impotent Rage against the Almighty, sitting in Heaven, and having them in Derision."

The preconceived theological ideas shown in such passages as the last sometimes give way to a sympathetic understanding of Satan's sufferings. Hume even becomes, occasionally, quite eloquent in his compassion [70]: "O foul dismal Descent and *Downfal!* A fierce Reflexion, and as furious and tormenting as hottest Hell it self! A Degradation to *ambitious Lucifer*, doubtless most grievous!" There are moments when he is able to feel the whole greatness of the rebellion against Heaven. His attitude is contrary to accepted opinion when he defends the application of the expression "godlike" to the hellish spirits [71]: "If *Homer* gave his *Hero* the title of Θεοείκελος, and *Virg. Æneas* be, *Os humerosque Deo similis*, these Mighty Spirits that durst Rebel against th' Almighty, may be well allowed the same Epithet." He protests very resolutely against the picture of Satan prefixed by his publishers to the edition of 1695 [72]), and incidentally he defines his own conception of Satan. But for the religious tinge in it, this conception would probably satisfy the more radical Miltonians of to-day who regard Satan as the main feature of the poem: "From Verse 591, to 594. and from thence to this, the Designer of Lucifer's Picture, prefix'd to this first Book, should have taken the Noble Lineaments of his Obscured and yet Glorious, Haughty Looks: He should have express'd his Furrow'd Face and Faded Cheek under those Lofty Brows of stedfast Courage and of wary Pride, vowing and waiting for Revenge: If he had hit these Lucky Stroaks, he might have spared his Horns and Asses Ears, so unsuitable to the Description of the Arch-Angel, that *Milton* has afforded him no hint of 'em, as not

---

[70]) IX. 165 *n.*
[71]) I. 358 *n.*
[72]) I. 603 *n.*

having, amongst his Idol-Deities, enrolled *Corniger Ammon.*"
His enthusiasm here apparently inspired the commentator
Richardson to a high-flown, but obviously sincere continuation
of this characterisation, which, however, does not go much
further than Hume in any essential points, in spite of Richardson's general tendency to exaggeration [73]).

There is little of interest in Hume's observations on the other
characters. I have already quoted his note on the modest,
decorous behaviour of Adam and Eve in my account of Hume's
views on τὸ πρέπον. The note is typical. God, the Messiah, the
angels, even Sin and Death fail to stimulate him to interesting
remarks. Here and there, but very rarely he succeeds in illuminating some stray features of the parents of mankind, generally
in a sober, neat manner, without venturing far beyond everyday
commonsense. His explanation of Adam's extreme pessimism
after the Fall seems plausible [74]): "That *Adam*... might reflect
on himself as most sinful... is not hard to be conceived: But
that he surpass'd all past Examples, which could be only the
fallen Angels, must be understood as an aggravation of his Guilt,
and the excessive Sense of, and Sorrow for it, by which he was
overwhelmed." There is some insight into human character in
his comparison of Eve looking at her reflection in the water with
Ovid's Narcissus [75]): "*Milton* has improved the Fable of *Ovid,*
by representing *Eve* like a She *Narcissus* admiring her self; and
has made it much more probable, that a Person who had never
seen any thing like her self, should be in love with her own faint
reflected Resemblance, than that a Man acquainted with the World
and himself, should be undone by so dull a Dotage." He may be
doing some injustice to Ovid whose narrative seems to aim rather
at decorative effect than at psychological truth but his interpretation of Milton's point of view is attractive.

Hume's religious feelings help him often to the truth.
Whatever Milton's abstract convictions were, his instinctive
religious attitude was certainly not destitute of the decorum and
the reverent piety of his contemporaries. Hume understands

---

[73]) Cf. chap. 5 sec. F.

[74]) X. 840 *n.*

[75]) IV. 461 *n.*

Milton in this respect; he must have breathed much of the same
mental atmosphere, and wrote not so very long after the publication of Milton's epic. He tells the story of the tower of Babel,
and of its being intended as a means of revenge for the flood,
and adds: "For which, there being no Foundation in the Historical Relation of *Moses*, Gen. 11 our Author thought it fitter to
come out of *Adam's*, than the *enlighten'd Angel's* mouth" [76]). He
does not fail to notice the inconsistency in Milton's assumption
that Abdiel in VI. 20 could think God ignorant of his experience
among the fallen Angels: *"Had thought to have reported;* This
is said *'Ανθρωπίνως*, after the manner of Men, for it is unconceiv-
able that an Angel (a Spirit of more pure and enlighten'd Perfection than Mankind is) should be a stranger to the *Omniscience
of GOD Almighty."* This is another one of the few instances
where Hume seems to express any criticism of Milton.

F. HUME ON MILTON'S TEXT.

Hume makes only a very few remarks on Milton's text. It
is clear that he could have no hand in the text of the Folio of
1695, for on one occasion he points out, with no suggestion of
personal responsibility, a mistake that is not corrected there.
The 1695 text spells "under bane", not "under banne" as in the
first edition (bk. IX. l. 923). Hume notices the correct reading,
which he explains as meaning "Unter Command and Injunction,
or under a Curse, not to touch it," adding "in the Fol. Edition,
it is misprinted, *Bane."* His quotation gives the correct form of
the word. There are some further differences from the readings
of 1695 in his notes, *e. g.* VIII. 529—30: "Transported I behold
transported Touch" where the comma after "behold" is omitted
although both the 1695 text and the first edition have it. This is
not merely a misprint, for Hume tries to explain the reading,
proposing several ingenious and rather curious interpretations:
"Pleas'd to excess, I find my Feeling pleasant to excess: Raised
above my self, I perceive my Feeling raised as far above it self:
Or carried beyond myself I perceive my sense of Touching
carried too beyond what's usual."

[76]) XII. 74 *n.*

In VII. 451 Hume anticipates one of the better observations of Bentley which has been accepted by later editors, but without mention of its first author. He shows the illogical character of "fowl living", pointing out that the "fowl" had already been referred to, and also that the reading is inconsistent with Scripture. In note X. 989 he discovers a wrong division of lines. This note is especially interesting as proving Hume's ability to appreciate the suggestive effect of metrical irregularities: *"Childless thou art, Childless remain;* A mistake of the Printer has made our Author seem ambitious to have imitated *Virgil* in some of *incomplete Verses;* or that he had a mind to shew *Eve's* vehement desire to stop and prevent the miserable Being of Mankind, by breaking of his Verse abruptly; but the next Verse being too long by what this falls short, plainly shews, that [*So Death*] is to be added to this. *Childless thou art, Childless remain: So Death."*

Hume makes an attempt to emend bk. III. l. 48, but not at all successfully. His arguments are Bentleian; he does not understand Milton's emotional, slightly hyperbolical manner of speaking and requires pedantic accuracy. His note on this matter might serve as an argument against those who accuse Bentley of dishonesty, for it shows how similar results were attained in a case where there was no bold hypothesis like that of Bentley to influence the judgement of the critic:

"Presented with a Universal Blanc; I cannot persuade myself but it should have been a *Universal Blot,* and that it is a mistake of the Printer. *Blanc,* is Fr. for White, and the Phrase, *Donner la carte Blanche à,* to send one a Blanc, is to submit absolutely to what Conditions the Conquerour shall set down: Now Blindness (as well described by Clouds and continual Darkness) does so fully import an entire Ignorance and Privation of Colour, that a Person born blind has doubtless no notion of any such thing; but for a Man that had for many years enjoyed his Eyes, to say, his Blindness had cut him off from the chearful ways of Men, and, instead of Nature's fair Book of Knowledge, had presented him with a Universal Blanc, like a piece of white Paper, unspotted and unstained with any Impression, his Memory retaining still the Idea's of all Things formerly seen, thô now as to his Eye-sight blotted out, seems absurd. The next Verse, *Of Natures Works to me expung'd and ras'd,* confirms, that it

ought to be an *Universal Blot;* for *Expung'*d, is of *Expungere,*
Lat. to blot out a written Word, by covering it with little Pricks
or Blots, and *Ras'd* is of *Radere,* Lat. to shave; the Romans, (who
writ on Waxed Tablets with Iron Styles) when they struck out
a Word, did *Tabulam* radere, rase it out."

Even Bentley's application of logic and philology was hardly
more regardless of the style of poetry.

3. BENTLEY'S EDITION OF "PARADISE LOST."

MILTON'S PARADISE LOST. A NEW EDITION, BY RICHARD BENTLEY, D. D. LONDON: Printed for JACOB TONSON; and for JOHN POULSON; and for J. DARBY, A. BETTESWORTH, and F. CLAY, in Trust for RICHARD, JAMES, and BETHEL WELLINGTON. MDCCXXXII.
4°: pp. [20] + 399 + [16]. Contents: p. [1] half-title; p. [3] title; pp. [5—11] preface; p. [12] "The Verse"; pp. [13—20] the argument; pp. 1—399 text and notes; pp. [1—16] index. With two portraits.

The first commentary on Milton after Hume's huge, undisciplined, encyclopædic work is thoroughly different in aim and execution. It is Bentley's famous commentary, as strictly textual in design as Hume's was explanatory, and as rigidly governed by one main principle as Hume's was diffuse and miscellaneous. Its preliminary history has been told many times, e. g. briefly and competently in Professor J. W. Mackail's recent Warton lecture on the subject [77]), so that it is unnecessary to go into details here. The evidence we possess seems to show that the work was not the result of long and patient preparation or premeditation. Fenton's suggestion in his edition of 1725 about the possibility of Milton's amanuenses or the printer having committed some textual blunders which remained uncorrected, may have caused Bentley to direct his attention to Milton's text. This, as well as the alleged advice of Queen Caroline to him to undertake the work, possibly alluded to by Bentley in his last note, "Non injussa cecini", seems to indicate that the decision to edit Milton came late

---

[77]) THE BRITISH ACADEMY WARTON LECTURE ON ENGLISH POETRY XV. Bentley's Milton By J. W. Mackail Fellow of the Academy [*From the Proceedings of the British Academy, Vol.* XI] London Published for the British Academy By Humphrey Milford, Oxford University Press, Amen House, E. C. *Price One Shilling and Sixpence net* [8°: pp. 21].

in life and perhaps not quite of Bentley's own accord. Professor Mackail's study of Bentley's MS. notes in especial seems to prove that the task was really carried out in a hurry and that much of the work in its final form may have been dictated [78]). This corroborates the statement made by Bentley in the preface that the notes were written extempore and sent to the press at once. Professor Mackail, though aware of all this, is somewhat oddly surprised by the contradictory statements and inaccuracies which he finds in the book [79]).

Bentley's quarrel with Trinity college, and his desire to win the favour of the public and the authorities before the opening of the next session of Parliament seem to have been the main causes of his haste. He hoped to reverse the judgement against himself of the previous year. The scarcity of notes on the two last books of the epic might be taken as additional evidence of hurry, although his own statement that this was due to the faultlessness of the text has some arguments in its favour. In these last books the romantic, erratic features of Milton's poetry almost completely disappear, and the narrative becomes mainly a summary of accepted scriptural and historical tradition.

Bentley's preface expounds the theory on which the edition is based. Milton's amanuenses, a phantom editor and the printer have all contributed mistakes, and the editor has had the audacity to alter and make additions, wherever the text did not please him. Milton in his persecuted condition, "poor, friendless, and what is worst of all, blind with a GUTTA SERENA", was unable to control him. The faults which result are monstrous, and such "as are beyond Example in any other printed Book." This is said regarding the supposed misprints only. The worst faults of all are the spurious insertions contributed by the poet's deceitful friend. "This Trick has been too frequently plaid; but especially in Works publish'd after an Author's Death. And poor *Milton* in that Condition, with Three-score Years Weight upon his Shoulders, might be reckoned more than half Dead."

Milton's pitiful state has caused other troubles as well, through the manifold inconsistencies it brought about in the work;

---

[78]) Mackail, p. 7.
[79]) Mackail, p. 16.

and Bentley makes a number of suggestions for amendment. The most notorious of these is his alteration of the last two lines of the poem.

Some of the absurdities involved in this theory are so crude and striking that many critics have denied Bentley's *bona fides*. He maintains that "the Proof-sheets of the First Edition were never read to *Milton:* who, unless he was as deaf as blind, could not possibly let pass such gross and palpable Faults. Nay, the Edition, when publish'd was never read to him in seven Years time. The First came out in 1667, and a Second in 1674; in which all the Faults of the Former are continued, with the Addition of some New ones." "But now if the Editor durst insert his Forgeries, even in the second Edition, when the Poem and its Author had slowly grown to a vast Reputation; what durst he not do in the First, under the Poet's Poverty, Infamy, and an universal Odium from the Royal and triumphant Party? Add to this a farther Confirmation: That when *Milton* afterwards publish'd his *Paradise Regain'd* and *Samson Agonistes;* that Edition is without Faults; because He was then in high Credit, and had chang'd his old Printer and Supervisor."

The preface to Pearce's reply, which appeared in the same year [80]), points out that Milton had many friends who were likely to have studied the work before its publication, and how improbable it was that nobody should have read it to the poet afterwards. Another even grosser blunder in Bentley's statement is pointed out by Pearce, namely, that "Paradise Regained" appeared before the second edition of "Paradise Lost", and that there was no reason why Milton should not have committed the correction of the latter poem to the preferable editor.

These mistakes can only be attributed either to great carelessness or to an intention to mislead the reader into accepting his theory. The fact that the preface seems to have been written very hastily, like the rest of the work, perhaps even more hastily, since the session of Parliament was drawing nearer and nearer, renders it not improbable that the former was the case. The last words of the preface, describing how the notes had been "put

---

[80]) Cf. chap. 4 sec. B.

to the Press as soon as made", appear to indicate that these were also the last words Bentley wrote before the appearance of the edition.

Bentley emphasizes the argument that the four alterations in the second edition, which according to him are the "sole Changes made" there (I. 505, V. 638, XI. 485, 551), are all for the worse. An inspection of Bentley's notes on these passages would seem to show that such a view was not impossible from his adopted stand-point. Prof. Mackail observes, however, that there are thirty-three such changes, and that Bentley only "seems to have got it into his head" that there were none beside these. Beeching's edition, which registers approximately this number of changes, leaving out of account such minor points as *e. g.* the alterations of *their* > *thir* in the first books, shows that most of these deviations from the original text affect one or two letters only. *None,* except the changes caused by the division into twelve books instead of ten (set apart as as special category by Bentley himself in note XI. 485), are at all comparable to the four alterations enumerated by Bentley, by which whole lines are changed and added. It is not surprising that Bentley did not take into account the slighter details as hardly worth special mention in the preface. What he calls the "sole Changes", is those that are really conspicuous. He may, for example, have regarded most of the rest as mere blunders of the printer. Prof. Mackail seems to ascribe too much importance to their omission. Bentley had lower standards of accuracy than present-day scholarship, but his attitude in this detail at any rate was more correct and probably also more sincere than Professor Mackail's statement might induce one to think. The "tampering with the evidence" Mackail mentions [81]) does not apply here. "All the Conjectures", says Bentley, "that attempt a Restoration of the Genuine *Milton*" are "cast into the Margin, and explan'd in the Notes. So that every Reader has his free Choice, whether he will accept or reject what is here offer'd him; and this without the least Disgust or Discontent in the Offerer" (Preface, sg. a_1v). Here, at the very outset, the commentator's attitude is frankly declared. Bentley's hot-headed, impatient temper, his seventy years, and the critical

---

[81]) p. 16.

habits acquired in a very different field of scholarship, sufficiently explain, perhaps, both his method and his theories.

Bentley's method is clearly stated in another passage of the preface. The emender of Horace, Terence, Plautus, the leader in the new movement of conjectural criticism, only follows the track pursued by him all his life-time when he asserts that "the Printer's Faults are corrigible by retrieving the Poet's own Words, not from a Manuscript (for none exists), but by Sagacity, and happy Conjecture", and that "the Editor's Interpolations are detected by their own Silliness and Unfitness; and easily cured by printing them in the *Italic* Letter, and inclosing them between two Hooks." The successful experience of a long life, his "real genius and perhaps unequalled power of divination in the field of conjectural criticism" [82]) had been tested in classical scholarship only, and Bentley failed in a department of inquiry new to him, evidently without suspecting that failure was possible in a literature apparently less difficult and more accessible than the classics.

A full elaboration and estimation of Bentley's hypotheses would require a considerable chapter to itself. Some notes on them may be found in the sections in this chapter on his cancellations and on his use of literary parallels. The one important result of his experiment was that it led him to scrutinize the whole of Milton's poem from one definite point of view, and that his violent, clear-cut, classicist standards were applied with great rigidity to nearly every detail of the poet's work. His opponents, therefore, found a solid basis to work upon, and, by merely trying to refute his statements and to prove the genuineness of the passages attacked by him, were compelled to meet reason with reason and sometimes to delve into the very heart of the literary problems of that period. Bentley's sagacity furnished him with so many reasons in support of his views that a neat rebuttal required serious work and careful comparison. All this became fruitful in the hands of less prejudiced, if less brillant students. The germ of his method was transferred into the field of English literary research, and bore fruit there.

---

[82]) J. Mähly, Richard Bentley, 1868. p. 1: "seine vielleicht einzig dastehende, wahrhaft geniale Divinationsgabe auf dem Gebiete der Conjecturalkritik."

A. BENTLEY'S LITERARY VIEWS AS EXHIBITED IN HIS TREATMENT OF MILTON'S STYLE.

Bentley's ideal of style coincides with that of the literary majority of his age. It is formulated incidentally in his note on P. L. VI. 219 where, while emending a passage which seemed tautological to him, he expresses a desire "To reconcile High Language with Philosophy and true Sense."

"True sense", as Bentley understands it, is a narrow concept, excluding almost any deviation from the simplest way of expression. It implies, amongst other things, an acute paralysis of the capacity for understanding metaphorical language and hidden associations, especially of an emotional character. It is in this direction that Bentley commits his grossest and most palpable mistakes. He lacks the imagination needed for reconstructing the experiences of a poet who creates his own imagery.

Even such a simple and common kind of metaphor as the representation of inanimate objects as animate is sufficient to raise Bentley's protest. Hume registered it among the few primitive types of metaphorical language included in his classification. It is no unusually bold specimen of this figure when Abdiel menaces Satan in P. L. VI. 188 with the words: "This greeting on thy impious Crest receive." Bentley's commonsense, however, is offended: "to call the *Crest*, an inanimate Metal, *Impious*, is something irregular." He alters it to the less daring expression "thy impious Head", although even here he does not wholly get rid of the metaphor. Examples of this kind abound in his notes. Book VI of *Paradise Lost*, where the greatness of the subject seems to inspire Milton's style to even higher flights than usual, troubles Bentley at almost every step. "Fierce ensigns" in VI. 356 offends him, because he knows that ensigns are "the tamest thing in the whole Battel." The war of the engines tearing the entrails of the air is considered an impossible image. Milton describes how

"... 'Twixt Host and Host but narrow space was left,
A dreadful interval..."   (P. L. VI. 105.)

Bentley notes: "How could the *Interval*, the empty Space betwixt Host and Host be call'd *dreadful?* Surely the Hosts themselves, and the blazing Edge of Battle must be much *more dreadful.*" This is an example of incompetence to handle *im-*

ponderabilia almost as striking as Bishop Newton's surprise that Milton should be so fond of that *little* bird, the nightingale [83]).

One of the reasons of his dislike for language of this stamp is stated in note VI. 528: *"Dawning Morn, Dawning Light* are standing Words in Poetry; but *Dawning Hills* are great Rarities." The expression is accordingly changed into something less opposed to Bentley's standards.

In all these cases Bentley struggles to get rid of the complex, intricate manner of thought and imagery in Milton. Yet his fondness for ratiocination and explanation sometimes induces him to put a less obvious expression instead of a simple and evident one. This is why "Still as Night Or Summer's Noon-tide air" in II. 309 becomes "Summer's noon-tide Hour", for "it was not the *Air*, that made the Silence and Stilness, but the *Hour;* when in hot Countries, the Sun shining fierce, both Men and Animals retire to Shade and Rest." The reason is preferred to the image.

Bentley's tendency to simplification and regularity destroys many of Milton's subtler distinctions of syntax. Bentley pleads for uniformity where Milton's expression varies according to the subdued vibrations and unexpected turns of feeling and thought which he is trying to render. These subtler shades disappear in Bentley's readings, even if the main logical outlines remain untouched.

Milton's treatment of the *verb* passes Bentley's understanding. He adduces two reasons for changing the subjunctive ·mode of III. 150 ["For should Man finally be lost? should Man"] into the indicative "shall". One of them is that the latter is found in l. 156 "Or shall the Adversary", the other, that the scriptural passage which seems to be imitated here has the indicative (Genes. XVIII. 25). The former argument is his starting-point and seems to be his main motive for the alteration. But in aiming at consistency he overlooks contextual differences. For the subjunctive occurs at the beginning of the Messiah's speech to the Father where he asks him half-hesitatingly about the destiny of Man:

> "For should Man finally be lost, should Man
> ...Fall circumvented thus by fraud...?"

---

[83]) Newton's edition of P. L., VII. 435 *n.*

He denies the possibility, beseeching the Father to refrain from
the destruction of mankind, and his next question is more urgent
and definite:

> "Or shall the Adversarie thus obtain
> His end, and frustrate thine, shall he fulfill
> His malice..."

This gradation from hesitation to certainty disappears in
Bentley's emendation.

Something very similar occurs on a much larger scale in
books XI and XII, where the vision of the future history of mankind is unfolded. The tenses used are intermittently the present
and the past, partly because Milton imitated the classical usage
of varying the past tense with the *præsens historicum*, but
sometimes because he wished to indicate the shifting angle of the
narrative. Bentley applies the same standard in both cases, and
rigidly regularizes the verbal forms. The former conception
seems to occur in XI. 644:

> "Part wield thir Arms, part ,courb the foaming Steed,
> Single or in Array of Battel rang'd
> Both Horse and Foot, nor idely mustring stood."

"The context shews, that he gave it STAND: as *Wield, Curb*",
is the conclusion at which Bentley arrives. Here he may have
been right. The case, however, appears to be different in various
other places, for example in XI. 688, where "such *were* these
Giants" is altered into "such *are*...", because, as Bentley says,
Michael is "speaking present in Vision, and not the Poet afterwards", and because the present tense was used a little while
before in l. 683. But at the beginning of his speech Michael is
referring to a vision which has hardly vanished and still seems
to be present to him. A few intervening lines of a more generalizing kind cause the freshness of the impression to ebb away,
and his general inference from the scene is expressed in a more
aloof manner in the past tense. Immediately afterwards, the
angel, while still speaking of the same event, already uses the
future form of the verb, no longer alluding to the imaginary
vision but thinking of the things that are actually to come. The
same is almost exactly true of the substitution of the present
tense for the past in XII. 81. Here the vision dealt with was

described some 15 lines earlier, and Adam has discussed it as if it were a matter immediately before him, whereupon Michael draws the final conclusion in the past tense. He passes on from the contemplation of the scene to more abstract considerations.

Pearce, who has a better sense of these shades of meaning, points out Bentley's failure to see the relative character of these grammatical forms in his remark on XII. 117, a passage where Bentley rejects the past tense because the narrative is dealing with the future. As Pearce rightly observes, the events told there belong to the past with regard to the general trend of the archangel's story.

Bentley fails to understand a side of Milton s syntax which should have been intelligible to him because of its connection with the poet's classical education. It is the involved structure of Milton's sentence, especially the elliptic expressions and parentheses [84]), the "ablativus absolutus" as Bentley and others still called it, etc. Part of this failure might be ascribed to Bentley's hurry. Pearce points out several places where Bentley misunderstands classical constructions. Thus "Nor sometimes forget" in III. 32 is identified by Bentley with "I always remember". Pearce observes "that *nec* and *neque* in *Latin* are the same as *& non*" (*i. e.* the construction would mean "I sometimes remember"). Much of the eccentricity of Bentley's commentary was due to his predilection for a matter-of-fact, terse and brief style, which seems to dim his understanding. His notes show his own way of writing. His opinions are indicated by his alteration of VI. 905 "Which *would be* all his *solace and revenge.* Rather thus:

THIS *would be* HIS GREAT *Solace and Revenge.*
This refers to the following Clause, as it should do: *Which* looks back to the preceding."

He splits the flow here. It appears as if Bentley had not been able to detach his understanding of classical peculiarities of language from the classics themselves. To him English was a spoken language, and his fealing for its literary qualities lagged behind. He could not grasp the spirit of Latinity as shown in Milton.

---

[84]) Cf. esp. III. 344 *& seq.* — a much-discussed example. Viz. also VIII. 500—7 where both text and punctuation are changed, XI. 807, *& c.*

His strong liking for a rigid, clear-cut order dictates one of his commonest idiosyncrasies, his steady battle with repetitions and tautologies. He goes, in this respect, to the very extreme, and is incapable of seeing the enhancing effect of most of Milton's repetitions of important words and phrases. Sometimes he may be right in his disapprobation of Milton's text, though not in his alteration of it. In VI. 580, to which he objects, the threefold repetition of "stood" in the same sentence "is", as Prof. Mackail confesses, "almost intolerable" 85). But this is an exception. The great majority of Bentley's objections to this figure are caused by his failure to see their significance. He does not understand the difference between "land" and "region" in V. 261. Pearce sees it more clearly: "I believe that M. meant by *Regions* larger Tracts than he meant by *Lands*, or whatever do not look like *Lands*." It seems to be a gradation, a rise from the narrower concept to the more comprehensive one.

The number of places where Bentley persecutes repetition is very great. P. L. II. 36, 67, 107, 264, 442 are a few chance instances. A normal example is that in II. 36 where "Firm Faith, and firm accord" is altered into "Firm faith and *fast* accord", although Milton most probably wished to emphasize the adjective. The emphatic character of the repetition is probably even more obvious in II. 107:

"his fatal Throne:
Which if not Victory is yet Revenge.
He ended frowning, and his look denounc'd
Desperate revenge, and Battel dangerous
To less then Gods. On th' other side up rose
Belial, in act more graceful and humane..."

Milton is repeating and developing his idea here: "Not victory but revenge... revenge and dangerous battle", opposing it to the figure of Belial, "in act more *graceful* and *humane*". Bentley takes no notice of the intensifying effect of the repetition, by which the contrast also is deepened; he simply suppresses it: "...since he had *Revenge* the very Sentence before, he could not, without forgetting himself, use it so soon again. I suspect he gave it,

Desperate RAGE and battel."

85) Cf. p. 18.

Even the handling of such an effective word as "dark" is misunderstood by him [86] : *"Darkness* and *dark* comes Three times within Four Lines. Better therefore here,

Thick Clouds and BLACK."

This hostile attitude to anything that might be regarded as superfluous is repeated in his observations on the general structure of Milton's epic. He disapproves of the reappearance of the description of Leviathan in book VII [87]), after it had been given in book I, forgetting the variations in the two passages and their impressive effect in both cases. In a similar manner, he thinks it "wrong Conduct" to foreshadow subsequent parts of the narrative because it decreases the feeling of surprise in the reader. The mention of the bridge through the abyss in II. 1023 is "want of Oeconomy", for "In Book the Xth, from Verse 285 for a Hundred [*i. e.* verses] and more, he [*i. e.* the poet] describes Poetically and pompously this same *Bridge* and *Intercourse"*. The rise of expectation, the suggestive effect achieved by such hints escapes his notice.

Bentley's principles, generally speaking, admit of only one deviation from his ordinary doctrine that "The simplest and nearest Word is the best" [88]). One artistic consideration occurs again and again — the ideal of "high language" mentioned at the beginning of this section. It is often an ideal of formalism and stilted expression, but not infrequently inclines to the better ideal of grandeur and intenseness combined with clarity. "Simplicity and grandeur" is Bentley's own formulation of it [89]). It is strongly opposed to the spirit of Italianate love-poetry and in so far coincides with the main tendencies of the style of "Paradise Lost". The traces of idyllic and effeminate romance which Bentley still finds in the work are condemned by him. He shows his views very violently while ascribing one of the supposed manifestations of this propensity to the editor [90]) : "your Woman *Flour* is but fit for a Madrigal; and the rest has a meanness of

---

[86]) II. 264 *n.*
[87]) I. 204 *n.*
[88]) V. 741 *n.*
[89]) X. 1092 *n.*
[90]) IV. 268 *n.*

Stile contemptible." Elsewhere, in censuring a descriptive passage of a similar kind, he at least admits the possibility that Milton sometimes indulged in this less heroic variety of style: "Our Author, through his whole Poem, had certainly that in his View, to make the Female Sex favour it. But here he seems to incline needlessly too much to *Eve's* outside, even with straining of his Verse" [91]).

He prefers the opposite tendency, sometimes crudely enough. The reading "SWALLOW'd in th' abortive Gulph" [92]) is substituted by him for the original text "plung'd in that abortive Gulph" because it is "More strong and formidable". This "heroic" inclination is even more manifest in some other places, *e. g.* in XI. 299 where the verb "to wound" in "Which might else in telling wound" is altered into "in telling stound".

Often he aims at mere academic oratory, as in XI. 278 *et seq.* where Adam's more resigned, less declaiming tone, indicated by the words "which I bred up with tender hand" and continued in the question:

"Who now shall reare ye to the Sun, or rank
Your Tribes, and water from th' ambrosial Fount?"

assumes a style with "more Pathos in it" through the repetition of the interrogative adverb:

"Who now shall rear you to the Sun? who rank."

Yet occasionally his emendations in this direction have some artistic value, though they may not improve on Milton's reading. In II. 33, where he changes the punctuation, he really seems to achieve some abrupt "'Passion and Force" in the rhythm, although the continuous power of Milton's flow is broken. Milton's text reads:

"for none sure will claim in hell
Precedence, none whose portion is so small
Of present pain, that with ambitious mind
Will covet more."

---

[91]) IV. 634 *n.*
[92]) II. 441.

Bentley emends:

> "For none sure will claim in Hell
> Precedence; None. Whose Portion is so small
> Of present Pain that with ambitious Mind
> He'll covet more?"

This is the "broken style", as he calls it in VI. 241, 243 *nn.*, which is emphasized in his attribution of asyndeta to a passionate manner of expression [93]).

In this sphere of intense, white-hot energy, indeed, Bentley almost forgets, sometimes, his narrowest prejudices, and even feels induced to acknowledge the right of imagination to transgress the rules. In his remark on one of these outbursts [94]) acknowledgement is made of the "Magniloquence of Stile, and Sublimity of Thought" exercised here "to admiration"; but though Bentley admits that "Poetic Fury is commonly both thought and allow'd to be regardless of Syntax", he is unable even here to refrain from the complaint that Milton is "deserting Propriety, while he's hunting after Sound and Tumor." It seems clear, however, that the austere, strong passion in Milton is the quality which most completely agrees with the tendency of Bentley's own energetic character. A curious emendation shows this very distinctly [95]). It is the passage where Bentley substitutes "Eternal Woe" for "Infernal world" out of his intense admiration for the strength which Milton had been able to put into Satan's character. He wishes to have it fully expressed in the style here: "But *Satan's* Character is the better kept up by his saluting and congratulating *Eternal Woe*. He knew well, that was his unchangeable Doom; and he was not scared with the mere Word. This paints him to the Life, his *obdurate Mind,* his *unconquerable Will,* His *Courage never to submit or yield.* So that to salute and welcome His own Punishment shows a Temper and Disposition truly *Satanical.*" Here, as happened to Hume, the grandeur of the sternest aspect of Milton's poetry, and of its fullest embodiment, the Character of Satan, conquers the conventional narrowness of the critic. Bentley's preface had showed what he admired in the poet — it was the mind which even at times of misfortune

---

[93]) I. 107 *n.*
[94]) VI. 212 *n.*
[95]) I. 251 *n.*

"could spatiate at large through the Compass of the whole Universe, and through all Heaven beyond it; could survey all Periods of Time from before the Creation to the Consummation of all Things."

In addition to these inherent qualities of Bentley's mind, there were a number of other causes of his imperfect understanding and appreciation of Milton. They have been pointed out by nearly all his critics. Bentley knew little of earlier English poetry, and was therefore a very incompetent critic of Milton's metre and language. This defect he shared with his age. The preliminary work for an adequate study of the older English authors had yet to be done.

Chaucer's "Troilus and Creseide" and "The Legend of Good Women", Spenser's "Faery Queene" and his minor poems ("Mother Hubbard's Tale", "Muiopotmos", the Hymns to Heavenly Love and Heavenly Beauty, the "Epithalamion"), Fairfax's Tasso, Sidney's "Arcadia" are mentioned by Bentley; but never Shakespeare and hardly ever any of the other Elizabethans. The names of Beaumont and Tom Coryat are used in jest only [96]).

"The Faery Queene" is named most frequently; Sidney's "Arcadia" and Fairfax are referred to several times. One important advance has indeed been made on Hume: Milton's earlier poems are cited (e. g. "Comus" in note I. 16, the "Nativity Ode" in note I. 252). His "History of Britain" also is taken notice of in a casual remark [97]). Yet Bentley did not gain much from this knowledge. The romance of the earlier works is never alluded to. "Paradise Regained" and "Samson Agonistes" are, naturally enough, much more frequently noticed.

Italian literature is almost entirely outside Bentley's scope. Ariosto is mentioned once in a remark which seems to be a literary commonplace [98]), and Boccaccio is referred to in connection with the name Demogorgon.

His ignorance of the older language is evident, and handicaps him heavily. His misunderstanding of *his* for an indication of personification, where it stands for 'its' [99]), is shared by such

---

[96]) IV. 714 *n.*
[97]) I. 252 *n.*
[98]) I. 16 *n.*
[99]) *e. g.* XI. 518.

careful critics as Pearce. But his ignorance, or carelessness, is striking when he misunderstands expressions such as "mortal" = "deadly" [100]). He has similar difficulties with "in behalf of" = "on account of" [101]), "a cry" [of hell-hounds] [102]), "speakable" = "able to speak" [103]), & c. The frequent Elizabethan use of "which" = "who" is not taken notice of in IV. 30 n. Similarly, the early use of "of" in the sense of "from" seems to be unfamiliar to Bentley [104]). These and similar deficiencies, naturally enough, prevented him from understanding the actual meaning of Milton.

Though Bentley, then, was not sufficiently equipped for the task of tracing Milton's native literary lineage, there are still signs that he had now and then devoted some interested attention to the little he knew of Milton's English predecessors. He quotes Spenser less frequently than Hume does, but his observations on him are acuter than Hume's, as his reading in English poetry seems to have been wider. Hume had studied Milton's cosmology, astronomy, & c. but only in their possible relations with professional science or with the speculations of mediæval divines and classical philosophers. Bentley in at least one note [105]) draws a parallel between Spenser's and Milton's conception of the universe, which shows a fair knowledge of Spenser's minor poems. Most of the poems of Spenser already mentioned occur in the compass of this note, in which Bentley tries to show that Milton's expression "the vault of heaven" is here wrong. He argues that neither Milton nor Spenser ever represents the habitation of God and the angels, which is evidently meant here; as vaulted, although the expression may be used with regard to the visible heaven, the sky. It is of some interest that Bentley should already have thought of a possible connection between the astronomy of Spenser's Hymns and that of Milton: a point emphasized quite recently by modern scholars like Mr. Edwin Greenlaw, welcomed as promising by such critics as M. Denis Saurat [106]).

[100]) XI. 366 n.
[101]) XI. 102 n.
[102]) II. 654 n.
[103]) IX. 563 n.
[104]) VI. 24 n.
[105]) I. 669 n.
[106]) Cf. Studies in Philology, July 1920, vol. XVII. pp. 320 & seq.: Edwin Greenlaw, Spenser's Influence on Paradise Lost. Cf. also Denis Saurat, Milton: Man and Thinker, Bibliography.

In spite of his very defective knowledge of archaisms Bentley
is quite aware of Milton's tendency to use old words, and even
undertakes to restore some supposed archaic expressions. His
alteration of "disturb" into "disturn" in I. 167 is based on
Chaucer's "Troilus and Creseide" of which he professes to have
studied several copies, as well as on the Italian form "distornare".
He observes: "And who knows not *Milton's* Inclination to
revive old Words, or even coin new ones, especially with the
Italian Stamp?" Hume mentioned Chaucer in a much more
casual way, and derived Milton's Italianisms mainly from the
French (cf. the chapter on Hume).

Bentley is able to correct the statement found in Hume that
"imparadized" is a word coined by Milton. He shows that,
besides occurring in Italian, it is used in Sir Ph. Sidney's
"Arcadia". Several other misstatements on supposed Miltonic
coinages, made by persons whom he does not mention, are equally
refuted ("to obey to", *e. g.* I. 337, he finds in Chaucer and Spenser, and "miscreated" II. 683 in Spenser). A certain respect both
for Spenser and Sir Philip Sidney is indicated by his frequent
quotations from them and his admitted attempt to reproduce
their diction (II. 517, 580, 855, VII. 373, 406 & c.). Some interest
in Old English studies is betrayed by a spelling such as "swerð"
(XI. 433), in spite of its grotesqueness and pedantry. Further
examples of these tendencies might be found, but all of them
remain on the surface, and Bentley's literary physiognomy is left
unchanged.

B. BENTLEY ON MILTON'S VERSE.

In the department of metre as elsewhere the problem of
correctness and regularity plays a predominant part in Bentley's
edition. His attitude is that of his time; his leaning towards
faultless, regular workmanship overmasters his appreciation of
a freer type of verse. His sympathy with intense, energetic
expression slightly lessens, it is true, the pedantry into which
he is apt to fall. He acknowledges that Milton "generally rather
aims at strong Expression, than smooth and flowing Numbers",
but in the very note in which this acknowledgment is made [107]

---

[107] III. 145 *n.*

he corrects a verse because it "is so rough, and walks so hobling, that it begs to be reliev'd."

Homer and Virgil had taught him that the subject makes it sometimes advisable to make the verse rough, and he praises Milton's "great Art and Judgment" in imitating this [108]). Yet note VI. 866 is more characteristic of his usual way of thinking: *"Burnt after them* to the bottomless *Pit*]. This is very strange Measure; unless he affected to make his Verse *bottomless* too, to express the Idea. But that Whim pursued, would produce strange Monsters in Verse." His sympathies are on the side of smooth measure as opposed to "absonous" verse [109]) and "harsh Measure, and Accent unnatural" [110]). He tries to regularize the metre as far as he can, and is consistent, for example, in altering the rhythm $\cup \cup --$ into the ordinary Iambic metre in such cases as, "Encamp their Legions, or with obscure wing" [111]). Here he adopts the inversion of the adjective: "wing obscure". The only instance of this rhythm noticed by Dr. Bridges, who has traced it systematically, and not changed by Bentley, is III. 564: "Through the pure marble Air his oblique way." This seems to be due to an oversight.

Rhymes, whether they are supposed internal rhymes, as in VIII. 244; which Bentley reads: "Tormént and loud lamént, and furious rage", or final, as in II. 220—221, are disagreable to Bentley.

A problem which greatly occupies him, is the connection between emphasis and accent. He repeatedly censures lines of which the emphatic word stands in a place which according to his theory should remain unstressed. His observation on III. 228 shows this clearly: the second line of the passage:

"Father, thy word is past, man shall find grace;
And shall grace not find means, that finds her way"
is changed to:
"And shall not Grace find Means? that finds her way",
because Bentley finds it wrong that "Grace, the Emphatical Word lies mute without Tone." The unusual rhythmic weight acquired

---

[108]) IV. 345 *n.*
[109]) VI. 34 *n.*
[110]) II. 226 *n.*
[111]) II. 132 *n.*

by the word through being placed in the stressed part of an inverted foot escapes Bentley's notice, because he scans the verse according to the accepted scheme. His way of marking the stress at the beginning of VI. 691 is a distinct proof of this: "Save whát Sin hath impair'd." Here again he complains that *"Sin* here, the most emphatical Word lies mute without Tone or Accent." Even the two successive "inverted feet" of this verse are not enough to warn Bentley that Milton hardly thought of the conventional metre while writing the line, and that "sin" in the poet's conception of the verse is more strongly emphasized than if it stood in the corresponding stressed place of a "regular" blank-verse line.

The only metrical liberty in Milton which is formally acknowledged and approved by Bentley, even to the point of his consistently using a mark to denote it, is what is usually called elision. It does not interfere with his standard of a perfectly regular Iambic pentameter, for he does not suppose the elided vowels to be pronouced at all, so that the number of syllables is not increased by them . He regards Milton's practice as an exact imitation of classical versification [112]): "our Author took a peculiar Liberty, from the *Greeks* and *Latins,* of throwing out the final Vowels, when the sequent Word began with another Vowel; which gave him an Easiness and Freedom in his Blank Verse, equal, if not superior, to Prose it self" [113]). This conception of elision induces him to spell XI. 236: "whom not t'offend." It compels him to emend IV. 839 where he does not know how to deal with the long vowel of "thee" in "Departed from thee and thou", for "he [= the author] would not strike the Vowels of *Thee* out here, to injure the very Thought without the least necessity." His own metrical practice does not seem to agree with his theory. Verse VII. 66 as emended by him ends as follows: "As one who', his drought / Yet scarce allay'd", & c. It is questionable how he expected "who', his" to be pronounced.

How rigidly Bentley's theory rejects the idea of supernumerary syllables, is shown by a considerable number of notes, *e. g.* VII. 385 where "With their bright luminaries that set and rose" is found impossible because "This Verse has a Syllable too

---

[112]) The matter is also clearly stated in Bentley's preface.
[113]) IV. 839 n.

5*

much; unless you'll contract *Luminaries* into Three Syllables. But *Milton* could not give it so." The same is repeated in XI. 373 and VIII. 591 where Bentley sees only the alternatives of the words "evil" and "reason" being "shrunk into one syllable", or the verse remaining irregular because it has one syllable too much.

This objection to supernumerary syllables combined with Bentley's conventional scansion of the verse and his theory of elision cause his peculiar reading of verse IV. 345: "Gambol'd before them, th' unwieldy' elephant", where he accentuates the first syllable of "unwieldy", although, as he especially remarks, "The Author knew the common Pronunciation to be in the Second; as VII. 411. *Wallowing unwieldy.*" This is the line in which Milton, according to Bentley, "made the Verse it self *unwieldy;* that the Reader might feel it, as well as understand it." This seems to be true, but Milton apparently effected this by combining the vocal glide of an elision with an additional syllable in "th' unwieldy", thus doubly loading the metre in the place where the sense required it. Bentley does not seem to be capable of imagin- ing an unelided additional syllable; he therefore assumes this unusual change of the word-accent and a new elision at the end of the word, which has to make the final vowel of "unwieldy" mute.

In this as well as in the previous cases, the precipitate appli- cation of theoretical standards not tested in practice leads Bentley to impossible conclusions, although he does not seem to have been conscious of the contradictions thus caused.

C. BENTLEY'S USE OF LITERARY PARALLELS FOR TEXTUAL PURPOSES.

Bentley's long and brilliant practice in reconstructing passages of classical poetry had supplied him with a bold and ingenious technique in the use of literary parallels for purposes of textual evidence. This kind of evidence is especially useful in Latin and Greek, where the linguistic instinct of the modern reader is otherwise often likely to fail. It was highly valuable there to be able to produce a quotation in favour of one's own reading.

This must serve to explain the primitive kind of evidence

often used by Bentley to prove his Miltonic emendations. He is fairly consistent in his substitution of Miltonic words and phrases only, but the analogy is sometimes so slight and the word so common, that the question remains how Bentley could so persistently repeat this kind of slipshod parallel. It becomes less surprising if one remembers that he had to correct the works of the ancients almost like a schoolmaster correcting inaccurate transcripts (cf. *e. g.* IX. 258 *n.* where "wish" is changed into "wish'd" and an instance of the latter form is quoted from IX. 421; in both cases Satan's wish to seduce Eve is expressed, but any closer analogy is absent).

Yet the deftness of his technique is often notable. He is so keenly interested in technical points and remote literary analogies occupy his mind so entirely that he seems to have little attention left for a quiet, balanced examination of the *contents* of Milton's poetry. He appears to forget the context and to follow the call of almost every new and curious though possibly very superficial and uncritical idea, being fully convinced that he is right in doing so.

Professor Mackail finds two valuable emendations which have been approved by most editors, and have made their way into the standard text, those of VII. 321 and 451 — "the swelling gourd" for "the smelling gourd" in VII. 321 and "soul" for "fowle" in VII. 451. It has been shown that some of the reasons for the second emendation were supplied by Hume, although he failed to do the constructive part of the work. Both corrections are based on a careful study of the probable literary models, and in both the alteration needed is so small that the original readings might be regarded as errors of the printer or amanuensis. Yet there are corrections which hardly any editor could accept, and which exhibit, nevertheless, the intenseness and inventiveness of Bentley's mind. He does not understand the expression "the *ridges* of grim war" in VI. 236 and proposes "the bridges" instead, deviating from his objection to metaphorical usage in favour of another deeply-rooted principle of his, that of the acceptance of classical traditions. He regards the expression as a translation of Homer's "Πολέμοιο γεφύρας", on the following grounds: "Γέφυραι are in common acceptation *Bridges:* in *Homer* they are the open Intervals between Rank and File. *To open* and *close such Bridges* is a Phrase intelligible." Only one letter has been added, the military analogy has some appearance of probability, the whole idea is so strikingly new that Bentley's more inventive than critical mind was satisfied.

An even less convincing correction where the classical parallel, however, is equally close, is found in II. 671. Bentley, who values Milton's learning, finds the passage unscholarly because ten furies are mentioned instead of three, and because death is described as "terrible as Hell" although the scene actually is in hell. His apparent conviction that poetic licence is a sign of absence of scholarship has to be kept in mind here. It seems to be supported by the closeness of the classical parallel once the obnoxious part has been omitted: "But the more to evince this Line to be spurious; the Two pieces of Verses,

> Black it stood as Night,
> And shook a dreadful Dart,

are one continued Sentence, translated literally from one in *Homer:*

> ʽΟ δ᾽ ἐρεμνῇ νυκτὶ ἐοικὼς
> Γυμνὸν τόξον ἔχων, καὶ ἐπὶ νευρῆφιν ὀιστόν."

Bentley's failure to see that literary imitation is not merely copying, misleads him here as in I. 621 and elsewhere.

D. BENTLEY'S CANCELLATIONS.

Bentley's most important alteration of Milton's text is the suppression of about seventy passages, ranging in length from one line to fifty-five (the description of the Paradise of Fools in book III). Nearly all of them he supposed to be the work of the editor who interfered with Milton's original. The observation in his preface, that the changes proposed should be taken only as suggestions, ought to be remembered, although the foot-notes in which they are recommended usually show no traces of this prefatory modesty.

Here more than anywhere else the question obtrudes itself, whether Bentley acted in good faith or no. It seems possible that he partly belived in his theory, and partly experimented, and was convinced by the numerous arguments discovered on afterthought. Success had made him self-confident, and he was hardly likely to entertain any doubts as to his competence in deciding textual problems. What he saw before him was simply another text like those of Horace or Terence or any of the other classical authors to whose works he had restored a shape, in spite of all the difficulties of corrupt tradition. Knowing much less about English literature than about the classics, and exposing himself much more to criticism because his author was so generally accessible, Bentley, nevertheless, was unable to give up the attitude of victorious superiority to which he had become accustomed. He conjectured as freely as in his edition of Horace, exercising the gift by which he had made his name.

All his prejudices become obvious in his cancellations. As Professor Mackail describes it: "His editor became 'an injudicious smatterer in Astronomy, Geography, Poetical Story, and Old Romances'. Bentley will have none of these. The desperate hook slashes right and left, and as he plies it, 'brightness falls from the air'. Out go, one after one, Milton's most splendid and most inimitable beauties" [114]). Nothing can be detracted from these words, nor can Bentley's artistic sense be rehabilitated. He suppresses Milton's long sonorous enumerations of mythological and historical names, missing in them the commonsense he likes, and unable to feel either their atmosphere or their phonetic beauty (cf. the notes on I. 306, I. 579, II. 635, II. 659, X. 524, & c.). What is not exactly logical, is eliminated; what does not accurately correspond with accepted history and science, is rejected as unscholarly (cf. I. 574, I. 717 — an anachronism, III. 35, III. 597 — objection to bad science). Pagan mythology is found unfit to be associated with sacred themes (IV. 705); romance and exotic descriptions are suppressed (II. 635, XI. 387, & c.); rationalistic considerations outweigh poetry (I. 351—355). All this has been dealt with so often that to repeat it would not be profitable. Yet certain frequently reappearing features in Bentley's editorial conduct here seem worth noticing and emphasizing.

One of his notes, in which he advances artistic objections, has recently been highly praised. "His note", says Prof. Grierson [115]), "on Milton's account of the dinner prepared for Raphael

---

[114]) Cf. p. 11.
[115]) Preface to Grierson's edition of P. L. 1925, p. XLVI.

and the latter's unhappy disquisition on angelic digestion" is "as
vigorous as, and more daring than a note by Dr. Johnson on
Shakespeare." This is the note on V. 395. Some of Bentley's
other objections to cancelled passages are sound in their way,
although they usually miss the essence of the poet. A note like
the following contains some reasonable argumentation, which
might almost seem convincing, if the style of the passage attacked
in it could be forgotten (on X. 731): "'Tis *Milton's* particular
Excellence, that he always keeps up τὸ Πρέπον, the just Character
of every Person that's introduc'd speaking. *Adam* here, *tost in
a troubled sea of Passions,* has a long Soliloquy with himself; the
Sentiments of which, if handled with a due Decorum, would raise
in his Readers an equal Concern with his own.

> ...*Si vis me flere, dolendum est
> Primùm ipsi tibi; tum tua me infortunia tangent.*

Now if we find *Adam* here, in that heavy Seriousness and Anxiety,
leaving his true Topics, and catching at Trifles, Quirks, Jingles,
and other such Prettinesses; we may boldly venture to say, Those
Lines are the Editor's, and not the Poet's." Bentley's sympathy
with pathos and intense expression, and his impatience with
everything that lessens the simplicity of outline, are not in
themselves preferences to be despised.

But these instances are isolated, and it is more from the
technical side that Bentley draws his reasons for cancellation.
One consideration must be emphasized — Bentley's insistence
that nothing unscholarly could have been written by Milton. This
was a dangerous criterion. The standards of scholarship, as well
as of science, had changed very considerably during the 58 years
since Milton died. Men of Bentley's own college, like Sir Isaac
Newton, as well as Bentley himself, had acted a decisive part in
these changes, yet Bentley seems to have failed to recognize the
difference of the times. Bentley, moreover, was untrained in the
historical consideration of an age not far enough to be regarded
as ancient. His outlook seems to have become historical only
when the period was sufficiently remote, like the times of classical
antiquity. Hume's notes show how unhistorically an erudite
scholar could handle things of the generation before his own.
Bentley in this respect has improved on Hume, but traces of the
same attitude may be found.

The main technical circumstance which seemed to support Bentley was the fact that the excisions required by his principles often produced a text which grammatically and metrically seemed less open to criticism. An instance of this kind may be found in VII. 463—474. Bentley suppresses the passage, finding the situation described there childish and impossible, but in addition to this lays special stress on criteria of metre and style. "I shall first join together the Lines that are genuine; and their Connexion will appear so inseparable, that the Lines intermediate must be voted spurious; though they were as elegant, as they 'll be found silly. He had spoke of the Generation of Beasts, both Wild and Tame:

> *Those rare and solitary, These in flocks*
> *Pasturing,* at once *and in broad herds, up sprung:*
> At once *came forth whatever creeps the ground*
> *Insect or Worm.*

Let any one, either gifted with Poetry, or conversant in good Poets, determine; if this Repetition, *At once, At once,* did not follow thus close under *Milton's* forming Stile, nothing intervening."

Bentley's use of the purely metrical test is of interest in this connection. The greater part of his cancellations — about 40 — involve only complete lines; the rest — about 30 — cause breaks in one or two verses; yet in nearly one half of these the fragments join without gap or excrescence. Bentley, it may be imagined, writing in great haste and applying his dogmas, must have been pleasantly surprised at the ease with which he attained to apparently acceptable results.

One reason for this manipulative success is Milton's habit of beginning and ending a brief, and sometimes a long, digression — usually constituting a syntactical unit of some kind — at the same place in the verse. An example of this may be found in I. 306—311 where the simile about Busiris and the Memphian chivalry begins and ends after the third accentuated syllable of the line. The same pause occurs two verses earlier in I. 304, and again in 301 and 299. Exactly the same rhythm is used in another cancellation in the same book, I. 717—722. A different pause, but equally favourable, is found in IV. 983—985. Something similar happens in VII. 481—484 where the coincidence is interesting, for the pause is not in a very usual place here, occurring before the last foot. Yet the most remarkable case of all is probably XI. 387—411 where the suppression of the long enumeration of kingdoms and cities leaves not the slightest metrical trace, though not a syllable outside the condemned catalogue has been cancelled.

A detailed study of these passages would transgress the scope of this survey. The impression produced by it would probably be (and is, so far as the present writer is concerned), that chance contributed to Bentley's infatuation, and confirmed him in the conviction of his infallibility.

4. THE RECEPTION OF BENTLEY'S EDITION.

A. THE BRIEFER RETORTS.

The reception of Bentley's edition was hostile. Details about some of the derisive poems and parodies published on the event may be read in Dr. Good's "Studies in the Milton Tradition" [116], a book which, however, does not say very much concerning the larger and weightier retorts. The articles in the periodicals of that time, especially in the "Grub-street Journal", are emphatic in rejecting and condemning Bentley's theories and emendations. The first larger review in the "Grub-street Journal" (No. 108) ridicules Bentley's logical blunders, *e. g.* his supposition that Milton's poverty and friendless condition compelled him to ask the help of an editor; for this "would rather induce a Man to write his own Copy."' The supposed sudden revival of prosperity which enabled Milton to find a better editor for "Paradise Regained" and "Samson Agonistes" is considered "strange to vulgar Apprehensions." The same writer, whose signature is J. T., shows in No. 113 that the second edition of "Paradise Lost" came later than "Paradise Regained", which implies that the improved assistance found for the latter poem, on Bentley's theory, should have been available for "Paradise Lost" also. No. 125 of the same periodical contains a letter attacking Bentley's assertion that his notes were written extempore and immediately sent to the printer. A certain Dr. Ashenhurst from Bristol is reported to have seen him preparing his commentary many years before, though it is not made clear whether actual work at the notes is meant. It is hinted, in this connection, that Bentley may have invented the apparition of an editor in order to avoid an open attack upon Milton. Extracts from Pearce's "Review" are given from July onward [117]), beside other criticisms in prose and verse.

---

[116]) Studies in the Milton tradition by John Walter Good... Published by the University of Illinois Urbana 1925 [8⁰ pp. 310]. See pp. 177—179.

[117]) The Grub-street Journal No. 131, 134, 146.

Two special publications besides Pearce's larger work deserve separate examination here as having some claims to the name of commentary [118]). One of them, an octavo pamphlet, uses Dean Swift's name, though only for part of the contents. The title-page reads as follows:

MILTON RESTOR'D AND BENTLEY DEPOS'D. CONTAINING, I. Some Observations on Dr. *Bentley's* Preface. II. His various Readings and notes on PARADISE LOST, and *Milton's* Text, set in opposite Columns, with Remarks thereon. III. PARADISE LOST, Attempted in Rime, Book I. Addressed to Dr. *Bentley*, From Dean SWIFT. *Sing, Heav'nly Muse, from Pedantry be free.* NUMB. I. LONDON: Printed for E. CURLL in the *Strand.* 1732. [Price 6 d.] 8⁰. pp. 30. On the last page the continuation of the work is promised.

An introductory remark on the rhymed paraphrase in which, according to the foot-note on p. 27. "the judicious *Rimer* has adher'd so closely to his Author, as to extend 25 of *Milton's* Verses to no more than 30 of his own", is really "From Dean Swift", namely from his "Letter of Advice to a Young Poet" [119]), where an attempt at "bestowing rhyme upon Milton's Paradise Lost" is mentioned.

The motto and the rhymed parody, & c. make it quite evident that the publication is mainly satirical. The pamphlet contains, as the title-page announces, a number of special notes on Bentley's commentary. They are not based on serious research, and abound in metaphors and exclamations. Bentley's ruthless method with its unproved statements is compared to "a Croud of Witnesses with cloudy Caps on..., but not *one Evidence* to prove a single Fact"... [120]). His presumption is ridiculed: "What a prodigious Man is Dr. *Bentley:* He corrects the Numbers of *Horace!* and raises the Sense of *Milton!*" [121]). Bentley's classical illustrations find praise [122]) but the flatness of his modern style

---

[118]) In this connection, see also: "OF VERBAL CRITICISM: AN EPISTLE TO MR. POPE OCCASIONED BY *Theobald's Shakespear,* and *Bentley's Milton...* LONDON... 1733..." (fol.: pp. [2] + 14).

[119]) Ed. Temple Scott, vol XI. p. 101.

[120]) I. 6 *n.*

[121]) I. 35 *n.*

[122]) I. 33 *n.*

is contrasted with Milton's archaic expressions which "preserve
the Majesty of his Verse" 123).

The writer appears to be an eager Royalist. He evidently
dislikes Milton's party, contesting in his preface Bentley's
description of the poet as lonely and "Obnoxious to the Government". The generosity of the royal Act of Oblivion and also of
the censor who permitted the publication of the poem, are
emphasized. Even the bookseller's point of view is presented
with greater sympathy than that of the poet. Bentley's complaint
of the scanty reward received by Milton is regarded as groundless: ten pounds is not "so poor a Price for a Book of this Bulk,
which in seven Years had but one Impression" 124).

The best part of the pamphlet is probably the passage of the
preface demanding the study of the authentic texts and condemning the devastating practice of adding new guesswork in each
edition until the original readings are badly corrupted: "...the
whole of *Milton's*, or any other Poem, extinguished by degrees,
and a new one set forth by Editors, challenge the Title not of
Notes, but of a Text *variorum*. To regulate the Work of a deceased
Author from various Readings in Manuscripts or printed Copies
is a laborious, but useful Undertaking: But this way of restoring,
i. e. interpolating by Guess, is so sacralegious [*sic*] an Intrusion,
that, as it had its Rise, so it is to be hoped it will have its Fall
with you."

The title-page of the second pamphlet, like that of "Milton
Restor'd", carries a derisive motto:

A Friendly LETTER to Dr. BENTLEY. Occasion'd by his
New Edition of PARADISE LOST. By a Gentleman of Christ-
Church College, *Oxon*. Monstrum horrendum, informe, ingens,
cui Lumen ademptum. VIRGIL. LONDON: Printed for J. RO-
BERTS, near the *Oxford-Arms* in *Warwick-Lane*. MDCCXXXII.
8⁰. pp. 64.

A second edition appeared in the same year. The author,
on the last page, signs himself "Semicolon". This pamphlet,
which now and then assumes a mock-friendly tone, is full of
personal attacks of an unpleasant kind, and its tone and style are
crude. Bentley's legal affairs are hinted at in the following

---

123) I. 46 *n.*
124) ibid.

manner: "Dear *Dicke*, give me thy Hand: I heartily congratulate thee on having had so little to do with Law... Every Reader will... be heartily sorry that you had not had an opportunity of looking into an *Indictment*, or standing a little in a *Court* of *Justice* befoe [*sic*] this was written" 125). Bentley's unrestrained manner is commented upon in a style no more chastened than his own: "S'life, Sir, are you mad? Did ever such a Piece of prophane Drollery come from a *Doctor of Divinity?*" 126).

The author's main attacks are directed against Bentley's pedantry and presumption. He is supposed to have "pilfer'd from a Rule in the Art of *Grubean Criticism*, which takes as the Foundation of all verbal Criticism these two Suppositions: First, That an Author *can never miss* making use of the *best Word* on every Occasion; the Second, *That a Critick cannot chuse but know which that is*" 127). His mistakes in biblical and even in classical lore are ridiculed: "Criticks... may villainously and maliciously Assert, that Dr. *Bentley*... understands his *Classicks* no better, than... he does his *Bible*" 128). Milton's words in P. L. III. 215: "just th' unjust to save", are traced back "to the Apostle, who makes use of the very Expression, *the Just for the Unjust*", and Bentley's inability to see this leads to the remark that he is " a mere *Novice* in his *own Employment;* nay, not so much as acquainted with *Chapter* and *Verse;* and a *Professor of Divinity* too: that's a Shame!" (III. 215 *n.*).

Broader and cruder remarks of this kind alternate with much that is intelligent and to the point; there are signs of thought and erudition. What strikes one more than anything is the resemblance of the more valuable and illuminating arguments to Pearce's "Review" of the same year. Todd, in the bibliography at the end of his edition, ascribes the pamphlet to Pearce, though not with certainty. Pearce was a Cambridge man, from Bentley's own college; but the Christ-Church of the title-page was not impossibly a disguise. His "Review" was published anonymously, though statements by people who knew him well, e. g. by Bishop Newton 129), make it certain that he was the author. Anonymity

125) Cf. pp. 9—10.
126) V. 414 *n*.
127) I. 6 *n*.
128) I. 16 *n*.
129) Cf. the preface to Newton's edition of "Paradise Lost", ed. 1749,

there was his only disguise. But he may have had some grudge against Bentley. His election to a fellowship at Trinity College, Cambridge, seems to have been first opposed by Bentley [130]), and he supported Dr. Colbatch and the fellows of Trinity in their struggle against the Master [131]). Monk doubts the Christ-Church of the title-page and suspects the pamphlet "to have come from a College with which Bentley was better acquainted" [132]).

The similarities between the more serious portions of Semi-colon's and Pearce's notes are not isolated and rare but occur throughout the pamphlet; if allowances be made for the radical differences of style, they are much more numerous than the disparities. The main argument of the first note in both, on the epithet "secret" in "the secret top Of *Oreb*, or of *Sinai*" [133]), is the same. Both publications defend the adjective, finding that it alludes to the clouds and darkness when Moses spoke with Jehovah. Milton's "rhyme" in I. 16 is explained by Semicolon as used "in the same Sense that the Ancients did their ‘$P\acute{v}\vartheta\mu o\varsigma$ and Rhythmus, viz. for Numbers, Metre and Verse in general." So Pearce observes that "we should here understand by *Rhime* not the *jingling sound* of *like Endings*, but Verse in general; the word being deriv'd from rythmus [*sic*], $\acute{\varrho}\acute{v}\vartheta\mu o\varsigma$." Not only the idea but even the expression here are similar. "Semicolon" ex-plains "puts on swift wings" as "moving forward swiftly with his wings". So Pearce: "he makes his wings move forward swiftly" [134]). The classical myth of Thamyris meets with the same interpretation from both commentators. "Semicolon" thinks that his "Lust for the muses" (which was Bentley's charge against him) meant "his extraordinary Love of Poetry"; Pearce explains it as "the Court which he made to them, or his violent Affection for Poetry" [135]). In both sets of notes the grouping together of prophets and poets in this passage is attributed to the

---

vol. I. sg. a₃r. Newton there acknowledges the ample assistance and advice given to him by Pearce, and speaks in the same breath of the latter as of the author of the "Review".

[130]) Cf. Monk's Life of Bentley, vol. I. 411.
[131]) Cf. Monk II, p. 79.
[132]) Cf. p. 322 of vol. II.
[133]) I. 6.
[134]) II. 631 *n*.
[135]) III. 35 *n*.

influence of the classical tradition which identified their pro-
fessions. Both of them prove the authenticity of the "Paradise
of Fools" episode by pointing to the mention of it in the argument
to book III [136]). A rather curious coincidence is found in the
explanation of the "Ministers of vengeance and pursuit" [137]).
According to Pearce this should mean the good angels pursuing
the rebels in spite of Christ's command, in VI. 802, to rest from
battle this day. That command, it is assumed, refers exclusively
to the battle, and not to the pursuit. The same interpretation is
found in "Semicolon's" note on the passage. The question
whether the special mention of rest for the day ("this day from
Battel rest") agrees with such an explanation, is not discussed
by either. Semicolon, it is true, sees another possibility, namely,
that the lightning, thunder and hail referred to immediately after
"Ministers" may have been personified by Milton. Pearce seems
to have been induced to accept the first of these explanations
because the passage, "Eternal wrauth Burnt after them to the
bottomless pit" [138]), is regarded by him as a hint at the pursuing
victors.

This is a mere selection from a much larger number of
coincidences. The differences are mainly in the manner of expression and in the degree of thoroughness, which is much
greater in Pearce's elaborate work. An example of their way
of expressing the same general idea may be found in I. 206 *n.*
where both expose the tautology of Bentley's emendation, "skinny
rind" for "skaly rind". They agree in giving picturesque
parallels which prove the absurdity of the expression though
Pearce does it cautiously and politely. In Semicolon's opinion,
the emendation is a good example of "one of the great Rules of
the *Bathos,* which requires that all Epithets should wholly coincide
with the nature of their Substantives; thus *liquid Water, windy
Air, dirty Earth,* and *burning Fire.*" He proposes the emendation
"skinny Skin". Pearce finds *"skinny...* a strange unpoetical
Epithet to be join'd to the metaphorical word rind: as if we
should call the *Shell* of a Nut, the *shelly rind.*"

The relation between the two publications is very similar

---

[136]) III. 444 *n.*
[137]) I. 169 *n.*
[138]) VI. 865 *n.*

to that between a brief, easy-going and hurried sketch and a serious and scholarly elaboration of it. The opposite assumption, of the superficial repetition in the lighter performance of the arguments of a more thorough work, seems less plausible. Pearce's book was studied and quoted immediately [139]) so that borrowings from it were not likely to pass as new.

B. PEARCE'S "REVIEW OF THE TEXT OF MILTON'S PARADISE LOST."

The publication of this book, which is the main and conclusive refutation of Bentley's emendations, was an important event in Milton criticism. Without discarding what was valuable in Bentley's attempt, it led the study of "Paradise Lost" back into the channels of orthodox research. It must have been written at great speed, as the early mention in the "Grub-street Journal" shows.

It appeared in three parts. The title-page of the first part is as follows [140]):

A REVIEW OF THE TEXT OF MILTON's *Paradise Lost:* In which the CHIEF of Dr. BENTLEY's EMENDATIONS Are Consider'd; And several other EMENDATIONS and OBSERVATIONS are offer'd to the Public. PART I. *Containing* REMARKS *upon the first* FOUR Books. LONDON: Printed for JOHN SHUCKBURGH; at the Sun, near the *Inner-Temple-Gate* in *Fleet-street.* M.DCC.XXXII.

The title-pages of the other two parts differ from the first only in the indication of their special contents:

PART II. Containing REMARKS *on the* V, VI, VII, *and* VIIIth Books.

And part III:

PART III. Containing REMARKS on the IX, X, XI, and XIIth Books. To which is added An APPENDIX to the Whole.

The third part has a note on the verso of the title-page indicating that the preface has been altered and "stitch'd up with

---

[139]) Cf. Grub-street Journal, 2 March 1732 (No. 113).

[140]) All three parts in octavo, part I containing pp. VIII+152, part II, pp. II + pp. [153—287] and part III, pp. II + pp. [289—400].

this Third Part, that Those who have bought the former Parts, may cancel the others, and place These in the room of them." A new general title-page is also added with the new preface 141) :

A REVIEW OF THE TEXT OF THE TWELVE BOOKS OF MILTON's *Paradise Lost:* In which the CHIEF of Dr. BENTLEY's EMENDATIONS Are Consider'd; And several other EMENDATIONS and OBSERVATIONS are offer'd to the Public. LONDON: Printed by JOHN SHUCKBURGH, at the *Sun,* near the *Inner-Temple-Gate* in *Fleetstreet.* M.DCC.XXXIII.

This is the final title. The main reason for the rewriting of part of the preface was evidently the need to correct a blunder regarding the first edition of "Paradise Lost" which was asserted to have been published "in 1669, (not in 1667, as Dr. *B.* says in his *Preface)*". Pearce had noticed in the meantime that there were variously dated title-pages of that edition, so that Bentley could not be said to be wrong. He gives an account of them in the rewritten preface.

Bentley is treated in it very respectfully. His great merits in scholarship are acknowledged. The author hopes that he *"will* not, he is sure *ought* not, to give Dr. *B.* any Offence." Pearce's care and caution are shown in the principles of Milton emendation professed by him: the alteration of words of a similar sound between which the blind poet probably could not distinguish, and of the punctuation where faults were more likely to occur. The improbability of the conjecture that no reliable person should have been found to help Milton, when Toland's Life mentions so many learned friends, is emphasized, and the idea of an editor who made alterations at his pleasure is therefore rejected. It is pointed out, as in the "Grub-street Journal" in No. 113, that "Paradise Regained" was prior to the second edition of "Paradise Lost", and the suggestion is made that the improved editorial conditions which benefited *"Paradise Regained"* may have been beneficial also to the second edition of the earlier work. An interesting feature is the reference to the dramatic schemes of "Paradise Lost" in the Cambridge MSS., and the connection of these schemes with Toland's mention of Milton's plan to write

---

141) The contents of the volume in its final form are: pp. VIII + 400. P. 1: the title-page; p. III—VII: the preface; p. VIII: errata; pp. 1—389: commentary; pp. 390—400: appendix (= additional notes).

a tragedy on that subject. Even Milton's possible models for the scheme are considered; it is thought probable that "M. took the first hint from an *Italian* Tragedy called *Il Paradiso perso*" of which Pearce had heard as having been written "many years before *M*. enter'd upon his Design."

Pearce's main qualifications for undertaking a revision of Bentley's edition were his critical, scholarly mind and his genuine appreciation of poetry. He seems to have been influenced by Addison's criticisms, for his note on P. L. II. 635, one of the best expressions of his attitude, largely repeats a remark from one of the "Spectator" articles [142]). The topic is Milton's Homeric and Virgilian practice of using digressive similes, the habit of first showing the points of resemblance between the objects compared and then, as Pearce puts it, "wandring into some unresembling Circumstances; which have no other relation to the Comparison, than that it gave him the Hint, and (as it were), set fire to the train of his Imagination." The allusion to the "fire of Imagination" indicates the essential difference from Bentley's attitude.

It is natural that the critic who writes this should be convinced of the legitimacy of metaphorical language: "in Poetry... a Metaphorical and more Remote word is often preferable to the Simplest and Nearest, because it throws the Diction still more out of Prose..." [143]). He approves the bold language in VI. 212. ("...the dismal hiss Of fiery Darts... flew") for here surely there is a place "where the Sublimity of the Thought will allow the Accuracy of Expression to give way to the Strength of it... There is a peculiar Force sometimes in ascribing that to a Circumstance of a Thing, which more properly belongs to the Thing itself; to the *Hiss*, which belongs to the Darts." The logically incorrect expression "darkness visible" is approvingly described as "Strong and Bold". This sympathy with the irrational and imaginative, the feeling for suggestions and remote hints makes Pearce a much better interpreter of the element of romance in Milton than Bentley. He sees its ennobling effect on the poem, and is horrified by the "vulgar Cast" which, *e. g.*, Bentley's proposed substitution of "places in our own Channel" for Bengala,

[142]) No. 303. Febr. 16. 1712.
[143]) V. 741.

6*

Ternate and Tidore would give to Milton's simile [144]). Nobleness is a positive quality (Bentley, as was shown, though he talked of grandeur, seldom saw it); the fleet in II. 635 & *seq.* could not be exchanged for "a Firstrate Man of War", as Bentley wished, because "*a Fleet* gives a nobler Image than a single Ship."

Pearce draws distinct bounds between poetry and fact. There is no harm in Milton's basing his narrative on insufficient historical evidence, as in the passage on Busiris, I. 306 & *c.*, cancelled by Bentley as fabulous invention: "As to *M.*'s making *Pharaoh* to be *Busiris*... there is Authority enough for to justify a Poet in doing so, tho' not an Historian: It has been suppos'd by some, and therefore *M.* might follow that Opinion."

Imagination and a poetic mind are more important than correctness. Pearce agrees with the substance of a note by Bentley censuring a "vitious construction" [145]), yet he adds immediately that "such small Faults are not only to be pardon'd but overlook'd in great Genius's." Even the classics are quoted to prove this: "Fabius VIII. 3. says of Cicero, *In vitium saepe incidit securus tam parvae observationis:* and in X. 1. *Neque id statim legenti persuasum sit omnia, quae magni auctores dixerint, esse perfecta, nam & labuntur interim & oneri cedunt.*"

"Semicolon" ridiculed Bentley for his insistence on Milton's faultlessness. The idea that passages which are only partly successful or even essentially failures should be spurious receives no countenance from Pearce. His dislike of certain parts of the poem does not prevent him from *emphasizing* their authenticity, as in his notes on IX. 10 and VII. 15. "Surely he [Milton] did not pretend to be without Fault, tho' we can never allow that this Poem has all those blemishes which the Doctor charges on those Books," is his retort to Bentley's comment on the latter of these passages.

This enlightenment, and what is new, the adoption of a rational historical method, helps Pearce to understand Milton's limitations and to appreciate them rightly. Bentley, who would

---

[144]) II. 635 *n.* Pearce is not troubled by the fantastic, composite character of Milton's Leviathan (I. 200) but calmly recognizes it — the monster being "as much a *Beast* as a Fish". His confidence, it is true, is backed here by the book of Job (ch. 14).

[145]) II. 47 *n.*

have the poet correct even in questions of astronomy and zoology,
without regard to Milton's period, was grieved by the lapse in
P. L. VIII. 145 where the spots of the moon seem to be regarded
as changeable, cloud-like substances, and found it very wrong
that Milton's conception of the life of bees did not coincide with
his own notions of natural history [146]). Pearce does not attempt
to defend the correctness of Milton's views, but gives, instead,
documentary evidence that such were the opinions of the poet's
contemporaries. An article by a certain Mr. Auzout in the
"Philosophical Transactions" for the year 1666 is considered by
him a possible source of Milton's astronomical misconceptions,
and Charles Butler's "curious Treatise upon Bees, entitled the
Feminine Monarchie, printed in 1634" is found to contain the
same views on bees as the disputed Miltonic passage. Pearce
reasonably enough concludes regarding the first of these discoveries that "M. who wrote this Poem about that time [= 1666],
might approve of *Auzout's* observation, tho' the Doctor and
I do not."

Pearce not only recognizes the validity of imagination and
the place in poetry of irrationality. He is able to follow Milton's
imagery in a considerable number of difficult places and has the
intuition to distinguish Milton's peculiar point of view in many
passages where Bentley most deplorably failed. He does not
shirk much patient and tiresome research to make sure of his
case, as in his study of Milton's topography in P. L. VIII. 652
& *seq.* — a passage of which Bentley questions the authenticity:

"So parted they, the Angel up to Heav'n
From the thick shade, and Adam to his Bowre".

Bentley wonders why the thick shade is mentioned, if Adam
has left his bower, and Pearce undertakes a close inquiry into
books IV and V, tending to prove that it was not the shade of the
bower but that of a forest walk in front of its entrance. With all
this care and conscientiousness Pearce is capable of much keen
and rapid insight. How completely a poet's intention can be
misunderstood, is shown by Bentley's attack on the description
of the creation of animals in book VII [147]). He derides the

[146]) VII. 490 n.
[147]) VII. 463 n.

"editor" for representing them as if they were devoid of life and movement, so that even the stag "For all his Swiftness... seems to have lain fast" in the earth whence he ought to have risen. Bentley's critic regards this as the representation of one single moment, referring to Addison's appreciation of the passage [148]) and stating his own opinion: "Mr. *Addison* thought that there was an *exquisite Spirit of Poetry* in the Description of the *Lion's* rising, and I will venture to say that in the account of the rest *M*.'s Genius plainly appears. The Doctor should have observ'd that *M*. is here describing only what happen'd to those several Animals, or what posture they were in at one single point of Time." This seems a very happy solution. Milton actually appears to be trying to visualize the details of one moment as clearly and graphically as possible, hinting at the same time by some little touches at the character of the movement, which, though not explicitly described, can be perceived as we perceive it, for example, in the posture of a statue. The German Lessing afterwards elaborated the same idea in his "Laocoon".

Pearce is conscious of the need to realize the visual appearance of things. This was valuable as a reaction against Bentley's tendency to intellectualization and general statement. The difference may be seen in Pearce's reply to Bentley's observation on I. 290 where the mention of concrete details after a vague general concept which logically covers them, is found inadmissible. Pearce vindicates the right to describe the particulars after the more inclusive term, as they raise the sense, being definitely represented as "Objects of the Artist's View".

Not only the external, visual side of the world, but also the vaguer qualities of the mind are studied by Pearce. Doubt and hesitation are acknowledged to be legitimate elements and subjects of poetry, like most other kinds of experience. Bentley may object to the uncertainty expressed by the verb in P. L. I. 228:

> "till on dry Land
> He lights, if it were Land that ever burn'd
> With solid, as the Lake with liquid fire..."

because "This Verb *were* instead of a Propriety about the Name, makes a Doubt about the Thing," for his poetic code demands

---

[148]) See Spectator No. 339, 29 March 1712.

bare, naked statement. His opponent, on the other hand, is prepared to put up with such dubiety: "surely it was a Doubt about
the Thing, which *M.* intended". If the imagery is vivid and well-
drawn, he is content: "...it raises the Thought more to Describe Things right, than to Name them properly".

Pearce passes from the mere admission into poetry of hesitation and uncertainty to the actual technique of handling them.
He solves, for example, Bentley's puzzle concerning the contradiction in Belial's manner of first putting a question and then
denying it [149]. It is an easy case of rhetorical question, but the
method of Pearce's solution is valuable, because he is conscious
of the mental operations which caused the apparent contradiction:
"it is no Contradiction, first to speak of a thing as Doubtfull, and
afterwards (as upon second thoughts, as upon better consideration) to pronounce it absolutely Certain. There is a peculiar
force and strength, when the Sentence thus rises; and the Argument is the Stronger, for not having been push'd with all its
weight at first." Bentley, who very rarely hesitated himself,
was not likely to undertake such a study of hesitation.

Beside having a genuine if not always very vivid imagination,
Pearce has a strong sense of form, of proportion, of the interdependence of the various parts of a structure, and he is fond
of tracing these relations. This faculty, which is at once keenly
analytic and strongly synthetic, enables him to study Milton's
scholarly style much more successfully than Bentley, whose
rash and narrow method of thinking generally concentrated on
one point without allowance for the elaborate interplay of Milton's thought. A note like the following shows Pearce's scrupulous care: "Excellence is a general word; ... he [= Milton]
branches the *Excellence* of Angels into two particulars, their
radiant Forms and their *high Power*" [150]. He delights in these
ramifications: "it is often a Beauty in Poetry to branch out the
general thought into its particulars" [151].

It is evident that this cast of mind is well adapted to understand the value of one of the main devices of Milton's style. This
is the device of gradation, an artifice perhaps more frequent in
Milton than in most poets, and highly typical of his manner.

---

[149] II. 151 *n.*
[150] V. 457 *n.*
[151] IV. 323 *n.* See also I. 290 *n.*

Pearce recognizes it in its simplest form, that of slightly varied repetition, as well as in its more difficult and hidden manifestations. Bentley's great hatred of repetition made him blind to its technique in Milton. Pearce sees clearly enough how the poet in using it avoids monotony by introducing *intensification* and *variation* instead of bare repetition, although he does not overlook the intensifying effect of many simple, unaltered repetitions [152]). It is not merely "issuing forth" in X. 537 as in X. 532, but "In Triumph issuing forth", "where the Addition of *In Triumph* heightens the Thought and improves it, and makes the *issuing forth* not the same thing as here."

Order and sense and development of thought are discovered by Pearce where Bentley saw only crude tautologies. Bentley found needless repetition in the expression "Illimitable without bound" [153]). Pearce suggests a pause after "a dark Illimitable Ocean", and thus shows that "without bound" belongs to another section of the period, where it forms the base of a well-built scale of ideas:

"a dark

Illimitable Ocean, without bound,

Without dimension, where length, breadth, and highth", &. c.

The representative, figurative meaning of words in a similar gradation is perceived in V. 326 ("each bough and brake, each plant and juiciest gourd") where Bentley wished to substitute a synonym of "bough" for "brake" ("each bough and branch"). The reply suggests that "bough" might be equivalent to "tree" (pars pro toto) and that the whole constitutes a decreasing sequence of concepts, the lowest step being reached in "gourd", which symbolizes "all kinds [of plants] that lie on the earth." There is even more discrimination in the analysis of VIII. 395 & c. where various pairs of animals are enumerated according to the increasing degree of difference between them, until the gradation reaches its climax in the greatest contrast of all, that between man and beast, between the rational and the irrational creature.

One of the best examples of this method has just been discussed in another connection. It is the study of the gradation of certainty in II. 151 *n*. But Pearce passes from the study of

---

[152]) See IX. 181 *n.* & c.
[153]) II. 892.

isolated passages to the examination of the poet's architectural designs in the building up of whole books of his epic, discovering the same peculiarities there. Bentley condemned the double description of the creation of whales in a note on VII. 391, even going so far as to desire the poet to deviate from Scripture to avoid this repetition — a solitary infraction of his principle of adherence to the Bible. He adds: "Could *Milton* say, *God created the great Whales, & c.* and himself afterwards create them again?" In reply to this Pearce points out very carefully and in detail how the book is built: "...*M.* in his account of the fourth, fifth and sixth day's Creation, takes a different method from what he does in his account of the divine work on the other days." Pearce's favourite figure occurs again in the description of this method of first giving "a short and general account of what was then created," and then "branching that account out into its several Particulars." His preoccupation with this method seems unmistakable.

Either Pearce knew more about older English literature than his references indicate, or he read the few books mentioned in his notes with close attention. His insight into many questions of style suggests an intimate study of older literary works. His two favourite sources for quotation and allusion are Spenser's "Faerie Queen" and Fairfax's Tasso, that is to say, works very well known to Bentley.

He does not refer very frequently to historical or encyclopædic works of a non-classical character. Sandys' Travels — a book quoted repeatedly by Hume — is mentioned in II. 1019 *n.* In the same note a "Historia Orbis Terrae" and "Hoffman. Lexicon" are employed to illustrate questions of geography and mythology. The two last titles are not given in full, which makes it hard to trace them. A few articles and books on astronomy and natural history have been referred to already. Cherefeddin Ali's "History of Timur Bec" in Petis de la Croix' French translation is used to explain oriental habits [154]). These and some others only indicate his method of illustration, not the scope of his reading, for Pearce seems to refrain from demonstrating his erudition, showing his knowledge of out-of-the-way subjects only where the matter requires it.

---

[154]) II. 3 *n.*

Milton's other works are not mentioned very often. It is more the intensity of Pearce's reading of Milton than its range that is impressive. His references to Milton's earlier pieces do not go beyond the limits found in Bentley's notes, but the remarks on them are sounder. "Comus" is the favourite. A new trait is the interest in the sonnets: the curious resemblance between P. L. VIII. 478 & seq. and the poet's sonnet to his deceased wife is noticed. The prose works are quoted repeatedly, e. g. IX. 44 n., VI. 552 n. — the "Reason of Church Gouvernment", IX. 163 n. — the "Treatise upon Education". But the sound, solid way in which most things in the book are treated, and even the reading shown in it, are remarkable if one remembers how shortly after Bentley's edition it was published.

Pearce's classical erudition was an indispensable weapon in the battle against Bentley. He is a typical classical scholar, sometimes even excessively so. What was said about his freedom from prejudice and his soundness of perspective needs qualification sometimes where the classics are concerned. The existence of a classical parallel seems to him sufficient in itself to support an emphatic change of the grammatical person in Milton [155]) and even Ovid's astronomy is apparently regarded as authoritative. "Dr. B. reads IN *Taurus rides,* and says, Does Taurus ride too, a Constellation fix'd? Yes, or else Ovid is wrong throughout his whole *Fasti,* where he describes the rising and setting of the Signs of the Zodiac" [156]). If his reverence for the classics interferes with the impartiality of some of his judgements, he is able, on the other hand, to make a number of competent remarks on Milton's treatment of classical lore. Bentley's objection to the mention of the gardens of Adonis in P. L. IX. 439 as unjustified by classical authority is met by a reference to Pliny's "Natural History" where the myth of the Hesperian gardens ruled by Adonis and Alcinous is dealt with (Nat. Hist. XIX. 4). Pliny supplies him with another retort, in the matter of the ellops, the hydrus, and other monsters in P. L. X. 525 & seq. Bentley attacks this passage as contrary to truth; his reviewer, quoting Pliny's *Natural History* and other works, proves that Milton only imitated a classical belief. Athanasius Kircher's treatise on

---

[155]) IV. 482 n.
[156]) I. 769 n.

Scylla and Charybdis [157] is used to defend the opinion that Scylla was a whirlpool [158]). Martianus Capella and Prudentius serve to illustrate the existence, in the ancient world, of the pronunciation "Serapis" [159]).

More than ordinary observation is shown in the comparison of the alternation of the plural and singular of the personal pronoun in Adam and Eve's prayer with the same manner of speech in the classical chorus [160]). The observation is corroborated by the occurrence of this feature in the chorus of SA., and even such a late commentator as Verity, who supports the view that Adam and Eve speak both for themselves, is not able to deny the possibility that Pearce's explanation may be right.

Some Latinisms are discovered in Milton's vocabulary. The equivalence of "memory" IV. 24 to *"recordatio*, or the thinking and reflecting upon any thing, as well present and future as past" evidently answers to the general meaning of the passage. The use of "conscience" in the sense of "consciousness", Lat. *conscientia*, ("the *conscience* of her worth" VIII. 502) is backed by a quotation from the English Bible (Hebrews X. 2). But Hume had already done a great deal more in this department, and Pearce's real innovations are to be found in the study of the influence exercised on Milton's style by the literature of later times.

That he was well aware of the commentator's duty to study the exact value of his author's words in the author's own time, is proved by VI. 189 *n.* where it is flatly described as "frivolous" to call a poet's expressions low and hackneyed unless it is clear that they were so at the time when he wrote. Spenser's letter to Lord Buckhurst in the introductory part of the "Faerie Queen" is used by him to prove the legitimacy of Milton's interpretation of "rhyme" as "verse" [161]); the pronunciation of "Michael" as a trisyllabic word in Milton is paralleled by the same phenomenon in the argument to the IXth book of Fairfax's Tasso [162]); and

---

[157]) Pearce gives no reference in which of A. Kircher's numerous works the treatise is found.

[158]) II. 1019 *n.*

[159]) I. 720 *n.*

[160]) V. 202 *n.*

[161]) I. 16 *n.*

[162]) II. 294 *n.*

the "scandalous fault" (as Bentley calls it) of pronouncing
Ægean for *Ægéan* is shown by quotations from the same source
to be in keeping with Elizabethan habits of speech [163]). Several
further notes are based on Elizabethan literature, but far more
often than not Pearce prefers to use purely logical arguments or
to quote Miltonic parallels. It is plain that he understands the
spirit of the older poetry, though he resorts to no elaborate
apparatus of references.

"Semicolon" had already observed that Bentley did not seem
to know the English Bible as intimately as was to be expected
from a professor of Divinity. Pearce's knowledge of it, and
possibly also of its original, seems to surpass Bentley's. He is
sufficiently well-versed in Biblical phraseology to refute Bentley's
explanations of a number of passages, *e. g.* of III. 335 and VIII.
264, where he carefully distinguishes between the meaning of
isolated words and that of the same words if used in some
traditional scriptural combination with other expressions
("Heaven and Earth" and "Heaven", "to live and move" and
"to move"). An interesting example of his study of biblical
language is his interpretation of "giant angels" in VII. 605.
Here his comparison of the expression with the corresponding
passage of the Hebrew Bible seems to lead him to a better understanding of the emotional back-ground of Milton's text. He
observes that the Hebrew word ("gibbor") means the disposition
and mind of the angels, "a Proud, Fierce and Aspiring temper"
not their size. That Pearce appears to be right — even though
Milton in his habitual way of doubling the meaning of words
may also allude to the classical giants, as some commentators
suppose — is asserted by Todd [164]), who discovers that a very
similar idea occurs almost immediately afterwards in "the proud
attempt Of Spirits apostat" [165]), which in turn resembles the
marginal reading of the corresponding place in the Latin
Version [166]). The later Latin of ecclesiastical ritual, which
seems to escape Bentley's attention, is not neglected. Bentley
condemns the description of Adam as following the angel Raphael

---

[163]) I. 745 *n.*
[164]) See Todd P. L. VII. 605 *n.*
[165]) Cf. ll. 609—610.
[166]) Gen. VI. 4.

"with benediction" [167]) because the word does not apply to the address of a superior to an inferior, as he maintains. Pearce's reply is that its meaning may be not "blessing" but merely "giving them good Words, or wishing them well", as in Ps. 109. 17, and he compares the signification of the corresponding verb in *"Benedicere Domino, to bless God...*, a common Phrase in Religious Offices".

He does not quite succeed in avoiding the attraction of linguistic professionalism. Bishop Kennet's "Glossary to Parochial Antiquities" [168]) is mentioned IX. 437, and there are cases where the use made by Pearce of philological theory resembles Bentley's whim of adopting Anglo-Saxon spellings. No more valid reason is given for defending Milton's "wile" in IX. 85 against Bentley's proposal to substitute the form "guile" than that both "are the same Words originally, only the first [*i. e.* "guile"] is written and pronounc'd after the French manner, the latter after the English; as are *Guarrant, Warrant, Guerre, War*, and a great many others": as if the distant origin of a word and not its actual meaning would determine whether it was fit to be used or not.

This, however, is exceptional. Pearce usually analyzes the actual meaning very keenly. He is not handicapped by the Bentleian narrowness of vision which generally perceives only the standard signification of expressions and finds it impossible that anything else should be conveyed by them. His broadmindedness admits unusual meanings, as it admits a much larger vocabulary than Bentley did. The latter seems to have liked and sometimes invented curious and "absonous" words of his own, mainly of a classical stamp [169]), but excluded "low" expressions, among

---

[167]) VIII. 644 *n.*

[168]) Pearce also refers to other linguistic sources. Thus Furetière's French dictionary is mentioned VI. 517 *n.*, the dictionary of the Academia della Crusca VI. 868 *n.*

[169]) See "infuscation" for "insurrection" II. 136, "Solennious" for "Mysterious" IV. 743, "terraqueous" for "self-ballanc't" VII. 242, & *c.* "Carities" = "all Relations of Consanguinity and Affinity", for Milton's "Charities", IV. 756, is apparently of Bentley's own coinage. The NED. does not mention it in this sense. Bentley expressly derives it from the Latin.

them nautical terms such as "larboard" [170]). Pearce disagrees, pointing to Dryden's, Virgil's and Milton's practice (see "veers" IX. 513, "moors... under the Lee" I. 207). He makes no apology at all for examining the influence of "vulgar Phrases" such as "I have him safe" or "He is safe asleep" on Milton's "Our great Forbidder, safe with all his Spies About him" [171]). This liberality extends to the acknowledgement of a much freer variation of the *meaning* of words. Hume had the same feeling for their shifting value, but he generally studied the interplay between their classical and their ordinary sense. Pearce usually starts from a close study of the general situation, examining his subject from a *more exclusively English* point of view and being mainly guided by the context. He tries to see all the tendencies of meaning that may be working in an expression and then to relate it to the situation, but as a rule without indulging in etymological calculations. To him "coast" in I. 306 need not necessarily mean the land only, as it does in Bentley's opinion, but may be used in a wider signification including "that part of the *Red-Sea* which was nearest to the Coast; and where it is probable that the Sedge in a storm lay the thickest on the Water", in accordance with Milton's description of "scatter'd sedge Afloat, when with fierce Winds Orion arm'd Hath vex'd the Red-Sea Coast whose waves orethrew Busiris".

Sometimes he is influenced in favour of the form considered by him more particularly Miltonic, as in his emendation of IV. 147—8. Milton reads:

"Of goodliest Trees loaden with fairest Fruit,
Blossoms and Fruits at once of golden hue."

Bentley's passion for regularity induces him to adopt the plural "fruits" in both verses, evidently because the word means a plurality of fruits. Pearce substitutes the singular for the plural, and shows by a number of parallels, one of them from "Comus", that Milton by the singular means fruits while still growing, and by the plural, when already gathered. He forgets that Milton need not necessarily have been *quite* consistent and

[170]) II. 1019. Perhaps with an eye on Addison's remark about technical terms, where "larboard" is also mentioned.
[171]) IX. 815.

that the parallelism of "blossoms and Fruits" may have suggested
the plural ending in the second line. A very enthusiastic statement of this preference for individualism in style occurs in a pronouncement on Milton's right to coin new words. The note
amounts almost to hero-worship, and implies the condemnation
of conventional styles of writing. "Surely so great a Poet as he
was, may be allow'd to coin words, or else who may? If he had
coin'd none, his Poem must have fail'd of much of the Grandeur
in Diction which it now has" [172]).

The freer spirit of seventeenth century language is recognized
in Pearce's syntactical observations. Sometimes he goes very
far, as when he considers it possible [173]) that the adverb "up"
in X. 503 might be understood as a verb ["But up and enter now
into full bliss"]. But he does see the general instability of the
older grammar, and successfully illustrates it. The notes on
II. 917, V. 368 and III. 54 examine irregularities in the connection
between the verb and its object, as in II. 917—918: "Into this
wild Abyss the warie fiend Stood on the brink of Hell and look'd
a while." The verbs of this passage require different constructions, but the noun follows the last verb. Bentley finds this
impossible; Pearce shows that all the cases referred to follow the
same rule, and that this must consequently be regarded as an
authentic peculiarity of Milton's style. It is to be understood
as only a device for expressing what could generally be stated by
using the present participle of the first verb, e. g. II. 918: "stood
and look'd" = standing looked, V. 368: "sit and taste" = sitting
taste.

He is conversant with Milton's elliptic manner: his habit,
e. g., of dropping the auxiliary "to be" (IV. 509), or of omitting
the preposition occasionally, if it is used in connection with a
verb, as in I. 282: "fall'n such a... heighth" (where Bentley
prefers "fall'n from such highth") or in I. 723: "Stood fixt her
stately highth" [174]). Milton's vigorous enthusiasm is considered
sufficient excuse for brevity of this kind, which might otherwise
have seemed objectionable. In VI. 311 the reader "had better...
allow the Poet the Liberty of dropping the Copulative... on

---

[172]) VI. 93 n.
[173]) IX. 169 n.
[174]) See Pearce's note on I. 282.

account of that Fire of Imagination which was kindled, and the height of that Noble Fury with which he was possess'd." The intricacy of Milton's parenthetical constructions and his "ablative absolute" does not puzzle him as it did Bentley. He solves the problem of the parenthesis "The multitude of Angels... uttering Joy, Heav'n rung" [175]) and sees that "Hesperian Fables true, If true, here only" [176]) is an independent insertion. However, he does not escape the fate of misinterpreting some of the more difficult elliptic expressions, *e. g.* III. 469 *& seq.:*

> "Others came single...
> *Empedocles...*
> *Cleombrotus*, and many more too long,
> Embryos and Idiots, Eremits and Friers
> White, Black and Grey, with all thir trumperie."

The phrase "and many more too long" disconcerts him, as well as the absence of a second verb relating to the nouns in the two following lines. He assumes the omission of a line immediately after these words, which supplied the verb and made up for the deficiency of the expression. But a similar ellipsis of a verb already used in connection with an earlier noun occurs in III. 534:

> "On high behests his Angels to and fro
> Pass'd frequent, and his eye with choice regard
> From *Paneas* the fount of *Jordans* flood
> To *Bëersaba...*"

The verb "pass'd" apparently relates to "his Angels" as well as to "his eye", as "came" seems to be the predicate of "Others" as well af of "Embryos and Idiots", *& c.* And the expression "many more too long" is found in "Paradise Regained" [177]), in a passage pointed out by Newton, which shows that the phrase must be authentic.

Pearce's persistent analysis and close study make him sometimes a too dogmatic believer in these instruments of literary method. He becomes sophisticated and tends on occasion to lose the fresh, intuitive perception of the general reader. The

---

[175]) III. 345—347.
[176]) IV. 250—251.
[177]) II. 188.

discovery of certain grammatical habits of Milton causes him to assume them where a simpler explanation would serve at least as well. Arriving at the conclusion that the possessive personal pronoun before a noun may be equivalent to the corresponding prepositional genetive used after the substantive (his = of him, our = of us), he applies the rule where it seems to be out of place. He interprets "how forgoe Thy sweet Converse and Love so dearly joyn'd" in IX. 909 as another way of putting the phrase: "the sweet Converse and Love *of Thee* so dearly joyn'd to Me", though "Love so dearly joyn'd" seems to be used here as the personification of an abstract noun; the grammatical relations suggested by Pearce would only fritter away the unity of impression. The same type of construction is assumed in II. 304, X. 368, IV. 129, VIII. 423, nearly all of which seem more easily explainable in the ordinary way.

The effect on the importance of words of their position in the sentence is seen in VII. 216 *n.* In this line "and thou Deep, peace" had been altered by Bentley into "and Peace, thou Deep". Pearce's opinion is that "the most significant and commanding word *Peace* should stand last in the sentence." The proportions of a period are measured in II. 857 *n.* where Bentley's proposal to cut out part of the text in order to bring two parallel cases of the word "here" more closely together is refuted by the observation that they already stand at the beginning of two short sentences. These considerations are primarily artistic: attention is not confined to the purely logical *meaning* of an expression. Sometimes, though rarely, the relations between character and expression are traced. Abrupt, irregular mental impulses are suspected, for example, in IV. 112 *n.* Pearce puts a dash instead of Milton's comma after "By Thee", reading: "By Thee — and more than half perhaps will reign." The explanation is that "Thus Satan will make an *Aposiopesis* (as the Grammarians call it), that is, will stop abruptly and leave out something, which he was going to say; in the room of which he adds boastingly, *and more than half perhaps will reign.*"

Many of Pearce's good qualities appear in his study of Milton's punctuation, of which an example has just been given. Bentley's edition had worked much havoc among Milton's stops. The notes on VII. 24, 27, 168, 413, VIII. 369, IX. 417, 436, 457 show Pearce's endeavour to put this right. In VIII. 369, Bentley inadvertently omitted a comma and decided that the sentence was "loose and gaping", which is refuted by Pearce. Some verv drastic alterations in Bentley's text of VII. 168 & *seq.*: a colon after *"infinitude"* in l. 169 (for a comma) and the change of a comma into a full stop after "to act or not" in l. 172, distort the passage beyond recognition. This is emended by Pearce, who also rejects the neat and regular, but unconvincing reading of Bentley in P. L. VII. 412 & *seq.* The shifting of a comma and the alteration of a few words had changed the passage very considerably ["...there Leviathan Hugest of living Creatures, on the Deep Stretcht like a Promontorie sleeps or swimmes, And seems a moving Land">... "Seems a fix'd Promontory when he sleeps; When swims, a Moving Land"]. Pearce justifies the original reading which is based on an acuter observation of nature: "in both cases, whether he [= Leviathan] was sleeping or swimming, whether he mov'd by his own force or the force of the Waves, he seem'd to be a *moving Land.*"

Sometimes, though rarely, metrical questions are discussed, but no very important principles are advanced. The facts are followed with some care, and attempts are made to state their laws if not their reasons. Milton's intentional neglect of smoothness and flow is recognized by Pearce, and it is shown that certain irregularities occur repeatedly: *e. g.* the "artificial negligence of Measure" at the beginning of lines [178]. On the other hand, Pearce seems to agree with Bentley's view that dissyllabic words like "ruin", "riot", "reason" may be "shrunk into one syllable" [179]. The problem of elision remains unsolved, though Bentley's reading "Eternity', whose Extent" [180], with the elision before a consonant, is condemned.

Taken as a whole, Pearce's commentary is of importance as combining some of the qualities that were most conspicuously absent in Bentley. His mind has artistic grasp. He is at the same time in sympathy with the freer spirit of seventeenth century poetry, and aware of the relativity of linguistic phenomena, of the complexity of their agents, of the variations of the meaning of words and phrases according to the changes of mood.

---

[178]) See III. 584 *n.*, V. 750 *n.*
[179]) I. 90, 248 *nn.*, VIII. 590 *n.*
[180]) XII. 556.

tradition and situation. To this sensitiveness are added the solid virtues of the painstaking, assiduous, analyzing scholar. The laudable qualities of Bentley, his scientific force, his acuteness and consistency, are, by Pearce, intelligently controlled. Without meaning to be exhaustive, Pearce established a reliable method of commenting.

5. THE COMMENTARY OF THE RICHARDSONS.

EXPLANATORY NOTES and REMARKS on MILTON's
Paradise Lost. BY J. RICHARDSON, Father and Son. With
the LIFE of the AUTHOR, and a Discourse on the POEM.
By J. R. Sen. LONDON: Printed for JAMES, JOHN, and
PAUL KNAPTON, at the *Crown* in *Ludgate-street*, near the
West-End of St. *Paul's*. MDCCXXXIV.
    8⁰, pp. [1] + CLXXXII + 546. *Contents:* p. [1], title;
pp. I—CLXIII, life of the poet and discourse on P. L.;
pp. CLXIV—CLXXXII, remarks on the commentary; pp. 1—
536, notes; pp. 537—541, misprints, alterations, additions,
errata; pp. 542—546, tables of subjects and descriptions and
a short abstract of the poem.
    Note: With a portrait of Milton.

A. THE RICHARDSONS: THEIR GENERAL QUALIFI-
CATION AND THE MAIN OBJECTS OF THEIR COM-
MENTARY.

The bulky volume of the Richardsons marks a new stage in
Milton annotation, perhaps even in Milton criticism. Only the
purely critical part of the book is discussed in the present chapter;
the numerous biographical facts as well as the description of
Milton's ways of composition and the history of "Paradise Lost"
found in the earlier part of the volume, are omitted here.
This work is much more the expression of a personal creed than
any of the earlier commentaries, far more so than Pearce's scholarly production, and is based on a much broader and profounder
conception of Milton's poetry than Bentley's edition can show.
Both Bentley and the Richardsons put distinctive personal force
into their work, but in principle they are radically opposed, and
the latter do not treat Bentley favourably in their introduction.
Bentley is not mentioned there, but his method is described in an
unmistakable way in p. CXXXVIII. Though the work does
honestly aim at giving a more or less full and impartial explan-

ation of the difficulties which the general reader might find in
"Paradise Lost" 181) the main impression produced by it is that
it records the personal experiences of the authors in reading
the poem.

The title-page defines the book as the outcome of the collaboration of two persons. It is divided into two main parts —
a Life of Milton (with a long critical section), and a commentary.
The former was written by the father, who in the last pages of
the prefatory matter explains the character of the joint work.
Father and son seem to have collaborated very closely on the
commentary: in remarking on the borrowings from other critics,
the elder Richardson describes how thoroughly every detail was
considered by both of them — "in the Same manner as if it had
been Suggested from Within; or by Me to My Son, or by my Son
to Me and... Altred, or Not as our Own Joynt Reason Dictated,
from Arguments our Own Conceptions furnish'd Us with" 182).

The father knew no Latin or Greek, or very little, as he confesses 183). His previous keen literary activity, however, which
was devoted mainly to the analysis and description of art 184),
and his reading in modern literature, had developed his critical
faculties and helped him to appreciate some features of Milton
which were not always intelligible to professional classical
scholars. Though he thinks that Milton did not study Italian
painting and sculpture very attentively 185), and though there
consequently could be no direct gain for his Milton research
from his studies of art, the mere fact of his having analyzed
artistic phenomena was likely to prove fruitful and stimulating,
when he came to annotate poetry. His practice as a painter had

181) See p. CLXIX.
182) Cf. p. CLXIX.
183) Cf. p. CXLI.
184) See DNB. article on Jonathan Richardson. He had published
several works on the theory of painting (1715, 1719) and, in collaboration
with his son, one on works of art in Italy (1722). Winkelmann is said to
have found the latter the best book on the subject. The ambitious scope of
Richardson's writings appears from the title of a work published in 1719:
"The Connoisseur. An Essay on the whole Art of Criticism as it relates
to Painting". The son whose Christian name was the same as his father's,
took up the same profession of portrait-painting, though not with equal
success.
185) Cf. p. XV.

given him some insight into the processes of artistic creation, and his friendship with eminent men [186]) of letters helped him also. His Milton studies seem to have profited from these literary connections, for the preface to the notes which follows immediately upon the Life mentions the aid of "Friends, the Best Qualify'd to Assist, Especially in those Sciences our Selves are the least acquainted with... Had we Leave to Name those Friends it would do Us Honour and our Work" [187]). The son had received a better education, and evidently supplied the classical learning: "My Son is my Learning... We make One Man... When therefore I, in my Own Person talk of Things which in my Separate Capacity I am known to be a Stranger to, let Me be Understood as the Complicated *Richardson*" [188]). "In what depends on the Knowledge of the Learned Languages my Son is my Telescope... 'tis by the help of This I have seen That in *Milton* which to Me Otherwise had been Invisible; though before I had my Instrument I saw a Sky of shining Stars, How much more Throng'd and Bright soever That Sky Now appears" [189]). It may be too bold to conclude from these sentences that the father contributed most of the general speculations. A perusal of the notes, however, seems to confirm that impression, for most of the reasoning and criticism is in the unbridled, exuberant, enthusiastic style of which these quoted passages are modest examples.

The work is inspired by a deep and lasting admiration for "Paradise Lost". Both father and son had been students of the poem for a very long time. Their book was undertaken only "after a Constant Love, and Continu'd Application to the Reading of *Paradise Lost* Almost ever Since we could read Any thing" [190]). The father, who had been exceedingly fond of Shakespeare, Cowley, Dryden and others, especially of the two first, "as I always was of the Muses", had not heard of Milton until, in his youth, he happened to find a copy of the poem in his

---

[186]) See DNB. on Richardson. Pope, Prior, Gay "and other conspicuous members of the literary world" are mentioned there as his friends.
[187]) Cf. p. CLXIX.
[188]) Cf. p. CXLI.
[189]) Ibid.
[190]) Cf. p. CLXIX.

master's, the painter Riley's studio [191]). He was dazzled with it, "so that from that Hour all the rest *(Shakespeare* excepted) Faded in my Estimation, or Vanish'd. I immediately began to Store up in my Mind Passages to Regale and Nourish my Mind with at All times" [192]).

But their Milton worship leads them much further than this. They know much about the other works of the poet, and state their valuation of them in very definite terms. Milton "Excell'd in Lyrick, Pastoral, Dramatick, Epic, and a Kind Purely Original, Such is his *Masque.* Comedy indeed he never attempted that we know of, nor Dogrel. Much Less any thing in the Least Profane, or Indecent" [193]). "Lycidas" is highly praised; "L'Allegro" and "Il Penseroso" receive special mention; the seriousness of his Latin verse and his love poems is pointed out with particular approval. After writing on "Comus", Richardson the elder observes: "As great an Encomium have I heard of *Lycidas* as a Pastoral, and That when *Theocritus* was not forgot; *Theocritus,* of whom *Virgil* was but an Imitator in his Pastorals, as he was of *Homer* in his *Æneis.* The *Allegro* and *Penseroso* are Exquisite Pictures. his Latin Poems have the Same Gravity and Dignity, and Most of them remarkably Excellent, though All Written while he was a Young Man, or *Almost Before.* even his Few Love Poems have a sort of Dignity and Gravity in them" [194]).

The references to the Latin poems are unexpectedly frequent, considering their former neglect [195]). They probably ought to be put to the son's credit. The poem on Shakespeare is quoted in IX. 461 *n.*; the prose is mentioned and quoted constantly, especially in the Life and the later parts of the commentary. The preface to the notes emphasizes the study of the whole body of Milton's literary work: "We have seen what he has said in Other Parts of his Work, or in Other Works of His, and brought him to be his own Expositor. We have Consider'd his Opinions

---

[191]) This contradicts the previous quotation, which is obviously one of Richardson's usual hyperbolical effusions.

[192]) Cf. pp. CXVIII—IX.

[193]) Cf. p. XIV.

[194]) Cf. p. XV—XVI.

[195]) *E. g.* El. III—IV. 158 *n.*, "Ad Salsillum" and "Mansus" — V. 161 *n.*, "Ad Patrem" — VII. 35 *n.*

and Turn of Mind, as particularly in Our Explanation of the Four Last Books" [196]. This general familiarity with Milton's whole literary output goes beyond what any previous critics had shown.

Milton was a learned writer, and "Paradise Lost" combines the fruit of his reading (p. CLII). The necessity to study his sources is therefore evident, and his sources are understood in their widest literary extent. Chaucer [197]), Spenser [198]), Shakespeare's "Othello" [199]), "Macbeth" [200]), the second part of "Henry IV" [201]), "Venus and Adonis" [202]), the Sonnets [203]) are among the works of older English poetry referred to by the Richardsons. It is especially interesting to note that he quotes a Shakespearian sonnet [204]) expressing one of the more contemplative and profound moods of the poet, to illustrate a "very Dreamy and Natural" passage in Milton, and that the place from "Macbeth" quoted in both the notes mentioned above is one of the weirdest in the play [205]). Iago's highly imaginative speech on "poppy and mandragora" [206]) has also impressed the commentators. In spite of all this, romance is condemned; the "Gothism found in the most Celebrated Modern Poets, *Chaucer, Spenser, Ariosto, Tasso, etc*" [207]) is not regarded with approval.

Italian poetry, the poetry of the country known to most painters of those Days, but only very cautiously explored by the earlier Milton commentators, is familiar to the Richardsons. Even the peculiarities of spelling in "the Old Italian Books by *Giolito*, or the *Guinti* and Some Others" are mentioned [208]). The references to Romance poetry go beyond Italian literature, for

---

[196]) Cf. p. CLXXII.
[197]) IX. 28 n., IV. 821 n.
[198]) Cf. Shep. Cal. V. 333 n., Translation of Virgil's "Culex", IV. 30 n., "Visions of the World's Vanity" V. 100 n., F. Q. VII. 364 n.
[199]) IX. 1046 n.
[200]) I. 62 n., V. 356 n.
[201]) IX. 330 n.
[202]) II. 846, VII. 364, 365 nn.
[203]) VIII. 478 n.
[204]) Sonnet 27, see VIII. 478 n.
[205]) On Banquo's sightless eyes, Macbeth III. IV.
[206]) III. 3.
[207]) IX. 28 n.
[208]) Cf. p. CLXXV.

Camoens is alluded to in VII. 364 *n.*, but this is exceptional. *Tasso* and *Ariosto* [209]) are no new discoveries but the name of Tasso's commentator *Scipio Gentili* seems to indicate some interest in Italian literary scholarship. Vida and Sannazaro are mentioned in V. 269 *n.* However, the best notes on Italian subjects deal with Dante. The sombre, infernal aspect of his poetry is taken notice of in I. 62 *n.* ["Eyes of Brass as *Dante* has given to Caron"] but most of the mentions are concerned with his descriptions of heaven and the angels [210]). The nature of the angels as described by Milton is supposed to be an imitation of Dante's notions [211]). Vivid, typically bold and graphic expressions of Dante [212]) are regarded as the probable source of Miltonic phrases [213]).

All this constitutes a considerable stock of new and valuable material for comparison. But the main asset of the Richardson's is not their erudition. Their love of poetry, their artistic temperament, combined with what the elder Richardson calls "Good Sense" [214]), are, or would appear to be, more essential. This certainly seems true of the father, whose copious statements in the Life and in the preface to the notes enable one to see his personality more clearly. He describes his interests [215]): "I have from my Infancy Lov'd and Practic'd Painting and Poetry; One I Possess'd as a Wife, the Other I kept Privately, and shall Continue to do So whilst I Live". They want to restore Milton's meaning in the interests of poetry and religion: "We found This Book, as a Picture of the greatest Master, Obscur'd for want of a Proper Light; We hold it Up to Them in Such a One; but we Abhor to do what is Too Often done by the Best Pictures,

---

[209]) IX. 28, V. 580, 269 *nn.*

[210]) Cf. I. 45, I. 610, V. 733 *nn.*

[211]) I. 45 *n.*

[212]) "Light'ning Divine, ineffable, serene" V. 731 is said to be probably derived from Dante's "Lampeggiò un Riso" (Rich. gives no reference) = "Flash'd, or Lighten'd a Smile"; "a Smile from Angelic or Divine Beings is suppos'd to give a Sudden Light and Lustre, to Flash Brightness. So Milton VIII. 367 ...On the contrary Evil Beings *Frown Darkness.* II. 719". Observations of this kind point out interesting similarities, even if the sources indicated may not always be right.

[213]) V. 733 *n.*

[214]) Cf. p. CLXV.

[215]) Cf. p. CLXXVIII.

We dare not Scour, much Less Retouch it" [216]). Yet to be able to do this a congenial mind is more needed than learning: "if a Poem is to be Read They will best Understand it, whether in the Original, or Translated or Explain'd and Remark'd upon, who have Most of the Poetical Genius by which it was Wrote, and which Those may be possess'd of who have not, or are not Known to have Attempted *to build the Lofty Rhyme*" [217]). Learning may even become a hindrance: "...'tis too Apt to Occasion a Self-Sufficiency and Arrogance upon Account of What is Quite Beside the Purpose in Hand; and where Another Kind of Reading, or perhaps Only Good Sense is Requisite; as This Last is Always without Comparison Preferable to All the Learning of the World, how Pertinent Soever" [218]). Richardson may easily have thought of his own respectable position in the intellectual world of his time, which had not been won by scholastic learning. An example of the "arrogant" scholar was near at hand in Bentley.

The Richardsons have made use of earlier works on the subject. This is admitted in the preface, but everything is professed to have been thought out very thoroughly so that "Our Thought is nevertheless our Own, Honestly Earn'd by the Sweat of our Brows" [219]). Here at least Hume's merits are acknowledged, for his commentary is mentioned as their chief source. The initials P. H. are explained to mean "Philip Humes" [220]).

B. THE INTRODUCTORY EXPOSITION OF THE LITERARY VIEWS OF THE ELDER RICHARDSON.

The latter part of the Life [221]) contains a survey of the character of Milton's poetry followed by a general theoretical discussion on poetry. Both show the critic's attitude in a clear light. It is advisable to follow Richardson's own arrangement and to deal with the particulars before going on to the general

---

[216]) Cf. p. CLXXVII.
[217]) Cf. p. CLXV.
[218]) Ibid.
[219]) Cf. p. CLXX.
[220]) Cf. p. CXVII, referred to on p. CLXXI.
[221]) Cf. pp. CXXXIX—CLXIII.

conclusions, for the writer's logical power seems inferior to his power of critical intuition. It is safer to explain the general statement by the genuine impressions received from first-hand literary experience than to deduce the details from main definitions which contradict each other, and may have been derived from other writers on literary theory. Most of these passages appear to be a passionate rehabilitation of the prerogatives of poetry impugned by Bentley.

Richardson's knowledge of Shakespeare and of Italian poetry supplies him with good examples of the radical difference between the styles of poetry and prose: "Poetry pretends to a Language of its Own. That of the Italian Poetry is so remarkably peculiar that a Man may Well understand a Prose Writer, and not a Poet" 222). The vocabulary, the phraseology, the arrangement of words — "Words, Tours of Expression, the Order of Them, All has something not Prosaic. This is Observable particularly in Shakespear" 223). But Richardson's preference for Milton is quite as evident here as elsewhere. Shakespeare's free and easy way in the selection of his subjects appears to him to be out of harmony with his verbal artistry. Something of the ideal of "high language" and high subjects, of the uniform sublimity of neo-classicism seems to be still discoverable in his views, and Milton's more academic ways attract him more strongly and find fuller acknowledgement: "Milton has Apply'd it [= the peculiar language of poetry] to that sublimity of Subject in which he perpetually Engages his Readers, above What *Shakespear* ever Aim'd at and where This is Peculiarly Necessary" 224).

The numerous classical elements in this poetically moulded style are clearly seen: "*Milton's* Language is English, but 'tis *Milton's* English; 'tis Latin, 'tis Greek English; not only the Words, the Phraseology, the Transpositions, but the Ancient Idiom is seen in All he Writes, So that a Learned Foreigner will think *Milton* the Easiest to be Understood of All the English Writers" 225). But only learned people could find him easy. The ordinary reader will want special comment, as he wants it

---

222) Cf. p. CXLIII.
223) Ibid.
224) Cf. p. CXLIII.
225) Cf. p. CXLII.

for understanding the language of the Gospels, according to Milton's own statement in the Tetrachordon [226]). However, this obscurity is "not that Vicious Obscurity which proceeds from a Muddled Inaccurate Head", it does not come "from Want of Words and Method and Skill to Convey them to Another", there is nothing in it of that "Sort of a Moon-Light Prospect over a Landscape at Best not Beautiful" [227]). On the contrary, „if a Good Writer is not Understood 'tis because his Reader is Unacquainted with or Incapable of the Subject, or will not Submit to do the Duty of a Reader, which is to Attend Carefully to what he Reads" [228]). This is especially hard in Milton's case where the reader "must be Always upon Duty" for "he is Surrounded with Sense, it rises in every Line, every Word is to the Purpose; there are no Lazy Intervals" [229]). There is nothing in Milton of the general fault of even the best Writers, in whose works "you Somtimes find Words and Sentences which hang on so Loosely you may Blow 'em off; *Milton's* are all Substance and Weight; Fewer would not have Serv'd the Turn, and More would have been Superfluous" [230]). Everything is deliberate, at once rich and economical, the conciseness admired by the first commentator on Milton is still the feature of his style pre-eminently emphasized by this critic of 39 years later.

The truth already fully recognised by Pearce, that each writer has his own particular style with its own laws, is confirmed by Richardson, and he does more than this — he tries to define the individual qualities of Milton's temperament on which his style rests: "There is Somthing in Every Man's [sic]... whereby he is Known, as by his Voice, Face, Gait, & c." In Milton it is "a certain Vigour, whether *Versing* or *Prosing*, which will Awaken Attention be She never so Drowsy, and then Persuade her to be Thankful though She was Disturb'd" [231]). It is a real fire burning in everything he wrote, glowing in his early work, found in his war-like pamphlets, flaming more intensely than ever in "Paradise Lost" where its heat is felt throughout

[226]) *Ibid.* reference to Toland's Ed. p. 365.
[227]) Cf. p. CXLV.
[228]) Cf. p. CXLIV.
[229]) *Ibid.*
[230]) *Ibid.*
[231]) Cf. p. CXLIV.

a wide range of moods and tendencies: "As his Mind was Rich in Ideas, and in Words of Various Languages to Cloathe them with and as he had a Vast Fire, Vigour and Zeal of Imagination, his Style must Necessarily Distinguish it Self; it Did so; and even in his Younger days, his Juvenile Poems, English, Latin, and Italian, have a Brilliant [*sic*] not Easily found Elsewhere; Nor is it not seen in his Controversial Prose Works; *Paradise Lost* wants it not, in which there are Specimens of All his Kinds of Styles, the Tender, the Fierce, the Narrative, the Reasoning, the Lofty, & c. So Early as when he Wrote for Divorce, though he Conceal'd his Name his Hand was known" [232]). Milton's own statement from his pamphlet on divorce is quoted here. It is evident how it is the mark of the poet's strong personality which particularly appeals to the critic.

Richardson has very thoroughly learned the lesson which Pearce taught, that *stimulating suggestion* is one of the main requirements of poetic diction. Plain outspokenness or minute volubility are by no means sufficient. Milton's sparing use of words seems to be connected with this law: "whoever will Possess His Ideas must Dig for them, and Oftentimes pretty far below the Surface" [233]). This presupposes much mental activity, much reading between the lines on the reader's part, for not only the poet's words but even his silence may be important. Homer, Longinus and Macrobius have made Richardson aware of this rule: "His Silence has the Same Effect, not only that he leaves Work for the Imagination when he has Entertain'd it, and Furnish'd it with Noble Materials..." [234]). For it also has a distinctly positive effect: Homer's works are distinguished both by "Readiness of Speech and Silent Majesty" [235]); "...by *Silent Majesty*, he [= Macrobius, who uses the word] seems to Mean with Longinus: 'His Leaving more to the Imagination than is Express'd'." This seems a good definition of the ways of the poet who in referring to the allusive manner of Spenser and others wrote of the "sage and solemn tunes... Of Forests, and

---

[232]) Cf. p. CXLIII.
[233]) Cf. p. CXLIV.
[234]) Cf. p. CXLIV.
[235]) Cf. p. CXLV.

inchantments drear, Where more is meant then meets the ear" [236]).

Originality and imagination are the principal concepts explicitly or implicitly referred to in these statements. They cause in the critic a very sceptical, even in many respects a positively revolutionary attitude to fixed rules and classifications in literature. If originality is one of the main conditions of poetry, the need for timid measures of precaution disappears. "Paradise Lost" may be different from anything in the poetry of the past: "... 'tis of no great Importance whether this be call'd an Heroic or a Divine Poem, or only, as the Author himself has call'd it in his Title-page, a Poem. What if it were a Composition Intirely New, and not reducible under any Known Denomination?" [237]). The greatness of the poem as well as its unique subject make it independent of the rules based solely upon the experiments of the past, even if those experiments were made by Homer and Virgil and the conclusions were drawn by Aristotle [238]): "if the Sublimity and Peculiarity of the Matter of this Poem, if its Superiority in that Respect has rais'd it above Some of the Rules given by *Aristotle,* or Whatever Other Criticks, and Gather'd From, or Founded on the *Iliad, Odyssey,* or *Æneid,* it has Distinguish'd it to its greater Glory; 'tis not only on Heroic Poem, but the Most So that Ever was Wrote" [239]). It is notable that the sacred character of the subject still plays almost as great a part in Richardson's valuation of the work as it did in Hume's estimation. However, the emphasis laid on Milton's genius seems quite as great: "*Milton* did not despise Rules, Such as were Built upon Reason, So far as those Establish'd Reach'd; but as his Free and Exalted Genius Aspir'd Beyond what had Yet been Attempted in the Choice of his Subject, Himself was his Own Rule when in Heights where None had gone before, and Higher than Which None Can Ever Go" [240]).

But Richardson's radicalism is not at all that of a fanatic who does not see the advantages of the opposite point of view. His observation that Milton did not disregard the laws of reason

---

[236]) Il P. 117—120.
[237]) Cf. p. CXLV.
[238]) Cf. p. CXLVII.
[239]) Cf. p. CXLVII.
[240]) *Ibid.*

shows this. Originality is by no means only being different from the rest. Tradition has its value, and what is useful in it, has to be assimilated, especially the heritage of classical literature. "Grace, Majesty and Simplicity" are among the qualities to be acquired from that source [241]). Milton has these features "to a Degree beyond what We have ever found in Any Modern Painter or Sculptor, not Excepting *Rafaelle* Himself" [242]). "...All his Images are Pure Antique. So that We read *Homer* and *Virgil* in reading Him" [243]). He is "an Ancient, but born two Thousand Years after his Time" [244]). Richardson is so far from under-estimating classical tradition that Greek and Latin still in his opinion are the preferable languages for poetry. Milton's English ranks next, partly because of its classical stamp. It is "the Best, next to Greek and Latin, to Convey those Images Himself Conceiv'd" [245]). Its classical character causes a strange, rare flavour: Milton's "Greek'd and Latiniz'd" language is made "as Uncommon and expressive as our Tongue could be, and yet Intelligible to us for whom he Wrote" [246]). The combination of all that is good in the past with the great new tradition of Christianity makes Milton's work incomparable. For poetry should improve mankind to make it happy. This is done by the aid of religion: "We have then in *Paradise Lost* a Collection, the Quintessence of All that is Excellent in Writing; Frequently Improv'd and Explain'd Better than by the Best of their Profess'd Commentators, but Never Debas'd; and a Sublimity which All other Human Writings put together have not. to Compleat All, He has made Use of All These, so as to be subservient to the Great End of Poetry, which is to Please and Inrich the Imagination, and to Mend the Heart, and make the Man Happy" [247]). Milton's best passages are "Such as None but the Noblest Genius could attain to, and That Assisted by a Religion Reveal'd by God Himself" [248]).

---

[241]) Cf p. CXLVIII.
[242]) *Ibid.*
[243]) *Ibid.*
[244]) Cf. p. CXLVII.
[245]) *Ibid.*
[246]) Cf. p. CXLVIII.
[247]) Cf. p. CLII.
[248]) *Ibid.*

The notion that Milton improved in imitating was expressed by Hume and others. Richardson adds a description of his method of assimilating the valuable parts of the productions of other poets. The transplanted passages are "as Gay and Fragrant as whence they were taken", "Genius and Judgment" make up for the neglect of invention 249). "What is Inserted Fits as well as in the Original Work; or if That is not Equal to *Milton's* Own, He makes it So by Raising its Native Character" 250). He prepares every borrowed effect so carefully as to make it absolutely his own, avoiding the badly calculated, imperfect adaptations so frequent in other poets. Many a bold allusion may be fine yet it "Offends the Imagination when it strikes upon it yet Unprepar'd; as in *Spencer*, B. II. Can. II. St. 22, where a Bear and Tyger are introduc'd as Fighting on the *Lybick* Ocean. *Milton's* Boldest Borrow'd Figures, as his Own, when they Awaken the Mind do it not with a Sudden Crash, but as with Musick; if they Surprize, they don't Startle Us. You will not find a Single Instance of Such Improprieties in Him" 251). Thus "all He touches becomes as if 'twas the Pure Gold of the Best Antiquity" 252). Milton has found the best way of doing what inevitably has to be done wherever perfection is to be achieved, for the departure from antiquity would mean the substitution of the inferior for the superior, of later deterioration for the thoughts and imagery of the youth of mankind when all that was excellent was once for all discovered and made use of in poetry 253).

The moderns, "Gothic" literature, Romance, belong to inferior categories: „Those who are unaccustom'd to this [= classical] Train of Thinking, may only please to Dip into *Chaucer*, *Spencer*, *Ariosto*, even *Tasso* or any of the Moderns, and observe what *Gothick* Figures and Things present Themselves to their Imagination, or what are Comparatively Mean" 254).

These were some of Richardson's main ideas on literature but expressed in a not too generalized form. He bases his conclusions on facts and observations and is so far reasonable and

---

249) Cf. p. CL.
250) *Ibid.*
251) Cf. p. CLI.
252) *Ibid.*
253) *Ibid.*
254) Cf. p. CXLVIII.

even convincing. But he also wishes to give a general definition
of poetry, which, as he remarks, is not given in Milton's own
statements about his works. The opinion he expresses is somewhat surprising: "Were I call'd upon to Define Poetry in
General... I would do it by saying 'tis ORNAMENT" [255]).
This means pleasure of a rather superficial kind, and this
principle is his only means of justifying the admission of fiction
into poetry: "This Implies Fiction, for Dress, Lace, Gold,
Jewels, etc. is not the Body. Poetry therefore is not Truth, but
Somthing More Agreeable, at least than Meer Truth" [256]). These
opinions seem to contradict his earlier insistence on the religious
element in poetry. However, a (probably unconscious) twist of
logic enables him to make even religion and morals subservient
to the aims of pleasure: "the Great End of Poetry... is to Please
and Inrich the Imagination, and to Mend the Heart, and make
the Man Happy" [257]). He does not distinguish sharply enough
between the happiness derived from "Dress, Lace, Gold" and
the intense gratification of purifying moral experience.

This is obvious from the inferences he draws from his definition that poetry is ornament or "Somthing More Agreeable...
than Meer Truth". He immediately shifts the emphasis to the
deeper aspects of poetry, illogically concluding that the business
of poetry "is, Consequently, to Awaken, to Please, to Allure;
'tis Address'd to the Imagination, to the Passions, and this
Supposes Energy as well as Beauty" [258]). According to this
sentence, poetry no longer could be mere ornament. Energy
appears to be the quality mainly emphasized here: "to Awaken,
to Please, to Allure" are treated as synonyms, but "to Awaken"
comes first. A passage extolling the pleasures of reading [259])
shows the comprehensiveness of Richardson's literary interests,
and the ever-present demand of stimulation. Reading fills the
mind, feeds it, rouses "the Intellectual Fire", puts "our Passions
into a more Vigorous Motion", instructs, amuses, gives what we
lack ourselves, inspires us with thought, feeding "the *Intellectual
Being*" which "has the Universe, and Beyond what is Real, even

---

[255]) Cf. p. CLV.
[256]) *Ibid.*
[257]) Cf. p. CLII.
[258]) Cf. p. CLV.
[259]) Cf. p. CLVIII—IX.

t! Immense Regions of Fancy to range and *Wander* in, and as it cannot be Limited by Time, it Expatiates Eternity." It gives us ᵃ!l kinds of experiences, those that are wholesome and noble as ᵃell as that kind which "pollutes the Mind with Black Exhalations, and Scorches, or Torments us" [260]). In spite of the stress he lays on the moral purpose of poetry, he acknowledges that, whatever objects it may aim at, good or evil, "'tis no Less, or More Poetry Still" [261]). Thus his radicalism tends to go very far. But the *best* kind of poetry is that which improves mankind [262]). Morals and religion come first but the rest cannot be excluded. Energy, passion appear to be the very essence of poetry.

If Richardson in spite of these much more adequate views was capable of identifying poetry with external embellishment, the cause may partly lie in his artistic temperament. He values the purely formal, sensuous elements of style. The discords, harmonies and patterns, "the Sound of the Words, their Harshness, Smoothness, or Other Properties, and the Ranging, and Mixing them, all help to Express aswell [*sic*] as their Signification" [263]). Imagination is the most important feature, and there may be a "Poetick Prose" as well as a "Prosaick Verse" but the form, the rhythm should never be ignored: "tho' the Verse Alone is not Poetry, 'tis, strictly speaking, Essential to it." An orator with "the Gaudiness and Splendour which Poetry demands", but "without the Musick of *Numerous Verse* would not be a Poet" [264]). Painting and Music seem to have deepened his appreciation of form as such: "Poetry Pleases by a Peculiarity and Majesty of Stile and Language; its Numbers, its Rime (if us'd, and Skilfully) Pleases as Musick does, and as Painting" [265]).

---

[260]) *Ibid.*
[261]) Cf. p. CLVI.
[262]) *Ibid.*
[263]) Cf. p. CXLIII.
[264]) Cf. p. CLV.
[265]) Cf. p. CLVI.

C. GENERAL LITERARY ASPECTS OF THE COMMENTARY.

The notes on individual passages are in general accordance with these prefatory statements. The established rules are regarded as somewhat irrelevant, individual liberty in poetry is welcomed and justified. Freer views on life, even on religion, appear natural and necessary; for the author is "Writing a Poem, not a System of Divinity or Philosophy... his Muse is Divine, but she is Also a Muse. He is Constant in his System, but 'tis a Poetical One" [266]). This is directed against the people who find it possible to make "Silly Objections when they Imagine Themselves Triumphing over their Author" [267]) — apparently an allusion to Bentley.

The very irregular style of the notes, and their habit of freely following every impulse of thought, is clearly reflected in the treatment of Milton's *digressions*. Excrescences are not condemned as superfluous if they are good in themselves. The general plan does not seem to admit of some of the particulars in the description of Satan's interplanetary journey [268]), yet even what is here "Over and Above the Principal Scope of it, comes in very Properly, Poetically, and beautifully". It would be undesirable for certain "irregular" passages to become more regular and neat and more in accord with the scheme which ordinary logic would expect. There are moods and frames of mind which can be adequately expressed by an imitation of their eccentricities. Hints at such views do occur in the commentary. The poet's digression on his blindness in P. L. III. 26—40 "is an Excursion of Thought, and not without its Poetical Beauty, as expressing the working of his Afflicted Mind better than if it had gone on more Regularly."

The tendency to study the concealed meaning of things, a vividness of imagination which understands the associations of words and is indispensable for appreciating Milton's allusive style enable the commentators to do justice to the Miltonic *catalogues*. They are not barren and bald to them, no mere

[266]) VII. 40 *n*.
[267]) *Ibid.*
[268]) II. 648 *n*.

8*

enumerations, no schoolmasterly whims, not even the longest and barest of them, the list of the great kingdoms and capitals of the world in book XI, the only one which is almost totally devoid of picturesque epithets and brief descriptive sentences aiding the imagination. Addison valued the catalogue of evil spirits in book I for "the very agreeable turn of Poetry, which rises in a great measure from its describing the places where they were worshipped, by those beautiful marks of rivers, so frequent among the ancient Poets." The list in book XI, on the contrary, stands and falls with the phonetic beauty of the names and the historical and geographical background suggested by them; but these are sufficient to kindle the commentator's mind [269]): "What a Picture does This Offer to the Imagination! ...This Landscape takes In all the Side of the Globe on which they Stood, the Various Climates, and Countries, the Future Seats of many vast Empires and Mighty Kingdoms and States..." The impression which the enumeration of the fallen angels in the first book produces on the Richardsons is deeper than merely that of a "very agreeable turn of Poetry." They seem to read more attentively between the lines. It is not only "an Artful and Entertaining History" to them; it is "of the Ancient Idolatry but Beautifully Pathetical" [270]). The admiring attitude to the legends of the ancients hinted at here is evident also in the other catalogues; the mythological names in IV. 268 & *seq.* are considered capable of making even the beauty of paradise more deeply felt.

Some of these lists of names are rich in mediæval romantic associations; for example the list of the kingdoms seen by Adam which was just discussed. They seem to be included in the annotators' praise. Their dislike of this type of poetry does not go nearly as far as Bentley's. The depreciation of "Gothic" poetry in the prefatory treatise does not prevent the critics from seeing the attraction of fine individual passages in that style where they happen to encounter them. The very "Gothic" matter of the Teutonic invasions described in I. 351 & 809 is praised for the "New and Great Images" presented there, though there is really very little classicism in the account of "the Northern Nations and Barbarous, Over stock'd with People" who send forth "Multitu-

---

[269]) XI. 378 *n.*
[270]) I. 392 *n.*

des, who (as *Shakespear* says) *cry'd Havock, and let Slip the Dogs of War"* [271]).

However, the impression strikes one very often that not this kind of romance but a greater, more peaceful and playful type of romantic poetry really appeals to them. Milton's Minor Poems may have helped to develop their taste for these matters. "Il Penseroso" is quoted in the note on the only place in "Paradise Lost" where fairy-folklore is dealt with at some length [272]) and the paraphrase in this note is certainly more in the slightly popular, easy-going style of the fairy-passages of "L'Allegro" than in the strictly measured, sonorous and somewhat solemn tone of the part of the epic under consideration there: the picture becomes "exceeding Pretty and Delightful", the fairies are "a Neat, Merry People", the moon "seems to stoop down the better to observe them, and to partake of the Pleasure".

The existence of such cases does not imply that the dignity of Milton's manner is not emphasized in the notes, but the Richardsons seem to have a genuine feeling for realism, even for humour. The grand style is superior in principle. Milton still only "does sometimes Stoop to what is Beneath his Ordinary Majesty" [273]). Certain kinds of realistic poetry are condemned, even the naturalism in the Homeric descriptions of warfare is treated with the same contempt as that with which Milton in the exordium to book IX of "Paradise Lost" "Glanc'd at *Homer's* perpetual Affectation of This Sort of Knowledge, which Certainly Debases his Poetry" [274]). Milton's poems, on the contrary, are "Crowded Close with Variety of what is Important and full of Dignity" [275]).

Wars are too closely associated with the degenerate wickedness of man. The Richardsons — perhaps only the elder Richardson — sympathize with a tendency in the literature of their time which prepared the way for the following generations and favoured the return to nature from the artificiality and ruthlessness of civilized life. The desire for idyllic, primitive plainness, the

---

[271]) I. 351 *n.*
[272]) I. 785 *n.*
[273]) V. 746 *n.*
[274]) IX. 29 *n.*
[275]) *Ibid.*

idealization of animals, are typical features of this tendency, and both occur in the notes of the Richardsons. Milton's suggestion of the existence of speech among animals is welcomed [276] : "but that They also have a Language, Certain Sounds Expressing the Various Passions of Love, Joy, Fear, Anger, & c. and are well understood by One Another, and by Us, is Indisputable." They have their share of intelligence: "They Thus Converse, and make known their Wants to all Their Useful Intents and Purposes, as well Altogether as Our Selves in what Concerns Us" [277]). Mankind is degenerate though we "perhaps might have been no Less Happy had our Language been Empty of a deal of the Jargon of Unprofitable Science, and the Uncertainty, Ambiguity, and Confusion, which has Occasion'd Infinite Perplexity, Folly, Wranglings, Wars, & c." [278]).

Here again the dislike of war appears. Simple, homely ideas attract the Richardsons much more. They like the metaphor of the earth "that spinning sleeps on her soft axle" [279]). "An Exceeding Apt Illustration, tho' taken from a Common, Mean Circumstance", and the manner of 18th century country realism of the type of the family scenes in Gray's "Elegy" bears some similarity to the primitive, but genuine idyl of Adam and Eve listening to the angel [280] : "...the Angel with Dignity has related a most Amazing piece of History, and our First Parents with Attention and Admiration express'd in their Beautyfull Countenances... [sic]."

Fun and humour are seen, and studied with some care. Satan's curious behaviour towards the end of his journey is explained in a humorous spirit, and the critic is anxious to corroborate his interpretation by referring to further comic features from various parts of the poem: "He [= Satan] throws Himself Directly Down and turns (as they say) Heel over Head all the Way, for This is the motion described, which Exactly is like the Spoke of a wheel. This Ridiculous motion is Beautifully apply'd to the Devil on This Occasion. So IV. 568. the Angel

---

[276]) VIII. 373 n.
[277]) Ibid.
[278]) Ibid.
[279]) P. L. VIII. 164.
[280]) VII. 50 n.

describes him *Bent all on Speed with an Aery Gate* and 129. *to have had a Mad Demeanor*, he seems to have been in a Sort of *Gamesome Mood* (as VI. 620) Glad that he is just at the end of his Journey" [281]).

The note expresses some pleasure at these grotesque traits. Hence the radical step of recognising the value of comic relief in sublime poetry, to which the recognition of the intensifying effect of comic contrast is added. This is remotely hinted at in the note on Milton's puns [282]) which in turn refers to an observation on VI. 206 where the whole matter is clearly stated: "There is Besides flung In a Repose, a Ludicrous Scene; but upon an Incident truly Great, and brought, not only to Refresh the Reader, it serves to Vary the Action, and by representing Those that were to be Ruin'd, with *Ruin upon Ruin, Rout on Rout, Confusion Worse Confounded* (I. 995) by shewing Them in *Gamesom Mood* (v. 622). This makes the Destruction appear, even That More Horrible." The value of the whole round of experience is thus understood more completely by the Richardsons than by the earlier commentators, with the exception of Hume, who in a simple-minded manner employed most things without being conscious of how they were to be used in literature.

The profession of the Richardsons has left some unmistakable traces in their manner of approach to Milton. The visual side of Milton's poetry is very strongly emphasized, often even over-emphasized. A list of Milton's "pictures", i. e. the main scenes of "Paradise Lost", regarded from a painter's point of view, is added to the cummentary. The luxury of Milton's descriptions attracted Hume strongly, but to the Richardsons the poet became pre-eminently an interpreter of the visual world who only through it passes on to the heart and mind: "in All he Writes, he is a Painter, he Directs his Discourse to the Eye, next to the Heart, he Sets the Picture of Things Before us with all the Strength and Beauty that Words can Image" [283]).

The excellence of Milton's combinations of colours is sometimes very well observed, yet certain expressions show how purely technical considerations peculiar only to the painter could be

---

[281]) III. 741 *n*.
[282]) VI. 557 *n*.
[283]) VII. 321 *n*.

ascribed to Milton by these critics. The angel descending to Adam and Eve in book VI with "his *Lucid Arms*, a Flowing Purple Drapery", as the note puts it in a very ornamental manner, is supposed to be represented on a richly coloured background in which "the Azure of the Sky, mix'd with the Glory of the Angel makes a Greenish Tinct, a *Jasper* Brightness," and "This with the *Radient* [*sic*] *White* Cloud gives an Idea of Colours most Delightful" 284), The glory of the angel here appears to be reduced to a yellow colour spot which in combination with blue yields green — a way of mixing colours on the pallet not suggested in Milton's description. It is true, some of the poet's expressions, such as "a Skie of Jasper" or: "draws Ore the blew Firmament a radiant white," remind one a little of the technicalities of painting.

Hume was interested in Milton's colour epithets and gave much attention to some of them, e. g. to "purple", as was shown. The Richardsons probably make the first attempt at a systematic comparative study of them in trying to define the colours Milton attributes to the morning sky 285). It is of some interest to note that the precision shown in this comparison is greater than is usually found in their inquiries: "Grey belongs to the Earlyest Dawn whilst the Beams of the Sun are yet too Distant to Warm th' *Uncolour'd Skie*. So V. 189. VII. 373. IX. 192. and *Lycidas* v. 25. 187". Then comes "the *Rosie Morning*... VI. 3. VII. 29. VIII. 511. XI. 175. when the Sun rises the Morning puts on her Saffron Robe, and This is the time Noted V. 139. IV. 642. Now is the *Rosie* Morning, Her Way lyes where spreads a General Rosyness, and shee as it were treads upon Roses". The evidence is collected so carefully that Milton's conception of this aspect of natural scenery is made vividly present to the reader's mind. Even "Lycidas" is studied here in order to illustrate one of the most attractive features in Milton's treatment of nature.

To the keener eye of the painter colours are likely to become more than mere ornament. They acquire a life of their own, sometimes perhaps of greater significance than the poet would allow. Colour symbolism easily becomes a problem of some actuality to those who deal with colours all their lives. To the

284) XI. 209 *n*.
285) V. 1 *n*.

Richardsons, the black mist accompanying Satan in paradise appears to be even more charged with meaning than Milton's text will warrant, although the direction of their hint seems to be right[286]): "Something Infernal broke through his Disguise. Grey and Blue Mists were Usual in This Garden, not Black Ones." Some other observations are even more suggestive. Hume had already explained that

"Should intermitted vengeance Arme again
His red right hand to plague us"[287])

probably referred to the thunder in God's hand; Bentley added the Horatian parallel "rubente dextra" (Od. 1, 2. 2, 3), thinking, however, that the image related to "Vengeance" and that therefore it should be "her" hand, not "his". Richardson sides with Hume, without mentioning him, but he adds a description of the associations evoked in himself by the colour adjective. A parallel from Virgil is quoted to describe the kind of image Milton probably intended to picture: "Virgil has also much the same, the Hand Glimmer'd with the Fire it Darted"[288]). However, more is meant by this than only the visual impression: "It may be Understood that the Hand of God was Red as a Sign of Wrath."

Portrait-painting has sharpened the eye of the commentators for the study of Milton's treatment of the human countenance. They see Satan "look with Horror Round him, Reflecting on the Place he has in Exchange for Heaven"[289]) and affirm with great certainty that Milton's description of "ire, envy and despair" as pale is right, emphasizing that "That is the most Diabolical Anger which is accompany'd with a Pale, Livid Countenance"[290]). The movements and gestures of the body are well discerned. Newton repeats as his own, and Todd reprints with Newton's signature, a note on Satan's flight through space[291]) explaining Satan's motions, first his dropping perpendicularly, in great haste, into the passage to the new creation, and then how he "being In, and not knowing where was the Seat of Man (for though 'tis said v. 530. Paradise was directly against the Gate of Heaven 'tis

---

[286]) IX. 180 n.
[287]) II. 173.
[288]) II. 173 n.
[289]) I. 242 n.
[290]) IV. 115 n.
[291]) III. 562 n.

plain *Satan* did not see it) ... Winds, Turns This way and That
Obliquely, as being upon the Search". The presentation of these
visual details is more vivid, their interpretation more intent on
bringing home the accompanying mental processes than nearly
everything in earlier Milton criticism, including Addison's
articles, who usually confines himself to more obvious and conventional features.

D. MILTON'S FORM: HIS LANGUAGE, SPELLING, AND VERSE.

The best part of the work done by the Richardsons consists
in critical remarks of a more general, intuitive order, such as
those discussed in the previous chapters. Minute research on
problems of language and metre is not their forte, although their
metrical views are interesting.

Their study of Milton's vocabulary is not very independent.
Hume and Pearce, and also Bentley, are frequently used by them
as sources. The additions are not very numerous. The exactness
of their adherence to their models might be illustrated by a note
on the expression "ardor" [292]). Hume interprets it as *"Ardor,
Lat.* Brightness, Fervency, Exceeding Love, *& c.* to which the
Angelick Excellency may well be assimulated, in respect of their
Purity, Activity and Zeal". The Richardsons explain that *"Ardor
in Latin implies Fervency, Exceeding Love, Eager Desire, Fiery
Nature, all included in the Idea of an Angel". The adjective in
the expression "Serried Shields" I. 548 means according to Hume:
"Lock'd one within another, link'd and clasp'd together", and
according to the Richardsons: "their Sides Clasp'd, Lock'd
together". Bentley's interpretation of "emblem" is adopted
IV. 703 *n.*

The view that Milton uses classical words in their original
sense, seems to have become a commonplace by now. The
Richardsons — probably the son, who contributed the remarks
on the classics — praise Milton's "Pure Latinity" as contrasted
with the commoner significations assumed by words in later and
"Baser Ages" [293]), which is in full agreement with the high

[292]) V. 249 *n.*
[293]) IV. 878 *n.*

estimation of classical antiquity expressed in the Life (quoted
p. 193). The "true Antique Sense" and "great Propriety" [294])
are combined in the use of "dispensed" (= Lat. dispensare, from
"penso", to weigh, meaning in Milton "to Distribute... Tasks
to every One", as the commentary explains). This interpretation
has been adopted by Verity and is new, as is also the explanation
of "counsels" I. 636 n. as "private Views" = "consilium" in
Latin. These and other remarks show that the younger Richardson at least knew something about classical scholarship, but the
acuteness of many of Hume's etymological remarks is absent.
Some details are added, but no perceptible methodical progress
is made.

The same applies to the examination of Milton's use of older
language. Pearce's care is absent here, and no interesting new
sources are discovered. Anglo-Saxon etymologies are given, but
they do not add anything important, and sometimes seem to be
borrowed from Hume [295]). Mediæval lore, the language of romance and Elizabethan speech are hardly touched on [296]) though
there are indications that the terminology of chivalry was not
unknown to them ("cover'd field" I. 763 compared with Fr.
"champ clos"). The impression produced by their notes on Milton's vocabulary is that they took no real interest in them.
Besides, there was no special object which compelled them to go
into these problems more thoroughly — nothing like Pearce's
aim of refuting Bentley, which implied a sound study of the
character of the expressions altered in Bentley's edition.

One important field of linguistic research, however, is culti-
vated by them more industriously then by their predecessors: they
make some interesting suggestions on Milton's borrowings from
the Italian. Thus they derive "made alt" (XI. 210) from the
Italian "far Alto", instead of spelling it "made halt": "See the
Vocab. Crusc. where *far Alto* is explain'd by *fermarsi* (Ital.)
Consistere (Lat.)." The derivation of "Ammiral" I. 294 from
the Italian is pointed out, though the form quoted is not "ammi-

---

[294]) XI. 766 n.
[295]) See I. 304 n. sedge < sæg, III. 1. Hail < Hæl.
[296]) See, however, e. g. VIII. 36 "a sumless journey" + Shakespeare,
Hen. V. Act 1: "Sumless Treasure", & c. and Spenser III. 10, 12.

raglia" but "Ammiraglio", meaning the commander of a fleet, not the ship of an admiral, which latter is meant by Milton (cf. NED). The mistake is at any rate less crude than that made by Hume who derives the word from "Gm. A͞miral, A͞mirael, the Chief Commander at Sea". Other notes e. g. on IV. 709, VIII. 3 show the same knowledge of Italian. These attempts were useful by calling attention to one of the real sources of Milton's style.

The remarks on syntax often bear the same flashlight character as the typical parts of the rest of the book. Pearce had sufficiently proved that Milton was fond of elliptic phrases, although he was puzzled by some of them. The study of Milton's language in the elder Richardson's critical introduction emphasized this feature. In the notes certain cases are explained which remained a riddle to Pearce. The conciseness of III. 474 ["Many more too long" — see above, p. 96] is seen by the Richardsons: "'tis his Concise manner; Let the Reader do Something for Himself." But the broadmindedness which is carried far enough here, becomes bizarre in the emotionalism of III. 344 n. The elaborate parenthetical construction of the period ["the multitude of Angels... uttering joy"] is destroyed for the sake of a more violent effect. L. 347 is pointed: "as from Blest Voices uttring Joy — Heav'n rung" <"As from blest voices, uttering joy, Heav'n rung." Here "uttering joy" is understood as the attribute of "blest voices", not as the verb of "the multitude of Angels", so that the latter expression remains without a verb. The explanation is a follows: "the Poet breaks off from speaking of the Angels, and in a Transport crys out Heaven rung, & c. Then more Calmly resumes the Thread of his Relation; Lowly Reverent, & c.". The commentator's enthusiasm overpowers his logic.

On the other hand, the writers are capable of interpreting the artistic meaning of certain unusual features of syntax. In II. 910 Milton starts a period: "Into this wilde Abyss", then describes Chaos and in II. 917 again resumes: "Into this wild Abyss", adding the verbs which finish the sentence. The commentator tries to follow the author's manner of thinking: "'tis Observable the Poet Himself seems to be Doing what he Describes, for the Period begins at 910. Then he goes not On Directly, but Lingers; giving an Idea of Chaos before he Enters into it. 'tis very Artfull; if his Stile is Somewhat Abrupt after Such Pondering it Better Paints the Image he Intended to give" 297).

Certain classical peculiarities of syntax in Milton are well observed, which may be due to the better training in matters of scholarship which the younger Richardson had received. The probability of an imitation of the Greek use of a participle after verbs of knowledge and perception in IX. 792 ("And knew not eating Death") is noticed, and a quotation from Oppian's Halieut. II. 106. given ("οὐδ᾽ ἐνόησαν σπεύδοντες ὄλεθρον"). Similar observations are those on the use of the positive for the superlative IX. 795 n. 298), on the hendiadys "joy And tidings" for "joyful tidings" X. 345 299), of "as" in a Latin sense X. 978 n. ("As in our evils" — cf. Cic. Ep. Fam. IV. 9. "Nam adhuc, & factum tuum probatur, &, ut in tali re, etiam Fortuna Laudatur"), & c. The work done in this field shows some observation and knowledge, and may have interested the younger Richardson more than etymological research and inquiries into Milton's vocabulary, where there appears to be somewhat less scope for subtler speculation. Care, some reading in learned works on the classics, and an attentive study of the situation, which here is one likely to attract the portrait painter, appear in XI. 248 n.:

"by his side
As in a glistering *Zodiac* hung the Sword,
Satan's dire dread, and in his hand the Spear."

Richardson explains the construction as being: "by his Side hung the Sword, and the Spear in his Hand." He interprets this as meaning either that the sword was hanging loosely in the belt and the spear was carried negligently in the advancing angel's hand, or that there was no verb to define the attitude of the spear. He refers to Markland, on Statius' *Sylv.* I. I. 79, for evidence that in ancient literature the verb was not applicable to all the members of a period. The style of these notes usually appears more moderate and careful than that of the father, as seen in the prefatory matter and approximately recognizable in many of the notes.

---

297) II. 917 n.

298) "Precious of all Trees" — Æn. IV. 576: Sequimur te Sancte Deorum, & c.

299) IV. 667 n.: parallel from the Æneid I. 640: "Munera Laetitiamque Dei" = "Munera Laeta" acc. to Rich.

The elder Richardson's interest in the qualities of verbal sound is indicated, among other evidence, by his eccentric use of capital letters. A more fruitful result of this interest is his understanding of the phonetic value of Milton's spellings and metric generally, in which he surpasses earlier critics. He follows his feeling for rhythm and his logical sense of the importance of words in using "Great Letters, wherever any particular Weight is to be laid on the Word" 300). Even at the beginning of a paragraph small letters are used where there is no stress on the word. The writer feels the significance of rhythm for the perception of the meaning, for "Sometimes Impressions are taken at First reading which are not Easily, if Ever Eradicated, though what the Writer was an Utter Stranger to" 301). A man capable of thus concentrating on the form of language was likely to understand that Milton's spellings were not always accidental or arbitrary but that e. g. "He, we, me, ye, are with a Double or a Single e, as the Emphasis lies upon them, or does not" 302). He sees Milton's scrupulousness in these matters. "Nay, a Neglect of This Kind is put into the Errata of the First Edition, the Fault is in II. 414" 303). However, he does not notice that Milton's form "thir" might be used for the unstressed variety of the word 304). Some of Milton's spellings are valued for the sake of authenticity and because the poet used them more or less consistently, but no inquiries are made into the reasons. "Sent, Thir, Perfet, Then (when a Comparative), *Soule, Eeven, Mindc, Don, Burden, & c.*" are enumerated in p. CXXXI, among which "sent" is explained as due to the etymology of the word ("Sentir Fr. It. sentire") 305).

Richardson is quite conscientious in his examination of these problems. To him they are a proof that Milton supervised the first edition, and the correction of occasional mistakes in the errata to this edition as well as the correction of these errata in the text of the second edition are further arguments used by him to corroborate his very decided notion that Milton's own editions

---

300) Cf. p. CLXXIV.
301) *Ibid.*
302) Cf. p. CXXXI.
303) Cf. p. CXXXII.
304) Cf. p. CXXX.
305) Cf. p. CXXX.

are to be regarded as authentic [306]) and that the second, thoroughly revised edition should be used as the standard one [307]).

The sound of words sometimes finds full justice in the notes, in accord with a statement already quoted from Richardson's general appreciation in the Life. The "Description of Drowsiness" in IV. 614 seems so suggestive to the writer that "Did not the Beauty of the Poetry keep the Mind Awake, the Words would Lull the Reader Insensibly". He believes to hear the sound of the thunder in I. 177. He admits that Milton may have chosen the less usual name Hermione for Harmonia because it was more sonorous [308]). The peculiarities of Milton's word-order seem to him to echo the meaning [309]): *"Homer* and *Virgil,* and after them the Best Poets have endeavour'd, besides the Words, to Express what they Conceiv'd, by the Order of them: This is done Here to a Degree perhaps beyond what is to be found Elsewhere; 'tis a Maze indeed! *a Wandring Maze!"* Even the rapidity or slowness of speech in Milton's text is measured by him, perhaps not correctly [310]), yet with an attempt to relate it to the characters: "the Speech of *Satan* appears to have been pronounc'd Slow at the Beginning, and so it ought to be Read; 'tis Answer'd Soon. *Satan* might Boast of What he had Done, or Dar'd to Do; 'Tother is not in That Humour, nor can One Moment Conceal the Dispair which Rack'd Him Equally with his Associate who endeavour'd to Conceal His." Richardson's appreciation of sensuous beauty and vividness thus ranges from his own art to the most typical features of another, and is, in its own department, a very considerable advance on earlier criticism.

As these remarks might suggest, the elder Richardson's examination of Milton's verse given in the life [311]), shows much discernment and is distinctly superior to that of his predecessors. He relies on his ear instead of applying classical theories. The analogy constantly occurring to him is that of music. Animals express their minds by sound, even a foreign language may seem less strange because its sound itself is full of significance. Verse

---

[306]) Cf. p. CLXXIV.
[307]) *Ibid.*
[308]) IX. 505 *n.*
[309]) II. 558 *n.*
[310]) I. 127 *n.*
[311]) Cf. p. CXXXIX.

and prose have their music which varies according to the subject.
Each kind of verse has its peculiar sound-value [312]): "Blank
Verse comes nearest to Prose, and as the Prose of Some Writers
Approaches Verse, *Milton's* Blank Verse, That of *Paradise Lost*,
has the Beauty of Both." He has read Milton's preface "On the
Verse" with much attention and understands the importance of
the free use of the pause and of run-on lines — features not
recognised by Bentley, and not even by Pearce, and afterwards
partly to be condemned so rigidly by Johnson: "it [i. e. blank-
verse] has the Sweetness of Measure without Stopping the Voice
at the end of the Line, or Any where else but as the Sense
requires; One Verse runs into Another, and the Period concludes
in any part of a Line Indifferently, and as if 'twas his Choice 'tis
very often Not at the End of One or of a Couplet, as is too Frequent with Those who write in Rime" [313]).

His explanation of the Miltonic elisions and contractions is
based entirely on the perceptions of the ear, with some theoretical
help from the laws of ancient prosody. This is new in Miltonic
annotation. The omission of the "contracted" or "elided" sounds
is not always complete; they are generally only pronounced so
shortly as not to upset the quantity of the verse. The result is
somewhat peculiar but fine: "He has frequently Eleven Syllables
in a Verse, but 'tis rarely So unless Those are no more in Quantity
than the Ten of Another.

> *Fall'n Cherube, to be Weak is Miserable*
> *Doing or Suffering: but of This be Sure,*

the *e* in the Middle of the Word *Suff'ring* must be Melted in the
Pronunciation, as if written Without it as here; and the two
Syllables made by that Vowel, and the *a* that follows in *Miserable*
are so Short as to be Equal to but One in any other part of the
Line. So

> *Assur'd me and still Assure though what thou tell'st*

here *Me* and *and* are both so Short, as to be more in Quantity
than if they were but One Syllable. to read right requires Some
Judgment, and some Experience in *Milton's* Manner who Abounds
More with These Instances than most English Poets; but, well
Read, the Musick of His Verse is Exceeding Delicate and Noble,

---

[312]) Cf. p. CXXXIX.
[313]) *Ibid.*

though Somwhat Peculiar to Himself; for He, (as in his
Language) has Profited Himself of the Greeks and Latins; His
Ictus, or *Cadence*, or Musick bears towards Them, as he has
form'd himself Upon Their Examples into Somthing of his Own
by his Own Ear, and which was a very Musical, Experienc'd and
Judicious One" [314]).

The quoted passage is remarkable, for it shows an understanding of Milton's verse far superior to that of many later
critics. One feels inclined to mention Newton who does not
distinguish between classical and English metre, creating even
more confusion than Bentley (see first note on P. L. I). The
quantitative principle in the treatment of supernumerary
syllables is recognized by Richardson but is not extended beyond
them, as was to be done by Newton.

E.   CERTAIN METHODICAL ABERRATIONS.

The preface to the commentary deals at some length with
its method of interpretation: "we have had but One Single Point
in View, That Important One, to give Our Author's Sense, as we
Conceiv'd He would have Explain'd Himself had he risen from
his Urn and Dictated to Us" [315]). The point is insisted upon, as
note XII. 583 proves: "whether Milton's Interpretation... is
Right or No, 'tis His, and we Think Applicable to the Passage
we are upon; Further is not Our Concern, who are, not giving
Our Own Meaning, but our Author's as far as we are Able." Yet
Milton was a poet, "if ever Human Nature could Boast it had
produc'd One". He knew "All That Poetry had Adorn'd The
World with" [316]). Hence the necessity to interpret him as a poet,
to understand him not indiscriminatingly, in the first chance
sense that occurs to the commentator, but in "a Poetic Sense,
either as what was found in Other Great Poets whence it Seem'd
Himself had receiv'd it; and innumerable Instances there might
be given of This Kind" — a method which was quite generally
applied by Hume, and often by Bentley — "Or where the
Thoughts seem'd to be his Own, we have Understood him in the

---

[314]) *Ibid.*
[315]) Cf. p. CLXXII.
[316]) Cf. p. CLXXIII.

Noblest Sense we could Attain to as believing That to be most
Probably His" [317]). Here the principle is definitely stated which
endangers the impartiality of the critic's judgment though it may
have been wholesome as an antidote against Bentley, and even
against certain notes in Pearce, "for a Poem, Such a One as This
Especially, is not to be Read, and Construed as an Act of Parliament, or a Mathematical Dissertation; *the things of the Spirit are
Spiritually Discern'd"* [318]).

It is clear that the reaction which had found a competent
justification through Pearce has achieved its climax here. Poetry
is to be understood as poetry, by intuition. Yet this may involve
the neglect of the more pedestrian but indispensable qualities of
patient research. The extreme idealization of the poet and the
substitution of the critic's individual inspiration, or of what he
thinks inspired, for the poet's real or apparent failures, is what
has to be avoided now. The principle may lead to quite as great
arbitrariness as Bentley's adherence to the rules though it seems
capable of doing more justice to the scope of Milton's imagination.

The commentators are generally strongly tempted by the more
picturesque and interesting interpretation, where they have
a choice, sometimes even where there should be no choice at all
because the facts too evidently support the less unusual explanation. Quaint exuberance or whimsicality of imagination appear
to be their most dangerous ideals. Sometimes they succeed in
overcoming the temptation, sometimes not. Hume's note on II.
511 showed that "globe" ["a Globe of fierie Seraphim"] was
probably a Latin military term. The note in the Richardsons' commentary eventually adopts the same opinion but not before proposing another explanation which complies more with the annotator's taste. He would like to understand "globe" in the ordinary
sense, for as the angels were spirits, and "Aloft in the Air, or on
Firm Ground was alike to them", they "may be conceiv'd Above,
Below, on Each Side, Around their *Mighty Paramount*". Milton's
habit of using Latinisms should make the other meaning more
acceptable, which is recognized by the Richardsons in the end.

As they devoted some attention to the possibility of the influence of Dante on Milton, it does not seem quite unlikely that

[317]) *Ibid.*
[318]) *Ibid.*

Dante's imagery in the "Paradiso" with its heavenly roses and strange luminous geometrical figures formed by the choirs of the blessed is reflected in the note. How unwillingly the soberer explanation is admitted, appears from another remark on a very similar case [319]). A passage from the "Reason of Church Government" [p. 205 ed. Toland] is quoted there according to which "cube" should be a military expression like "globe" ["one great Cube, the Main Phalanx" — quoted acc. to Rich.]. In spite of this evidence, the meaning preferred is that of a cube which "consists of Angels on All the Four Sides, and Above", intended to hide the infernal engines. That the less fantastic interpretation is at least quite as probable here as in the former case, does not seem to trouble the writer. He prefers what, he thinks, is more imaginative, according to his principle stated before, believing that "the Sense we have chose is more Poetical as giving a Greater, and more Uncommon Idea".

At times the artistic principle which induces him to neglect such philological details is right in a general way. Hume and Pearce had shown that "Alchymie" (II. 517) was used as the name of a metal (Hume was not certain of its character), and even Bentley referred to this meaning, however, rejecting the word for another expression of his own. These details are passed over in the note of the Richardsons. They propose another "Vastly Poetical" signification, this probably being "the Name of the Art which is the Sublimer part of Chymistry, the Transmutation of Metals". Milton here, according to them, "names no particular Metal but leaves the Imagination at Large, Any Metal possible to be produc'd by that Mysterious Art; 'tis a Metanomy [sic], the Efficient for the Effect"... The argument is attractive and in keeping with Milton's predilection for grand, vague effects, but the existence of the other meaning makes the issue highly questionable.

Even Verity's edition interprets "His Ministers of vengeance and pursuit" (I. 170) as meaning "the good angels" though "essentially the expulsion of the rebels was due to the Messiah", "sole victor" (VI. 880), possibly basing the interpretation on Pearce's opinion that the Messiah had ordered his army to abstain from battle but not from pursuit. Verity seems to over-

---

[319]) VI. 552 n.

look the opinion first brought forward by the "Gentleman from Christ-Church", "Semicolon", that this might simply be a personification of the forces of nature, hail and lightning, which are mentioned immediately after. The Richardsons appear to be quite right in rejecting Pearce's explanation and may have been ignorant of "Semicolon's" pamphlet. They propose a new way of interpreting the passage, which is striking because of the attention it pays to the subconscious, irregular impulses of the mind. It is in its own small way a study in hallucination and shows a tendency which now and then occurs in the notes of the Richardsons, though not very often in such a distinct form. Satan and Moloch are represented as *imagining* that they were pursued by the angels: they were "Too much Terryfied to look Behind them, and Too much Confounded to Judge of what was doing Above them" [320]). Even Chaos partakes of the terror. "All three of them, or if there were a Million of Such, should not induce Us to Believe Thus was the Fact; They only say what their Terrify'd Imaginations Suggested to them" [321]). Such notes as this open new ways of inquiry although they may be wrong in themselves. The Richardsons are beginning to deal with aberrations of the mind, with the concealed, curious and abnormal.

These eccentric, but interesting inclinations are perhaps even more distinctly shown in the analysis of the expression "darkness visible" [322]). Hume explained it simply enough as the expression of an ordinary visual perception, and Pearce appreciated the boldness of the wording without seeing anything peculiar in the meaning. The Richardsons indulge in elaborate theories which rest on some interesting observations, but even more on certain misconceptions.

The substance of this note is that Milton deliberately pictured a kind of fire which emanates darkness ("...from those flames No light, but rather darkness visible Serv'd only to discover sights of woe..."), and that this darkness is only a horrid background to show the terror of the place to the damned angels: "this Fire was created on Purpose, to Torment the Rebel Angels." The figures on this background are distinctly visible because

---

[320]) I. 169 *n.*
[321]) *Ibid.*
[322]) I. 62 *n.*

"their Tincts are Inherent, and not owing to what is Foreign to them as Light is to us. Why may we not suppose there may exist Beings of a Luminous Nature, and therefore Visible but which may Not have a Necessary Power to disperse Light? or that such Power may be Suspended in Hell?" [323]).

This opinion is based on the XVIIth chapter, v. 5, of the *Book of Wisdom* from which some quotations are given: "no Power of Fire might give them Light: Neither could the bright Flames of the Stars endure to lighten that horrible Night. Only there appeared unto them a Fire kindled of it self, very dreadful." The writer also mentions v. 14 of the same chapter which "speaks of Night intollerable, and which came out of the Bottoms of inevitable Hell".

The analogy is close in many respects, and Milton may have had these passages in view. But that he did not do it in the deliberate, consistent manner assumed by the annotators, seems to be proved by another passage which is especially commented upon by them. It is I. 182 where "the seat of desolation" is "voyd of light, Save what the glimmering of these livid flames Casts pale and dreadful". The writers see very clearly that this appears to contradict their former suppositions. They save themselves out of the trouble by assuming that the power of light denied to the flames in the other passage could very well be allowed them in the description of another part of Hell. The not impossible explanation that Milton, if he was at all thinking of the Scriptural scenery, might have used its imagery only to strengthen the suggestive power of a metaphorical expression, without any further implications, does not occur to them.

The ascription to the poet of these curious arbitrary ways, the readiness to indulge in conjecture and, without sufficient ground, to attribute to him elaborate scientific theories which elsewhere seem to be contradicted by his own text, appear, in the present case, to have been largely caused by the strong impression produced on the Richardsons by the depreciated "Gothic" writers. The note describes the "Faint, Ghostlike, Frightful Apparitions, with Stone Eyes as *Spencer,* or Eyes of Brass as *Dante* has given to *Caron,* or as *Banquo's* Ghost in *Shakespear,* Eyes that have no Speculation but are staring and

[323]) *Ibid.*

fix'd" [324]). The imagination of the critics is stronger than their faithfulness to their principles and their adherence to logic. If their method does not clarify the reader's understanding, they at least seem to belong to those who prepared the way for the "Revival of Imagination".

F. MILTON'S CHARACTERS.

The Richardsons are the first commentators to deal in detail with Milton's characters. Many of their longest notes treat of them. Much in these observations is commonplace, much again new and of a quaint flavour peculiar to these critics. Exclamations and exaggerations abound here as almost everywhere else in the most typical parts of the book.

Satan and the other fallen angels are sometimes handled in the somewhat rough manner of the more characteristical remarks of Hume. Milton's reference to the contrast between heavenly and infernal spirits in IV. 118, in the annotator's opinion, "admirably heightens the Accursed Character of *Satan*". IV. 383 *n.* notes "a Boast of *Satan* Magnifying his Own Grandeur". But the great genuine vigour of his character is very distinctly felt [325]): "He took Fire at the Mention of Submission" and is "full of Pride and Scorn". Like that of the other leading characters, Satan's appearance, or rather the commentator's conception of his appearance, is dwelt upon in detail, in a way showing distinct traces of Hume's note on the same passage, which was provoked by the vulgarizing illustrations in the 17th century editions of "Paradise Lost" [326]). This note (quoted at the end of the section on Milton's characters in the chapter on Hume) which proposed a loftier conception of Satan than the usual representation of him as a common devil, is reflected in the similar protest of the Richardsons against the "Horns, Sawcer Eyes, Ugly Faces, Tayls, Cloven Feet, & c." and in their desire to have him designed in a more appropriate way. His portrait should represent "Virgin Beauty with Masculine Strength and Vigour, all in the Utmost Conceivable Degree, the Strength and Vigour little Impair'd, but

[324]) I. 62 *n.*
[325]) I. 110 *n.*
[326]) I. 600 *n.*

the Beauty Wither'd, Ruin'd by Age, Disease and Scarrs; and by
Guile, Envy, Malice, Rage, Lust, Grief, Despair, & c." Guido and
Raphael were unable to do this. "*Michael Angelo* was more Fit
for it, and he has done Vastly beyond any Other, and without
falling Deep into the Common Follies" but even his work is "not
what *Milton* has directed us to Imagine" [327]). The poets of the
past equally failed. "Tasso has gone into the Horns, Tayls, & c.
No Man has Ever Thought in This (as in Other Respects) like
Milton. O that he had Painted!" However, the writer does not
fall in this description into the very extreme of vague abstractions
and hyperbolic language. His pictorial imagination suggests to
him the possibly even too realistic idea of drawing Satan and the
reprobate angels in tattered, torn clothes — a remainder of the
very style attacked by him.

The fallen spirits have many laudable qualities. Note II. 496
relates "An Instance of... [a] Vertue Really Practic'd in Hell;
we hear of no Dissension among Themselves". They "had still
a Sense that there was a Beauty in Hazarding Themselves for the
Common Good though Really they Acted upon a Selfish Principle" [328]). And the melancholy tone which seems so distinct
in the description of the abstruse debates of the fallen angels,
even though the representation of their teachings as "Vain wisdom all, and false Philosophie" [329]) may indicate a satirical intention on the part of the poet, is fully understood and echoed
by the commentator. He tries to picture their discussions [330]):
"Though the Text does not Say it, the Reader will from the Words
naturally be led to imagine Some were Retir'd, in Thought, as well
as from the Company, and Reason'd and Debated, Discours'd
within Themselves, on these Perplexing, but Important Suttle-
ties: this gives a very Proper Image here, a very Melancholly and
Touching One."

The description of the good angels revels in superlatives.
Their picture should show "a Propriety, Elegance and Gayety
beyond anything to be seen in the Works of the Greatest Masters,
beyond what Colours, even those of Silks, Flowers, or precious

---

[327]) *Ibid.*
[328]) II. 482 *n.*
[329]) II. 565.
[330]) II. 558 *n.*

Stones, can shew" [331]). Their beauty should be inexpressible:
"When the Imagination is Rais'd as much as Possible, let it still
Know More is Unconceiv'd; Let the Lark Sing after he is Lost
in Air" [332]). The ecstasy of these notes goes far beyond the
temperate manner of the age, even beyond the manner of Milton,
whose strict, definite outlines keep most of the pictures of his
angels very distinct and clear, though he had mastered the art
of evocative vagueness where necessary, as the Richardsons were
well aware (see II. 517 *n.*, quoted before).

They are, in theory, equally aware of his usual concrete
manner, as seems to be proved by the remark on IX. 102 which
ascribes to everything in Milton's poetry some degree of materiality [333]). Only the description of God Father is excepted
and the exception is justified by the quotations given in another
note [334]) : *"a shape Divine, Presence Divine,* a *Bright Vision* as
VIII. 295, 314, 367". The commentator here acts on the prefatory
principle quoted elsewhere [335]) that spiritual things should be
spiritually discerned: "the Utmost Conceivable Majesty and
Beauty of Age without the least Decay", "an Idea of Immateria-
lity Seeming to be in Such a Form, and Surrounded with and
Penetrated by Glory" should be represented instead of the usual
frail old man of the painters. The same indifference to tradition
in painting, the same demand of spiritual qualities appear in the
portrait of Christ who should bear the Father's likeness but only
in an inward way: "the Paternal Majesty, shining in the Filial
Divinity..." — a dignity and beauty "Less Youthful and More
Majestic" than the angels. Here the analysis becomes more
trustworthy, it is no mere uncritical ebullition as in the
description of the angels, the impressions seem to be formulated
in accord with the critic's actual observations, although the
documentation is not thorough.

The greatest arbitrariness is openly admitted in the treatment of Adam and Eve, in spite of an earlier remark in the same

[331]) *Ibid.*
[332]) *Ibid.*
[333]) The importance of little concrete details is well realized III. 438 *n.*:
"*Heylin* in his *Cosmogr.* gave *Milton* These Waggons driv'n with as Ships;
to make the thing more probable the Poet has added that they were of Cane."
[334]) III. 51 *n.*
[335]) Cf. p. 225.

note demanding as great accuracy as possible in the interpretation of the poet's meaning [336]). After a long extolling passage the proposal is made to draw Adam with the indispensable symbcl "of a Man in his Perfection", of "the Force and Maturity of Manhood" — a beard. It is admitted that this could not be the poet's intention yet it appears as if the professed tendency to understand everything in the most poetical sense possible had caused this idea, and after all, "We are at Liberty to do for Our selves as we think fit" [337]).

It is of some interest to find that the Richardsons already seem to regard Adam as a partial representation of Milton himself, at least in certain details The note just quoted mentions the resemblance between Adam's long hanging hair and that of Milton, and calls attention to Milton's pride in his appearance. Newton elaborated the remark, adding some interesting details [338]).

The development of some of the characters is traced neatly enough. The signs of the approaching Fall are noticed long before the event takes place. The commentator sees how carefully it is prepared [339]), how the events develop "Exceeding Plausible", step by step [340]). The harmony between Adam and Eve is disturbed gradually, before anything really fatal has yet happened. A slight dissension, a "Little-suspected Cause" [341]), "by Insensible Steps... produc'd a Melancholy Effect, which produc'd a Much worse". Similar discrimination is shown in [342]) "Observing how Artful and Judicious *Milton* is in bringing On the Great Change wrought in Both their Hearts by the Divine Spirit; their Minds are Humbled, Soften'd, Prepar'd by Degrees; according to III. 188." Sometimes it seems to be assumed that Milton consistently observed the laws of psychological probability in describing his characters, e. g. VIII. 19 n. that Adam "must be Alway understood as speaking as things Appear'd to Him, and to the Knowledge he had". However, the point is not pressed

---

[336]) IV. 321 n.
[337]) Ibid.
[338]) IV. 305 n.
[339]) IX. 271, 372 nn.
[340]) IX. 372 n.
[341]) Ibid.
[342]) X. 947 n.

too far. Adam's considerable learning in bk. VIII is not censured as exaggerated; on the contrary, it even seems to be underestimated. The improbability of the supposition that the first man on earth could acquire all the knowledge mentioned there does not even enter the commentator's mind. It is found natural that Adam at the beginning of his life in Paradise is not well up in learned matters, "not being Yet Better Instructed, and *Eve* is as Naturally Fully Satisfy'd with her Husband's Superior Understanding", but "'twas another Sort of Conversation when *Adam* Enquir'd of the Angel concerning these Heavenly Bodies, VIII. 15. but Neither Then was he Taught much more philosophy of This Kind, but far Better" [343]).

This note shows, among other things, how deftly the Richardsons occasionally observe little touches of character. They appear to know how the skilful addition of realism here and there makes the whole picture much more convincing. Eve, elsewhere eulogized as being beyond the reach of any painter's imagination [344]), is, at the soberer moments of the annotators, found to have her human limitations; *e. g.* [345]) her "Housewifely Vanity". While receiving her angel guest, she is eager to show "How she can Entertain rather than How Grateful she is to Heaven. *Milton* has made her Thoughts Turn All That way, as it immediately follows". But an excuse is found for this: "it was in Obedience to her Husband". These light, observant remarks make up for the heaviness sometimes so perceptible in the exalted moods of the critics, though even that exaltation is stimulating in its own way and leads out of stagnation because it is genuine.

---

[343]) IV. 667 *n.*
[344]) IV. 321 *n.*
[345]) V. 328 *n.*

6. FRANCIS PECK'S "NEW MEMOIRS".

NEW MEMOIRS OF THE Life and Poetical Works OF Mr. JOHN MILTON: WITH I. An Examination of *Milton's* Stile: And, II. Explanatory & Critical Notes on divers Passages of *Milton & Shakespeare:* By the Editor. III. *Baptistes:* A Sacred Dramatic Poem, *in Defence of Liberty;* as, written in *Latin,* by Mr. *George Buchanan;* Translated into *English,* by Mr. *John Milton;* & first published in 1641. BY ORDER OF THE HOUSE OF COMMONS. IV. The Parallel, or Archbishop *Laud* & Cardinal *Wolsey* compared: a Vision, by *Milton.* V. The Legend of Sir *Nicholas Throckmorton,* Kt. Chief Butler of *England,* who died of poison, *Anno* 1570. an Historical Poem: By (his nephew) Sir *Thomas Throckmorton,* Kt. VI. *Herod* the Great: a Poem: By the Editor. VII. The Resurrection, a Poem in Imitation of *Milton:* by a Friend. And, VIII. A Discourse on the Harmony of the Spheres: by *Milton.* The Whole illustrated with proper Prefaces & Notes, By FRANCIS PECK, M. A. Adorned with the Head of *Milton* (from a Painting in the Hands of the Editor) & the Print of a medal struck in honor of him by Mr. Auditor *Benson.* LONDON: Printed MDCCXL.

4⁰: pp. [2] + VI + [4] + 437 (the last numeration includes "Baptistes" and the "Parallel"; the rest of the volume different in different copies, in spite of the indications in the title-page). "NEW MEMOIRS OF THE Life and Poetical Works of Mr. JOHN MILTON" occupies pp. I—VI and 1—264 of the first part and contains: p. I, half-title; pp. III—IV, dedctn to Speaker Onslow; pp. V—VI, Preface; and 27 chapters (pp. 1—264). The "Explanatory and critical notes" on Milton cf. pp. 132—208. Eight poems are dealt with individually as follows: p. 11, the Nativity Ode; pp. 11—22, "Comus"; pp. 22—26, "L'Allegro"; pp. 26—31, "Il Penseroso"; pp. 31—36, "Lycidas"; pp. 37—70, "Paradise Lost"; pp. 70—85, "Paradise Regained"; pp. 85—86, "Samson Agonistes". Pp. 105—132 contain "An Examination of Milton's stile [*sic*]".

The story of the origin of Peck's commentary is quite different from that of the earlier collections of Milton notes. The previous annotators dealt with the acknowledged works of Milton, or rather almost exclusively with "Paradise Lost", whereas Peck's starting-

point is quite unexpected. The supposed discovery of a new work
of the poet induces him to go through nearly the whole Milton
corpus to make sure of the authenticity of his find. Even the
authors of the remote past are studied by him in this connection.
With the relish of the real antiquary Peck grows absorbed in his
studies, accumulating a great amount of material. He composes
a commentary on the chief poetical works of Milton, and even
devotes a long chapter to Shakespeare's plays, in the search for
literary parallels. The specimens of Shakespearean notes which
he prints are only a selection from a larger number.

Peck's intentions are explained in a preface, which is dedicated to Speaker Onslow. He had found a translation of George
Buchanan's Latin play "Baptistes", which he attributed to Milton
for reasons stated in his preface to the version. It was a useful
result of his quest for evidence about the play that he recognized
the need of a thorough-going knowledge of all the works of an
author in order to pronounce on any one. This is evidently what
induced him to undertake the new task of examining in detail
Milton's minor poems. He defines his attitude as follows: "...to
understand both that poem [= the "Baptistes"] & HIM the better,
I read over the rest of His *poetical,* & most of His *prose* Works.
Besides which I dipped, & often pretty deep, into a great variety
of other books, where I thought I might find any thing for my
purpose" [346]. The underlining of "him" apparently indicates
that Peck felt the need of making a solid study of the poet's personality before judging his works.

The objects of his observations are tentatively summed up in
the preface where he states that they were written: "I. Some to
ascertain MILTON'S orthography. 2. Some to distinguish his
pastoral words. 3. Some to shew how he corrects himself. 4. Some
to observe how he follows & improves upon SPENSER &
SHAKESPEARE. 5. Some by way of glossary. 6. Some to
explain the poetical history & fables alluded to. 7. Some to point
out some particular passages of the classics there imitated. 8. Some
to mark some extraordinary beauties of his own. And, 9. Some to
justifie some few emendations & shew what they are." This
description is not quite accurate, for some of the points mentioned
first are by no means of the first prominence in the book. The

[346]) Cf. preface, p. V.

remarks on Milton's spellings and on his corrections of his own works are not nearly so conspicuous as the preface would represent them to be. The latter subject, particularly, is only slightly touched upon in a few scattered observations, though these deal with the Trinity MS., and are so far of much interest. Milton's imitations of Spenser and Shakespeare and of various other modern and mediæval authors are studied, together with a number of other matters not mentioned in the summary.

Most of the problems enumerated are old, though there may be found some glimpses of a new method in Peck's way of treating them. Neither Milton's orthography nor his mythological and literary allusions nor his archaisms were left unnoticed by Peck's predecessors. His "pastoral" words are most of them simply archaic expressions, though here and there with a possible reference to pastoral peculiarities, as the notes on them show [347]). The study of "some extraordinary beauties" of Milton appears to indicate the desire to arrive at an individual artistic appreciation of the poet, and in some of the notes this aim is achieved. Peck's emendations are neither numerous nor remarkable, but it is to his credit that he makes occasional use of the Trinity College MS. The study of Milton's "corrections of himself", though he does not go far with it, is perhaps the most interesting feature of the whole work. Here again the Cambridge MS. is used. Bentley dealt with the main differences between the two first editions of P. L., but his point of view was extremely one-sided, and he had no MSS. to rely upon. Unfortunately, Peck makes comparatively little use of his opportunities.

Nevertheless, in the few remarks falling under this head, the rudiments of a documented study of Milton's method of composition are to be found. A bold attempt in the same direction is the experiment made by Peck to show the possibility of reconstructing the original play which he believes to have been the basis of "Paradise Lost". In this endeavour he totally fails because of his inability to proceed critically and cautiously. He proves, however, his capacity for occasional quick combination and divination in such cases as the study of the rhymes of "Lycidas".

The book is a medley of notes, rather than a regular commentary. Its somewhat casual and unsystematic manner of composition

---

[347]) Cf. below sect. B. of this chapter.

makes even the special chapters on the individual poetic works of Milton for the most part mere agglomerations of scattered remarks on miscellaneous problems. It is difficult to separate them from the "Explanatory and Critical Notes" proper which are found in a chapter of their own. The whole must be studied in order to define Peck's views and method.

The present chapter deals only with the literary part of the work. The biographical part demands separate treatment, and the various miscellaneous works included in the volume are left out of account. The bibliographical and textual observations, which abound, are examined here only in so far as they touch on points of literary criticism.

Peck's treatment of the apocryphal works of Milton as well as the translation of his "Discourse on the Harmony of the Spheres" are omitted in the present dissertation. They scarcely belong to the domain of serious scholarship. But it has to be allowed that the critic's many-sided interests which are revealed everywhere, undoubtedly left their mark on the amateurish, groping, but sometimes very curious and ingenious method of the book.

A. PECK'S VIEWS ON MILTON'S POETICAL CHARACTER AND ON HIS PRINCIPAL WORKS.

The first chapter of Peck's work contains some paragraphs which aim at a summary definition of the character of Milton's poetry. After drawing, in his elaborate fashion, a comparison between the characteristics of a fine poem, a fine picture and a fine house [348]) he sums up the substance of Milton's writings, describing it as "the true in poetry" [349]). His definition distinguishes between: (1) the simple, (2) the ideal, and (3) the compound true. The first of these is found in the appearanec of reality; the second in the combination of the perfections of various models, mainly "from the antique"; and the third in "the highest excellency of the art" united with "the perfect imitation of the Fine Nature". In this last kind all is probable, because true; all is surprising "because all is curious & extraordinary"; all is

---

[348]) Cf. p. 2.
[349]) Cf. p. 3.

impressive (but not forced) because "the wonderful & the perfect" and "the natural" are combined. Milton's poetry is classed with this type.

The general theory of poetry described here is by no means new. Very close parallels may be found, for example, in Dryden [350]), who in his "Parallel of Poetry and Painting" 1695 tends to identify poetry with selective imitation. Dryden starts from a comparison between pictorial and poetic technique, just as Peck compares the relative merits of fine paintings and fine poems. Both seem to be influenced by the idea of a picture, forgetting that the painter is necessarily more a copyist of nature than the poet, who deals with words and ideas instead of the visible appearance of things. Dryden puts his point very definitely: "To imitate Nature well in whatsoever subject, is the perfection of both arts; and that picture, and that poem, which comes nearest to the resemblance of Nature, is the best" [351]). The idea of "fine nature" is distinctly formulated in the following passage: "[Poetry and Painting] are not only true imitations of Nature, but of the best Nature, of that which is wrought up to a nobler pitch. They present us with images more perfect than the life in any individual; and we have the pleasure to see all the scattered beauties of Nature united by a happy chemistry, without its deformities or faults" [352]). Peck's main addition to this is the somewhat academic notion that the so-called "ideal true" is mainly derived "from the antique".

The chief defect of this theory reveals at the same time one of the principal differences between Richardson's and Peck's descriptions of Milton's poetic character. The idea of imitation is made so prominent on this theory that the personality of the poet with its original flashes of intuition creating a new kind of reality — Richardson's "intellectual fire" [353]) — is in danger of being forgotten. Even the highest manifestation of poetic truth, Peck's "compound true", seems to be based on a combination of two kinds of imitation, and the value of poetry to depend on the

---

[350]) That Peck had studied Dryden's critical writings, appears from various references and quotations, *e. g.* p. 32, where the "Preface to Juvenal" is mentioned, and id. p. 61—62.

[351]) *Ibid.* p. 137.

[352]) Prof. W. P. Ker's edition of Dryden's Essays, 1926, vol. II, p. 136.

[353]) Cf. above, p. 113.

closeness with which its models are reproduced. It is possible, however, that a more independent treatment of nature and of literary models was intended to be conveyed by the adjectives "curious and extraordinary", which are used by Peck to characterise the impression of the best type of "the True in poetry".

Richardson emphasised the importance of imagination and inspiration in Milton's works, but did not pay enough attention to the value of deliberate artistic calculation in the composition of a poem of the range and size of "Paradise Lost". The tendency to lay too much stress on the deliberate aspects of composition and to leave too little room to subconscious, spontaneous creation, is plain enough in these utterances of Peck, and is carried almost to extremity in certain other parts of his first chapter. A special paragraph is written to prove that "Milton affected to be thought all nature, yet was indeed almost all art" (argument to chap. I). Peck's slightly modified quotation from Pope's preface to his translation of the Iliad (Peck, p. 4) seems to express his own views in likening "SHAKESPEARE (who was indeed all *nature*) to a flash of lightning; & MILTON (who was almost all *art*) to a furnace, kept up, by an uncommon ardor, to a continual glow". Instead of discussing the problem whether Milton did not belong to that class of authors who spend much time on polishing and perfecting what had been quickly composed, he appears to think of him as taking endless pains, and as doing so without any strong, spontaneous initial inspiration. In this spirit, he calls attention to the Trinity College MS., "corrected in an infinite number of places, sometimes three or four times over". Milton's own statements that he had the gift of easy, fluent composition are met by him with disbelief [354]: In order to justify his attitude, Peck undertakes an original examination of Milton's prose style. The circumstance that many authors undoubtedly have to use special devices for creating the illusion of spontaneity, makes his attempt intelligible:

"To make this [*i. e.* his way of composition] appear yet more natural, he very artfully slides into his prose works a great

---

[354] Cf. P. L. III. 37: „thoughts, that voluntarie move Harmonious numbers"; IX. 24: "my unpremeditated Verse", and the passage in **Ap. Smect.** where the author, according to Peck's quotation, describes how the words came "tripping about him at command".

number of verses, seemingly as if they fell from him whether he
would or no... He thus addresses the *Remonstrant*,

Go on, dissembling *Joab*, as still your use is;
Call brother, & smite; call brother, & smite;
Till it be said of you as was of *Herod*,
A man had better be your hog than brother!

Many other such passages might be produced: his prose works
are full of them" [355]).

We might equally well or better regard this passage as
a spontaneous outburst of indignation and anger, if we consider
the violent character of Milton's controversial prose. The
crudities in the above-quoted verses might impress one as the
result of unrestrained emotion. Pope's suggestion, as well as the
general character of the poetry of his time with its regular and
punctilious technique, seem to have blinded Peck to the nature
of bold off-hand composition.

In his treatment of Milton's individual poems Peck generally
refrains from stating any definite view on the works taken as
wholes. He analyses various stray features, and accumulates
miscellaneous notes. In most of his chapters on the principal
poetical productions of Milton, the main literary estimate is given
at the start, in a stereotyped phrase. He names, as "Mr. Milton's
nine most celebrated English Poems", the Nativity Ode, "Comus",
"L'Allegro", "Il Penseroso", "Lycidas", the "Baptistes", "Paradise
Lost", "Paradise Regained" and "Samson Agonistes". Each of
these works is dealt with in a special chapter, except the "Baptistes", which has special treatment. On these works, as a rule,
he prefers to quote the opinions of others — though there are
remarkable exceptions, e. g., his treatment of the rhymes of "Lycidas" [356]). Addison's, Dryden's, Atterbury's, Pope's, Voltaire's,
Richardson's and Warburton's pronouncements on "Paradise
Lost" are duly given (pp. 61—64), some of them at considerable
length. The views of Richardson are thus favoured, and so are
those of Pope, with expressions of admiration for "that wonderful
creature, that ever delightful and inimitable genius" — an utterance which seems further to support the view that Peck's notions
of Milton's art have been considerably influenced by Pope.

[355]) "Animadv. on the Remonstrant's Defence", I. p. 150, evid. from
Toland's edition, which is usually quoted by Peck.
[356]) Cf. pp. 32—33.

Now and again Peck speaks for himself, as in the very decided protest against the depreciation of "Paradise Regained" — a protest which he accompanies with an interesting analysis of the probable reason for the neglect of the work [357]).

Toland is quoted as declaring in his Life of Milton, that "Paradise Regained" was "generally esteemed much inferior to PARADISE LOST: which he [Milton] could not endure, being quite of another mind. Yet this occasioned somebody to say, wittily enough, That *MILTON* might be *seen* in PARADISE LOST, but not in PARADISE REGAIN'D". Fenton's Life already contains a more ɛmphatic observation on the matter: *"But, Oh! what a falling off was there.* — Of which I will say no more, than that there is scarecely a more remarkable instance of the frailty of human reason, than our author gave in *preferring* this poem to PARADISE LOST; nor a more instructive caution to the best writers, to be very diffident in deciding the merit of their own productions." Peck subjoins a third quotation, from Richardson, which states the case even more explicitly: „His time was now [*i. e.* after the restoration] employed in writing and publishing, particularly PARADISE LOST, &, after that, PARADISE RE-GAIN'D & SAMSON AGONISTES. The *last* of these is worthy of him. The *other* of any one else. If it be true that he *preferred* this to the *first* of the three, what shall we say?"

Peck's own opinion on the matter is that "Mr. *Toland.* first printed an unlucky jest, which much hurt the reputation of the PARADISE REGAIN'D among those who had rather sit down contented with other people's judgments, than be at the pains to make a judgment for themselves, tho' very able to do it." He thinks that Toland influenced Fenton, and Fenton Richardson, who was swayed by the previous opinions, "& therefore did not weigh the beauties of it [= the poem] so attentively, as he should have done. And indeed, when a good thing is once decried (as this divine poem was by nothing at all at first, I verily believe, but a mere witticism) we are all but too ready to joyn with the pack, &, right or wrong, to hunt it down" [358]).

This burst of independence is unusual, and it appears that

---

[357]) Cf. pp. 81 *et seq.*
[358]) Cf. p. 83.

Peck's main reason for valuing "Paradise Regained" is merely the skill shown by the author in evolving an epic poem out of so limited a subject. He emphasises "what a spatious field the poet hath in the PARADISE LOST; what a narrow one, in the PARADISE REGAIN'D" [359]), admiring "how the author could spin it out into four such beautiful books as he did, which, next to the PARADISE LOST, make it absolutely the best poem yet extant in our language" [360]). The references to Bentley made here and there in the course of the work [361]) lead one to think that he may have been influenced here by Bentley's brief remark on "Paradise Regained" [362]), where the same idea is expressed more concisely. The subject of the poem is called there "a dry, barren, and narrow ground, to build an epic poem on", though the handling is praised: "In that work he [= Milton] has amplified his scanty materials to a surprising dignity; but yet, being cramp'd down by a wrong choice, without the expected applause."

Peck is interested in the question whether the poem should be considered complete or not but instead of offering an answer himself, he writes a letter to "*William Cowper* Esq. Clerk of the Parliaments", asking him for a decision. The reply is suggestive and compares the plan of "Paradise Regained" with those of the *Iliad* and *Æneid*. Both of them break off as soon as the turning-point is reached: "It is these breaks, & leaving things to be imagined, & c. that, with the use of some other figures, make a poem differ from a dry history" [363]). In the first, it is enough to show the promised land to the reader, in the latter he has to be put in possession. This sensible explanation, which, instead of judging by standards, takes into account the effect upon the reader, is quoted by Peck without comment.

Some independence is shown by Peck in the discussion of the poetic category to which "Paradise Lost" belongs. Here Peck keeps in mind Milton's own liberality of view, and adopts an attitude not dissimilar to that of Richardson. Richardson did not approve of the extreme importance attributed to such classi-

---

[359]) Cf. p. 82.
[360]) *Ibid.*
[361]) *E. g.* the quotation of Bentley's note on repetitions of longer passages in Milton in § XXXI of Peck's chapter on the poet's style.
[362]) X. 182 *n.*
[363]) Cf. p. 80—81.

fications, but acknowledged the poet's right to create his own literary species [364]). Peck, like Richardson, let Milton speak on this point for himself, quoting from the "Reason of Church Government" [365]) his statement of the two epic varieties: the traditional epic based on Homer, Virgil, Tasso and the book of Job, and a freer kind which does not follow the rules of Aristotle, but of nature, "which, in them that know art & use judgment, is no transgression, but an inriching of art..." [366]). Milton's plans of heroical epics on Arthur and Alfred are supposed to belong to the former group, "Paradise Lost" and "Paradise Regained" to the latter.

Peck makes an interesting attempt to trace, by means of the Trinity College MS., Milton's poetic development. The conclusions he draws are sometimes too bold, but now and then he seems to hit some truth. The epic schemes just touched upon are examined in this speculative way, and the Trinity MS. is used to throw light on their character. According to Peck, the "two large heroic poems" would have been written in imitation of Homer — the poem on Arthur alluded to in "Manso" and in the "Epitaphium Damonis" on the model of the Iliad, and the epic upon Alfred on that of the Odyssey. The circumstance that the note on the latter scheme found in the Cambridge MS. compares Alfred's exploits to those of Ulysses, makes a further comparison with Homer very natural, and the war-like ring of the references to the Arthurian epic in the Latin poems renders probable the association with the Iliad. Peck goes further, trying to calculate the degree in which these schemes were suited to Milton's genius, and preferring the subject of Alfred in accordance with Milton's own later confession, in Bk. IX of P. L. [367]), of his dislike of noisy heroic subjects: "Had he wrote these two poems, he would undoubtedly have introduced abundance of fine machinery into the former, by the assistance of MERLIN; & yet perhaps have shone more in the latter, as the story would have been more peaceful, & consequently more roomy for adventures of another sort than that of the first. For battles & races & tiltings & feastings are things

---

364) Cf. above, p. 110.
365) Toland's ed. p. 222.
366) Cf. p. 6.
367) Cf. p. 87.

which, as our author himself very freely tells us, he had no manner of fancy to treat of." Both conjectures receive a fractional support from Milton's own statements, for Merlin is mentioned in the passage in the "Epitaphium Damonis". But, of course, the whole inquiry is extremely questionable.

The dramatic sketches in the Trinity MS. receive more attention than any other part of it, perhaps because of the scope they afford to conjecture. They are the only section of the MS. of which a full transcript is made by Peck [368]). He makes a close study of them, concentrating mainly on the drafts of "Paradise Lost". The fact that the subject of the epic appears in four schemes, *i. e.* more often than any other subject, and that three of these drafts open the long list of sacred themes, induces Peck to assume, somewhat precipitately, "that, besides the bare plans, he [= Milton] also wrote a good deal of the Drama itself (perhaps all) & then took it to pieces, & threw the main of it into this work" [369]).

This conjecture does not contradict E. Phillips's statement that Milton had actually written some verses of such a drama, which were inserted at the beginning of book IV of the epic; but Peck unfortunately does not base his assertions on reliable data. One of his main arguments is the existence of a portrait, which, as he supposes, represents Milton in his youth with a book entitled "Paradise Lost". This in his opinion "amounts almost to a demonstration that he had begun and made some progress in a dramatic poem of *that name,* when he was even so very young" [370]). Instead of asking if the painting really represented the poet, and if so, whether it was authentic, he even decides that the book on this portrait must necessarily have been that highly hypothetical drama, regarding this as a "wonderful instance of his forward parts & most early ripeness of judgment" [371]).

Trusting to such evidence, he begins to reconstruct the play, finding that "with the help of the plans which he hath left us, it were easie to throw the PARADISE LOST back again into

---

[368]) Cf. pp. 88—96.
[369]) Cf. p. 37.
[370]) Cf. p. 40.
[371]) *Ibid.*

a dramatic poem" [372]). He thinks he "could give the whole so; or very near it", but for the moment he offers " only

ADAM UNPARADIS'D.

Act IV. Scene II."

The imaginary division into acts and scenes seems to be based on the fourth draft, which is similarly entitled "Adam unparadiz'd" and was originally left undivided, but could be divided with some plausibility on the analogy of the three earlier sketches. Peck seems to have so divided it. In reprinting the scheme he provides it with a division which recalls Milton's division of the earlier plans. The fourth act deals with Adam and Eve's quarrel after the fall, and this is the subject of the reconstructed scene. It incorporates the latter part of bk. X of the epic, which consists mainly of dialogues and soliloquies, and has relatively few epic intervals. It was this, no doubt, which led Peck to select this particular part of the poem for the demonstration of his method. He starts with verse 720 of the book and goes on nearly to the end. The narrative passages are replaced by stage-directions. The result is a more or less acceptable dramatic scene, but the stage-directions are out of keeping. Some are excessively theatrical, and the gestures proposed in them are radically different from the intense, genuine and noble character of Milton's conception of the scene. In the very beginning, *e. g.:* "*Enter* Adam, with his arms across, and Eve following him at a distance; he casts up his eyes to heaven —" The worst example is the stage-direction substituted for ll. 865—7, where Milton's Eve tries to comfort Adam but is rejected by him "with stern regard".

"Soft words to his fierce passion she assay'd.
But her with stern regard he thus repell'd.
Out of my sight, thou Serpent..."

Peck naturally enough substitutes gestures and movements for Milton's sentiments, but listen to his grotesque interpretation: "Eve *rises* and *approaches to pacifie him. He kicks at her.*"

The twelfth chapter of Peck's book, where Milton's plans are reprinted, contains also some conjectures on his dramatic intentions in general, and on the probable direction which his development as a playwright would have taken, had it not been checked

---

[372]) Cf. p. 41.

by "the mean, narrow-spirited temper of the times" and Milton's own "stepping into business &... into years" [373]). According to Peck, Milton desired "to have rivalled, nay to have outdone *Shakespeare* & Johnson" (*i. e.* Ben Jonson). He does not draw any comparison between Shakespeare's and Milton's characters as dramatists, but only points to a draft in the Cambridge MS. proving Milton's "design of writing the Tragedy of *Macbeth* anew, after it had been so admirably well done by SHAKESPEARE" [374]). The preface to "Sejanus" is quoted where Jonson emphasises the need of "truth of argument, dignity of persons, gravity & hight of elocution, fulnesse & frequencie of sentence", and Peck concludes that "what he only promised, MILTON (as we may see by his SAMSON) in part performed". He regrets that the spirit of the age and the circumstances of his own personal life prevented Milton from doing what he might have accomplished "with a beauty & a grandeur above all the moderns" [375]).

Peck made other experiments. He divides "Samson Agonistes" and "Comus" into acts, and even subdivides "Samson" into 18 scenes [376]). This procedure disagrees with Milton's own statement in the preface to "Samson": "Division into Act and Scene referring chiefly to the Stage (to which this work never was intended) is here omitted". On the other hand, Milton's remark that "It suffices if the whole Drama be found not produc't beyond the fift Act" [377]) shows that he was not quite forgetful of the traditional scheme of classical tragedy in composing the work, and that Peck did not act entirely without authorization.

There are other traces here and there of his interest in Milton's stage effects. He collects information about the actors at the first performance of "Comus" [378]) and tries to get some idea of its scenic arrangement. The stage-direction following on l. 957 of the poem states that there enter "Countrey-Dancers, after them the attendant Spirit, with the two Brothers and the Lady". Hence, the contrast between the "duck or nod" mentioned in l. 960 and

---

[373]) Cf. p. 96.
[374]) Cf. p. 96.
[375]) *Ibid.*
[376]) "Paradise Regained" and "Comus" are provided also with detailed arguments after the fashion of "Paradise Lost".
[377]) *Ibid.*
[378]) Cf. pp. 12, 153.

the "other trippings... of lighter toes" is interpreted as follows:
"By *ducks* & *nods* our author sneers at the country people's
awkward way of dancing. And, the *two brothers* & the *lady* being
now to dance, describes their elegant way of moving by — *trippings* — *lighter toes* — *court guise, & c.*" [379]). The interest which
Peck took in the fate of Comus as a stage work is shown also by
the quotation from the "Universal Spectator" (N. 454) giving an
account of its production by Dalton in 1738 [380]).

B. PECK ON MILTON'S STYLE AND LANGUAGE.

The chapter on Milton's style aims at a much stricter logical
arrangement and at fuller illustration than any previous handling
of the subject. The views on Milton's ways of expression
scattered here and there among Peck's miscellaneous notes are
condensed and to a certain extent systematized in this chapter.
A great deal of it is mere compilation, and the earlier analyses of
Milton's style, particularly Addison's article in the "Spectator"
(N. 285) and the notices dealing with Milton's language in Anthony
Blackwall's "Introduction to the Classics" [381]) are freely drawn
upon. But Peck has at least the merit of wishing to be thorough.
The argument to the chapter reads as follows [382]):

"An Examination of *Milton's* style: viz. 1. *He sometimes, tho'
rarely* lengthens *a word.* 2. *He very often* shortens *a word.*
3. *He often* softens *a word.* 4. *He often makes use of* old *words.*
5. *When he wants a proper word to express his sense, he coins
a* new *one.* 6. *He very often* drops *a word.* 7. *He sometimes*
repeats *a word.* 8. *He naturalizes many* Greek *words;* 9. & *almost
innumerable* Latin *words.* 10. *He often introduces* technical
words. 11. *Of his elisions, melting of syllables, & using something*

---

379) Cf. p. 153.

380) Cf. p. 21.

381) The title of the third edition — the only edition that could be found
in Oxford — is as follows: An Introduction to the Classics; containing
a short discourse on their excellencies; and directions how to Study Them
to Advantage. With An Essay, on the nature and use Of those Emphatical
and Beautiful figures which give Strength and Ornament to writing. By
Anthony Blackwall; M. A.... London, M.DCC.XXV. [12⁰].

382) Cf. p. 105.

like an English *dactyl foot.* 12. *He often makes the* substantive
an adjective, 13. *or verb,* 14. *or participle,* 15. *or adverb;* 16. *or
places it between two adjectives.* 17. *He often makes the* adjective
a substantive, 18. *or verb,* 19. *or adverb;* 20. *or puts it after the
substantive,* 21. *or before the infinitive mood.* 22. *He often makes
the* verb *a substantive,* 23. *or adjective,* 24. *or participle;* 25. *or
puts it between two accusatives.* 26. *He sometimes makes the*
participle *an adjective,* 27. *or adverb.* 28. *He very often uses the*
complex *epithet;* 29. *& as often the* continuative *epithet, substantive, or verb.* 30. *Of his transpositions.* 31. *return of the same,
or very near the same, words & lines.* 32. *The justness of his
metaphors;* 33. *fineness of his simile's* [*sic*]; 34. *liveliness of his
descriptions;* 35. *inimitable beautifulness of his poetic preventions;*
36. *boldness of his other figures as* (I.) *the metonymie,* 37. (II.)
irony, 38. (III.) *catachresis,* 39. (IV.) *exclamation,* 40. (V.) *correction,* 41. (VI.) *apostrophe,* 42. (VII.) *suspension,* 43. (VIII.)
prosopopoeia, 44. (IX.) *transition,* 45. (X.) *sentence,* 46. (XI.)
epiphonema. 47. *His admirable mixtures of opposite passions;*
48. *delightful imitations of the ancients,* 49. *& of Scripture.*
50. *Conclusion."*

The gradual transition from the study of simpler to more complex phenomena is evident. §§ 1—3 deal with phonetic alterations of single words; §§ 4, 5, 8, 9, 10 with the character of Milton's vocabulary. The formulation of the contents of §§ 6—7 in the argument seems to indicate that these were meant to deal with some of the simplest cases of the syntactic treatment of single words: their omission or repetition. However, in the former paragraph the problem is wider and includes the question of Milton's elliptic style, though this is not dwelt upon very attentively. § 11, which treats of prosody, seems somewhat out of place in the midst of a discussion of the character of single words, which is continued in §§ 12—27. Though most of these paragraphs deal with the use of one part of speech in the meaning of another, a few notes on the ways of combining different parts of speech are interspersed. §§ 28—29 continue the treatment of Milton's combinations of words. In § 30 a syntactic phenomenon of a more complicated kind, *viz.* the alteration of the habitual word-order. is illustrated. The next paragraph examines repetitions, yet not of single words as § 7 did, but of whole phrases or verses or groups of verses. In the rest of the chapter, except at the very end, more involved features of style are studied, and the concluding paragraphs fall quite beyond the scope of the chapter.

The matter of the chapter is much less satisfactory than its plan. The definitions are often mere quotations from other critics, made without independent comment. Though the general idea of a systematic chapter on Milton's style, with abundant illustrations, is new (Addison's attempt is hap-hazard and under-illustrated) Peck shows little power or originality.

The two first paragraphs, on the lengthening and shortening of words, are apparently an elaboration of Addison's observations in No. 285 of "The Spectator". The examples given by Addison are all found in Peck. Moreover, quotations from the same number of the "Spectator" appear in other parts of the chapter, e. g. in the section on the coining of new words by Milton. Though Addison's remark starts from the metrical consideration of the length of words, this criterion is soon supplemented by another which has nothing whatever to do with the number of syllables in a word, *viz.* the question of the commonness or uncommonness of the expressions used by the poet. Thus, for example, the use of "eremit" for "heremit", which is referred to by Addison as well as Peck, may be caused by the desire for a less common word or by metrical considerations or by both. The adoption of "Hesebon" P. L. I. 408 for "Heshbon" [383]) might be explained in the same way, or possibly by phonetic considerations, e. g. the tendency to avoid the sound sh, which is pointed out by Masson [384]) who mentions the use of "Basan" for "Bashan" [385]), "Sittim" for "Shittim" [386]) & c. & c. In any case, the length of these words is by no means their only remarkable feature, as Addison expressly emphasizes, and Peck is wrong in putting them under this heading as if it were all but certain that this was the quality which induced Milton to use them. It seems probable that Peck carelessly took the category and part of the examples from Addison, without troubling to study their treatment by the critic. His own illustrations are dealt with in the same mechanical manner. Such words as "supernal", "ingrate", "insatiate" are regarded as mere

[383]) E. g. Numb. XXI. 26.
[384]) Cf. p. 171 of Masson's ed. of Milton's Poetical Works, vol. III, Macmillan, 1893.
[385]) P. L. I. 398.
[386]) P. L. I. 413.

shortened varieties of "supernatural", "ungrateful" and "unsatiated", without any notice being taken of the differences of origin and atmosphere.

The examples of the "softening" of words illustrate the very feature which was overlooked by Peck in the paragraphs just discussed, *i. e.* the avoiding of harsh sounds and combinations of sounds, and are sometimes aptly chosen, *e. g.* "ammiral" for "admiral"[387]),and apparently,also,"far-fet" for "fat-fetch'd"[388]). On the other hand, the identification of "cressets" P. L. I. 728 with "crescents" only shows Peck's ignorance of the meaning of the word. A few further surprises of this type are found in his next paragraph on Milton's use of old words, *e. g.* the identification of "lore" with "lure"[389]). The majority of Peck's examples are, however, well chosen, being words of a distinctly archaic or possibly provincial stamp, such as "to tine", "bosky", "welkin", "purfled", "pranckt" & *c.* The explanations generally come close to the truth, and show, on the whole, some knowledge of the older language.

Addison's defence of Milton's coinages of new words (Spect. No. 285) which is quoted by Peck, seems to have stimulated him to study the question, though his illustrations are not borrowed from Addison. The expressions "honied" Il P. 142, "canie" P. L. III. 439, "roseat" P. L. V. 643, "hosting" (sb.) P. L. VI. 93, "infuriate" (adj. pple.) P. L. VI. 486, "Atheous" P. R. I. 487, "arrowie" P. R. III. 324, "endorst" P. R. III. 329, are cited as instances. Of these, "canie" [= cany], "infuriate" and "arrowie" in the Miltonic sense [= "consisting of arrows" as distinguished from "resembling an arrow"] are not registered by the NED. before Milton. The rest do occur before their appearance in Milton's works, some of them even very early, but of "atheous" there is

---

[387]) P. L. I. 294.

[388]) P. R. II. 401.

[389]) A few similar lapses occur elsewhere, in the notes on the individual poems. A typical case is the explanation of "dingle" in Comus (Co. 312 *n.*). Being unacquainted with the fact that the word is used as a noun, Peck decides that "it is an adjective and agrees with *dell*" [in: "I know each lane, and every alley green, Dingle, or bushy dell of this wilde Wood"]. "Both together signifie a low deep place, where briars hang thick & long, &, if I may so speak, *dingle-dangle* over one's head, & which, consequently, if not well known & carefully avoided, would, in the night, go near to tear one's eye out."

only one instance previous to Milton, and "to endorse" does not appear to have been used seriously in the literal sense of the word before Milton adopted it. The results of Peck's investigation are creditable, when one considers the absence of satisfactory lexicographical works at his time [390]).

His lists of Græcisms and Latinisms can hardly have been meant to show exclusively Miltonic innovations, for the very first Greek expression quoted by him, "cynosure", is expressly exemplified elsewhere in his book by an instance taken from Burton's "Anatomy of Melancholy" [391]). Peck must have been conscious that some of them at least were known before Milton. The illustrations which he gives of elliptic constructions are not particularly striking after Pearce, and the opinion that the removal of all superfluities of language "is indeed one of the greatest arts in composition" is stated far less categorically than in Richardson's handling of the same problem [392]). The examples of the repetition of single words contribute nothing of interest. In the paragraph on Milton's use of technical terms no new ideas are added to Peck's quotations from Addison [393]) and Spence [394]), save in the remarks on Milton's knowledge of the technicalities of music.

The paragraph on prosody is examined in another place, together with the above observations. The treatment of Milton's use of one part of speech for another contains some mistakes, but is notable as making allowances for freer habits of style. Though the inquiry was not new, and even Hume mentions the use of adjectives as nouns, Peck's systematic grouping is meritorious. He has tried to include every possible case, and in certain respects has done rather too much than too little. He tries to demonstrate the possibility of changing almost every part of speech into nearly

---

[390]) In this connection, mention should be made of the chance notes on Milton's spelling found here and there. Some of them are accurate enough, e. g. the remark that the noun "even" and its cognates (evening, etc.) are generally spelt with a double e, whereas the adverb (true only of the emphatic adverb) has one e (p. 137); id. that "Ore" (= "ore of a metal") is generally spelt with a capital (p. 144). Peck sees in the spelling "oughly" a symbolic representation of the meaning (p. 150).

[391]) Cf. p. 141.

[392]) See above, p. 108.

[393]) Spect. No. 297.

[394]) On the Odyssey, p. 170 acc. to Peck.

every other. This is valuable as a recognition of the great liberties
found especially in Elizabethan English. Attention is called to
such peculiarities as the following: "the roses bushing round"
P. L. IX. 426; "tempest the Ocean" P. L. VII. 412; "without
disturb" ibid. VI. 549; "Thy sweet Converse and Love" ibid. IX.
909; "At Feed or Fountain" ibid. IX. 597. Several of the forms
cited by Peck are misinterpreted. Thus, "divine" in "divine of
something ill" 395) is defined as a verb used as a participle,
without any notice being taken of the Latin adjective "divinus",
e. g. in Horace's "Ars Poetica" 218, 219 "divina futuri... sen-
tentia" 396). "Adorn" in P. L. VIII. 576 ("Made so adorn for
thy delight the more") is classed as the adjective use of
a verb though it may be an imitation of the Italian adjective
"adorno" 397), or else an example of an abbreviated participle of
the type of "infuriate" 398) which is found so frequently in Milton.
Peck apparently does not understand this form, for "forfeit" in
"this now fenceless world Forfeit to Death" 399) where all symptoms of the type are found is described as the substitution of
a verb for a participle, which is quite a different thing from the
abbreviation of a participle on the analogy of the corresponding
forms borrowed from the Latin.

In spite of these and other blunders, there are some good
observations: "bushing" e. g., in the passage quoted above, he
connects with "bush", instead of adopting the corrupt and conventional reading "blushing" ["the roses blushing round"] as in
Bentley's edition.

The notes on Milton's ways of combining different parts of
speech contain some good illustrations of certain important
characteristics of the poet's word-order. The habit of placing
the adjective after the noun 400) is the least typically Miltonic
feature among these. On the other hand, the position of a noun

---

395) P. L. IX. 845.

396) Cf. Verity's ed. of. P. L., IX. 845 n.; see also Newton, P. L.
IX. 845 n.

397) Cf. Newton, P. L. VIII. 576 n.

398) Cf. above p. 155.

399) P. L. X. 304.

400) E. g. "Inmate bad" IX. 494.

between two adjectives [401]) or of a verb between two accusatives [402]) are notable points and are well exemplified.

These and some further syntactic remarks seem to have been suggested by an observation in Addison's article on Milton's language [403]) where the following devices for raising the style are enumerated: "Under this head may be reckoned the placing the adjective after the substantive, the transposition of words, the turning the adjective into a substantive, with several other foreign modes of speech which this poet has naturalized, to give his verse the greater sound, and throw it out of prose" [404]). These stray suggestions of Addison seem to be industriously enlarged upon and illustrated by Peck.

A long list of Milton's compound epithets is followed by a number of Shakespearean examples showing that this device was common among the Elizabethans, and no mere echo of the style of classical antiquity, as might be judged from Hume's treatment of the matter [405]). Another connecting link between Milton and Shakespeare is found in the "continuative epithet, substantive or verb", i. e. the consecutive use of co-ordinate verbs, nouns or epithets. Special notice is taken of Milton's manner of composing lines consisting only of three such words [406]). His inversions of the usual word-order receive more attention here than in the earlier commentaries. Some extreme cases of this tendency, e. g. P. L. XII. 412: "to death condemnd A shameful and accurst", partly explain Peck's eagerness to see such transposition even where some other explanation is more satisfactory. P. L. IX. 202: "The hands dispatch of two Gardning so wide" is explained as: "the dispatch of two hands" & c. though there is hardly much reason to connect "two" with "hands", instead of interpreting it as signifying "Adam and Eve". Peck likes these inversions all the better for their boldness. His most enthusiastic remark refers

---

[401] E. g. "sad occasion dear" Lyc. 6.

[402] E. g. VI. 713: "my Almightie Arms Gird on and Sword upon thy puissant Thigh."

[403] Spect. No. 285.

[404] Ed. 1822 of the "Spectator".

[405] See above, p. 40.

[406] E. g. P. L. II. 185: "Unrespited, unpitied, unrepreevd".

to P. R. I. 171: "But this surpasses all the rest, & is greatly beautiful.

— the hand
Sung with the voice, & this the argument. P. R. I. 171.
For, — *the voice sung with the hand, & c.*"

In both cases the verb applies to "the hand" as well as to "the voice", so that Peck's interpretation does not solve the difficulty. The illustrations given in Todd's edition make it probable that "to sing" is used in the Latin sense of "cano" which also means "to perform on any instrument". If so, no unusual transposition need be assumed.

The repetitions of whole groups of words and longer passages were already observed by others, *e. g.* by Bentley [407]). However, the "turn of words" in S. A. 961 ("then winds and seas, yet winds to seas") which is quoted in this connection, is a good instance of modified repetition and supplements Pearce's observations on cases of a somewhat similar type.

In addition to these notes on the more strictly formal elements of Milton's language, a considerable number of remarks deal with his figures of style. This is apparently the least independent part of the chapter, for nearly all definitions and illustrations are taken from Anthony Blackwall's work, as is partly acknowledged in the foot-notes. This book, though quoting Milton more frequently than any other English writer, is essentially a manual of literary theory pursuing its own line of argument, which is that of giving a systematic synopsis of the main literary categories, not a detailed study of Milton's peculiarities of style. Its Miltonic illustrations, although sometimes interesting enough, are casual. Peck seems to be unconscious of the need of altering Blackwall's scheme or adding more suitable illustrations. Blackwall's explanatory and illustrative matter is transcribed by him almost exactly in the original order, except for the omission of remarks with non-Miltonic examples, so that the original system is mutilated without the substitution of an equivalent.

Blackwall's list of tropes includes: the metaphor, the allegory, the metonymy, the synecdoche, the hyperbole, the irony and the catachresis. Of these, only the metaphor, the metonymy, the irony and the catachresis, which are illustrated from Milton, are

[407]) Cf. X. 1092 *n.*

represented in Peck's chapter. The paragraph on the first of these is borrowed from Vossius, the definitions and illustrations of the rest being from Blackwall. A typical instance of Peck's neglect of the inner connection between Blackwall's categories is shown in the treatment of a special group of figures expressing various stages of hesitation: "doubt", "correction", "suppression", "omission" [408]). Here again Peck's reason for dealing with only one of these, *viz.* "correction", is evidently that only this figure is exemplified from Milton in Blackwall's book.

The paragraph describing the chief kinds of sentences, the "direct and plain" and the "indirect and disguised" varieties, is also from Blackwall, but at least the former type finds a new illustration: "be lowlie wise" [409]). The example of the more difficult variety is borrowed. This appears to characterize the average intentness of Peck's endeavour to do independent work in this part of his book.

Beside these notes relating to style, various observations are found which touch on style only indirectly, as for example the remark on the vividness of Milton's descriptions [410]). While the notes on Scriptural and classical borrowings in Milton contain nothing new, those on "mixtures of opposite passions" are of some interest, as they refer to a typical feature, *e. g.* in the observation on the phrase: "Grinn'd horrible a gastly smile" [411]). Peck admires the passage despite his narrow ideal of beauty and „Fine Nature".

C. PECK'S STUDY OF MILTON'S MS. CORRECTIONS. HIS EMENDATIONS.

Peck's emendations and the few remarks made by him on Milton's "corrections of himself" (cf. his preface) show certain aspects of his conception of style and also of his critical method. He used the Trinity MS. to prove his view of the artificiality of Milton's manner [412]). In another place he tries to trace Milton's

---

[408]) Cf. pp. 191—197 ed. 1725 of Blackwall.
[409]) P. L. VIII. 173.
[410]) Cf. p. 125.
[411]) P. L. II. 845 *et seq.*
[412]) Cf. above p. 144.

ways of thought from the corrections in that MS.: "There is
hardly a more agreeable research than to observe how any great
author (such as MILTON) corrects himself" [413]. However, the
note we quote from shows that his knowledge of the language of
older literature, and apparently even of the Bible, was insufficient
for drawing any reliable conclusions. He examines the alteration
of Co. 608 & c.

> "Or drag him by the curls & cleave his scalpe
> downe to the hips"

into its present form:

> "Or drag him by the curls, to a foul death,
> Curs'd as his life."

"But here our author afterwards found he had committed an
egregious mistake. He had threatned to drag *Comus* by his
curled hair, & then to *cleave his scalpe*, i. e. his *bald* pate. Now
curles upon a *bald pate* is a good joke. He therefore altered the
two last lines (as we see by Edit. 1673) to what we read
above" [414]. He forgets, or does not know, that the Bible uses the
expression "the hairy scalp" [415]), of which there are several
examples in the NED. The question whether Milton's alteration
may not have been caused by the desire to adopt a less crudely
realistic style, as many other changes in the same poem would
indicate, is not discussed.

The Trinity College MS. is used for the solution of textual
problems, which, of course, involve problems of literary psycho-
logy and style. In his emendation of "Comus" l. 553 [416]) Peck
runs counter to the authority of the original editions, accepting
the Cambridge reading "drowsie-flighted steeds" (the hyphen is
added by Peck; the original reading = "drousie flighted steeds")
instead of the usual "drowsie frighted steeds". His argument is
that "They must be clever animals which can be *drowsie* and
frighted at the same time! The great MILTON could not be guilty
of such a gross absurdity. It was the printer's fault & none of
his." It seems that Peck did not make allowances for Milton's
bold combinations of ideas. Newton accepts the reading of the
Cambridge MS. whereas Warton and Todd keep to the printed

---

[413]) Cf. p. 148.
[414]) *Ibid.*
[415]) *E. g.* Ps. 68. 21.
[416]) Co. 561 *n.*

11

authorities, the former explaining the printed reading as meaning not simultaneous qualities but two successive stages of consciousness [417]). Todd points to the improbability that Milton should have failed to alter the reading if it was a misprint [418]). While the later commentators are critical and cautious in their judgments, Peck's preference of the MS. reading is shared by a recent critic such as A. W. Verity (ed. of Comus, l. 553 *n.*), so that his boldness is not so unique here as in some of the cases already discussed. Verity finds that *"drowsy-flighted* gives a more picturesque conception... and it appears most improbable that Milton should have changed the line so manifestly for the worse."

Peck's views are here shared by careful critics, which is intelligible, as he has MS. sources to support his conjecture. In certain other cases he seems to lack critical judgment. In Il P. 151 *n.* "Above, about, or underneath" is altered into: "...and underneath" because of *"Cassio's* pious salutation to *Desdemona,* whereof these fine lines are almost a direct copy.

> *Hail to thee, lady! & the grace of heav'n,*
> *Before, behind thee, and on ev'ry hand,*
> *Enwheel thee round. —"*

This is the well-known method of basing an emendation on a supposed model of the poet, but Peck neglects that not a single word in Shakespeare's verse is identical with any in Milton's, and that the similarity of meaning and context is too slight to justify definite alterations. He also fails to prove the faultiness of the earlier reading. His lack of tact and taste is seen in the idea of altering Lyc. 75 according to the standards of "elegant" poetry. The association of the furies, instead of the traditional fates, with the "abhorred shears" strikes him as impossible. Without considering Milton's motives, e. g. his apparent intention to produce an effect of grim ugliness, Peck decides that the beings described by the poet "may be elegantly called *fairies"* [419]).

D. PECK ON MILTON'S VERSE.

Though Peck, as was shown above, finds Milton's poetic method artificial and laborious, the chapter where these views are expressed, contains some passages on the inspiring influence

---

[417]) Cf. p. 200, ed. 1785.
[418]) Co. 553 *n.*
[419]) Cf. p. 168.

exerted on the poet by his passion for music: "it may be premised, that he fetches more flights & beautiful images from that science than any other *English* poet whatsoever" [420]. Peck tries to trace this influence in the imagery of Milton's works as well as in the technique of his verse, especially in his analysis of the rhymes of "Lycidas", starting with the assumption that Milton was a trained musician.

He is convinced that the poet not only loved music as a soothing or stimulating influence, as indicated by such passages as Co. 555 *et seq.*, that "wonderful description of a fine song by a fine voice at a distance... one of the most sublime passages in all *Milton*" [421]) or by P. L. I. 549 *et seq.* where the author shows "the *great power of music to* encourage armies to engage & fight deliberately, like the antient heroes" [422]), but also that he had a competent knowledge of the technicalities of music. In L'All. 135 & c. ("Ever, against eating cares" *et seq.*) he sees the description of a fugue, and the poet's way of depicting an organ in P. L. I. 709 & c. convinces him of Milton's ability to take this instrument "to pieces, & clean it, & put it together again, without any other person to help him" [423]). This view, which agrees with the accounts of Milton's skill in music given by the early biographers, *e. g.* by Aubrey, is the cause of Peck's bold application of musical analogies in the pages devoted to the study of "Lycidas" and the "rhime and mystery concealed in it" [424]). In this analysis, Peck goes beyond Richardson's comparison of Milton's poetical technique to that of music [425]).

Dryden's depreciation of Milton's rhymes in his preface to Juvenal, which is referred to by Peck, apparently caused the younger critic to adopt the opposite view with such determination. Here for once Peck is methodical and consistent and intelligently tries to vindicate Milton's deliberate workmanship, studying the facts more carefully and in some respects more acutely than *e. g.* Dr. Johnson did in his dogmatic condemnation of the supposed irregularity and harshness of the verse of "Lycidas". He attempts

---

[420] Cf. p. 8.
[421] Co. 566 *n.*
[422] Cf. p. 8.
[423] Cf. p. 111.
[424] Cf. pp. 32—33.
[425] See above, chap. 5, sec. D.

to show that this irregular scheme was not adopted "because Mr.
Milton could not help it" but "because Mr. *Milton* designed it" [426]).

In his view the lack of regularity is only apparent and the
arrangement of the rhymes has its definite laws. Though their
places are not fixed so that they are "thrown oft from each other,
by the intervention of other lines & Rhimes, to a great distance",
most of the verse endings have "their return or answer at the end
of some verse in the some [*sic*] paragraph", without being connected with any line in any other paragraph. This, in Peck's
opinion, is an attempt "to give, tho' secretly, a poetical image or
draught of the mathematical Canon of Music". The paragraphs
are likened to musical bars, the rhymes to chords, the unrhymed
lines to discords in the same bar. Milton's skill on the organ is
mentioned in order to show that "the odd dispersion of the
rhimes... may not improperly be compared to that beautiful way
of sprinkling the keys, for which some masters of it are so justly
famous" [427]). It may be difficult to decide whether these musical
analogies really influenced Milton's technique. Nevertheless, the
regularity of the rhyming scheme and the part played by the
unrhymed lines are plausibly explained by Peck. His valuation
of poetic originality, or perhaps ingenuity, is seen in the inference
that the author appears to have been "resolved to let the world
see, how that he was both a perfect master of rhime, & could also
express something by it, which no body else ever thought of."

Milton's liberal treatment of metre, *e. g.* the rhythmical
variety of "L'Allegro" and "Il Penseroso", is appreciated by Peck.
He ascribes the poet's deviations from the ordinary monotonous
beat of equal numbers of stresses and syllables to the influence of
the matter of the twin poems. The metre there is "not always
the same, but varied as the subject & words suggested; every
hint of all which that great master was always ready to catch
at" [428]). The elisions in Milton are described according to the
actual impressions of Peck's ear. A final *y* before an initial vowel
"seems not to be cut off, but rather to remain" [429]). Milton
thereby "gives a particular softness to the foot, & makes it read

---

[426]) Cf. p. 32.
[427]) Cf. p. 32.
[428]) Cf. p. 30.
[429]) Cf. p. 112.

like an *English* dactyl" [430]). However, sometimes Peck shows his
usual absence of consideration and caution, as in the note on
Co. 807 [431]). In this remark, the last word of the verse, "direct"
("This is meer moral babble, and direct Against the canon laws
of our foundation") is regarded as an elided form of "directly"
before a vowel in the beginning of the next line, as if the consonant *l* could be swallowed by the elision. Peck apparently forgets
what he has himself observed in a different connection, that adjective forms are often used by Milton in an adverbial sense [432]).

E. PECK'S REMARKS ON THE HISTORICAL, SOCIAL AND LITERARY SETTING OF MILTON'S WORKS.

Peck's antiquarian bent is closely connected with his interest
in obsolete and quaint expressions. One of his main merits is the
comparison of Milton's poetry with the older literature of England
and with its folklore and romantic traditions. His inquiries in
this department remind one of Hume's amateurish, rambling
antiquarianism, though he pays more attention to English matters, however, without neglecting the study of the Fathers of the
Church, the classics and later foreign authors.

Peck seems to know very intimately the country-side with the
customs and traditions of its past and present, as well as the ways
of the continental peoples. Sometimes he uses his knowledge of
foreign lore for explaining the origin of English traditions, as in
tracing back the word "rebeck" to the name of an Italian or
French instrument of dancing music [433]). In explaining the adjective "blithe" [434]), he refers to Danish popular amusements and
customs: "the Danes call the month of *February blüde manet*, the
merry month; from the *Carnival*, or modern *Bacchanalia*, which
always falls some time in that month". He studies the history of
the morris-dance [435]), trying to ascertain the date of its introduction into England and to define what is in it of native and what
of foreign origin. The name is derived by him from "moorish",

---

[430]) *Ibid.*
[431]) Cf. p. 151.
[432]) Cf. chapter on style, § 19.
[433]) L'A. 94 *n.*
[434]) L'A. 24 *n.*
[435]) Co. 115 *n.*

more or less in accordance with the evidence now found in the NED, whereas the dance itself is supposed to have been introduced at the time of Edward III, when John of Gaunt returned from Spain, the figure of "Maid Marian" being regarded as a national contribution to the borrowed custom. Vivid illustrations are adduced from Shakespeare [436]) but Peck's method of copious historical and literary documentation is marred here, as in many other cases, by his antiquarian enthusiasm, which causes him to introduce irrelevant detail, e. g. the description of a horse ballet at the court of the emperor Maximilian.

Peck makes use of recent authorities to verify the meaning of mediæval terms, such as "palmer" and "pilgrim". Thus, Shakespeare's and Milton's use of these expressions is compared with Sir Isaac Newton's interpretation of them in his "Observations on the Apocalypse" [437]). Several quotations are also given to show that neither of these poets noticed the special technical meaning of these words. In dealing with the curfew, Peck mentions the legend of its introduction at the time of William the Conqueror [438]).

These and similar inquiries into the social and historical setting of Milton's poetry prepare the way for later scholars, such as Thomas Warton. This applies also to the notes on folklore and popular superstitions. Peck, who seems to have been fond of everything quaint and fantastic, evidently felt attracted by romances and fairy-tales. His treatment of the "Legend of Sir Nicholas Throckmorton" in the same volume is a fair instance of this tendency, but it appears also in his Miltonic notes. In connection with the above remark on the curfew he quotes Shakespeare's passage on Flibbertigibbet in "King Lear" [439]) as well as an allusion to the appearance of fairies at curfew-time in "The Tempest" [440]). Shakespeare's treatment of old traditions of this stamp in "Hamlet" is appreciated [441]): "Shakespeare touches this old imaginary circumstance, of spirits & ghosts ceasing to walk at the *first cock* crow, very beautifully." The stories

---

[436]) Mids. N. D., II Hen. VI, Twelfth Night, & c.
[437]) Cf. p. 269 of the work, according to Peck.
[438]) Co. 438 *n.*
[439]) Co. 438 *n.*
[440]) *Ibid.*
[441]) L'A. 115 *n.*

of the Rosicrucians on the "swart faeries of the mine" are drawn upon to illustrate "Comus" [442]. Reginald Scot's "Discovery of Witchcraft" is studied for the sake of the information it gives about the legend of Robin Goodfellow [443]), concerning which a ballad from the Pepys collection at Cambridge is reprinted in full in Peck's chapter on "L'Allegro". His interest in these matters does not seem to be purely literary, for he speaks of Robin Goodfellow as still actually seen in Scotland, where he says his name to have been changed to that of "Brownie" [444]). The more adventurous aspects of romance have been studied by Peck in several languages, and he quotes out-of-the-way foreign synonyms of a typical word such as "bandit", showing his interest in picturesque popular idioms of this type [445]).

Elaborate historical, geographical and mythological works supply him with material on local legends and traditions. Selden's commentary on Drayton's "Polyolbion", Henry Rowland's "Mona antiqua restaurata" (Dublin 1723, acc. to Peck), Spenser's catalogue of rivers in the "Faerie Queen" are used to explain the allusions in "Lycidas" [446]), *"Holingshed, Stow, & our author's Hist. of England"* in order to elucidate the legend of Locrine in "Comus" [447]). But various far less solemn matters are also dealt with, *e. g.* the details of the meal set before Christ by the Tempter [448]). The main part of this note was contributed to Peck by a "curious lady", as he calls her, who seems to have made a special study of ancient cookery at the festivities of Cardinal Wolsey and Elizabethan society. She writes with professional accuracy how *"Grey* ambre is the ambre our author here speaks of, & melts like butter". This serves as an example of Peck's endeavour to collect independently or through his informants literally everything likely to explain the background of Milton's works. Pearce saw

---

[442]) Co. 438 *n.*

[443]) L'A. 100 *n.*

[444]) L'A. 100 *n.*

[445]) „*Bandite*, or *bandito*, from *bando*, Ital. *edictum publicum; &* bandire, *edicto publico proscribere;* originally, from the Anglo-Saxon, *abannan;* to proclaim or publish: an outlaw or fugitive: called in the *Low-Countries*, Free-booters; in *Germany*, nightingales; in *Spain*, Bandilero's [*sic*]; in the north of *England*, Moss-Troopers; in *Ireland*, Tories." (Co. 426 *n.*)

[446]) Lyc. 50 *n.*

[447]) Co. 841 *n.*

[448]) P. R. II. 335 *n.*

the necessity of accurate historical research but had little time for it, being engaged in problems of a more exclusively philological and textual character. Peck tries to make up for this neglect.

Many of these inquiries are diversified by references to, and quotations from Milton's poetic predecessors. The number of names is not very considerable but some of them are new. Balladry [449]), Drayton's [450]), Ben Jonson's [451]), Chaucer's [452]), and Spenser's [453]) names are alluded to. Peck's knowledge of the two last-mentioned enables him to identify the references to them in "Il Penseroso" [454]). The now generally accepted interpretation of "Where more is meant than meets the ear" [455]) as referring to the style of allegory is already given here.

Old popular books such as Purchas's "Pilgrimage" [456]) and the "Anatomy of Melancholy" by "ROBERT BURTON (better known by the name of DEMOCRITUS JUNIOR) S. T. B. Student of *Christ's Church,* & Rector of *Segrave* in *Leicestershire",* as Peck minutely describes him [457]), find mention. The latter, which appears to agree with Peck's inconsistent, miscellaneous method, is alluded to repeatedly. The resemblance between the poem on melancholy prefixed to the first edition of Burton's work, and Milton's "L'Allegro" and "Il Penseroso", which was mentioned later on by Warton without any reference to Peck's book, is already pointed out by the latter [458]). One of the more lyrical passages of Burton is quoted to illustrate Milton's use of the word "cynosure" [459]) : "'Tis the general humor of all lovers; she is his stern, his pole-star, his guide; his *cynosure,* his *Hesperus* & *Vesperus,"* & c.

But the aptest and most numerous quotations are from Shakespeare. Peck's preface showed how greatly he was interested in the poet. The fact that a special chapter is given exclusively

---

[449]) Cf. p. 23.
[450]) Lyc. 50 *n.*
[451]) Cf. p. 96.
[452]) Il P. 109 *n.*
[453]) Lyc. 50 *n.* & *c.* & *c.*
[454]) Cf. Il P. 109, 116 *nn.*
[455]) Il P. 120.
[456]) Cf. p. 200.
[457]) Cf. p. 27.
[458]) Cf. pp. 27 *et seq.*
[459]) Co. 343 *n.*

to Shakespeare is good proof, particularly as Peck describes the chapter as only part of a much larger collection of observations [460]). His references to Shakespeare are, accordingly, more varied than those of the earlier commentators. Besides the great tragedies, the comedies and less popular tragical plays are often mentioned [461]). Some of his Shakespearean references have been alluded to above. The quaint and easy style of the comedies seems to have attracted him. Mrs. Page's expression "tricking" [462]) is taken due notice of, and Shakespeare's vocabulary of dances and merriments is traced with great interest [463]). The typically Elizabethan wit of Shakespeare's dialogue, the grace and movement of his fairy-scenes find much attention, as in the comparison of the vivid description of the dance in Co. 960—962: "Here be... Other trippings to be trod Of lighter toes" with the very similar expressions in Ariel's and Oberon's speeches [464]). That these parallels deal with a very typical feature of the period, which may, perhaps, be associated with the Elizabethan passion for festivities, seems evident from the great number of cognate expressions adduced by Warton in his notes on the same passage of "Comus", in addition to the instances quoted by Peck, whom Warton does not mention [465]). Peck's personal interest in amusements of this kind, as indicated by his numerous remarks on them (some of these were quoted above), seems to qualify him for the study of the cheerful aspects of Elizabethan poetry.

There is little critical analysis in most of these notes. Even some of the most conspicuous contrasts in Peck's parallel passages are passed over without mention, as e. g. the difference between the description of Harapha's clumsy approach in S. A. 1067 and of Diomede's "aspiration" that "lifts him from the earth" in "Troilus and Cressida"... [466]). But the intimate knowledge of

---

[460]) Cf. above p. 140.

[461]) For instance "Much Ado about Nothing", Co. 438 n., "The Comedy of Errors", ibid., "Measure for Measure", Co. 408 n., "As you Like it", Co. 143 n.

[462]) "Go get us properties and tricking for our fairies", cf. Il P. 121 n.

[463]) Cf. Co. 143 n., on "measure", and Co. 115 n., on the morris-dance, as described above.

[464]) "Each one, tripping on his toe" & . Tp. and: "And this ditty after me Sing and dance it trippingly", Mids. N. Dr.

[465]) Ed. of Poems upon Several Occasions, 1785, pp. 253—4.

[466]) S. A. 1067 n.

Shakespeare shown by many of Peck's remarks supplied some of
the later annotators with valuable material, which was relatively
rarely acknowledged. Comparisons between the description of
the pain of alternate heat and cold in P. L. II. 595 & c. and a
similar passage in "Measure for Measure" [467]), as well as between
Adam's reflections on death and the soliloquies in "Hamlet" [468])
are drawn both by Peck and Newton.

Peck's study of Milton's classical models is less important,
mainly because more work had already been done in this department, except in regard to the minor poems. In his illustration of
these, Peck had to make a new start. Some of the Virgilian
passages mentioned in his notes on "Lycidas" form part and
parcel of nearly every modern Milton commentary, e. g. Virg. Ecl.
X. 3: "neget quis carmina Gallo", which is supposed to be the
model of Lyc. 10, and Virg. Ecl. III. 26: "non tu in triviis, indocte,
solebas Stridenti miserum stipula disperdere carmen?" compared
by Peck with Lyc. 123 & c. Other parallels have found less general favour, e. g. those between "L'Allegro" and various parts
of the "Calendae" of Statius [469]).

The ancients are not overestimated, as a rule. Deviations
from classical models are accepted as legitimate, if they are
justified by the result, e. g. in Milton's treatment of the legend
of Alpheus: "our author here makes *Alpheus* to sink into the
earth at the stern voice and speech of *S. Peter*. Which thought
is very beautiful, and a much better reason for his disappearing
than his supposed pursuit of *Arethusa*" [470]).

A considerable number of notes deal with the Fathers of the
Church, in accordance with the special mention made of them in
Peck's preface. He mainly attempts to trace the sources of Milton's
religious views. The origin of sin [471]), the problem of Satan's
punishment [472]), the doctrines of Origenes [473]) are dealt with
side by side with extracts apparently selected merely for their

---

[467] "Ay, but to die, and go we know not where" & c. Peck P. L. II.
586 *n.*, Newton P. L. II. 603 *n.*
[468] Peck P. L. X. 782 *n.*, Newton P. L. X. 813 *n.*
[469] L'A. 1 *n.*, 118 *n.*, 131 *n.*
[470] Lyc. 132 *n.*
[471] P. L. VII. 548 *n.*
[472] P. L. XII. 545 *n.*
[473] P. L. V. 414 *n.*

value as anecdotes, *e. g.* the story from Rivinus, "De Serpente seductore" [474]), assigned to Rabbi Acha by the author of the book. It relates how all creatures and even the creator himself received their names from man. The connection with Milton's line: "And thou thir Nature know'st, and gav'st them Names" [475]) is not convincing, for Milton's source is probably found in Genesis II. 19, 20.

Certain notes treat of parallels to Milton in the Romance literatures. "Lycidas" and Dante are compared [476]) but even such relatively little-known authors as Ferrante Pallavicino find mention. The satire on the corruption of Christianity in "Il Divorzio Celeste", a work attributed to Pallavicino, is referred to as a parallel to the attacks on the clergy in "Lycidas" [477]). However, it is questionable whether Peck knew the original, for, as his foot-note indicates, he had used Boyle's "Critical Dictionary". A very long quotation from Mateo Aleman's "Guzman Alfarache", (pp. 52—57), also from a translation, contains some close similarities to certain passages of "Paradise Lost", which have been passed over by Newton and Todd. The place quoted by Peck describes in an allegorical form the origin of discontent on earth. Jupiter gives the God Content to mankind, who soon forget their former deity and worship only their new idol. The gods meet to decide how to punish the trespassers, and Momus proposes merciless destruction. Only Apollo's opposition saves the guilty, but their idol is taken away and Discontent put in its place. To deceive mankind, the latter is shaped exactly like Content. The desperate crowd "tug hard" for their old god but forget their fury on perceiving his likeness among them. Such is the story related in the quotation. The resemblance to Milton appears in Apollo's speech in defence of mankind which very strongly reminds one of P. L. III. 144—166 [478]). The coincidences might be

---

[474]) Lipsiae 1686 4⁰. p. 49 according to Peck.
[475]) P. L. VII. 493.
[476]) Lyc. 123 *n.*
[477]) Lyc. 108 *n.*
[478]) "If thou destroy the world, in vaine then are those things which thou hast therein created. And it were imperfection in thee to unmake that which thou hast already made, only for to amend that which thou now findest amisse; much lesse would I have thee to repent thy selfe that thou hast made man. For that will be but to discredit thy selfe, and thine owne worke. Besides, how can it stand with the power and goodnesse of a *Creator*, to take

partly due to the similarity of the situations, *e. g.* the idea of the inappropriateness of the creator's cruelty to his own creatures. But the further argument that destroying the beings created by oneself is a sign of imperfection, and the discussion of the question of free-will immediately after in Aleman add interesting new points of resemblance to the passage in "Paradise Lost", which is preceded by the speech of the Father on the problems of free-will and predestination. The general situation — the description of a council in heaven in both cases —, and the parallel between Apollo, the son of Jupiter, and the son of God both pleading for the offending party, increase the similarity. The tone is epic and solemn in both, with the exception of the description of the last quarrel and a few other passages in Aleman.

The deficiencies of Peck's method appear in his inferences. Milton might possibly have remembered the happy life of mankind with their deity Content in his description of Adam and Eve in paradise, but he did not imitate it, as Peck appears to suggest. A far greater lapse, however, is his view that the grotesque "struggle which mankind made to retain their God *Content* among them" may be regarded as "a lively intimation of the great reluctance wherewith our first parents left the happy garden" — a judgment which disregards the enormous differences of style and sentiment and makes far too much of the very natural fact that the departure from paradise did not take place without reluctance and hesitation.

---

too strict a course against his *creature*, & to exceede, by extraordinarie means, in his chastisements"

    (See p. 58 of Aleman's Guzman Alfarache, transl. by John Davies of Kidwell, 1630, at Oxford, acc. to Peck).

Almost immediately after, the question of free-will is touched. "If thou give them it, they must necessarily then be such manner of men as their forefathers were. And if thou do not give it them, they shall not be men."

7. JAMES PATERSON AND "RAYMOND DE ST. MAUR".

A COMPLETE COMMENTARY, WITH *Etymological, Explanatory, Critical* and *Classical* NOTES ON MILTON'S Paradise Lost: explaining 1. All the *Hebrew, Chaldaic, Arabic, Syriac, Phoenician, Egyptian, Greek, Latin, Italian, Spanish, Portuguese, Danish, Russian, Tatarian, Saxon, Teutonic* (or *German) Dutch, Norman* (or *Old French) Old English* (or *Scottish) Indian, American* and *Miltonian* Words, i. e. Those of the Author's own Coining, thro' the whole *Poem.* 2. All the difficult Terms of *Divinity, Philosophy, Mathematics, Astronomy, Astrology, History, Geography, Architecture, Navigation, Anatomy, Surgery, Chemistry, Alchemy, Hunting, Hawking, Gardening,* and other *Human Arts* and *Sciencos* [*sic*]. 3. All the fine *Epithets*, the *Mythology* (or *Fables)* of the Antients [*sic*] all the *Figures* of *Grammar* and *Rhetoric, Comparisons, Similies, Digressions,* different *Persons;* and setting all the *Transposed Sentences in* a plain *English Prose Order,* with many new *Tneological, Critical, Historical* and *Political Observations,* never published before. For without such a *Work* the *Poem* is useless to most Readers of it. *In Magnis voluisse sat est.* Tibull. By JAMES PATERSON, M. A. And PHILOLOGIST. LONDON: Printed by the Proprietor, R. WALKER, in *Fleet-Lane.* MDCCXLIV.

12⁰: pp. [4] + 512. *Contents:* p. [1], title; p. [3], the King's declaration of Paterson's copyright; p. [4], abbreviations; pp. 1—8, preface; pp. 9—512, commentary.

THE STATE of INNOCENCE: AND FALL of MAN. Described in MILTON'S PARADISE LOST. Render'd into PROSE. With Historical, Philosophical and Explanatory NOTES. From the *French* of the Learned RAYMOND DE ST. MAUR. By a GENTLEMAN of OXFORD. LONDON: Printed for T. OSBORNE, in *Gray's-Inn,* and J. HILDYARD, at York. MDCCXLV.

8⁰: pp. IV + 436 + [31]. *Contents:* p. I, title; pp. III—IV, preface; pp. 1—436, text with notes; pp. [1—19], index; pp. [20—23], list of similes; pp. [25—31], index to notes.

The second edition in 1755: MILTON'S PARADISE
LOST, OR, THE FALL OF MAN: WITH Historical, Philosophical, Critical, and Explanatory NOTES. From the Learned
RAYMOND DE ST. MAUR. WHEREIN the Technical Terms
in the Arts and Sciences are explained; the original Signification
of the Names of Men, Cities, Animals, &c. and from what
Language derived, rendered easy and intelligible. ALSO THE
Mythological Fables of the Heathens, wherever referr'd to,
historically related; difficult Passages cleared of their Obscurity;
and the Whole reduced to the Standard of the *English* Idiom.
In TWELVE BOOKS. Embellished with a great Number of
Copper-Plates. LONDON: Printed for H. OWEN, White-
Fryars, Fleet-street; and C. SYMPSON, at the *Bible-ware-
house, Chancery-lane.* MDCCLV. < 8⁰: pp. 430 + [18]; the
preface here somewhat abridged >.

In the edition of 1767, which seems to be identical with
the previous one, except for the illustrations and some possible
slight differences in the text, the title-page differs in its latter
part: IN TWELVE BOOKS. Embellished with Fourteen
Copper Plates. LONDON: Printed and Sold by J. BEDFORD,
at the *Crown*, in St. *Paul's Church Yard*, and C. SYMPSON,
in *Stone-Cutter-street, Fleet-Market.* *MDCCLXVII* < 8⁰:
pp. 430 + [18] >.

The Scottish edition of 1770, which gives the full preface
of 1745, has the following title-page: THE STATE OF IN-
NOCENCE, AND FALL OF MAN, DESCRIBED IN MIL-
TON'S PARADISE LOST. Rendered into PROSE. With
Historical, Philosophical, and Explanatory NOTES. From the
FRENCH of the Learned RAYMOND DE ST. MAUR. By a
GENTLEMAN of OXFORD. ABERDEEN: Printed and
sold by JOHN BOYLE. MDCCLXX. [12⁰: pp. VIII + 428].

These are the only editions containing both paraphrase
and notes. Selections of "St. Maur's" notes have been reprinted
various times together with notes by other commentators.

The French translation by "Raymond de St. Maur" appear-
ed first in 1729 with the following title: Le PARADIS PERDU
DE MILTON. POEME HEROIQUE. TRADUIT DE L'AN-
GLOIS. Avec les Remarques de Mr. ADDISSON. TOME I.
A PARIS,
chez (CAILLEAU, Quay des Augustins, à Saint André.
   (BRUNET Fils, Grand-Salle du Palais, au cinquième
   (pilier, au S. Esprit.
   (BORDELET, rue S. Jacques, vis-à-vis le College des
   (Jesuites, à S. Ignace.
   (HENRY, rue Saint Jacques, vis-à-vis S. Yves.
MDCCXXIX. Avec Approbation & Privilège du Roy. [3 vols.
12⁰].

Paterson's notes and "The State of Innocence" have to be dealt with together, for the commentary contained in the latter publication is almost entirely identical with part of the former, except for some slight alterations or casual differences. The difficulty is that the title-page of the "State of Innocence" calls the notes to this work a translation "From the *French* of the Learned RAYMOND DE ST. MAUR", *i. e.* Nicolas François Dupré de St. Maur, member of the French Academy and author of a translation of "Paradise Lost" published in 1729. One feels inclined to assume that Paterson had in some way or other plagiarized from St. Maur's work, though it is impossible to suppose that the authors of both publications used the French original independently, for then the translations would have differed. On the other hand, Paterson hardly could have made use of a work by another writer which was published a year later, unless the date of the "State of Innocence" is fictitious or he was able to examine the translator's MS. before it appeared, which is improbable. The other assumption, that the translation from the French is a plagiarism from Paterson's original work, seems also to present difficulties, but there can be no doubt as to the identity of most of the notes, which extends to very minute details, including technicalities.

The material found in the Bodleian and in the British Museum does not seem sufficient for a definite solution of the problem how far Paterson and the "gentleman of Oxford" depend on Dupré de St. Maur. The French translation of Milton by the latter is found in the British Museum, but only in a few editions, none of which alter the impression that the French notes cannot be regarded as identical with the commentary professing to be their English version.

The annotations to the French translation are not so numerous as those of the "State of Innocence", not to mention Paterson's larger work, and are generally much briefer and less elaborate. A number of biblical and classical references and allusions to rather obvious facts are found both in the French and English commentaries, but most of them are too commonplace to justify the assumption of any interdependence between these works. The literary criticism, the parallels from the literatures of the Latin nations, the references to French historical works & c. in St. Maur's notes are not found in the English "version", and it appears questionable whether the English commentator ever had studied the French book with any attention.

"The State of Innocence", and consequently also Paterson's commentary, contain some typically English matter which could scarcely have been translated from the French, so that if there were any French sources, these were probably adapted very freely. This is suggested by the allusions to English translations of foreign books, *e. g.* p. 390 to a work by "M. *Christ. d'Acugna*, translated into English, 1699", to reference books used by English scholars, *e. g.* p. 34 [479]), to "Potter's Antiq. of *Greece*, vol. 1. p. 328" or to travel books *& c.* by English authors, which were hardly popular enough in France to be used for purposes of illustration by a French commentator [480]). Sir Walter Raleigh, who is mentioned p. 385, was more likely to be quoted by a French student of English literature, but the comparison of foreign places and conditions to English, in a manner which seems to assume the reader's familiarity with English life, indicates the hand of an Englishman, as in the note on "Ispahan" [481]: "...the river *Zenderu*, which is as broad and deep as the River *Thames* is at London"; or in another note on p. 101: *"Bosphorus... Lat.* from the *Gr. i. e. The Passage of an Ox*, as we say *Oxford."* The reference to an English provincial paper as well as the whole point of view in the note on "Columbus" p. 314 are even less French than these: "But it [= America] was first discovered about 300 years before, *A. D.* 1170, by *Madoc* a valiant Prince and Son of *Owen Guinneth* King of Wales; as is related by *Lynwric Ap Grano, Galyn Owen, Peter Martyr, Humphrey Lloyd, David Powell,* Sir *John Price, Richard Hackluyt,* Sir *Thomas Herbert, & c.* which was farther confirmed by the Reverend Mr. *Morgan Jones,* Chaplain of *South-Carolina,* who lived four Months with the *Doeg Indians,* and conversed with them in the Old *British* Language. Lastly, that Prince *Madoc* was buried in *Mexico,* appears by the Epitaph on his Monument lately found there. See the *Gloucester Journal* and *Daily Post,* &c. *March* 6, 1740."

It does not appear impossible that St. Maur's name was used for advertising the "State of Innocence". This may have con-

---

[479]) Note on Adonis.
[480]) Cf. *e. g.* "Cockburn's Journeys", p. 58.
[481]) Cf. p. 381.

tributed to the success of the enterprise, which found more favour
with the public than Paterson's work, to judge from the number
of its editions, although this result may have been at least partly
due to the prose-paraphrase of "Paradise Lost" in the "State of
Innocence", and to the absence of most of the learned notes,
especially the philological observations found in Paterson's book,
which were cumbersome enough to deter the common reader.

If the notes should not be a translation from the French, as
seems at least probable after the above, there remain the possibilities that one of the two English commentaries was plagiarized
from the other, or that both are by the same author, or that the
two writers used some third unknown source. As there are no
direct reasons to assume the last, and as a plagiarism of the
first type would probably have been too bold to pass unnoticed,
the second conjecture should be examined first, particularly as
the prefaces and even the title-pages of the two works provide
some interesting evidence in support of this idea.

The technical execution of the notes peculiar to Paterson's
work resembles that of the rest. The identity of the abbreviations
and of the method of enumerating the languages regarded as the
sources of Milton's words without quoting any examples from
these languages, & c., confirm the impression that the author was
the same. But these are not the only coincidences. The preface
to the "State of Innocence" shows great similarity to the preface,
and especially to the text of the title-page, of Paterson, both as
regards matter and expression. Paterson enumerates in his title-
page a list of the languages dealt with in his etymological notes,
the first six of the series being "the *Hebrew, Chaldaic, Arabic,
Syriac, Phoenician, Egyptian*". The "Gentleman of Oxford"
similarly demands from the competent reader of Milton a knowledge of "the *Hebrew, Chaldee, Arabic, Syriac, Phoenician* and
Egyptian, and all the dead Languages, with the *living* and *modern* ones, in all their different Dialects." The selection and order
are identical, and Paterson shares with the "Gentleman" the
tendency towards philological completeness, for his list includes
"*Tatarian*, ... *Indian*" and "*American*... Words", and his preface apologizes for the incomplete information given as to remote
or ancient languages, emphasizing the need of thorough etymological inquiries for the "Improvement in Learning to future
Ages". The "Gentleman of Oxford's" list of the other subjects

of his notes, the "difficult Terms in the *Mathematicks, History, Astronomy, Astrology, Geography, Architecture, Navigation, Anatomy, Alchymy, Divinity,* and all other human Arts and Sciences", is almost literally identical with the second part of the enumeration on Paterson's title-page. The "fine Epithets", the *"Figures* of *Grammar* and *Rhetoric",* the *"Transposed Sentences"* set "in a plain *English Prose Order"* mentioned in the third section of his list are found also in the preface to the „State of Innocence", where "Paradise Lost" is described as "wrote in the highest Stile of heroic Poetry", and its "Thoughts, many of them express'd by Figures of *Grammar* and *Rhetoric",* as "full of *Digressions* and *Sentences transposed".* Both works profess to take into consideration the needs of foreigners who know little English. "The State of Innocence" is said to have been written "that all *English* Readers may have the like Pleasure... and to help Foreigners, whose small Acquaintance with our Language might otherwise prevent their Intelligence of the finest.Poem that ever was wrote" (preface). Paterson aims at "the *Satisfaction* of the *Unlearned,* that know not the *Use* of *Dictionaries;* and of *Foreigners,* who are Strangers to the *Original Language* of *Milton"* [482]).

These similarities are too considerable to be accidental. Especially the verbal coincidences suggest that the author was the same in both cases. There are also other connecting links. Paterson speaks in his preface of having originally intended to publish an annotated edition of "Paradise Lost": *"At first I proposed to publish this* Commentary *along with the* Original Poem, *with* Alphabetical, Numerical Notes, *and other* References *on the* Margin *of the* Book; like *the* Scholastical Notes *upon the* Classics. *But being opposed in the Design, I modell'd it into this* Form." "The State of Innocence" is to a very considerable extent the realization of this plan, though, it is true, with some technical deviations, as the use of foot-notes instead of marginal notes, perhaps owing to practical considerations, and with the cardinal difference that it is not an edition of the original text of the poem but a simplified paraphrase. This involves the absence of elaborate discussions of style and language, as most verbal and syntactic difficulties have disappeared.

[482]) Cf. p. V.

Even the idea of a prose paraphrase is intimated in Paterson's preface. He maintains that he has "placed all the transposed Sentences into *a natural or plain* English Prose-Order, *but generally by Way of a short* Paraphrase, *not in the same* Words *of the* Poem, *for a certain* Reason *known to myself*". It seems difficult to trace this mysterious reason, but if Paterson had carried out his intention, a large part of the poem would apparently have been paraphrased in the free manner typical of "The State of Innocence", tending rather towards popular simplicity than close adherence to Milton's text. As Paterson has, in his paraphrastic way, reconstructed the natural order of only a few selected passages, there is little material for a comparison with the later work. In the preface to the latter, such a partial paraphrase is considered unsatisfactory, but it is described in terms which might well apply to what Paterson did. "It was not thought sufficient to pick out Lines here and there, and explain them only, for it is impossible to know which Part may be difficult to each Reader." Hence, another method is chosen by the author, "for which Reason, the whole is render'd into plain and intelligible Prose, the Sense preserv'd, and nothing omitted that may make it clear to all Readers." The mere "picking out of lines" practised by Paterson is replaced by a more thorough method.

Though Paterson's paraphrastic attempts are neither numerous nor long, and should be expected to differ from the corresponding parts of the complete paraphrase, where the context influences the wording, there are many remarkable resemblances not suggested by the original. The nearly complete identity of some of these deviations from Milton, which often seem too unfelicitous and unimportant to have been deliberately borrowed, could hardly have been caused by unconscious imitation. A few examples (all from books I and II) are given in the following:

1) P. L. I. 44—47 — one of the first paraphrased passages in Paterson:

"Him the Almighty Power
Hurld headlong flaming from th' Ethereal Skie
With hideous ruine and combustion down
To bottomless perdition."

Paterson renders it: "The Almighty Power of God hurled or threw Satan and his Accomplices headlong from the highest

12*

180

Heavens, with most dreadful Ruin and Burning, down to the bottomless Pit and everlasting Destruction..." [483]).

„The State of Innocence" uses some of the typical expressions of this rendering: "...for the Power of the ALMIGHTY cast him down from the Heavens, with most dreadful Ruin, and Burning, down to the bottomless Pit, and everlasting Destruction..." [484]).

„Dreadful ruin and burning" for "hideous ruin and combustion" is no surprising coincidence, considering the closeness of the paraphrase to the original. On the other hand, the curious method of dividing the bold expression "bottomless perdition" into its component parts and supplementing either of these with a more conventional specimen of the wanting syntactic element, evidently in order to make the sense more intelligible, could hardly have independently occurred to both paraphrasts.

2) The rendering of P. L. I. 305—6:
"When with fierce Winds *Orion* arm'd
Hath vext the Red-Sea Coast..."
is identical in both works, except in the punctuation. Paterson's paraphrase reads: *"When Orion attended with boisterous Winds, hath vexed the Coast of the Red Sea."* The substitution of "boisterous" for "fierce" and "attended" for "arm'd" is not suggested by Milton.

3) I. 659—660: "But these thoughts Full Counsel must mature".

Both Paterson and the "Gentleman of Oxford" enlarge "full Counsel" into "full Counsel [= Council] and good Deliberation", obviously for the sake of greater plainness. Both substitute "must bring to perfection" for "must mature". Neither of these renderings seems inevitable from the point of view of the original text.

4) II. 11: "Powers and Dominions, Deities of Heav'n". Both renderings have: "...ye Powers and other Inhabitants of Heaven". The latter part of this apostrophe differs entirely from Milton's text and has no special merits which might have caused one of the two paraphrasts to borrow it deliberately from the other.

---

[483]) I. 46 *n.*
[484]) Cf. p. 5.

5) II. 513: "A Globe of fierie Seraphim" is rendered in both works: "A Company of fiery Seraphim".

Thus not only the notes but also the prefaces, title-pages and paraphrases of the two works contain close similarities. The derivation from the French appears to be fictitious, and the *nom de plume* "A Gentleman of Oxford" may have been adopted by anyone. There is hardly anything to controvert the assumption that the same author wrote these books, especially as even the plans stated but left unexecuted in the earlier seem to have been carried out in the later work.

Paterson may be supposed to have decided to popularize his enterprise by omitting the more learned notes and adding a simplified paraphrase to attract the more indolent or less educated class of readers. The possibly not very satisfactory reception by the public of the earlier volume, which was not printed again, may have caused his later anonymity. This conjecture only suggests one possible way of explaining the curious publication in the course of two years of two partly identical works, apparently by the same author.

Various suggestions have been made regarding the „State of Innocence". Thus, its paraphrase has been regarded as a re-translation from the French into English; George Steevens apparently alludes to it in an observation on the crude blunders of the French scholars and students of Shakespeare [485]): "The late Mr. Thomas Osborne, Counseller, (whose exploits are celebrated by the author of the *Dunciad*) being ignorant in what form or language our *Paradise Lost* was written, employed one of his gazetteers to render it from a French translation into English prose." Osborne is the publisher of the "State of Innocence", and its numerous editions may have made it an object of some notoriety. D'Israeli's "Curiosities of Literature" [486]) repeats this story but without mentioning names or referring to Steevens: "There is a *prose version* of his "Paradise Lost", which was innocently *translated* from the French version of his epic!" In Todd's Milton bibliography [487]) Steevens's remark is mentioned in connection with the "State of Innocence", but no effort is made to controvert the notion.

---

[485]) Shak. ed. 1793 vol. I. p. 72—73.
[486]) Cf. ed. 1849 vol. I. p. 340.
[487]) Poetical Works of Milton, vol. IV. ed. 1842, p. 540.

Paterson's notes are undoubtedly based on the original text, as is clearly shown by his observations on Milton's vocabulary, which will be dealt with below. If his commentary and the "State of Innocence" were written by the same person, the conjecture that the paraphrase could have been ignorantly made from a foreign language loses all probability. But the paraphrase itself shows its origin clearly enough. Milton writes in P. L. II. 629 *et seq.*:

> "Mean while the Adversary of God and Man,
> *Satan* with thoughts inflam'd of highest design,
> Puts on swift wings, and toward the Gates of Hell
> Explores his solitary flight..."

The prose is as follows [488]) : "Satan, the Adversary of God and Man, with Thoughts enflam'd with highest Designs puts on swift Wings, and takes his solitary Flight towards the Gates of Hell." Very few words are altered, nearly all the typical expressions and partly even the rhythm of the original being preserved.

The notion that the work was done without a knowledge of the "form or language" in which "Paradise Lost" was composed, is contradicted by the preface where the very first sentences describe it as a poem, leaving no doubt that it was written in English verse. Thus, it is emphatically asserted that "this Work [*i. e.* the paraphrase] is not done to insinuate, that it is superior or any Way equal to the Poetry of PARADISE LOST". One of its objects, as was shown, is to help foreigners with little knowledge of Milton's language. The mistake made by Todd and, as it seems, also by the others is probably due to a vague association of the book with some French original, without any inquiries into the nature of this connection.

The DNB has a misleading remark on the authorship of the book. It is ascribed to George Smith Green [489]), "an eccentric eighteenth-century watchmaker of Oxford, with a turn for literary study". The authorities referred to by the biographer of the DNB (J. B—y, *i. e.* James Burnley) are: "Notes and Queries", 3rd series, X. 47; Baker's "Biographia Dramatica"; and Disraeli's "Curiosities of Literature".

---

[488]) St. of Inn., p. 86.
[489]) In the article on G. S. Green.

183

The anonymous contributor to "Notes and Queries" who unfortunately forgets to make a due statement of his authorities, rightly corrects the name of "Raymond de St. Maur" into "Nicholas Francis Dupré de St. Maur", yet writes as follows of the "State of Innocence": "This new version of the *Paradise Lost*, which was conceived to 'bring that amazing work somewhat nearer the summit of perfection', was the production of George Smith Green, an eccentric watchmaker at Oxford..." This does not differ from the information given by the DNB.

Disraeli's "Curiosities of Literature" (*ubi supra*) refers to Green, but in a different connection: „One Green published a specimen af a *new version* of the "Paradise Lost" into blank verse! For this purpose he has utterly ruined the harmony of Milton's cadences, by what he conceived to be 'bringing that amazing work somewhat *nearer the summit of perfection'*." The same information is given in Baker's "Biographia Dramatica" 490), which is in part almost literally identical with the above.

These remarks evidently relate to a work entitled: "A NEW VERSION OF THE PARADISE LOST: or, MILTON PARAPHRASED. IN WHICH THE MEASURE and VERSIFICATION are *corrected* and *harmonized*; the OBSCURITIES *elucidated;* and the FAULTS of which the Author stands accused by *Addison*, and other [*sic*] of the Criticks, are removed...... By a GENTLEMAN of OXFORD. OXFORD: Printed by W. JACKSON...... 1756 ...." (8⁰). Todd assigns the pamphlet to Green 491), referring to Farmer's "Essay on the Learning of Shakespeare", 3rd ed. p. 27. The fact that both Baker and Disraeli have the quotation given by the contributor to the *N & Q.* leads one to the conjecture that this latter may have taken it from them but failed to notice that it related to the metrical version, which in Disraeli's book is mentioned almost in the same breath with the prose paraphrase. The rest of the correspondent's data on Green's character and works agree with those in Baker's book, which was likely to be consulted by anyone. The oversight, though crude, is not improbable, since the DNB repeats the association of Green with the prose rendering, forgetting to mention the metrical work at all.

---

490) Ed. 1812, article on G. S. Green.
491) IV. ed. of Milton's Works, 1842, vol. IV, p. 540.

It seems convenient to study the notes included in the "State of Innocence" separately from those peculiar to the earlier work, if solely for the purpose of giving an idea of the contents of the book. Everything said of the commentary of the "State of Innocence" naturally applies also to the corresponding parts of the other work. The "State of Innocence" contains most of the historical, geographical and miscellaneous information given in Paterson's notes, omitting, as was said, nearly all the philological remarks. As in the case of Hume, the commentator does not confine himself to the interpretation and elucidation of the text but accumulates irrelevant information, though with a neater method and greater accuracy than Hume. A favourable example is the following picturesque geographical note, which may have helped the readers towards a fuller appreciation of the imaginative effect of Milton's allusion, besides being far more accurate than the corresponding notes of the earlier commentators [492]: "The Pike of *Teneriffe* is one of the highest Mountains upon our Globe; a Mass of Rocks heaped confusedly together, like a rough *Pyramid*; computed to be between three or at most four Miles perpendicularly above the Sea; and about fifteen Miles to them that ascend it. It may be seen 120 *English* Miles offat [*sic*] Sea, in clear Weather." Hume described the mountain as 15 miles, Richardson as 45 miles in height [493]. Newton, who may be supposed to have read this note, has the same computation as the "State of Innocence", assuming the height to be "15 miles from the very first ascent of the hill till you come thro' the various turnings and windings to the top of all" [494]. His punctiliousness exceeds even that of the annotator of "The State of Innocence", for, as he asserts, he has consulted "a gentleman who measur'd it", who assured him "that the perpendicular highth of it is no more than one mile and three quarters."

That apparent endeavour to be accurate does not save the anonymous commentator from committing bad mistakes. The above-mentioned remark on the clergyman who conversed with the aborigines of America "in the Old *British* Language" shows great credulity. Some statements are very bold, e. g. a remark on the

---

[492]) Cf. p. 171, on P. L. IV. 987.
[493]) Cf. their notes on the passage.
[494]) IV. 987 *n.*

Chinese language [495]) : "The *Chinese* have about 60,000 Letters, yet not above 300 Words". The exaggeration in the following description of whales [496]) is scarcely intentional: "The Whales live in these cold Northern Seas, and also in the cold Coast of *Pataegonia*, near the Straits of *Magellan*, in great Abundance; but rarely in the warm, because of their excessive Fatness; for they would melt and be parboiled in hot Waters."

The view of Hume and others that the thought of classical antiquity was derived from the Bible is found repeatedly. Homer is admitted to have been "the wittiest Man that ever liv'd, who had none to imitate", however, with the exception of *"Moses*, from whom he took his best Thoughts"... Solomon is the source from which *"Pythagoras, Socrates, Plato, Aristotle, Trismegistus & c.* borrow'd their Principles of Philosophy". A certain prudish narrowmindedness spoils the critic's enjoyment of the Olympian games, which are praised for their humane character, "abating the Immodesty of the Players, who were all naked" [497]).

Some advance appears in the treatment of mediæval matters, which is more careful than in Hume's, Richardson's or Pearce's notes, not to mention those of Bentley. Only mediæval religion was treated more fully by Hume. Peck's many-sided interest in questions of folklore, chivalry and mediæval life in general, is absent, but events of the remote past are related with some competence. A fair example is the note on the introduction of jousting in England and Germany [498]). Old poetry is scarcely alluded to.

Milton's deviations from the facts of history meet with less pedantry than the annotator's attitude to classical morals would lead one to expect. As in Hume [499]), it is pointed out [500]) that the"Expedition and Fall of *Charles* the Great, with his Nobles at *Fontarabia*, related by M. *John Turpin*, is entirely false and fabulous." Yet as in Pearce, poetic inaccuracy is excused, though the present commentator shows more anxiety to seek support from the ancients: "But Poets do not regard Exactness of History

[495]) Cf. p. 122.
[496]) Cf. p. 13.
[497]) Cf. p. 80 *n*.
[498]) Cf. p. 46 *n*., on P. L. I. 583.
[499]) P. L. I.
[500]) Cf. p. 48.

nor Chronology, provided a Fiction may help them out, and please
their Readers. For *Æneas* was 300 Years after Queen *Dido*, tho'
Virgil makes them contemporary, as St. *Austin* proves in his
Book, Of the City of God, and G. *Hornius* in his Arca Noae.
P. 358."

The critical remarks seldom go beyond commonplace general-
izations and comparisons of Milton with the poets of classical
antiquity. It is found that Milton "hath exceeded *Homer* himself,
and *Virgil* also in *Epic* Poem, both in the Grandeur of his
Subject, in his Learning, Characters, and every Thing else" [501].
Here it is still the subject, not the execution, which is mentioned
first, and Milton's erudition comes next, which is perhaps
significant, for the same attitude appears in another note where
Milton's description of the Pandæmonium is compared with an
Ovidian passage [502]: "*Milton's* pregnant Imagination, Wit,
Elocution, and Learning, in the Composition and Description of
this Court, have far outdone *Ovid's* in his Description of the
Sun, and of all other ancient Poets; so that nothing extant among
them comes up to this." And once more, in the final remark on
book I [503], "all human Learning" is said to have been surpassed
by this Miltonic description.

Philology is one of the main characteristics of Paterson's book.
The fact that the title puts the etymological notes before the
"Explanatory, Critical and Classical" remarks, shows the
importance ascribed to this section. This may be due to the
influence on Paterson of classical editorship, a feature of
which notice has already been taken. The whole work is
intended to rival the commentaries on ancient literature. Since
"*The* Iliads *and* Odysses [*sic*] *of* Homer, *and the Works of* Virgil
have had the Honour of a thousand Commentators", Paterson
thinks it "*necessary to add such* a Commentary *to this* [= *P. L.*]
as the great Work *required*" [504].

The above philological tendency appears throughout the preface. The æsthetic speculations of the "judicious Mr. Addison" and
the textual criticism of the "learned Dr. Bentley" and that other
"learned Author" who wrote a confutation of Bentley, *i. e.* appar-

---

) Cf. p. 108.
502) Cf. p. 57.
503) Cf. p. 59.
504) Cf. preface, the beginning.

ently Pearce, are all described as *"of a quite different* Nature *from my Design."* Only two annotators, *"a very learned and judicious Gentleman of* North Britain, *signed* P. H. *for* Peter Home", whose commentary appeared *"about 50 Years ago"*, *i. e.* evidently "P. H. φιλοποιητης"* (1695—1744), and Richardson, are acknowledged to *"have attempted something of this Kind"* [505]), and stress is laid on the philological part of their work. Hume's notes are regarded as not practical enough, "useless to the Unlearned", because in Paterson's opinion they cite too many foreign words and indulge too much in *"long and tedious* Quotations *out of the* Greek, Latin, *and* Italian Authors" — but also as of no avail to the learned, who already possess the original works. Paterson's ideal of completeness is extravagant, for even Hume is censured by him as passing by *"many* Original Words *in the* Poem *untranslated (tho' he has done others of them well and with great Learning)."* But even less favourable is the comment on the volume of the Richardsons, in which words are found to be set down *"over and over, without any* Explication", and others enlarged upon *"with long* Paraphrases, Quotations *and* Breaks, *where there is no need... Parturiuntur* [*sic*] *Montes!"* The biographical part of their book is criticized even more severely than this: *"Alas! How mean is this, in Comparison of* Cowley's *Life, by the* Rev. *Dr.* Sprat, *late Bishop of* Rochester: *'Tis a Pity that he had not written* Milton's *Life also."*

Paterson evidently tries to be more practical, but though he, instead of quoting foreign words, only mentions the languages from which he believes the words used by Milton to be derived, he certainly does not confine himself to the explanation of difficult cases. According to his preface, he has *"translated almost every* Foreign Word *into proper* English, *express'd them all in the same* Number, Time, Mood, *and* Person, *as they stand in the* Poem *itself; with two, three or four* Words *of the same* Signification, *but better known to the* Unlearned." Everything has to be explained so thoroughly as to make the work *"more serviceable to the meanest* Capacities *and* Strangers". He seems to be thinking of a real encyclopædia: *„And to render this* Work *more complete, I have explained also many other* Foreign Words, *as they occurred*

---

[505]) It is of some interest to observe the lack of variety in Paterson's above epithets: "judicious", "learned", "very learned and judicious".

in my Notes; *but are not in MILTON'S* Poem." The unintelligent reader's needs are provided for by the special mention *"of every* New Person *or* Subject *of each* new Paragraph, *where it was not very obvious and plain; that the* Reader *may the more readily* understand *what he reads, and may retain the Threads of the* History *in his Memory, as he goes on."* This anxious pursuit of simplicity leads the commentator to curious extremes. Thus, the expression "the brow of some high-climbing Hill" [506]) is explained as follows: *"Brow; Sax. Dut.* O. E. That Part of the *Face* of a Man about the Eyes; the Top or Height of any thing. Here, the *Side* of an *Hill;* by a *Fig.* of *Rhet."* Even the word "bird" is explained: according to Paterson, it denotes "Any Fowl large or small" [507]).

One section of Paterson's philological notes is of greater interest. In his title-page he refers to *"Miltonian Words, i. e.* Those of the Author's own Coining". The idea of examining these is not new, as the cases of Hume and Peck prove, but Paterson does this with greater consistency, and the abbreviation *"Milt.",* meaning "Miltonian", is found in many notes. Very often he succeeds in bringing to light expressions created by Milton, revived by him after a considerable interval of oblivion, or used only very seldom before him, to judge from the data of the NED. It is true that more often than not the words described by him as new coinages are found at least once or twice before Milton, but it has to be considered that the lexicographical apparatus of those times was not comparable to that of to-day. Often there seem to have been weighty reasons to ascribe the origin of such words to Milton, at least from the point of view of the average 18th century scholar, since many of these expressions had assumed a peculiar Miltonic flavour, possibly owing to the influence of the imitations of Milton's poetry. The observation that the contemporary poetical style followed Milton in the use of these peculiarities, was likely to induce the less careful critic to put them down as created by Milton. Instances of these and other types of supposed or real Miltonisms are traced in the following attempt at a rough characterization of Paterson's work in this department.

---

[506]) III. 546 *n.*
[507]) III. 38 *n.*

The following cases of apparently genuine Miltonic coinages recognized as such by Paterson should be enumerated here: "horrent" [508]), "hymning" [509]), "ill-mated" [510]), "imbrute" [511]), "inabstinence" [512]), "obtrusive" [513]), "pontifical" in the sence of "bridge-making" [514]), "self-depraved" [515]), "self-begot" [516]), "serpent-error" [517]), "unbenighted" as the negation of "benighted" [518]), "unbesought" [519]), "undazzled" [520]), "unfumed" [521]), "unimmortal" [522]), "unimplored" [523]), "unlibidinous" [524]), "unoriginal" — "having no Creation, Beginning" & c. [525]), "unreprieved" [526]).

The number of compounds and negative adjectives or participles is conspicuous. This is understandable, for it was comparatively easy to recognize the individual character of compounds, which are less difficult to form, and therefore more likely to be invented under the influence of a passing mood, than other words. The negative adjectives and participles are a special feature of Milton's style, and his peculiar coinages of this type (e. g. "unimmortal" which is found in the NED only once after Milton, in 1876) were easily recognizable. They appear to be characteristic of the long, grand flow of many passages in "Paradise Lost".

The data of the NED suggest to what an extent some of the above words seemed to bear the stamp of Milton's style. "To imbrute" is quoted twice from Milton: once from "Comus" l. 468,

[508]) II. 514 n.
[509]) III. 417 n.
[510]) XI. 683. n.
[511]) IX. 165 n.
[512]) XI. 476 n.
[513]) VIII. 504 n.
[514]) X. 313 n.
[515]) III. 130 n.
[516]) V. 860 n.
[517]) VII. 302 n.
[518]) X. 682 n.
[519]) X. 1058 n.
[520]) III. 614 n.
[521]) V. 349 n.
[522]) X. 611 n.
[523]) III. 231 n.
[524]) V. 449 n.
[525]) X. 477 n.
[526]) II. 185 n.

which is the first case registered, after which follow two cases of "to embrutish" (in one case spelt with an *i*) and one of "to imbrute", all from non-Miltonic sources; the next, Miltonic, case is from P. L. IX. 166. The only later instance previous to 1744 is from Young's "Night Thoughts": "Embruted ev'ry faculty divine", where both the nature of the example (cf. P. L. IX. 166: "This essence to incarnate and imbrute, That to the height of Deitie aspir'd") and the general connection of Young's blank-verse poetry with Milton lead to the conjecture that the word might be a Miltonism.

Two Miltonic examples are given of the form "hymning". Neither the verb [527]) nor the verbal noun [528]) is found previous to Milton. The next instance is from Dryden's dramatization of P. L., "The State of Innocence", IV. 1: "None of all his hymning guards are nigh", which is followed by three quotations from Pope. The general character of Dryden's work suggests that the expression may have been imitated from Milton, which appears also to be true of at least one (Essay on Man III. 156: "In the same temple... All vocal beings hymn'd their equal God") and probably also of another quotation from Pope (Iliad XXIV. 83: "Where this minstrel-god... amid the quire Stood proud to hymn, and tune his youthful lyre"), whose indebtedness to Milton is generally acknowledged. The two last-quoted examples treat of the exalted hymning of deities, like the passages in "Paradise Lost". Paterson surely knew Pope's works and may have felt the probability af a derivation from Milton.

Some of the expressions of the present group occur only once in the NED which makes it intelligible that they struck Paterson as unique, *e. g.* "ill-mated", "self-depraved", "serpent-error", "un-libidinous", "unoriginal" (in the sense specified above), "un-benighted" (*id.*). The same applies to the cases where further examples are found only after Paterson, *e. g.* "inabstinence" (only later instance 1863), "obtrusive" (next case 1798), "pontifical" = "bridge-making" (next and only further example by Ruskin 1887), "unfumed" (the only case beside P. L. V. 349: "the shrub un-fum'd" is from a work on photography 1891: "to print... on un-fumed paper"), "unimmortal" (see above).

---

[527]) P. L. VI. 96.
[528]) P. L. III. 417.

191

Paterson appears to come close to the truth in those cases where only one instance previous to Milton is found, as *e. g.* of "lonely" [529]), "rubied" [530]), "self-raised" [531]), "viewless" = "invisible" [532]), "unadored" [533]), "unmeditated" [534]), "uninvented" [535]), "unshed" [536]) = "not shed or poured out" (the only earlier example in 1450!). Examples of words, of which there are two or three cases prior to Milton, are: "illimitable" [537]), "prevenient" [538]), "uncreated" [539]), "unprevented" [540]), "unexampled" [541]), "undying" [542]), "unbuild" [543]). In such cases, Milton's use of the words had presumably given them the peculiar flavour most easily distinguishable to the 18th century reader. The word "lonely", for example, which in the NED is quoted from Shakespeare's "Coriolanus" ("a lonely Dragon"), and whereof the abstract noun is found in Sidney's "Arcadia" ("a tedious lonelinesse"), seems to have been definitely naturalized owing to Milton, from whom the next examples of either form are taken. Nearly all cases of "lonely" found in Milton's poetry are quoted in the dictionary to illustrate his various ways of employing it, and the instances given are undoubtedly more characteristic than those from Sidney and Shakespeare. Milton connects it with the scenery typical of the 18th century descriptions of solitude: "the lonely mountains" [544]), "som high lonely Towr, Where I may oft out-watch the *Bear*" [545]), "the misled and lonely Traveller" [546]). The "Night and

[529]) II. 828 *n.*
[530]) V. 633 *n.*
[531]) I. 634 *n.*
[532]) III. 518 *n.*
[533]) I. 738 *n.*
[534]) V. 149 *n.*
[535]) VI. 470 *n.*
[536]) XII. 176 *n.*
[537]) II. 892.
[538]) XI. 3. *n.*
[539]) II. 150 *n.*
[540]) III. 231 *n.*
[541]) III. 410 *n.*
[542]) VI. 739 *n.*
[543]) XII. 526 *n.*
[544]) No. 181.
[545]) Il P. 86.
[546]) Co. 200.

lonely Contemplation" in Gray's "Elegy", l. 73, where the whole scenery with its ivied towers and dignified rural attributes reminds one of "Il Penseroso" and "L'Allegro", is a typical example of the contemplative, grave use of the word apparently introduced by Milton. "Illimitable", which in Milton may be imitated from Spenser's "Hymn of Heavenly Love" where it is registered first ("The heavens illimitable height"), seems, in turn, to have influenced the example immediately following (Pope's Odyssey XX. 75: "Tost thro' the void illimitable space") where the Miltonic device of putting a short adjective before this polysyllabic word is repeated (see Milton's only case of it: "a dark Illimitable Ocean without bound", P. L. II. 892). Pope appears also to have revived Milton's use of "barbaric" (P. L. II. 4: "Barbaric Pearl and Gold", Pope *Temp. Fame* 94: "With diamond flaming, and Barbaric gold"), a word likewise classed by Paterson as "Miltonian" [547]). Similar cases where the 18th century examples of the NED seem to confirm that Milton's manner of using formerly known expressions had been adopted by leading authors, are numerous and make it intelligible that Paterson considered them the poet's intellectual property. Sometimes it even seems that through the mis¬ interpretation of Miltonic passages new shades of meaning were created, which Paterson regarded as the authentic acceptations. "Limitary" [548]) ("Then when I am thy captive talk of chaines, Proud limitarie Cherube" — a hapax legomenon) is defined by him as meaning: "Bounded within Limits... A Word of Disdain". None of the examples previous to Milton contain any notion of contempt. His own example is classed by the NED as signifying "Of or pertaining to a limit or boundary", which suits the context, though it is admitted that the word may mean "subject to limits; limited in action, range, etc....", *i. e.* exactly what Paterson believes to be its sense. The two following cases — both of them classed with the second group — seem to indicate depreciation. One of these, from Dryden's "State of Innocence" ("Let me with him contend, On whom your limitary powers depend") seems to allude to the above-quoted Miltonic passage,

---

[547]) II. 4 *n.*
[548]) P. L. IV. 971.

the other, from C. Pitt [549]), is unmistakably contemptuous and
might also be derived from Milton, considering its hymnic style.
Paterson appears to be right in attributing to Milton a shade
of meaning which, even if not his own, is apparently due to his
unintentional influence.

A considerable percentage of Paterson's "Miltonian" words
seem to have been rare in the 17th century before the publication
of P. L. though they may have been frequent at earlier periods.
To this group belong "battailous" [550]), "to illumine" [551]), "in-
terrupt" $\doteq$ "broken off" [552]), "miscreated" [553]), "ponent" [554]),
& c. The general conclusion would probably be that this department of Paterson's investigations contains much thoughtful
observation, surpassing the rest of his work, and even now
leading the careful student to interesting discoveries both as to
Milton's peculiarities of language and 18th century idiosyncrasies of style. Sometimes one feels inclined to describe him as
ignorant of important features of Elizabethan language, as in
his attribution to Milton of the introduction of "gan" for
"began" [555]), a form found in Spenser's "Shepherd's Calendar",
Shakespeare's "Cymbeline", "Macbeth", & c., or of such a typical
Spenserian word as "impurpled" III. 364 n. Milton's use of it
in this passage is strongly reminiscent of Spenser (cf. the latter's
F. Q. III. VII. 17: "wildings... Whose sides empurpled were
with smyling red" and Milton: "the bright Pavement... Im-
purpl'd with Celestial Roses smil'd"). The same is true of the
classification as a Miltonic novelty of a common Elizabethan
expression found even much earlier, in "Cursor Mundi" and
Chaucer, such as "emprise" [556]), or a word used in a famous
Shakespearean passage, such as "oblivious" = "causing forget-
fulness" [557]). But the limitations of the learned apparatus
available at that time should not be forgotten.

[549]) Callimachus' Hymn to Jupiter 119: "What no inferior Limitary
King Could in a length of Years to Ripeness bring."
    [550]) VI. 81 n.
    [551]) I. 23 n.
    [552]) III. 84 n.
    [553]) II. 683 n.
    [554]) X. 703.
    [555]) VI. 60 n.
    [556]) XI. 642 n.
    [557]) Cf. Macb. V. III. 43: "Some sweet Oblivious Antidote".

At the end of his preface Paterson expresses the desire *"That this* Work *will display fully the* Benefit *and the* Ornaments *of this incomparable* Poem, *to the Satisfaction, I hope, of every curious Admirer of* Paradise Lost". This seems to promise a critical interpretation of the poem, but his few literary remarks do not go far. His statement in the preface that he has *"shewed all the* Similes *or* Comparisons, *pointed out all* Figures *of* Grammar *and* Rhetoric, *with the* Digressions" can only refer to his registration of them, for it is not easy to find in his book even the rudiments of an analytical treatment. The monotonous formula "by a *Fig.* of *Rhet.*" only means that the expression is used in another than its ordinary sense.‌ As a rule, no comments are given.

The few observations on style show some toleration of poetic liberty, but no signs whatever of the radicalism of Pearce, Richardson or Peck. The inverted adjective (P. L. I. 61 *n.,* on "a Dungeon horrible... flam'd") is praised as an ornament of poetry: "Here, *Milton* places the *Adjective* after the *Substantive,* for an *horrible Dungeon flam'd;* which is seldom done in *English Prose,* yet it raiseth the Stile very much, and is a Beauty to the *Language* of a *Poet.*" Paterson acknowledges the cumulative effect of Milton's digressive similes, which were already appreciated by Addison, despite their lack of strict logical consistency (I. 283 *n.,* on the long sequence of similes): "Here is a Cluster of *Comparisons;* all brought by our *Poet,* to embellish and aggrandize *Satan;* that he might both please and delight *the Reader.*" Here as elsewhere Paterson appreciates the abundance of Milton's imagery but without much discrimination, as, *e. g.,* in speaking of an "elegant" description of Hell [558]), which reminds one of Peck's substitution of "fairies" for "furies" as more elegant [559]).

Milton's authority appears to reconcile Paterson to some of his repetitions, *e. g.* in II. 986 *n.* where "ancient" is found to be "four Times repeated in this *Page,* which would be a Blemish in any *Poet* but *Milton.*" Nevertheless, he evidently does not realize the emphatic effect produced by such repetitions, for he definitely states his disapproval of an impressive case of this

---

[558]) II. 522 *n.*
[559]) See above p. 162.

195

kind 560) : *"Revisit...* The *Word* is very proper; but *Milton* repeats it four Times within these two Pages, which is a Fault in *Poetry*, and in *Prose* also." This pronouncement, reminiscent of Bentley's hatred of repetition, ignores that the structure of the period depends on the parallel effect of the repeated words ("Thee I revisit" is found in III. 13 and 21 — a whole group of words being here repeated, probably in order to make the parallelism more conspicuous) and that the last, negative repetition ("...but thou Revisit'st not these eyes" III. 23) emphasizes the contrast to the affirmation expressed by the previous cases of the verb.

The notes to each book are followed by a final observation where the commentator's impressions are summed up. Their monotony and poverty of ideas is unusual, but they evidently show what Paterson valued in the poet, for the same features are dwelt upon over and over again. Milton's learning is the main object of Paterson's admiration. The summary of the notes to book I shows this very definitely. The book is said to contain "more of the *Hebrew, Arabic, Phoenician,* and other *Oriental Languages;* more *Antiquity, History* (both *Divine* and *Human*), *Mythology* or *Fables* of the *Poets;* more antient *Geography, & c.* than any of the following *Books;* Altho' the whole *Poem* is filled with more Learning of every Sort, than is contained in any *Volume* extant; in the most *sublime,* elegant, well connected and short Compass." Similar estimates of Milton's erudition are subjoined to the notes of most books . The literary criticism is somewhat vague and full of sonorous superlatives. Thus, the character and speeches of the fallen angels in book I are called "wonderful and astonishing, most proper and masterly", whereas the whole Book is "a most finished Piece of surprising *Poetry, Wit* and *Imagination...* most pleasant, useful and entertaining".

The educational value of "Paradise Lost" is one of the main qualities praised by the commentator. The expressions "most pleasant, useful and entertaining" show this . The *résumé of* book XI mentions its "useful Instructions in Morality and Natural Philosophy", although Paterson here refers to Addison's censure of the excessive allusiveness and the exaggerated display

560) III. 13 *n.*

13*

of learning which are found to obscure the poem to the average reader. The religious influence of the work is valued. It is regarded as "a most excellent *Instruction* to all *Sinners*, that have a sincere Mind to *repent* and be saved, from the just Wrath of *God* hanging over their *Heads*, on the Account of their *Iniquities*."

Nevertheless, Paterson sides with those who prefer Milton's description of the infernal characters to that of God and the inhabitants of Heaven. The reason referred to is the same as that mentioned by Addison [561]), *i. e.* the indescribable grandeur of the divine beings, which exceeds the poet's powers. "The *Poet* sets off the *Devils* every where more excellently, than he doth *God;* And no Wonder; for he is *infinite, incomprehensible,* and *ineffable* in every Respect. Job 11. 7. As it is said of *Polycletus* the *Sculptor,* that he represented *Men* better than they are; but he did not come up to the Majesty of the Gods" [562]). Satan 'is described in exactly the same spirit as by Hume. *i. e.* though he is "a *Devil* indeed; full of *Pride, Malice, Revenge, Obstinacy* and utmost *Confusion,* under his *woful Fall* and *Torments*" [563]), the poet "paints him out with all the *Beauties* of *Imagination* and *Elocution,* in his monstrous *Stature, Looks, & c.* which represent him more conspicuous and terrible; to strike the *Reader's* Fancy" [564]). Paterson feels the effectiveness of the bold, large outlines of Milton's descriptions. The representation of the "mighty, long and profound Astonishment" of the fallen Angels who spent nine days and nights "Thunder-struck and confounded at their *Dismal Fall*", is found to exceed "all human Imagination, and all the Astonishment or Consternation that ever was or will be again" [565]).

---

[561]) Cf. The Spectator No. 315.
[562]) Summary of bk. II.
[563]) I. 84 *n.*
[564]) I. 192 *n.*
[565]) I. 50 *n.*

8. JOHN HAWKEY'S EDITIONS.

PARADISE LOST. A POEM IN TWELVE BOOKS. The AUTHOR JOHN MILTON. Compared with the Authentic Editions, And Revised by JOHN HAWKEY, Editor of the Latin Classics. DUBLIN: Printed by S. POWELL, for the EDITOR. MDCCXLVII.

8^0: [1], title; pp. I—II, advertisement; 1—394, text and half-titles of the books of the poem; [1—6], a list of various readings and emendations with notes to them.

The aims of this edition are textual. It is an attempt to give a text "freed from all blunders and absurdities" by consulting the two first editions [566]). Hawkey [567]) is, on the whole, very careful and even tries to follow the original punctuation, deviating from it mainly in occasionally adding a comma. The spelling is normalized, but now and then Miltonic peculiarities are retained. The edition would not fall under the subject of the present treatise but for a number of notes at the end, dealing with emendations. Hawkey adheres fairly rigorously to the authentic texts, accepting only about a couple of Bentley's emendations and preferring e. g. even the reading "medal or stone" in P. L. III. 592 to the more logical "metal or stone", because the first editions have the former. No infallibility on the author's part is assumed but the editor emphasizes that he thinks him very careful even with regard to insignificant details. An instance of carelessness is III. 33 ("Those other two equal'd with me in Fate" — a line preceding an enumeration of four persons) where the apparent logical lapse is ascribed to "poetic rapture". Hawkey refrains on principle from altering such "incuriæ". Milton's language is studied carefully in doubtful cases, as e. g.

---

[566]) Cf. preface.

[567]) John Hawkey (1703—1759), educated at Trinity College, Dublin, editor of Virgil, Horace, Terence &c., translator of Xenophon (cf. DNB).

IV. 115 ("Thrice chang'd with pale, ire, envie and despair")
where Pearce had changed the substantive to an adjective by
removing the comma between it and the following noun. Hawkey
shows that X. 1009 has the same substantive ("di'd her Cheeks
with pale"). This example evinces not only care but also some
insight into the Elizabethan liberty of expression. The same
tendency to take into account the author's peculiarities appears
in the defence of Milton's spelling "Bearth" for "birth" in
IX. 624.

The whole trend of the edition is toward recognition of the
poet's authority, in the spirit of Pearce's commentary. Hawkey
follows the same principles in his edition of "Paradise Regained"
which appeared in 1752 [568]).

---

[568]) PARADISE REGAINED. A POEM IN FOUR BOOKS. With
the other POETICAL WORKS OF JOHN MILTON. Compared with the
best Editions, And Revised by JOHN HAWKEY, Editor of the Latin
Classics. DUBLIN: Printed by S. POWELL, for the EDITOR. MDCCLII.
8⁰: pp. 391.
No notes.

9. BISHOP NEWTON AND HIS COLLABORATORS.

PARADISE LOST. A POEM, IN TWELVE BOOKS. The AUTHOR JOHN MILTON. A NEW EDITION, With NOTES of various AUTHORS, By THOMAS NEWTON, D. D. VOLUME the FIRST. LONDON: Printed for J. and R. TONSON and S. DRAPER in the *Strand*. MDCCXLIX.

4⁰: 2 vols: pp. [18] + LXVI + 16 + [12] + 459; pp. 444 + [132]. *Contents:* Vol. I: p. [1], title; pp. [3—10], dedictn to the Earl of Bath; pp. [11—18], preface; pp. I—LXI, life of Milton; pp. LXII—LXIII, S. Barrow's; and pp. LXIV—LXV, A. Marvell's verses on P. L.; p. LXVI, "The Verse"; pp. 1—16, Addison's Critique; pp. [1—12], list of subscribers; pp. 1—459, text of bks. I—VI with notes. Vol. II: p. [1], title; pp. 3—432, text and notes to bks. VII—XII; pp. 433—444, appendix containing some additional notes; pp. [1—16], subject index; pp. [17—132], "A Verbal Index". The edition contains one plate to each book of the poem, and two portraits.

In "THE SECOND EDITION", that of 1750, some further publishers are mentioned in the imprint. The number of plates is the same, except that there is only one portrait of the author <8⁰, pp. [23] + LXXXV + [27] + 510; pp. 456 + [212]>. The edition contains no list of subscribers. The arrangement of the matter is in all other respects as above, except for the insertion of the additional notes in their proper places, under the text, and a postscript on the Lauder affair, dated Dec. 5. 1750 (cf. vol. II, pp. 449—456). The next edition, that of 1754, 4⁰, contains some further matter on the Lauder case. The main interpolations and forgeries of Lauder are added to the Postscript (vol. II, pp. 455—460). Otherwise, the arrangement is as before. The first volume has [18] + LXIX + [21] + 491, the second 460 + [116] pages. In this edition there are two portraits, as well as one plate to each book of the poem (in the B. Mus. copy Richardson's portrait of Milton is pasted on a blank-leaf at the end of the second volume).

J. Baskerville's editions of 1758 and 1759 are also printed "for J. and R. Tonson" like the previous ones, but they contain no notes. The edition of 1760, which is mentioned in connection with Newton's name in the British Museum catalogue, seems to have been lost or mislaid. It is possible that Newton's fourth and fifth editions are to be looked for among these last [569]). *The edition of 1763*, 8⁰, "THE SIXTH EDITION", has the following imprint: "LONDON: Printed for *J.* and *R. Tonson, B. Dodd, H. Woodfell, J. Rivington, R. Baldwin, T. Longman, L. Hawes, Clark and Collins, E. Dilly, T. Caston, C. Corbet, T. Lownds,* and the Executors of *J. Richardson.* MDCCLXIII". Otherwise the title is as in Newton's first edition. The number of pages is [23] + LXXXVI + [26] + 510 in the first, and 463 + [182] in the second volume. The matter is, on the whole, the same as in 1754 and the number of portraits and plates illustrating the text is also identical. *In the 1770 edition*, Newton's new episcopal dignity is alluded to in the title: "...THE SEVENTH EDITION, WITH NOTES of various AUTHORS, By THOMAS NEWTON, D. D. Now Lord Bishop of BRISTOL. VOLUME THE FIRST. LONDON: Printed for J. BEECROFT, W. STRAHAN, J. and F. RIVINGTON... MDCCLXX." <8⁰, 2 vols: vol. I. pp. [23] + LXXXVI + [26] + 510; vol. II. pp. 463 + [182]>. The matter and the number of plates are the same. *The edition of 1778* ("The EIGHTH EDITION" according to the title-page, published "IN TWO VOLUMES... LONDON: Printed for W. STRAHAN, J. F. and C. RIVINGTON, L. DAVIS... MDCCLXXVIII", 8⁰, number of pages and illustrations as in the previous edition, but containing one portrait only) seems to differ only in the title, like *that of 1790* ("Late Lord Bishop of Bristol" substituted after the editor's name, the imprint different: "LONDON: Printed for J. F. and C. RIVINGTON, L. DAVIS, B. WHITE and SON... MDCCXC", 8⁰, number of pages and plates the same). In 1795 an abridged 12⁰ edition appeared in three volumes, with a "Preface to the Pocket Edition, with the Notes of Various Authors", signed C. M. in pp. V—IX of vol. I. [570]).

---

[569]) Todd's bibliography (ed. 1842, Vol. IV) mentions an 8-vo ed. by Newton, published in 1757. No particulars are given as to the place or publisher.

[570]) The title of the first volume is as follows: PARADISE LOST. A POEM, IN TWELVE BOOKS. THE AUTHOR JOHN MILTON. PRINTED FROM THE TEXT OF TONSON'S CORRECT EDITION OF 1711. A NEW EDITION, WITH NOTES AND THE LIFE OF THE AUTHOR, IN THREE VOLUMES, BY THOMAS NEWTON, D. D. LATE LORD BISHOP OF BRISTOL, AND OTHERS. VOL.I. LONDON: PRINTED FOR THE PROPRIETORS. 1795." The third volume has a special title: "NOTES ON THE PARADISE LOST OF JOHN MILTON, BY NEWTON, BENTLEY, RICHARDSON, HUME, ADDISON, WARBURTON, THYER, PEARCE, & c. VOL. III. LONDON: PRINTED FOR THE PROPRIE- TORS. 1795." <Vol. I: pp. IX + 298; vol. II: pp. [II] + 270; vol. III:

This preface states that "the aim of the Editor has been to
observe a proper medium between the meagreness of some Annotators and the excessive profusion of Newton, who has certainly overloaded his Publication with a number of remarks
unnecessary, trite, and frivolous" (pp. VIII—IX).

PARADISE REGAIN'D. A POEM, IN FOUR BOOKS. To
which is added SAMSON AGONISTES: AND POEMS upon
SEVERAL OCCASIONS. THE AUTHOR JOHN MILTON.
A NEW EDITION, With NOTES of various AUTHORS, By
THOMAS NEWTON, D. D. LONDON: Printed for J. and R.
TONSON and S. DRAPER in the *Strand*. MDCCLII.

4^0: pp. [8] + 690 + [2]. *Contents:* p. [1], title; pp. [3—6],
preface; pp. [7—8], table of contents; pp. 1—189, "Paradise
Regained" with notes; pp. 190—305, "Samson Agonistes", with
notes; pp. 307—690, the minor poems, including the translations and Latin and Greek verses, with notes, and, on pp. 581
—587, a transcript of the dramatic drafts in the Trinity College MS.; pp. [1—2], an index of the less common words
explained and illustrated in the notes. 5 plates illustrate the
poems, one portrait is prefixed to the volume, another (in the
Brit. Mus. copy) pasted on a blank leaf following the text.
"The SECOND EDITION", "Printed for *J. and R. Tonson* and *S. Draper;* and for *T. Longman, S. Birt, C. Hitch,
R. Ware, J. Hodges, C. Corbet, J. Brindley,* and *J. Ward.*
MDCCLIII", appeared in two 8^0 volumes, <pp. [8] + 335 and
[7] + 386 + [4]>, with the same matter but some rearrange-
ments due to the division into two parts. The first volume
contains the preliminary matter, P. R., S. A. and the Trinity
drafts, the second volume the rest as above. The edition has
six plates, one of these a portrait.
In 1773, the poem was brought out in exactly the same
form, with the same number of pages and plates (after the
name of the editor, "Now LORD BISHOP of BRISTOL" is
inserted, and the imprint is: "LONDON: Printed for
J. BEECROFT, W. STRAHAN, J. and F. RIVINGTON...
MDCCLXXIII"). *The edition of 1777* differs as to the size, but
the matter is arranged in the same way. It is a 4^0 volume
containing [8] + 690 + [2] pages, "Printed for W. STRAHAN,
J. F. and C. RIVINGTON, B. WHITE, T. CASLON...
MDCCLXXVII", as the title-page indicates. *In 1785* the size
of the edition is again 8^0, the number of volumes, pages and

pp. [II] + 248>. The general arrangement is as before but vol. I contains
bks. I—V, vol. II bks. VI—XII, the verbal index and dedication are omitted,
and the notes have been transferred to the third volume.

illustrations and the arrangement being exactly the same as
in 1753.

Newton's important edition — as a variorum edition, the first
attempt to collect all the valuable work so far done in the field of
Milton annotation — was modelled on similar publications by
classical scholars. "My design in the present edition is to publish
the Paradise Lost, as the work of a classic author cum notis
variorum" [571]), is Newton's description of his idea. This applies
equally to the subsequent volumes containing the rest of Milton's
poetical works. Newton wished the publication to become a pendant
to the "new and correct editions of the works of approved
authors", defending his plan of undertaking with regard to English
literature what others had done in the department of classical
scholarship. He insists on the need for an accurate text based on
Milton's authentic editions, instead of that indefinite "floting [sic]
in the wide ocean of conjecture" which distinguishes the labours
of the editors of Shakespeare [572]).

Despite this very sound doctrine, Newton's practice is not
entirely without subjective arbitrariness. The punctuation follows Milton more or less strictly, for Newton finds his pointing
"generally right", assuming that the poet and his friends had
carefully supervised it, but in the spellings a somewhat unsatis-
factorily defined distinction is drawn between those peculiar to
Milton and those general at his time [573]). Newton states it as his
principle to adopt what is right and to reject what is wrong,
transcribing the excellences but not the errors of the authentic
editions [574]). This is a dangerous ideal as long as the concepts
of right and wrong are not very carefully defined. Fortunately,
Newton generally manages to refrain from the Bentleian attitude
of omniscience, confining himself to normalizing the spellings
without introducing any peculiarities of his own, or at least usually
explaining his deviations from this method in foot-notes. Not
infrequently typical Miltonic spellings are retained.

Newton is not always fair to his predecessors. His prefaces

---

[571]) Vol. I, sig. a_2r of 1-st ed. of Newton.
[572]) Vol. I, sig. a_2r, op. cit.
[573]) *Ibid.* & sig. a_2v.
[574]) Sig. a_2v.

profess to give a survey of their work but some important sources
are omitted. Thus, Peck is not mentioned in the preface to "Paradise Lost". Newton had made use of several of his parallels
and syntactic observations [575]), and the grudging acknowledgement
of his indebtedness to Peck in the preface to the edition of "Paradise Regained" and the Minor Poems does not make up for this
neglect. Newton admits having "pickt out some grains from
among the chaff of Mr. Peck's remarks" [576]), a judgment which
seems too severe on Peck, as Newton has borrowed more than he
cares to acknowledge. But the injustice done to Hume is far more
serious. Our appendix, which traces the main debts to the earlier
commentators in Newton's notes to book II of "Paradise Lost",
should make this clear. Newton's references to Hume are
extremely slighting. He admits that he "laid the foundation"
but "laid it among infinite heaps of rubbish". His work is described as a "dull dictionary of the most common words, a tedious
fardel of the most trivial observations", though it is also found
to contain "a great deal that is useful", there being "gold among
its dross" [577]). The main objection to be made to this criticism
is that Newton has found far more gold among the dross than
he ever admits, much more than in Peck's book, generally without
even an indication of it.

The importance of Addison's essays is acknowledged by their
wholesale insertion in the work, partly as a separate treatise and
partly as foot-notes. A number of the sounder remarks of Bentley,
whose attempts to rewrite Milton's poetry Newton calls „most
miserable bungling work", are reprinted, but the part his critic
Pearce takes in the edition is much greater. He is admitted to
have "perused and corrected" the MS. and assisted Newton "from
the beginning to the end" [578]). His notes are drawn upon rather
copiously and receive ample praise as being "a pattern to all future
critics, of sound learning and just reasoning joined with the
greatest candor and gentleness of manners" [579]). The comments
of the Richardsons are found sometimes to hit "the true meaning

[575]) Cf. below.
[576]) P. R. Vol. I, sig. A_3r, ed. 1752.
[577]) P. L. Vol. I, sig. a_2v, ed. 1749.
[578]) Vol. I, sig. a_3r, ed. 1749.
[579]) *Ibid.*

of the author surprisingly", though they contain some "strange inequalities" and "extravagances". Nearly everything valuable in them has been made use of, either with or without acknowledgement. The other published sources mentioned in the preface to "Paradise Lost" are: Warburton's notes to the first three books of the poem in the "History of the Works of the Learned" [580]); the pamphlets "An Essay upon Milton's Imitations of the Ancients" and "Letters concerning Poetical Translations", of which especially the latter is important as having provided Newton with most of his better metrical remarks [581]); and the "learned Mr. Upton's Critical Observations on Shakespeare" [582]) containing some chance notes on Milton. It is difficult to ascertain all Newton's debts, particularly to works not mainly concerned with criticism of Milton. He says himself: "like the bee, I have been studious of gathering sweets wherever I could find them growing" [583]). Paterson and the so-called "St. Maur" are not mentioned. Newton's silence as to many of his borrowings from Hume and Peck justifies the assumption that he may have used other unacknowledged sources. In the present treatise, only his indebtedness to his acknowledged predecessors in Milton annotation is traced consistently. An attempt has been made by the present writer to find out as exactly as possible what is Newton's own and

---

[580]) Anonymous, in April 1740, pp. 273—280. Mainly against Bentley.

[581]) An ESSAY upon MILTON'S IMITATIONS OF THE ANCIENTS, IN HIS PARADISE LOST. With some Observations on the *Paradise Regain'd.* [Motto]. LONDON: Printed for J. ROBERTS in *Warwick-Lane.* MDCCXLI. Price One Shilling.

8⁰: pp. [2] + 62.

LETTERS CONCERNING Poetical Translations, AND VIRGIL'S and MILTON'S ARTS OF VERSE, & c. LONDON. Printed for J. ROBERTS, near the *Oxford-Arms* in *Warwick-Lane.* MDCCXXXLX.

8⁰: pp. [4] + 83.

The Bodleian copy bears the inscription "Ar: Onslow. The Gift of the Author, Mr. Auditor Benson." Todd, the DNB & c. also ascribe the pamphlet to William Benson, the same to whom Peck dedicated his "New Memoirs, & c."

[582]) CRITICAL OBSERVATIONS ON SHAKESPEARE. By JOHN UPTON Prebendary of *Rochester* [Motto] LONDON: Printed for G. HAWKINS, in *Fleet-street.* M,DCC,XLVI.

8⁰: pp. IV + 346 + [16] + [2].

Contains some notes on Milton. 2d ed. 1748, 8⁰.

[583]) Vol. I, sig. a_3v, ed. 1749.

what is merely borrowed. It has been necessary to eliminate all
mere reformulations or abridgements of earlier matter, concentrating
exclusively on what seemed to be original work. As there is
relatively little of the latter, the results may appear disappointing.
Many an interesting point may seem to have been unduly omitted,
though in most cases this would probably be due to the fact that
the observation concerned is borrowed. The appendix on book II
was partly written to support this statement.

Newton's prefaces mention the people who had sent him special
contributions. The edition of "Paradise Lost" contains such mainly
by Heylin, Jortin, Warburton, the younger Richardson, Thyer,
"the Librarian at Manchester... a man of great learning, and
as great humanity", and some anonymous persons [584]. Some
oral remarks made by the Speaker of the House of Commons [585]
are also taken into consideration. Heylin, according to Newton,
had himself proposed to publish a new edition of "Paradise Lost",
but, hearing of Bentley's plan, had communicated to him the notes
already written for that purpose. Bentley is said to have exploited
them without any acknowledgment. Points unused by Bentley
which suited Newton, were extracted by the latter from Heylin's
MS. Jortin's remarks, which were conveyed to Newton by Pearce
and deal mainly with Milton's imitations of the classics, are highly
praised by the editor, though no special characterization of
Jortin's virtues as a critic is given. The contributions of Warburton, who, as Newton observes, recommends his Milton edition
in the preface to his Shakespeare [586], are found to be similar to
light sketches of great masters in painting, "...worth more than
the labor'd pieces of others" [587], and great praise is given to Warburton's conjectural experiments in Shakespeare criticism [588].

---

[584] Heylin is apparently John Heylyn (1685?—1759), educated at
Trinity College, Cambridge, D. D. 1728, editor of theological works, sermons,
& c. Called the 'Mystic Doctor' (cf. DNB). John Jortin (1698—1770),
educated at Jesus College, Cant., wrote "The Life of Erasmus" 1758, "Remarks on Spenser", & c. Robert Thyer (1709—1781), born at Manchester,
of Brasenose, Oxford, editor of Samuel Butler's "Remains", was Chetham
librarian at Manchester.

[585] P. L. Vol. I, sig. a_4v, ed. 1749.

[586] Cf. preface to Newton's P. L., sig. a_3v, ed. 1749.

[587] *Ibid.*

[588] *Ib.* sig. a_2r.

Only slight use is said to have been made of the younger Richardson's "very copious collection of fine passages out of ancient and modern authors, by which Milton profited", because of the late arrival of these notes [589]. Thyer had originally composed a great number of observations in an interleaved copy of Milton, which, as Newton writes, was unfortunately dropped on the road while being sent to him, so that Thyer had to restore them as best he could.

Newton describes the main objects of his notes [590]). He says he has written them: (1) to establish "the true genuin [*sic*] text of Milton" and to discuss the various readings; (2) "to illustrate the sense and meaning, to point out the beauties and defects of sentiment and character, and to commend or censure the conduct of the poem" — that is to say, to explain Milton's work and give a critical account of it; (3) to examine the style and language, the uncommon words, as well as the uncommon significations of common expressions; (4) to study the metre, the pauses, the "adaptness of the sound to the sense"; (5) to point out Milton's imitations or allusions. He originally intended to deal with these matters in separate essays to be prefixed to the work but found the method of foot-notes more convenient, as enabling the reader to peruse the criticisms in connection with the passages to which they refer. The above objects, as stated in the preface, contain nothing very new, which entirely agrees with Newton's general eclectic manner. His independent contributions to knowledge and critical method have to be traced from the notes themselves, and can be found out only by a very minute examination of these, since they are interspersed with too much that is borrowed or imitated.

The same principles apply to the edition of the rest of Milton's poetical works. Newton's preface points out that pioneer-work had to be done here, as no detailed commentary upon these works had so far been attempted. Meadowcourt's notes on "Paradise Regained", which had been published separately, were very slight [591]). So the materials found in Newton's edition are nearly

---

589) *Ib.* sig. a_4r.
590) *Ib.* sig. a_4v.
591) A CRITIQUE ON MILTON'S PARADISE REGAIN'D. — simul et jucunda et idonea dicere vitae. LONDON: Printed for HENRY LINTOT,

all of them new. Warburton, Jortin, Thyer, the younger Richardson continue their special contributions, and Peck is also quoted. Sympson and Calton of Marton in Lincolnshire are new names [592]). Some of these seem to be particularly qualified to comment on Milton's early poems, e. g. Thyer, who, as a great "master of the Italian language and Italian poetry, which in Spenser's time was the study and delight of all the men of letters", is urgently advised to "gratify the public with his equally learned [sic] equally elegant observations" upon Spenser [593]). Only some chance remarks are contributed by Sympson, a critic described by Newton as "particularly well read in our old English authors, as appears from his share in the late excellent edition of Beaumont's and Fletcher's works". Newton calls him his friend and acknowledges that Sympson has assisted him in his edition of "Paradise Lost", but without specifying the character of this assistance [594]).

The Latin and Greek poems, which are included in the edition, are left without a commentary. The Trinity College Manuscript has been made use of, particularly for the sake of the dramatic schemes already reprinted in Birch's edition of Milton's prose and in Peck's "New Memoirs". The text is based on the editions published at Milton's lifetime, yet not without the alteration of

---

at the *Cross-Keys*, against *St. Dunstan's* Church in *Fleet-street*. MDCCXXXII. (Price One Shilling.)

4^0: 2 leaves, blank, unnumbered, — 1 leaf, unnumbered, containing the title, — pp. 30, text.

A Critical Dissertation with NOTES ON MILTON'S PARADISE REGAIN'D. By the Reverend Mr. MEADOWCOURT, Canon of *Worcester*. [motto as above] The SECOND EDITION, corrected. LONDON: Printed for A. MILLAR, opposite *Catherine-Street* in the *Strand:* And Sold by M. COOPER, at the *Globe* in *Pater-noster-Row*. 1748. (Price One Shilling.)

8^0: pp. 49 (blank-leaves torn off in Brit. Mus. copy). The same as the preceding with some additions, but otherwise no perceptible alterations. The DNB (*i. e.* Gerald le Grys Norgate) calls the author, Richard Meadowcourt (1695—1760), "a sympathetic and a learned critic" but "deficient in insight".

[592]) Both absent in DNB. Sympson edited the 1750 edition of Beaumont and Fletcher together with Theobald, Seward, and others.

[593]) P. R. Vol. I, sig. A$_2$v, ed. 1752.

[594]) *Ibid.*

"what", as Newton thinks, "the author himself would have corrected" [595]).

The study of Newton's life of Milton, which is prefixed to the edition of "Paradise Lost", does not concern us here. In the following, the notes of Newton's collaborators are examined first [596]), since they form part of the basis he had to work upon, and therefore are likely to have influenced him. Newton's share in the Lauder controversy is passed over as having too little to do with the development of serious Milton criticism.

A. ROBERT THYER.

Thyer is perhaps the most conspicuous among the new contributors to Newton's Milton edition, both as regards the number and the value of his notes, which deal with "Paradise Lost" as well as with the rest of Milton's poetical works. Newton's prefaces make full acknowledgment of the fact. According to the preface to "Paradise Lost" [597]), Newton did not know Thyer personally, though, as has been shown, he describes him as "a man of great learning, and as great humanity". The same source states that Thyer's original contributions to Newton's commentary were lost by an accident, though the author afterwards restored as much as he could, "sending a sheet or two full of remarks almost every post for several weeks together". A few notes which arrived too late were added in an appendix in the first edition, but afterwards they were inserted in their proper places.

"Good sense, and learning, and ingenuity" are the qualities praised by Newton in Thyer's remarks [598]). Thyer's classical scholarship appears to be considerable, but he does not deal widely with older English literature. An important asset is his knowledge

---

[595]) *Ib.* sig. A_2r.

[596]) The younger Richardson and Heylin are not dealt with separately. As is shown in the above, only fragments of their collections were used by Newton. It would be difficult to attach great value to their contributions, which consist mainly of literary parallels, with little analysis. Richardson's comments on "Lycidas" are more varied, and evince a genuine though not very original sense of poetic beauty.

[597]) Sig. a_4, ed. 1749.

[598]) Cf. preface to P. R., sig. A_2v, ed. 1752.

of Italian [599]). It has been pointed out that Newton for this reason advised him to edit Spenser [600]). The above characterization seems to be correct. Thyer has commonsense and clever ideas as well as a wide knowledge of history and literature, and takes a genuine human and artistic interest in Milton's personality and poetry [601]). The harmonious combination of these qualities makes him superior to Newton as a critic, and places him above Newton's other contributors, though some of these may exhibit their erudition more ostentatiously or excel in certain points. Thyer's intellect is balanced and free from pedantry, though not quite unprejudiced. A considerable artistic instinct adds the necessary literary touch, though he never indulges in unrestrained enthusiasm. On the other hand, he generally manages to keep free from a fault peculiar to many commentators, that of accumulating facts without sufficiently explaining their artistic significance.

Thyer is still subject to some of the limitations of his period. He is not yet able to distinguish with sufficient clearness between the conditions of his own time and those of Milton's and seems to expect from the poet a knowledge of the scientific achievements of the eighteenth century — almost as Bentley did, forgetting like Bentley that h'e is dealing with poetry [602]). It is not surprising, on the other hand, that he dislikes what he regards as a very crude anachronism, *viz.* the introduction of "cuirassiers" into a description of the world at the time of Christ [603]). Though Newton

---

[599]) Cf. preface to P. R., sig. A$_3$r.

[600]) That Thyer's knowledge of the Italians surpassed that of the average amateur, seems to be indicated by his discoveries of Italian phraseology in Milton. Milton's "dun air", in P. L. III. 72, is derived by him from the Italian "aer bruno", the image of the sun "smiting the open field" (P. L. IV. 244) is compared with Ariosto's "Percote il sol ardente il vicin colle", the "high disdain" of P. L. I. 98 with "alto sdegno", & c.

[601]) Some of Thyer's remarks on the influence of the circumstances of Milton's life on his poetry are subtle and observant. He connects the weakness of Milton's eyes with the "very singular" notice "which he takes of the twilight, whenever he has occasion to speak of the evening" (P. L. IV. 598 *n.*). Thyer's description of the twilight shows his sensitiveness to nature. He speaks of "something so agreeable in that soft and gentle light", and of the "peculiar fragrance" that "attends it in the summer months" (*Ibid.*).

[602]) Cf. P. L. X. 659 *n.*

[603]) P. R. III. 328 *n.*

adduces some evidence to refute this, there can hardly be any doubt that Thyer, who had not seen this evidence, wrote in good faith. Here his point of view is intelligible, for in this passage Milton apparently aims at historical exactness, which makes anachronism out of place [604]). Nevertheless, Thyer has moments when he is prepared to forgive even blunders for the sake of a "fine strain of poetry", as in P. L. X. 245 *n.* where the artistic effect is made possible by the introduction of a "now exploded notion". Milton's unauthorized genealogy of the Graces in "L'Allegro" finds not merely forgiveness but even praise, as it "suited the nature of his subject better" [605]). However, Thyer becomes apologetic in discussing Milton's description of mediæval "tilts and torneaments" in the same poem. The fact that the poet describes things no longer in use at his period is excused mainly because his critic takes into account "how short a time they had laid aside, and what a considerable figure they make in Milton's favorite authors" [606]), that is to say, largely because the anachronism is very slight, though Thyer evidently finds it blamable in itself. Here the case is different from the first example discussed in this connection, for the world depicted in "L'Allegro" and "Il Penseroso" obviously does not pretend to be a reproduction of the world as actually seen, but rather of an idealized domain modelled partly on pastoral poetry and partly on classical antiquity (cf. the classical names), on romance, & c. It may not be judged by the standards of consistent realism — exactly as "Lycidas" can only be understood if the scenery is regarded as a very free combination of the present with the national as well as the classical past. It is evident that Thyer's instinctive leaning towards a more liberal attitude is struggling with the concepts inherited from contemporary literature, causing the above inconsistencies. In certain cases Milton's poetic licences are approved as far as they enhance the effect, whereas at other times conventions handicap the critic.

The intellectual discipline shown in the theorizing and argumentative parts of Milton's poetry might be expected to appeal to Thyer's scholarly mind. Nevertheless, his artistic sensitiveness

---

[604]) Cf. also S. A. 934 *n.*
[605]) L'A. 14 *n.*
[606]) L'A. 119 *n.*

makes it surprising to find his principles so entirely in agreement with the didacticism of his contemporaries. Instruction, in Thyer's opinion, still remains one of the main objects of poetry. He admires it, "in how short a compass" Milton "has compris'd, and with what strength and clearness he has express'd the various actings of God towards mankind, and the most sublime and deep truths both of the Jewish and Christian theology" [607]). Poetry in his view even becomes a sort of *ancilla theologiae*, for he remarks with apparent approval that Milton "is scarcely ever so far hurried on by the fire of his Muse, as to forget the main end of all good writing, the recommendation of virtue and religion" [608]).

In spite of these express statements, Thyer's artistic instincts seem to carry him in the opposite direction, that of art for art's sake. The inconsistency is the same here as in his treatment of anachronisms. The key-note of his remarks on „Paradise Regained" is apparently the desire to prove that the poet is constantly aiming at imaginative effects, the didactic and intellectual touch of the whole depending mainly on the subject. Like Bentley [609]), Thyer admires Milton's skill in overcoming the narrowness of his theme [610]), and attempts to analyse his method. In this connection, he states his fundamental conception of epic poetry, which is not profound and disagrees with the attitude often found in his critical practice. According to this formulation, an epic poem "ought to consist of a proper and happy mixture of the instructive and the delightful" [611]) — a view which is in keeping with the main trend of his age when no deeper emotional gratification was demanded from poetry, the main emotion expected being easy pleasure. Yet Thyer's quest for imaginative excellence is somewhat too impassioned to fit in with this eulogy of the golden mean. He is anxious to trace the elements of pure artistry hidden behind the more obvious rationalist and didactic style of "Paradise Regained", and tries (in contradistinction to Newton — cf. below) to vindicate the competence and spontaneity of Milton's imagination, finding the main difference

---

[607]) P. L. XII. 11 *n.*
[608]) P. L. VI. 661 *n.*
[609]) Cf. P. L. X. 182 *n.* in Bentley's ed.
[610]) P. R. II. 1 *n.*
[611]) *Ibid.*

between the two epics in their subjects [612]). The "argumentative cast" of the theme paralyses Milton's muse, who nevertheless "emerges upon every favorable occasion, and like the sun from under a cloud bursts out into the same bright vein of poetry, which shines out more frequently, tho' not more strongly, in the Paradise Lost" [613]).

This is in accord with Thyer's comment on Lord Shaftesbury's opinion that, as the annotator quotes him, "Milton's beauties generally depend upon solid thought, strong reasoning, noble passion, and a continued thread of moral doctrin" [614]), i. e. a definition which, though admitting the poet's emotional power, shifts the centre of gravity towards reason and morality, in the manner just shown in Thyer's own remarks. Here Thyer objects to this application of the principles which elsewhere he so readily acknowledges, criticizing Shaftesbury from the point of view of pure poetry. He calls attention to Milton's art of working up a simple idea "into half a score of as fine lines as any in the whole poem" which show "what an exalted fancy and mere force of poetry can do" [615]). The "picturesque manner of Spenser" [616]), whom Thyer so frequently quotes, as well as the Italians, may have taught him to appreciate this "exalted fancy". His high valuation of "Lycidas" shows the same tendency. Newton prefers "L'Allegro" and "Il Penseroso" to "Lycidas" owing to some irregularities in the latter [617]). In Thyer's opinion it is exactly the "natural and agreeable wildness and irregularity which runs quite through it" which gives „the greatest grace" to the whole [618]). He ascribes these qualities to "the warm affection which Milton had for his friend, and the extreme grief he was in for the loss of him." This has been doubted by various critics, e. g. by Thomas Warton [619]). But the important part of Thyer's remark is the theoretical attitude implied in it. He recognizes the rights of emotion even if it clashes with the rules. "Grief is

[612]) Cf. P. R. II. 1 n. end, P. R. II. 363 n.
[613]) P. R. IV. 237 n.
[614]) P. L. VII. 98 n.
[615]) Ibid.
[616]) P. L. XI. 489 n.
[617]) L'A. 45 n.
[618]) Lyc. 193 n.
[619]) See Warton's final note to "Lycidas".

eloquent, but not formal", is his conclusion. He was not the man
to side with merely formal poetry.

His appreciation of the spontaneous, lyrical element in Milton
is elsewhere stated even more clearly than in the above observation. He likes the poet's delight in sacred music [620]), praising
him for his freedom from the prejudices of the Puritans, "the
enthusiastic madness of that fanatic age against Church Music" [621]). The outbursts of Milton's imaginative powers are referred to with much warmth in a remark on his allusions to this art.
Thyer emphasizes how his "imagination glows with a particular
brightness ... where he has occasion to describe the power of
music" [622]). The words "sudden", "rapturous" recur very frequently in similar observations, e. g. when Thyer speaks of the
"rapturous start of the poet's fancy" [623]), or when he responds
to Milton's delectable revellings in visual impressions [624]) : "There
is in my opinion great beauty in this abrupt and rapturous start
of the poet's imagination, as it ... carries a very pretty allusion
to those sudden gleams of vernal delight which break in upon the
mind at the sight of a fine prospect."

This is the right frame of mind for the appreciation of unexpected and bold expressions. "Satan bowing low His grey
dissimulation", a passage which "your little word-catching critic
will very probably censure, but readers of true taste admire", is
described as "a true instance of the *feliciter audet*" [625]), and
another impressive poetic licence of the same kind is found in
the expression: "...while the hand Sung with the voice" [626]).

Too high-flown conceits in the Italian manner are nevertheless repugnant to Thyer's taste. His admiration for imaginative
qualities has its limits where the imagination forgets all moderation. Certain exceptional cases of baroque profusion happen to
appeal to him, e. g. Marino's skill in varying the same idea
through six stanzas [627]), even though he finds Milton's "graver

---

[620]) Il P. 161 *n.*
[621]) *Ibid.*
[622]) L'A. 135 *n.*
[623]) Il P. 61 *n.*
[624]) L'A. 69 *n.*
[625]) P. R. I. 497 *n.*
[626]) l. 171, *ibid.*
[627]) Cf. P. L. VIII. 476 *n.*

turn" and the "divine character" of his subject incompatible with this style [628]). He is impressed by Marino's "surprising redundancy of fancy and beauty of expression", but the heavier manifestations of the same tendency, such as Boiardo's long description of heraldry and decorative detail, are condemned [629]). Certain limits have to be observed, otherwise the result strikes him as "rant and rhapsody" [630]). What one "may easily imagine might have really happen'd" [631]) is what he values in the description of Eve where Satan admires her, preparing for the temptation.

This Italian prolixity is opposed by Thyer for very sound psychological considerations. He knows that the main object of a poetical text is to stimulate the mind. In applying this knowledge to Milton's criticism he foreshadows the attitude of Warton [632]), who, however, draws the inevitable conclusions as to the value of certain poetic devices, whereas Thyer states the main principle only. In his opinion, the Italians "have never said enough whilst any thing remains unsaid" [633]). Instead of intensifying the impression, this volubility only weakens it, impairing the reader's mental activity. "When once enough is said to excite in the reader's mind a proper idea of what the poet is representing, whatever is added, however beautiful, serves only to teize the fancy instead of pleasing it, and rather cools than improves that glow of pleasure, which arises in the mind upon the contemplation of any surprising scene of nature well painted out" [634]). The ideal representation gives few circumstances "but selected with great judgment, and expressed with no less spirit and beauty" [635]). Thus, the very basis of Thyer's conception of poetry leads him to the recognition of classicist moderation, preventing him, at the same time, from deviating into classicist dogmatism, the main emphasis being laid on the activity of the mind and not on dead rules.

The elasticity and vividness of Thyer's imagination enable

---

[628]) *Ibid.*
[629]) P. L. IX. 34 *n.*
[630]) P. L. IX. 457 *n.*
[631]) *Ibid.*
[632]) Cf. below, chapter on Warton.
[633]) P. L. IX. 457 *n.*
[634]) *Ibid.*
[635]) *Ibid.*

him to trace the impulses of Milton's characters, the interplay
of their varying moods. The reserve and moderation of the commentator's manner agree with the fact that he succeeds mainly
in the treatment of quiet, delicate emotions. The "piety of the
saint, and the tenderness of the mother", *i. e.* of the Virgin
Mary [636]), her anxiety and self-restraint, are described with a
keen sense of the continuously changing flow of her emotions.
Thyer sees "that sudden start of fond impatience in the third line,
But where delays he now? breaking in so abruptly upon the com-
pos'd resignation express'd in the preceding ones", as well as
"her suddenly checking herself, and resuming her calm and
resign'd character again" [637]). Descriptions of conflicting or
apparently contradictory feelings seem to attract him. Warburton did not understand the expression: "dim sadness ... mixt
With pitie, violated not thir bliss" [638]). He sees a contradiction
in the passage: "the latter passion [he evidently means pity] is
so far from alleviating the former, that it adds weight to it" [639]).
Thyer sees the possibility of combining such seemingly incompatible emotions as pity and bliss, speaking of the "blessedness of
a benevolent temper" [640]). The emotional character of the word
"fervent" [641]) is analysed with much delicacy, the situation being
carefully examined. Its subdued though not unimpassioned tone
is ascribed to the mental state typical of the sinless life in Paradise. It is found to "imply some emotion" yet to carry nothing
in its idea inconsistent with that "subserviency of the passions,
which subsisted before the fall". Thyer's tendency to study complicated emotional states of mind appears in all the above instances.
Sometimes his sensitiveness verges on sentimentality, *e. g.* when
the scene of Adam's reconcilement to his wife [642]) is described as
"extremely beautiful, I had almost said, beyond any thing in the
whole poem," so that "that reader must have a very sour and un-
friendly turn of mind, whose heart does not *relent* with Adam's..."
"Samson Agonistes" evidently impresses Thyer very deeply,

[636]) P. R. II. 93 *n.*
[637]) *Ibid.*
[638]) P. L. X. 23 *n.*
[639]) *Ibid.*
[640]) *Ibid.*
[641]) P. L. IX. 342 *n.*
[642]) P. L. X. 940 *n.*

and his notes show that his critical powers did not flag in dealing with its outbursts of violent and unrestrained emotion, despite his predilection for more idyllic features. Here again the tendency to study irregular, shifting moods appears, and the word "sudden" is used repeatedly in a characteristic manner.

"Something vastly grand and noble" is found in Samson's "sudden gust of indignation and passionate self-reproach" upon a mention of his former weakness of mind [643]). The "wildness" appreciated by Thyer in "Lycidas" is valued by him in "Samson Agonistes" also, though no traces of the "agreeable" quality which he praised in the early poem are found in the play. In defending the recurrence of certain ideas in the speeches of Samson he uses almost exactly the same words as in the above-quoted note on "Lycidas": "Grief though eloquent is not tied to forms, and is besides apt in its own nature frequently to recur to and repeat its source and object" [644]). The rough, impulsive character of Samson's speech is traced in the structure of the verse: "Those sudden starts of impatience are very natural to persons in such circumstances, and this rough and unequal measure of the verses is very well suited to it" [645]).

Despite some inconsistencies between his conservative principles and his unconventional feeling for imaginative excellence, Thyer, on the whole, remains one of the subtlest commentators on Milton in the whole century, mainly through his artistic sense and his faculty for delicate description. Not so much his theories as his practice contribute to a deeper insight into the achievements of Milton as an artist, though his recognition of the impression on the mind as the main criterion of the value of a literary work is far in advance of the somewhat helpless dogmatism of Newton himself, showing the beginnings of a more adequate theoretical attitude.

B. BISHOP WARBURTON.

Warburton's notes, which are not very numerous, deal less with technical matters and more with artistic problems than those of Newton's other contributors, with the sole exception of

---

[643]) S. A. 411.
[644]) S. A. 633 n. Cf. also S. A. 340 n.
[645]) S. A. 606 n.

Thyer. Warburton's individual, eccentric manner does not lessen the stimulating effect of his remarks, though at times his attitude may be obviously wrong.

He has some religious prejudices against Milton and objects to the application of human analogies to divine things [646]). The "unreasonable as well as untheological" supposition that God gave to man the knowledge of his fellow-creatures before that of the nature of the creator himself [647]), and the doctrine of the spiritualization of matter [648]) are both received with little favour.

Warburton's views on the character of literary creation are somewhat simple-minded and short-sighted. He appears to be ignorant of Virgil's untiring labour at the Æneid and of Milton's long preparations for "Paradise Lost". His opinion of these works and of the Homeric epics is that they were the result of sudden eruptions of inspiration: "each of these poems was struck out at a heat and came to perfection from its first essay" [649]). This is the very reverse of the attitude of Peck and Pope who assumed very little spontaneity in Milton [650]). Inspiration is regarded as all-powerful, patient, assiduous work is ignored. This is the typical point of view of the extreme advocate of the imagination.

The same lack of critical restraint causes Warburton to forget the relativity of the value of all human achievement. He dogmatically extols the two ancient poets and Milton as the culmination of epic poetry, and finds them to have exhausted all spheres of human action, Homer having treated of "the province of *morality*, Virgil of *politics*", so that nothing is left for Milton "but that of religion" [651]). The conclusion of the note is very categorical: "Here then the grand scene closes, and all further improvement of the epic is at an end." Joseph Warton derides this notion as "totally groundless and chimerical", attacking Warburton's doctrinairian narrowmindedness [652]).

Warburton's knowledge of Elizabethan poetry may have in-

---

[646]) P. L. VIII. 221.
[647]) P. L. VIII. 357 *n*.
[648]) Co. 462 *n*.
[649]) P. L. IX. 28 *n*.
[650]) Cf. above, on Peck.
[651]) IX. 28 *n*.
[652]) Todd's ed., P. L. IX. 28 *n*.

15*

fluenced his taste. His over-valuation of poetic inspiration might
at least in part be due to this 653). The same fact might also
explain his fondness for conceits, in which respect he differs from
most Milton commentators of that period. The ingenious play
of the imagination seems to interest him more than any considerations of moderation and restraint. Milton's conceits are
even developed considerably further, with a readiness betraying
the critic's predilection for this style, as in Co. 249 n. where
Warburton in dealing with the image of sound floating on the
wings of silence introduces a new high-flown idea, that of the
hostility of silence and sound: "This is extremely poetical, and
insinuates this sublime idea and imagery, that even silence herself was content to convey her mortal enemy, sound, on her wings,
so greatly was she charmed with its harmony". Shakespeare seems
to have taught Warburton to do justice to the Elizabethan richness of "Comus". Warburton even prefers to the rest the passages
imitated from Shakespeare. The "brighter vein of poetry" and
the "ease and delicacy of expression very superior to his
[= Milton's] natural manner" found in the echoes of Shakespeare's fairy scenes are dwelt on with especial emphasis 654).
This is the reverse of Newton's attitude 655). Originality is valued
by Warburton, even in the treatment of classical tradition. To
his mind, Milton's genealogy of Echo 656) is "much nobler and
more poetical than any of the ancient mythology". The mixture
of mediæval fable and classical mythology in "Comus" is not
condemned 657). Some of these notes seem to lead out of the age
of reason into the twilight spheres of Young and Macpherson.
Such is the remark describing how "darkness sets the imagination

---

653) His Shakespeare notes seem to prove this. In his remark on "the
sea-maid's music" in MidsND. he describes Shakespeare's power of carrying
his readers into fairyland, his being "borne away by the magic of his
enthusiasm" and hurrying one "with him into these ancient regions of poetry,
by that power of verse which we may well fancy to be like what, — Olim
fauni vatesque canebant". Traces of this enthusiastic attitude appear in
Warburton's Milton criticism, though the scarcity of his notes makes it
difficult to form a definite idea of his views.
654) Co. 1 n.
655) Cf. below.
656) Co. 241 n.
657) Co. 46 n.

at work, to create ideal forms and beings" 658). Warburton's lack of critical reserve fortunately did not impair his ability to appreciate individuality and imagination.

C. JOHN JORTIN.

Jortin's Milton notes are pre-eminently those of a classical scholar. He discusses problems of classical textual criticism which relate little to Milton 659). Classical parallels from obscure authors are not infrequent. P. L. I. 199 *n.* mentions in the space of a few lines Pomponius Mela, Nonnus, Pindar, Farnaby's commentary on Ovid, & c., and in P. R. III. 47 *n.*, a note called by Newton immediately before "a learned collection out of the Heathen moralists", Jortin hurries through Plato, Tacitus, Seneca, Cicero, Epictete and Marcus Aurelius to give a survey of the ancient ideas of glory. English poets are seldom mentioned 660). His remarks make somewhat dull reading but his principles are less pedantic than his style. "Vulgar errors" and legends are admitted into verse because they "adorn the poems" 661). Inconsistencies in Milton's early work which enhance the poetic effect, such as the tendency of this "most antipapistical" poet and his like to "canonize and then to invoke their friends as saints" 662) appeal to the critic. Some sensitive observation of nature appears in his explanation of Lyc. 142 ("the rathe primrose that forsaken dies", Lyc. 142 *n.*). He seems to have observed that the primrose, as an early flower, "continues till it is put out of countenance by those which are more beautiful, and so *dies forsaken* and neglected". This may not be correct — it is questioned by Thomas Warton 663) — but it is not the idea of a pedant.

Some of Jortin's emendations could, however, hardly be regarded as free from pedantry. P. R. I. 402 *n.* alters "each mans"

---

658) L'A. 6 *n.*
659) P. L. XI. 565 *n.*
660) Cf. P. L. II. 684, Il P. 151 *n.*
661) P. R. I. 456 *n.*
662) Lyc. 183 *n.*
663) Cf. his note to this passage.

into "each one's" mainly because the expression refers to Satan, who is not a "man". Jortin entirely forgets the anthropomorphism of human language, which uses in a metaphorical sense expressions that could scarcely be replaced by more definite words without adding a touch of academic dulness. The more concrete though less precise expression may heighten the vividness of the passage. Moreover, Satan appears, in this particular place, to be speaking not only of himself but also of men — the "companions of his misery" to whom the previous lines referred.

The weight of Jortin's critical remarks is hardly sufficient to justify Newton's assertion in his preface to the edition of "Paradise Lost" [664]) that "every thing that proceeds from him is of value, whether in poetry, criticism or divinity", though his erudition seems to be solid enough and though certain indications of an unbiassed critical attitude may be discovered.

D. RICHARD MEADOWCOURT.

Meadowcourt whose "Critique on Milton's Paradise Re-gain'd" [665]) was published, as has been said, in 1732 and 1748, has contributed only a few notes, which add little that is of any importance, though some of them show his considerable reading [666]). His sense of actual facts and knowledge of local English traditions are shown to much advantage in his explanation of the probable allusion to St. Michael's in Lyc. 159 & c., but his feeling for poetical qualities is primitive. The above-mentioned pamphlet had already proved that his standpoint was perfectly in keeping with the spirit of the period, in a manner reminding one of the rationalist and classicist exaggerations of Bentley's commentary which was published in the same year. According to Meadowcourt, the object of poetry is instruction. In order to attract attention, as he thinks, instruction must be accompanied by pleasure, and for the purpose of achieving pleasure, the whole technique of poetry has been invented: ..."the secondary Aim of Poets has

---

[664]) Vol. I. sig. a$_4$r.

[665]) Cf. above, introd. part of this chapter.

[666]) Cf. P. R. II. 313 n. on the names of *Thebes* and *Thebez*, and P. R. IV. 564 n.

always been to please, in order to instruct with greater Success. Hence have they invented Harmony in Sounds, and different Measures of Verse: From hence sprung Figures and Tropes, and all the Ornaments of Language: From hence the whole Art of Poetry derives its Birth" [667]). The main value of "Paradise Regained" from the standpoint of this theory is naturally its didacticism and theoretical wisdom ("A Performance that abounds with such instructive Doctrines, and with Sentiments of Morality so just, so useful, and so refined, the World has not yet receiv'd" — *ibid.* p. 2). There is very little penetration in Meadowcourt's analysis of the characters of the poem. Satan is the typical cunning tempter and Christ's behaviour "becoming a Person of Divine Extraction" [668]). Milton's "Similitudes and Allusions" as far as derived "from Romance and Fable" and "thereby mixing up suppos'd Realities with unacknowledg'd Fictions" are regarded as "disfiguring and deforming his Subject", "lessening what he should augment; and overlaying thick Shade where he ought to throw on the strongest Light" [669]). The frankness and outspokenness of this artistic utilitarianism and classicism is that of a clergyman apparently more intent on professional sermonizing and instruction than on the study of literary subtleties.

E. CALTON.

Some learning and diligence do not make up for Calton's inability to do justice to the terseness of Milton's style. He finds it too complicated, and is puzzled by the poet's "unnatural conciseness" and "exceedingly elleiptical" [sic] language [670]). This is not only a matter of taste. His attitude is evidently caused by his inability to understand Milton's method of expression. Calton seems to have been spoiled by the smooth and easy manner of his contemporaries. He is unable to follow Milton's less obvious but more substantial style. Certain passages, hardly very difficult, impress him as inexplicable. P. R. I. 19 *n.* evidently misinterprets

[667]) Cf. p. 1 of ed. 1732.
[668]) *Ibid.* p. 3.
[669]) Cf. p. 28.
[670]) P. R. II. 60 *n.*

the meaning of the passage: "Now had the great Proclaimer... cri'd Repentance, and Heavens Kingdom nigh at hand To all Baptiz'd". Calton relates "To all Baptiz'd" to both accusatives of the verb "cri'd", failing to note that it might possibly refer to the second only (= heaven's kingdom *which is* nigh at hand to all baptized). His interpretation involves the incongruity that the prophet attempted to convert those who, as a sign of their conversion, had already been baptized: "Whereas in the nature of things as well as in the Gospel history, his preaching must be, and was, preparatory to his baptism" 671). All these difficulties disappear, if the comma after "repentance" is taken into consideration and "To all Baptiz'd" related only to the second accusative, as Newton proposes.

A similar difficulty is discussed in P. R. II. 419 *n.* The passage has no verb which might according to ordinary standards of language be supposed to govern the accusative "Multitude" in line 419 ("Or at thy heels the dizzy Multitude"). The construction is obviously elliptic. Calton does not acknowledge the Miltonic reading and boldly proposes an emendation, which normalizes the grammar but endangers the metre: "Or at thy heels to keep the dizzy multitude". He attempts to save the situation by pointing out the existence in Milton of hypercatalectic verses 672). His attitude is here rather liberal, for he acknowledges that "Milton's verses are not always to be measur'd by counting syllables on the fingers' ends". Newton's opinion is precisely the reverse: he is liberal as to the grammatical and conservative as to the metrical point, objecting to the hypercatalectic verse but accepting "the *dizzy multitude* as the accusative case after the verb *gain,* making favorable allowances for a little inaccuracy of expression".

The conventionalism of Calton's views on language and the inconsiderate boldness of his emendations remind one of Bentley's editorial practice.

---

671) *Ibid.*
672) He refers to S. A. 655, 868 and P. L. IX. 249.

F. SYMPSON.

Sympson's notes, which are relatively few, evince a good deal of erudition but he shows a lack of insight, particularly in some of his emendations. P. R. II. 319 *n.* where he alters the text because he apparently does not study the context with sufficient care, is a typical example of his attitude. Newton in the same note points out his blunder. An equal lack of care and penetration appears in P. R. II. 177 *n.*

Sympson's views on Milton's verse, however, have their very definite merits. He does justice to the rich, varied metre of the songs of the chorus in "Samson Agonistes", comparing them with the tedious regularity of Ben Jonson's imitations of the classical chorus: "Old Ben's are of a poor similar regular contexture; our author's truly Grecian and noble, diversified with all the measures our language and poetry are capable of"... [673]). It is true that he qualifies this praise by doubting if these metres could possibly be pronounced in the manner designed by Milton [674]). Slight remarks on the stage pronunciation of Milton's verse — directions for asides — are found in Co. 756, 800 *nn.* The liberalism of Sympson's prosodical views seems to be due to his study of the Elizabethans [675]).

G. NEWTON'S CRITICAL QUALIFICATION AND OPINIONS.

In Newton we find a typical erudite divine, a man of more culture and intelligence than originality. He is more skilful in adapting and summing up the opinions of others than in formulating any of his own and a very large part of his notes is a mere restatement of the substance of earlier remarks in a scholarly style. His erudition is as solid as his style and method. He is competent in the ordinary branches of academic learning, particularly in classical scholarship and Scriptural lore, and his knowledge of English literature is not contemptible although it bears few

---

[673]) S. A. 147 *n.*
[674]) *Ibid.*
[675]) Cf. above, introd. part of this chapter.

traces of the spirit of adventurous research which distinguished Peck and was to distinguish the Miltonic studies of Thomas Warton. Any comparison with the erudition of Warton would be out of place. While Newton is no more than a learned, cultured man with no mean intelligence, Warton is the very incarnation of eager, sensitive literary antiquarianism.

Shakespeare and Spenser are Newton's favourite authors, to judge from the frequency of his references to them, wherein he follows the model of his predecessors. One of his last notes on "Paradise Lost" dwells on his reasons for referring so often to Shakespeare. It considers Milton's admiration for him as well as the national pride in his works: "And throughout the course of our remarks we have been the more willing to explain and illustrate our author by similar expressions and sentiments in Shakespeare, not only because Milton was a great reader and admirer of his works, but also because we conceive Shakespear and Milton to be two of the most extraordinary geniuses and greatest poets, whom any country or any time has produced" [676]). As a result, allusions to Shakespeare are probably more conspicuous than in any earlier Milton commentary, with the possible exception of that of Peck. The sonnets [677]) and narrative poems [678]) and some of the poems wrongly attributed at that time to Shakespeare [679]) are mentioned and partly quoted [680]). Spenser's "Faery Queen" is alluded to very frequently [681]) and now and then one finds references to the other poems [682]).

Newton seldom mentions mediæval authors. He has references to the "Canterbury Tales" [683]) as in most commentaries.

---

[676]) Cf. P. L. XII. 630 n.

[677]) Cf. Co. 695 n.

[678]) E. g. Venus and Adonis, cf. Co. 743 n.

[679]) Cf. L'A. 151 n. on the "two beautiful little pieces of Shakespeare, entitled The Passionate Shepherd to his Love, and the Nymph's Reply to the Shepherd".

[680]) Newton knew the two last-mentioned poems from Warburton's notes on the "Merry Wives of Windsor", as he himself observes.

[681]) Cf. Il P. 109 n., Arc. 57 n., N. O. 64 n., & c. & c.

[682]) "The Shepherd's Calendar" Co. 542 n., Lyc. 114 n., "Epithalamion" P. L. V. 711 n., "Muiopotmos" P. R. II. 401 n., the "Hymn of Heavenly Love" P. L. I. 17 n. and the "Hymn of Heavenly Beauty" ibid., "Colin Clout's Come Home Again" P. L. II. 489 n., & c. & c.

[683]) Cf. P. R. II. 401 n., Il P. 7 n., id. 109 n., & c.

Geoffrey of Monmouth [684]) and "The Cuckoo and the Nightingale" [685]) are a greater surprise. On the whole, in his mentions of, and quotations from, earlier authors, Newton adds relatively little to the research of his predecessors. Sidney (his "Arcadia" is mentioned repeatedly, *e. g.*, together with the "Defence of Poetry", in P. R. II. 401 *n.*), as has been shown, was well-known even to Bentley. Ben Jonson [686]), Fairfax's Tasso [687]), Harrington's Ariost [688]), to enumerate the most conspicuous favourites of Newton among the authors not yet mentioned, were familiar to many of the earlier Milton students discussed in the present treatise. Beaumont and Fletcher [689]), but quite especially J. Fletcher's "The Faithful Shepherdess" (see particularly the notes to "Comus") should be added to the above. Their occurrence is even less striking than that of the rest, for one of the editors of their works, Sympson, contributed to Newton's notes and is called his friend in the preface to "Paradise Regained". Taken as a whole, Newton's knowledge of older authors is not contemptible but it hardly opens up any new paths. The editor evidently confined himself to the study of those writers who interested the larger circles of the literary public of that time.

Italian names, except those of Tasso and Ariost, are not frequent, though, judging from his quotations and comments upon them, Newton seems to have known Italian. Well-read informants sometimes supply him with curious and unexpected parallels, for example the "ingenious friend" who communicates with regard to P. L. IV. 750 *et seq.* "that this address to wedded love is borrow'd from one of Tasso's letters, *O dolce conguintione* [sic!] *de'cuori, a* [sic!] *soave unione de gli animi nostri, o legitimo nodo, & c.*" Some of Newton's remarks on Italian poetry will be dealt with below.

The study of Milton's MSS. enables Newton to call attention to many corrupt readings (cf. particularly the notes on the sonnets). And besides purely literary studies, much miscellaneous

---

[684]) P. L. I. 575 *n.*
[685]) Son. I. 1 *n.*
[686]) Cf. L'A. 132 *n.*, P. R. II. 401 *n.*, P. L. V. 439 *n.*, & c.
[687]) Cf. P. L. I. 105 *n.*, II. 628 *n.*, & c. & c.
[688]) Cf. P. R. II. 6 *n.*, P. R. IV. 541 *n.*
[689]) Cf. *e. g.* P. R. II. 344 *n.*

delving into special works was needed, pre-eminently into geo-graphical and historical publications, but to enumerate these would be valueless. Classical historians and geographers like Josephus [690]), Valerius Maximus [691]), Polybius [692]), Livy [693]), Strabo [694]), & c. & c., are referred to or quoted at greath length. Modern works, such as Dr. Shaw's "physical observations on Arabia Petræa", as Newton calls it [695]), Tavernier's "Travels into Persia" [696]), & c., are consulted, particularly in the notes to the numerous geographical allusions in "Paradise Regained". Nevertheless, Newton's learning cannot be called exceptional. He has done respectable work, but even the undisciplined Peck's inquisitiveness seems to lead more frequently to interesting discoveries than the somewhat conventional scholarship of Newton.

His treatment of "Paradise Regained", "Samson Agonistes" and the Minor Poems is somewhat less thorough than that of "Paradise Lost", apparently because the preliminary work done by his predecessors was incomparably slighter in this case. In treating of Milton's minor productions, Newton was compelled to proceed more independently and thus to expose all the deficiencies of his method and erudition.

The academic conservatism and dogmatism of Newton's attitude appear rather clearly in his treatment of Milton's personal life and views. And since some of his remarks on these latter are very typical, they should be dealt with before the purely critical part of Newton's work. It is true that his careful, conscientious research is concerned more with the establishment of the actual facts of Milton's life and the explanation of the personal and topical allusions in his poetry than with tracing their influence on the author's art. Especially the edition of the Minor Poems where the personal element is so conspicuous, affords Newton ample opportunity of exploring Milton's personal history, though

---

[690]) P. R. II. 423 *n.*
[691]) P. R. II. 199 *n.*
[692]) *Ibid.*
[693]) *Ibid.*
[694]) P. R. III. 253 *n.*
[695]) P. R. I. 340 *n.*
[696]) Cf. P. R. I. 323 *n.*

his work in this field cannot in any way be compared to that of Warton [697]).

A considerable part of the notes falling under this personal category deal with Milton's religious views. In spite of some flashes of liberalism, they are typical of Newton's conservative outlook, and his fundamental opinions are stated very clearly, e. g. the view that "they are only would-be-wits, who do not believe and worship a God" [698]). He even ventures the debatable statement that "The greatest geniuses in all ages from Homer to Milton appear plainly by their writing to have been men of piety and religion" [699]). He accordingly takes great pains to prove that Milton was orthodox in the main points of religious doctrine and seems to be anxious to controvert the opinion that the poet may have adhered to Arianism. The passage: "Equal to God, and equally enjoying God-like fruition" [700]) is used to emphasize that "This deserves notice as an instance of Milton's orthodoxy with relation to the divinity of God the Son". The same "truly orthodox" tendency appears in P. L. VII. 602 n. Yet Newton also finds features which, in his opinion, deserve censure. He opposes most resolutely the theory of the spiritualization of matter: "Our author should have considered things better, for by attributing his own false notions in philosophy to an Arch-Angel he has really lessen'd the character, which he intended to raise" [701]). The conclusion reached towards the end of this note apparently implies a reproach to Milton for thinking too logically and systematically in theological matters: "For Milton, as he was too much of a materialist in his philosophy, so was too much of a systematist in his divinity". Even such problems of theology as whether the angels did actually eat or no are seriously discussed by Newton, and decided in the affirmative [702]).

This does not mean that the presence of strong evidence should not at times induce Newton to adopt more liberal views on certain matters, e. g. on the problem whether Milton regarded

---

[697]) Cf. below, chapter on Warton.
[698]) P. L. IX. 199 n.
[699]) Ibid.
[700]) P. L. III. 306—7.
[701]) P. L. V. 478 n.
[702]) P. L. V. 435 n.

himself as inspired from above [703]). Heylin seems to doubt how far the poet's invocation of the Holy Ghost to inspire him is admissible, trying to prove that the concept of "inspiration" ought to be interpreted in a larger sense [704]). The biographical data collected by Newton led him to the conclusion that Milton understood it literally, which view is supported by similar invocations in earlier poetry.

Newton's general lack of enthusiasm appears in his observations on Milton's love of freedom, e. g. in P. L. XI. 798 n. (on the verse: "Shall with thir freedom lost all vertu loose"). There is here no trace of the exaggerated emotionalism of the Richardsons. One thinks, rather, of a somewhat narrow-minded, almost schoolmaster-like attitude: "Milton everywhere shows his love of liberty, and here he observes very rightly that the loss of liberty is soon follow'd by the loss of all virtue and religion. There are such sentiments in several parts of his prose works, as well as in Aristotle and other masters of politics" [705]). This treatment of one of the main passions of Milton's life — the description of his frequent hot-headed battles for the cause of liberty as merely' some "such sentiments in several parts of his prose-works" — is typical. The reserve and conservatism of this note appear in many of Newton's remarks, where the more radical features of the poet's art are described, though he sometimes succeeds in doing justice to the less orthodox characteristics of Milton.

He shares the exaggerated respect for the authority of' classical antiquity so often found in Milton annotation — however, with the reservation that he (like many of his predecessors) regards Milton's genius as able to carry him even beyond the competition of the classics. Classical precedents suffice to justify peculiarities which in themselves seem to clash with Newton's literary principles. The ancients are the "best poets" whose authority has to be respected [706]). The only arguments used in P. L. II. 965 n. to defend Milton's introduction of "shadowy" allegorical beings is that Virgil, Seneca, Claudian & c. did similar things and that Virgil's descriptions of them are pleasing. Hence

---

[703]) P. L. I. 17 n.
[704]) Ibid.
[705]) P. L. XI. 798 n.
[706]) P. L. IX. 462 n.

the conclusion that "it is impossible to be pleased with Virgil and to be displeased with Milton" 707). The reason *why* Virgil appeals to the reader does not interest the commentator, the particulars of the two cases are not examined by him at all. However, it must be remembered that Newton later on, towards the end of his edition of "Paradise Lost" 708), chances to deal with the problem once more, making up in some degree for his superficiality 709).

Things that are not found in the works of the ancients appear to be objectionable for this very reason, though Milton's greatness is sometimes deemed sufficient to justify his independence. Newton gives serious consideration to the condemnatory verdict passed by some critics on Milton's description of his own personal misfortune at the beginning of book IX of "Paradise Lost", for, as he says, "we find no such digression in the Iliad or Æneid; it is a liberty that can be taken only by such a genius as Milton" 710). However, it is a sign of advance on the simple-minded recognition of classical authority by some of his predecessors that Newton tries to point out its reason, attributing it to the influence of traditional education: the classical associations become so familiar as to be made "such an essential part of poetry" that they can be hardly separated from it 711). This recognition of the fact that the value of a classical style depends on the influence of convention should be equivalent to recognizing the relativity of this style, though Newton generally forgets this.

But his study of the ancients produced more than the merely negative result of a prejudiced outlook. The examination of Vergil and probably also of others taught him that the value of poetry is not mainly in the novelty of its themes but even more in its manner of treating these. Classicists such as Pope may have led him to the same conclusion. Similes need not be new if they are poetic 712). Milton's imitations are important literary achievements, so Newton analyses these, finding that Milton, the "universal scholar", who "took hints from the Moderns as well as the Ancients", "was a great genius, but a great genius form'd by

---

707) *Ibid.*
708) P. L. X. 230 *n.*
709) Cf. below.
710) P. L. IX. 1 *n.*
711) P. L. XI. 8 *n.*
712) P. L. V. 708 *n.*

reading; and as it was said of Virgil, he collected gold out of the dung of other authors" [713]). He was great enough to improve even on the greatest models, not merely on little-known writers such as Odoricus Valmarana to whom Newton supposes him to be indebted [714]). The idea is not new but Newton's treatment of it adds some interesting items to the observations of earlier writers. The greater subtlety of the analogies and allusions in Milton's recast of the Homeric and Virgilian descriptions of the heavenly scales of fate [715]) justifies Newton's inference that this is no "imitating servilely" the excellence of his models but rather the creation of a new original through the poet's "manner of varying and improving" them. Milton succeeds in assimilating the style of his original so entirely and so creatively that he surpasses his model. The description of the heavenly battle is found to be "very much in Homer's manner", but though Milton owes much to the ancient poet, he exceeds him: "Homer taught him to excel Homer" [716]). Newton's trained mind sees Milton's technical superiority to Homer, the deliberate, intelligent art substituted by him for some of Homer's rigid conventionalities. Homer's heralds often deliver their messages in literally the same expressions in which they receive them. Even "in the heat and hurry of battle" they repeat them word for word, "and sometimes a thing is repeated so often that it becomes almost tedious" [717]). Milton, on the contrary, borrows "all the beauty and simplicity of Homer, without any of his faults" [718]). Instead of a single speech, he repeats parts of various earlier speeches, which have their peculiar significance, for they emphasize matters important for the development of the poem, and the repeated words are originally the utterances of God himself whose expressions piety forbids to alter. (Cf. ll. 96—98 and 48 of the same book.)

There is very little emotionalism in Newton's attitude. Some of his analyses are keen, but Thyer's artistic sensibility is almost entirely absent. It is therefore not the emotional aspect of

---

[713]) P. L. V. 689 n.
[714]) Ibid.
[715]) P. L. IV. 1003 n.
[716]) P. L. VI. 239 n.
[717]) P. L. XI. 261 n.
[718]) Ibid.

Milton's works that attracts Newton most, though at least one of his notes deals with the sweeping effect of the "highth and fury" of the poet's descriptions [719]), which cause him to forget the rules. He takes a keener interest in purely intellectual and technical problems, sometimes becoming almost pedantic in the treatment of relatively unimportant details. Thus, he finds Virgil's and Milton's lists of warriors to fall short of "Homer's excellence and beauty", merely because they happen to mention the names of persons who take no part in the subsequent action [720]). On the other hand, the accuracy lacking there is sometimes found by Newton in Milton's similes. He praises these as "very apposite" and corresponding "exactly in all the particulars" [721]).

Newton does not go so far in his demand for regularity as to deny to poetry the use of uncommon language, though it is not quite so certain what he thinks of uncommon matter [722]) : unusual, artificial imagery, such as the sophisticated "horses tails and sphinxes and dragons and other terrible animals on the helmets of the ancient heroes", or the Chimæra on the crest of Turnus [723]), is found to be inferior to Milton's simpler personification of horror sitting plumed on Satan's crest [724]). The classicist ideal of grand, impassioned simplicity appears to be more congenial to Newton than most artistic doctrines. The parallel to Bentley is obvious (cf. above). According to Newton, "Nothing in all the ancient tragedies is more moving and pathetic" than Adam's passionate desire to die after the fall [725]). Milton's "great and masterly" manner is preferred to that of Ovid, for "the Roman poet has lessen'd the grandeur of his by puerile conceits and quaint antitheses" [726]). However, the extremes of passion have to be avoided. The "folly and impiety of Eve", which might easily impress one as "extravagant and monstrous", appear to

---

[719]) P. L. VI. 856 n.
[720]) P. L. I. 506 n.
[721]) P. L. III. 431 n.
[722]) P. L. III. 555 n.: "poetry delights to say the most common things in an uncommon manner".
[723]) Æn. VII. 785.
[724]) P. L. IV. 989 n.
[725]) P. L. X. 859 n.
[726]) P. L. II. 898 n.

Newton to be bearable only in a diluted form [727]). "Decorum"
remains predominant: Homer's description of the conjugal love
of Jupiter and Juno is indecent but Milton has been able to make
a "moral lesson" out of an "impious fiction" [728]). The general
drift carries somewhat too obviously towards the standards of
the more commonplace and conventional criticism of the period.

Certain prejudiced views Newton seems to have derived
directly from Bentley. The preliminary mention of the infernal
bridge in P. L. II. 1023 *et seq.* (which may be regarded as the
careful preparation of an important point), is condemned as
"wrong conduct and want of oeconomy for the whole poem"
because it lessons the surprise in book X — an important
additional argument being that "we cannot recollect a parallel
instance in Homer or Virgil, or any authorised poet" [729]). The
first of the above quotations from this note echoes Bentley's own
words and reflects this critic's unusual dislike of repetitions of
any kind. Newton's sense of epic dignity is offended by the
passage on the Limbo of Vanity which strikes him as "fitter for
a mock-heroic poem than for the true epic" [730]). The element of
grim mockery which lends a certain imaginative breadth and
sweep to the description escapes him altogether. He distinguishes
far more strictly between the poetic categories than was the
fashion of Milton's time. The mixed style, which is so characteristic of Milton's teachers, the Elizabethans, appears to be repugnant
to Newton.

Unusual *events* are met with approval if they are not of the
most extreme kind. The kind appealing to Newton is apparently
that described by him as both "natural and surprising" [731]). But
only Newton's careful manner of expression distinguishes his condemnation of the romances of chivalry from the similar observations of Bentley [732]). His regret of Milton's early fondness for
romances goes so far as to make him express the desire that these
"had better never been read" by the poet [733]). This is far more

---

[727]) P. L. IX. 739 *n.*
[728]) P. L. IX. 1029 *n.*
[729]) P. L. II. 1023 *n.*
[730]) P. L. III. 459 *n.*
[731]) P. L. IV. 359 *n.*
[732]) P. L. I. 575 *n.*, cf. also above, chapter on Bentley.
[733]) *Ibid.*

conservative than Thyer's attitude, but some resemblance to the statements of Thyer [734]) is found in Newton's desire that poetry should be sensible, pleasurable and in conformity to the Bible, or, as he puts it, "agreeable to reason and revelation" and "pleasing to the imagination" [735]). It is evident that real historical events correspond more exactly than fiction to the first of these requirements. Hence Newton's preference of some of the imitations of Homer in "Paradise Lost" to Homer himself, for the former are said to represent "real histories and matters of fact" [736]).

Thus, poetry to Newton remains essentially a means of pleasure and instruction. It may not deviate too far into extravagances and should take into account all the demands of religious orthodoxy, refraining from fiction, except where classicist convention has made the latter an habitual ornament. The absence of emotionalism, the interest in technical problems, the insistence on perfection and elaboration instead of novelty, are typical features of classicism. The admission of certain chance irregularities shows only that the liberal tendencies discoverable in most of the previous commentators, who had nearly all been studied by Newton, had left their marks on his attitude.

This is not the best frame of mind to bring to a study of Milton's early poetry. It is true that Newton admired these poems, as he admired Handel's music to some of them. He is deeply impressed by these compositions: "That great artist [= Handel] has done... justice to our author's L'Allegro and Il Penseroso, as if the same spirit possessed both masters, and as if the God of music and of verse was still one and the same" [737]). The poems in the volume of 1695 receive high praise: "and if he had left no other monuments of his poetical genius behind him, these would have been sufficient to render his name immortal" [738]).

Yet some of the main features of these poems now regarded

---

[734]) While discussing the rarity of descriptive passages in "Paradise Regained", Thyer, as has been shown, finds that an epic poem "ought to consist of a proper and happy mixture of the instructive and the delightful" — P. R. II. 1 *n.* — but he obviously lays stress on the latter element which is by no means opposed to the character of romance.

[735]) P. L. IV. 671 *n.*

[736]) P. L. XI. 660 *n.*

[737]) Vol. I, p. LXII; ed. 1750 of P. L.

[738]) Cf. p. XXVI, opus cit.

16*

as valuable are depreciated by him. Their whimsical manner which Milton drew from the Elizabethans strikes him as mere youthful fermentation. He quotes and translates Cicero's approval of this quality as the foreboding of a rich maturity (De Orat.): "...in a young genius there should always be something to lop and prune away" — but it ought not to be forgotten that this may have been partly due to Newton's usual tendency to quote widely, sometimes with only a very loose application to the text, the more so as this is a classical quotation, a device common in academic disquisitions [739]). In some other, apparently more independent, notes, Milton's use of figurative language is treated more superciliously. In Co. 732 *n.* it is called "exceeding childish". "The Cynosure of neighbouring eyes" is regarded as "an affected expression" [740]). The somewhat contemptuous description of the heavy humour of the poems on the university carrier as "that sort of wit, which was then in request at Cambridge" [741]) is certainly more justified.

The imagery of the "fanciful Italians", "allegorical poets or painters" [742]), meets with little sympathy, though the disciplined style of the Italian sonnet appeals to Newton. Petrarca is praised "for the tenderness and delicacy of his passion, as well as for the beauty and elegance of his sentiments and language" [743]), but the more masculine virtues of some of Milton's own sonnets are not overlooked, either: a bold and heroic couplet in the sonnet to Cromwell is extolled as "two glorious lines" [744]). The more capricious masculinity of grotesque Elizabethan realism (the Trinity MS. reading of Co. 608: "and cleave his scalpe downe to the hips"), which is abundantly illustrated by Newton himself from the plays of Ben Jonson and Shakespeare, is nevertheless condemned. The authority of Shakespeare does not seem to weigh with him so much as that of the "authoriz'd" classical writers.

This is seen in his comparison of Milton's and Shakespeare's fairy-scenes. Warburton's knowledge and appreciation of Shakespeare enabled him to relish the ease of his romances,

---

[739]) Co. 557 *n.*
[740]) L'A. 80 *n.*
[741]) U. C. I and II, note.
[742]) Il P. 52 *n.*
[743]) Son. I *n.*
[744]) Sonnet to Cromwell, 5 *n.*

preferring Milton's imitations of them to his independent writing [745]). Newton arrives at exactly the opposite conclusion as to the respective merits of the two authors. Milton's guardian-spirit in "Comus" is considered superior to Shakespeare's Ariel, much stress being laid on the fact that the poet "was well acquainted with the Platonic notions of Spirits or Demons" [746]). Here, Milton's learned apparatus seems to incline the scales in his favour.

Newton quite naturally regards "Paradise Lost" as the crowning achievement of Milton's poetry. It is "the flower of epic poetry, and the noblest effort of genius" [747]), though the other poems "are no less excellent in their kind", and, if not equally sublime, "are at least equally beautiful and pleasing to the imagination" [748]). "Paradise Regained" is described as more even in execution, "more argumentative" and perhaps also "superior in sentiment" but distinctly inferior as regards imaginative qualities [749]), though Milton's skill in adorning the barrenness of the subject is acknowledged [750]). If Thyer found that Milton attained to his former perfection wherever the subject admitted of it [751]), Newton assumes that he even tried to avoid any chance of comparison with his former work, being too conscious of the inferiority of his second epic [752]). Thyer was in love with the rich imagery of some passages in "Paradise Regained" whereas Newton takes little notice of it. This appears to be typical of the fundamental difference between the two.

It seems to be true that the very plan of the epic encouraged an argumentative style and that a superabundance of descriptive matter might have obscured the main design of the poem. A strict refraining from poetical embroidery was suited to the theorizing matter — though a number of passages show, as Thyer no doubt very rightly pointed out, that Milton could take up his old style when he thought fit.

---

[745]) Cf. above.
[746]) Co. 1 *n.*
[747]) Preface to P. R., sig. A$_2$r, ed. 1752.
[748]) *Ibid.*
[749]) Life, p. XLIII, ed. 1749.
[750]) P. R. II. 6 *n.*
[751]) Cf. above.
[752]) P. R. I. 44, 500 *nn.*

The less ornate, abstract style which predominates leads to the creation of a generalized type of imagery — agreeing with Newton's somewhat devitalized though not unscholarly taste. Newton describes a particular kind of it, referring to Milton's manner of combining the features of various individuals: "as Apelles from the different beauties of several nymphs of Greece drew his portrait of Venus, the Goddess of beauty" [753]. This device, reminiscent of Peck's ideal of "compound beauty" [754], is, in accordance with Newton's academic taste, regarded as "the best method that can be taken of describing general characters".

Newton's classical trend appears in his interest in literary classification. He attempts a definition of the poetic category to which "Paradise Regained" belongs [755], though he does not sufficiently examine how far Milton's views on this question influenced the actual plan and execution of the work. This formal method of approach is justified up to a point, for Milton himself speaks of the various classes of epic poems in his "Reason of Church Government" [756], distinguishing between a larger, classical, and a somewhat briefer, didactic type of epic. Newton points to the resemblance of the work to the book of Job, which Milton mentions as an instance of the less traditional variety. Both works are found to have in common the subject ("a good man triumphing over temptation"), the dialogue form and the moralizing, reflecting character. Hence, "Paradise Regained" is regarded as a specimen of the latter species. This idea is already found in Peck, but Newton, in his usual manner, elaborates the parallel.

In the notes to "Samson Agonistes" his method of almost purely formal criticism is modified in certain cases. The work impresses him very strongly [757] but not for its academic perfections. He dwells repeatedly on its sincerity, on the genuine feeling caused by the fact that Milton here partly describes his own old age. The close resemblance between the subject of the play and Milton's situation after the restoration was noticed by

[753] P. R. III. 71 *n*.
[754] Cf. above, chapter on Peck.
[755] P. R. IV. 624 *n*.
[756] See the introd. to the second book, cf. our chapter on Peck.
[757] Cf. S. A. 3 *n*.

others, *e. g.* by Peck, but Newton's analysis of its connection with the artistic character of the work reveals new prospects. He regrets [758]) that Milton by philosophizing overmuch impairs the impressiveness of Samson's complaint on his blindness, and finds it inferior to the very similar complaint in the beginning of "Paradise Lost", as only in the latter the poet speaks in his own person and gives direct expression to his feelings. Nevertheless, Milton in other parts of the play is found to describe "what he thought in some of his melancholy hours" [759]), writing so well because he does it "from his own feeling and experience", so that "the very flow of the verses is melancholy and excellently adapted to the subject" [760]). It seems as if the powerful impression produced on Newton by the work had at least temporarily changed his literary ideals, so that intense, genuine personal feeling supersedes the formalism of his usual doctrines.

That the "academic" aspects of the tragedy are not forgotten, is, in the present case, more than natural, considering the importance attributed by Milton himself to the similarities between his own work and the drama of classical antiquity. Newton refers to Horace's "Ars poetica" in order to define the rôle of the chorus [761]). He compares the idea of making the characters take for prophecies the unwitting words of others with similar features in the ancients [762]). Important questions of dramatic structure are discussed, *e. g.* the gradual revelation of the action (the persons serving to reveal it being scarcely conscious of the matter — a good observation on the connection between the behaviour of the *dramatis personae* and the development of the plot), as well as the device of leading the expectation of a happy solution to its climax immediately before the catastrophe takes place. Here again Newton finds much opportunity for exerting his purely logical, intellectual faculties. His usual overvaluation of the ancients seems to have disappeared. Though he acknowledges that the play is written "in the very spirit" of the classical drama, he regards it no more than "Paradise Lost" as a mere imitation: in his opinion it "equals, if not exceeds, any of the most

---

[758]) S. A. 90 *n.*
[759]) S. A. 594 *n.*
[760]) *Ibid.*
[761]) S. A. 210 *n.*
[762]) S. A. 472 *n.*

perfect tragedies, which were ever exhibited on the Athenian stage when Greece was in its glory" 763), the only argument in favour of the Greek tragedy being that it is two thousand years older 764). But more significant than his recognition of the literary perfection of the work, in which he is certainly not alone, is the importance here attributed to the intensely personal, emotional elements of Milton's art.

H. NEWTON'S OBSERVATIONS ON MILTON'S STYLE AND LANGUAGE.

Newton's treatment of Milton's style seems to depend in some degree on Pearce. Pearce's close connection with the enterprise, and particularly his revision of the notes, may have influenced this aspect of them. The cautious method, the accurate documentation, the unemotional manner of expression all remind one of Pearce, though Newton is less acute and adds less material to the stock accumulated by editors earlier than Pearce, besides accepting the conventions of his own time much more readily than the latter.

His adherence to the accepted standards appears in his handling of Miltons's spellings. They are usually normalized though many of the original forms are retained, in accordance with the preface 765). His conventional attitude at times apparently causes him to neglect the phonetic value of Milton's orthography in favour of the usual norms or, which is typical of his learned tendencies, in favour of the etymological forms. On the other hand, certain unusual spellings which seem to be of a purely spectacular interest, are kept intact. These matters are interesting, as Newton's notes show that he regarded them as of considerable importance. The alteration of "voutsafe" into "vouchsafe" in P. L. II. 332 illustrates his occasional disregard of the phonetic aspect. Though he admits that Milton's form "is rather of a softer sound", the other spelling is preferred as being "more agreeable to the etymology of the word". The same

---

763) Life, p. LXII.
764) S. A. 3 n.
765) Cf. above.

tendency is conspicous in his substitution of the harsh form
"perfect" for Milton's "perfet" [766]), which is to a considerable
extent due to Newton's classical prejudices. He somewhat contemptuously rejects the form borrowed from the derivative
modern languages (he mentions the French "parfait" and the
Italian "perfetto"), following the principle that "in general it
is better surely to derive our language from the original Latin
than to make it only the copy of a copy" [767]). This is done
despite his conviction that "there are several such words that
want mollifying in our language" [768]).

The occasional care of Newton in questions of the language
of older English poetry is probably best seen in his treatment
of Milton's old accents, particularly of those of classical
origin. His other linguistic remarks are less interesting, as a
rule, but in this department he takes care to study the usage
of the Elizabethans, especially of Spenser and Fairfax. He has
evidently made good use of the verbal index added to his edition
of "Paradise Lost", e. g. in his study of the stress of "blasphemous". He shows from P. L. V. 809 and VI. 360 that Milton
apparently accentuated the second syllable of the word [769]).
The only further example in Milton's poetry (in P. R. IV. 181)
is not mentioned, probably because there was no exact index to
the other works. The form is illustrated from Spenser. Similar
observations [770]) are found repeatedly.

---

[766]) P. L. V. 399 — cf. Peck's chapter on style, § 3, on the problem of
the "softening" of words.

[767]) The following list of not quite common Miltonic spellings retained
by Newton in book I of "Paradise Lost", which for various reasons appear
to be of interest, might help to realize the intentions of the editor: "advent-
rous" l. 13, "rhime" l. 16, "center" l. 74, "beest" l. 84, "skaly" l. 206,
"Farewel" l. 249, "watry" l. 397, "fertil" l. 468, "swage" l. 556, "dazling"
l. 564, "Sluc'd" l. 702, "jocond" l. 787. Some of these may have been left
in the text accidentally, but the above-mentioned remark in Newton's preface
makes it likely that the retention of at least part of them was deliberate.
Such forms as "skaly", "swage", "beest" may have attracted Newton by their
picturesqueness, as it is not quite clear what peculiar phonetic meaning he
may have ascribed to them.

[768]) P. L. III. 627 n.

[769]) P. L. V. 809 n.

[770]) On "future" P. L. X. 840 n., "Proserpin" ib. IV. 268 n., "surface"
ib. VI. 472 n., "prostrate" ib. VI. 841 n.

Newton's objection to what is unusual, and consequently to most things peculiar to his author, except in so far as the taste of the eighteenth century had accepted them, appears in his notes on the poet's manner of expression. Milton's borrowings from the style of the romances of chivalry are treated with the same dislike as his early enthusiasm for them [771]. "Soldan" instead of "Sultan", "Panim" instead of "Pagan", "Rhene" and "Danaw" instead of "Rhine" and "Danube" — all of them forms occurring in romantic poetry, as Newton probably knew, for at least "Soldan" and "Panim" are shown by him to be found in Spenser — are met with disapproval [772]. He seems to ignore the archaic atmosphere apparently aimed at in these and other expressions [773]. Uncommonness of style is attacked by him, in the spirit of Bentley. The use of uncommon words, "when the common ones would suit the measure as well", is found to be mere affectation [774]. Milton's supposed belief that this "added to the dignity of his language" is received sarcastically. Newton finds no affectation in other expressions equally uncommon but taken from the sphere of classical antiquity. He must have felt the pleasing associations of classical words more keenly than those of a romantic vocabulary, exactly as he understood the atmosphere of classical mythology better than that of the fictions of romance [775]. "Frizl'd hair implicit" [776] finds his approval. Here he even decides that the unusual words improve the style: "The subject is low, and therefore he [= Milton] is forc'd to raise the expression" (*ibid.*) — this in spite of a certain artificiality and preciosity in the metaphor. The probable classical origin of the phrase seems to impress him here, for he explains it himself as alluding to the ancient sense of "coma" [here = "leaves, twigs and branches"]. Again another device of style imparting to the language a certain "cast of antiquity" due to classical and biblical associations, is praised in P. L. IV. 660 *n*.

Newton's conservatism does not go so far as to deny to Milton

---

[771] Cf. above.
[772] P. L. I. 764 *n*.
[773] Cf. the references to Aspramont, Montalban, & c. in I. 583 *et seq.*
[774] P. L. I. 764 *n*.
[775] Cf. above.
[776] P. L. VII. 323 *n*.

the right of coining new words. "Hosting" [777]) is found to be a "very expressive word" the coinage of which is justified because "the occasion is so new and extraordinary". It has, however, to be taken into account that Newton's opinion may not be independent, for Pearce had already defended this expression, vindicating the poet's right of verbal invention.

Peck appears to have been Newton's model in his treatment of Milton's use of one part of speech in the sense of another. Both the approach to the problem and its illustration resemble those in Peck's book, as particularly P. L. IX. 227 *n.* shows, where nearly every detail seems to have been taken from Peck's remarks [778]) although Newton's method is rather more analytical [779]).

Milton's word-order, which had been dealt with repeatedly [780]), is discussed in some of the more characteristic remarks of Newton. It is natural that the perfectly "regular" device of Milton's symmetrical arrangements of words does not fail to appeal to Newton [781]). The emphatic effect produced by the position of identical, synonymous or contrasted expressions first at the beginning and then at the end of a syntactic unit is pointed out by him [782]). A case of similar though even more rigid symmetry is found in P. L. II. 559, where the addition of epithets to the repeated nouns varies and deepens the impression. Newton's interpretation of this device is largely borrowed from Richardson [783]) who, like Newton, mentions the analogy of the "mazes" of the mind described there to the "Wandring Maze" of the word-order. Newton here uses his habitual method of elaborating the suggestions of earlier critics. He adds some observations on the technical aspect of the matter, indicating that the peculiar effect is caused by the "turn of the words", *i. e.* by their inver-

---

[777]) P. L. VI. 93 *n.*

[778]) Cf. Peck, chapter on style.

[779]) Cf. also P. L. IX. 169 *n.*

[780]) Cf. above, and see Peck's section on this problem in his chapter on Milton's style.

[781]) Cf. P. L. II. 737, X. 572 *nn.*

[782]) Cf. P. L. X. 570 *n.* — here the contrast between: "so oft they fell" — "once lapst".

[783]) P. L. II. 558 *n.*

sion, and showing the strengthening of the nouns by means of characteristic adjectives [784]).

Despite the endeavours of his predecessors to do justice to Milton's elliptic style, Newton still feels uncertain as to some cases of it. An interesting example is P. L. III. 49 *n.* Lines 46—50 [785]) apparently constitute a number of parallel participial clauses subordinated to the pronoun "me" [786]) and an absolute sentence which is co-ordinated with these clauses, though not very clearly, and though it does not formally depend on the pronoun. Verity describes it as "an absolute construction, added rather loosely as a sort of climax to the whole sentence" [787]), quoting several convincing examples of similar carelessly connected absolute participial constructions [788]).

Pearce, who had his special reasons, (he evidently disliked, as did Bentley, the inaccuracy of the expression "A universal blank of Nature's works"), proposed to alter "Of Nature's" into "All Nature's". Newton likes the emendation, but for considerations of his own. He is puzzled by the absence of a link to connect the last part of the period with what precedes: "... it is not easy to say what the conjunction *And* copulates *wisdom* to". It appears that the possibility of bold omissions of conjunctions like those exemplified by Verity does not even occur to him. There have also been other explanations. Todd [789]) recommends to regard

---

[784]). Another feature of Milton's word-order, which was also dealt with by Peck (chapter on style § XXV), *viz.* the position of a verb between two accusatives governed by it, is discussed by a "great man" who remains anonymous (P. L. VI. 713 *n.*). He proposes an emendation restoring the ordinary syntax, without respecting Milton's individual style, though this latter seems particularly suitable here, if only for the retardation of the otherwise possibly too colloquial flow of the passage. Newton quotes his opinion without the least sign of disagreement.

[785])   ..... ever-during dark
        Surrounds me, from the chearful waies of men
        Cut off, and for the Book of knowledg fair
        Presented with a Universal blanc
        Of Natures works to mee expung'd and ras'd,
        And wisdome at one entrance quite shut out.

[786]) l. 46.

[787]) Ed. of P. L., III. 50 *n.*

[788]) From Lyc. 128, 129, and the "Animadversions".

[789]) P. L. III. 48 *n.*

243

"wisdom as the genetive case; of nature's works, and *of* wisdom
& c." but he adds no parallels to support his conjecture. Yet even
according to this interpretation the construction would remain
elliptic. Newton apparently regarded the matter too much from
the point of view of the everyday languge of his time in which
the use of ellipses had become less general.

The same lack of historical perspective is shown by his
explanation of the unusual accusative in "muttering thunder" 790).
Newton describes it as an "ablative case absolute", though in this
case the verb ought to follow the noun. Dunster proposes the more
natural solution that thunder is an accusative, which is confirmed
by the parallel cited by Todd from Co. 804: ... "the wrath of *Jove*
Speaks thunder" 791).

It would be unfair to assert that the majority of Newton's
remarks contain only negative features like the above. A considerable number of notes help to throw light on points of style.
Even the emotional background of certain syntactical irregularities is taken into account, as in P. L. X. 758 *n.* where the changes
of the grammatical person in Adam's soliloquy are described. The
"change of passions" and the "change of persons" seem indeed to
go hand in hand, as Newton maintains. Adam partly talks of
himself in the ordinary manner, using the first person, and partly
addresses himself in the second person, whenever he becomes
particularly emotional or rhetorical 792).

A structural device evidently designed to keep a long and
involved sentence clear is described in P. L. VI. 472 *n.* The nominative "which of us" 793) is so wide apart from the verb belonging to it that a new nominative ("whose eye", l. 476) has to be
thrown in.

Emotional influences on the structure of sentences are taken
into consideration where the breaking, splitting influence of haste
is described. This had been done by others 794) but Newton traces
this feature with particular attention. The "hurry of the Angels"
is supposed to have caused the "short periods, without any partic-

---

790) P. L. IX. 1002 *n.*
791) Cf. Todd's note on the same passage.
792) Cf. Verity P. L. X. 758: *"thou didst,* addressing himself, not his
Maker, as in 743—55. The abrupt transitions show his emotion."
793) VI. 472.
794) Cf. above, on Bentley.

les to connect them" in P. L. VI. 507 *et seq.* [795]). Similar cases of *asyndeta* were already taken notice of by Bentley [796]). A short sentence following a long period appears to denote a similar mood in P. L. IV. 560. Newton finds "This abruptness ... very elegant and proper to express the haste that he [= Uriel] was in" [797]). The "broken" style of P. L. IX. 1162 [798]) is explained in a very similar manner: "As Adam is now first angry, his speech is abrupt and his sentences broken". The lack of a link to connect P. L. V. 211 ("On to thir mornings rural work"...) with the preceding lines displeases both Bentley and Pearce. They try to emend it resp. to explain it away. Even Pearce would prefer a smoother construction. Newton accepts the irregularity, finding a sufficient explanation in the impression of haste it produces, though at the same time he tentatively proposes an "easy alteration".

The opposite tendency, that of retardation, of producing the effect of slowness, is discussed in a note dealing with a special device of Milton, which, it is true, falls beyond the scope of syntax. Milton in depicting Vulcan's fall in P. L. I. 742 *et seq.* dwells carefully on the various moments of the fall, apparently in order to make its duration more intensely felt. Here the effect of *concrete details* is well traced, with a penetration which strikes one sometimes though not frequently in Newton's notes on matters requiring no very deep psychological insight.

In the above, only a selection was given of Newton's more typical remarks on technical problems of style. They should suffice to give some idea of his methods of observation and analysis. His classical propensities, his respect for the authority of the Bible, appear here as almost everywhere else. His deficient understanding of some of the fundamental peculiarities of Milton often prevents his conscientious research from attaining to considerable results. "Regular" features suit him better than irregularities, as, for example, his treatment of Milton's word-order shows. His study of the psychological agents influencing Milton's syntax does not go very far, but even here some details

---

[795]) P. L. VI. 507 *n.*
[796]) Cf. above, on Bentley, as before.
[797]) P. L. IV. 560 *n.*
[798]) Cf. *n. ibid.*

are shown quite successfully, as the preceding pages may have proved.

Beside Newton's own notes, there are scattered all over his commentary a number of observations by unknown contributors, in which there is more insight and skill of illustration than in his own remarks. His preface to the edition of "Paradise Lost" [799]) mentions the receipt of some contributions by people who wished to remain anonymous or were unknown to him. In the passage on the Paradise of Fools [800]) the apparently defective phrase "many more too long", which seems to lack a verb and a connecting-link with the next verse, leads Pearce to the conjecture that a line must have been omitted. According to Newton's note, a "very ingenious person" supposes this to be a mere "appearance of inaccuracy and negligence" designed "to express his [= Milton's] contempt of their *trumpery* as he calls it, by hustling it all together in this disorder and confusion". The supposition, whether right or wrong, takes into account the general mood of the passage. That Pearce's conjecture does not correspond with the facts, is definitely proved by a reference to P. R. II. 188—9 where exactly the same phrase is found, being divided between two lines, so as to make any insertion impossible.

A remarkable figure, a typical "irregularity", is described and excellently illustrated in another anonymous note [801]). The contributor (called by Newton "a very learned and ingenious friend") accepts as genuine and intentional the apparently incongruous device of first treating of the part of some larger unit and then unexpectedly continuing as if not the part but the whole was meant ["th' Eternal eye... saw Rebellion rising... And smiling to his only Son thus said"]. That this is not only a chance whim or casual slip but quite probably a device common to the period of Milton or of his immediate predecessors is indicated by some quotations from Spenser's "Epithalamion". Spenser describes "Her long loose yellow locks" which "Do like a golden mantle her attire", but at the same time "being crowned with a garland green, *Seem* like some maiden queen", and similarly "Her modest eyes" that "blush to hear her praises sung so loud,

---

[799]) Ed. 1749, sig. a$_4$v.
[800]) P. L. III. 473.
[801]) P. L. V. 711 *n*.

So far from being proud". Here one and the same device occurs twice in the same stanza and therefore could hardly be attributed to a mere accident. The historical method used here makes it more than probable that the same is true of the Miltonic passage.

J. NEWTON ON MILTON'S CHARACTERS.

It sometimes happens that Newton feels attracted by the extreme, violent features of Milton's characters. He is evidently impressed by the "truly diabolical sentiment", as he called it, of Satan's menaces of revenge: „So he can but be any ways reveng'd, he does not value tho' his revenge recoil on himself" [802]). But such cases of involuntary admiration for grandeur as such, no matter whether it takes a form which is traditionally good or evil, are exceptional. Newton's general moderation agrees better with the Aristotelian doctrine used by him to justify the poet's sympathetic treatment of Satan: "...herein he has follow'd the rule of Aristotle in his Poetics, chapter 15, that the manner should be as good as the nature of the subject will possibly admit. A Devil all made up of wickedness would be too shocking to any reader or writer" [803]). It is apparently this "shocking" quality which most of all deters Newton. He prefers gentler features. It is instructive to compare his interpretation of Adam's question to Raphael in P. L. V. 467 with Dunster's explanation in Todd's edition of Milton. Adam's "wary speech" describes the angel's condescension to eat earthly food, as if it were equal to the repasts of Heaven. He concludes by exclaiming: "yet what compare?". Newton interprets this as an indirect, respectful expression of his desire to know whether there could be any comparison between those two kinds of repasts, whereas Dunster regards it as "the exclamation of admiration at the superior joys of Heaven, as suggested by the superior nature, the 'radiant form and divine effulgence', of his heavenly visitor". Both interpretations seem plausible but Newton's insistence on Adam's modesty and reserve is typical.

---

[802]) P. L. IX. 173 n.
[803]) P. L. II. 483 n.

It is no exceptional feature if Milton makes his characters express his own personal opinions instead of conforming to the rules of verisimilitude. Newton notices the inconsistencies in Milton's representation of Adam. He condemns Adam's anachronistic utterances, the notions of a "Peripatetick" expressed in his despairing soliloquy after the fall [804]) as well as the "trifles, quirks, jingles, and other such prettinesses" incompatible with his character. His inference is that this is a blunder on the poet's part: "Aliquando bonus dormitat Homerus". It is true that his note follows Bentley's corresponding remark very closely but he apparently assimilates the latter's opinions so as actually to make them his own. Nevertheless, he is surprised sixty lines later [805]) at Adam's statement that contradictions are impossible in God, as they are arguments "Of weakness, not of Power". Instead of regarding this introduction of complicated philosophy as one of the usual inconsistencies of Milton, he speculates as to where Adam might have heard this scholastic doctrine, as if he were a real being, not the creation of a poet. He draws the inference that he must have learned it from the angels: "we must suppose that it was *held* likewise by the Angels, of whom he might have learned it in discourse". One might regard this as irony, did not Newton elsewhere in all earnest discuss the question whether the angels use food or not, arriving at an affirmative conclusion [806]). He apparently deals with the whole matter as if it were real, instead of regarding the anachronism of Adam's scholastic mode of thought as an instance of Homer nodding.

At times Newton shows greater ability to understand the relativity of all characterization, insisting less on the necessity of verisimilitude and taking into account the general character of the work. It has already been shown that the only excuse he found in P. L. II. 965 *n.* for Milton's introduction of the improbable allegorical figures of Sin and Death was the occurrence of similar characters in ancient poetry. In a later note Newton points out that nearly all the events take place in the invisible world, and that "such fictitious beings may better have a place there", as the actions of Sin and Death are "at least as probable as those ascribed

[804]) P. L. X. 740 *n.*
[805]) P. L. X. 800 *n.*
[806]) Cf. P. L. V. 435 *n.* and above.

to the good or evil Angels" [807]). This unusual concession to the imagination is, however, supported by the authority of the Bible, in accordance with Newton's habit of taking recourse either to the Scriptures or the classics: "...the characters of Sin and Death are perfectly agreeable to the hints and sketches, which are given of them in Scripture" [808]). The view that fiction as such is justified in itself, apart from any accepted literary models, seems to be foreign to Newton.

However, even the authority of the Bible is insufficient to reconcile Newton to some of the cruder expressions used by Milton's God, which have approximate parallels in Scripture. In P. L. X. 616 *n.* he finds the metaphors in the speech of God to his heavenly audience "wonderfully coarse indeed" and "beneath the dignity of an epic poem" as well as "unbecoming the majesty of the divine Speaker". There is naturally less objection to these offences against the "grand style" where they occur in the speeches of the infernal angels. The much-censured puns in book VI of "Paradise Lost" are excused where they happen to be made by Belial, whereas this "sportive manner" is found to agree very little with the temper of some of the less depraved fallen spirits (such as Beelzebub or Moloch, cf. P. L. VI. 620 *n.*). Dunster afterwards points out (*ibid.*, ed. Todd) that not only Belial but even Satan, that more heroic spirit, uses this style. Newton, though he does not defend Satan's behaviour [809]), quotes without any objection Thyer's remark on the appropriateness of this manner to the rebellious angels: "such kind of insulting wit being most peculiar to proud contemptuous Spirits" [810]). He apparently agrees with this observation, but it is typical that the actual formulation of this freer attitude is by Thyer.

Sometimes Newton goes deep into a situation, calculating minutely the gestures and even the metre used to express the moods of Milton's characters. His keen sense of concrete details, which has to make up for his lack of Thyer's sensitiveness to shifting, complicated frames of mind, is his greatest help here, *e. g.* in a note objecting to Bentley's alteration of P. L. VI. 189

---

[807]) P. L. X. 230 *n.*
[808]) *Ibid.*
[809]) Cf. P. L. VI. 568 *n.*
[810]) *Ibid.*

("So saying, a noble stroke he lifted high"> "So said" ... & c.). Milton's very dramatic reading which in one moment comprizes two actions — those of speaking and striking — appeals more to Newton than "Dr. Bentley's reading *So said*, as if he had not aim'd his blow, till after he had spoken" [811]). The intenseness of the situation is traced also in the metre. "Saying" adds a vibration to the line, expressing the agitation of the speaker, or, as Newton puts it, *"Saying* is here contracted into one syllable, or is to be pronounc'd as two short ones, which very well expresses the eagerness of the angel".

Yet these excursions into independent observation are far less conspicuous than Newton's ordinary commonplace accentuation of decorum and conventional beauty. Eve's modest behaviour, her retirement from the abstruse conversations of Adam and the angel, are in conformity to his ideals [812]), though he is not unconscious of the greater classicist principle of dignity and grandeur, for in the same note he dwells on the combination of "majesty and grace" with the "lowliness" of Eve's deport. Nevertheless, this remains a somewhat homely ideal compared with Satan's superhuman greatness which apparently was somewhat beyond the range of the critical code of Newton.

K. NEWTON'S VIEWS ON MILTON'S VERSE.

Newton's treatment of Milton's verse is very considerably influenced by the "Letters concerning Poetical Translations" [813]), a work repeatedly quoted by him [814]). This pamphlet contains a number of interesting observations, and the remarks borrowed from it differ from Newton's own notes in their greater insight and livelier style. Most of them deal with problems of metre and euphony. They should be examined here, as their influence on Newton's own views is obvious.

The briefest formulation of what is probably the main metrical principle of Newton is found in his note on the two last

---

[811]) P. L. VI. 189 *n.*
[812]) P. L. VIII. 40 *n.*
[813]) Cf. above, footnote.
[814]) Cf. *e. g.* P. L. XI. 141, 707 *nn.*

lines of "Paradise Lost". It is the principle of metrical variety achieved by a varied disposition of the pauses: "the varying of the pauses, which is the life and soul of all versification in all languages". "It is this chiefly which makes Virgil's verse better than Ovid's, and Milton's superior to any other English poet's" (*ibid.*). Newton most resolutely opposes the monotony of the French practice, possibly thinking also of Pope whom he mentions in a similar connection in his first note to the poem. The lack of variety in the pauses is in his view the only reason why "the French heroic verse has never, and can never come up to the English". The monotonous French pauses in his opinion "either offend the reader, or lull him asleep" (*ibid.*). Newton's radicalism is surprising considering his habitual conservatism but it loses some of its strikingness by being traced back to a passage in "Poet. Transl." which differs from Newton's note only in its style 815).

The practice of English poetry may be taken as proof that the more liberal attitude is justified, as its influence on literature has been more fertile than that of the narrow standards of conservative critics. Newton deals with the matter in his first note to "Paradise Lost" 816). There he expressly contradicts a remark made by Pope in a letter to Walsh, according to which "in any smooth English verse of ten syllables, there is naturally a pause at the fourth, fifth, or sixth syllable, and upon the judicious change and management of these depends the variety of versification". Milton, on the contrary, uses pauses in all parts of the verse, "and scarce ever suffers it [= the pause] to rest upon the same syllable in more than two, and seldom in so many as two, verses together", "by which means he is master of greater harmony than any other English poet". These statements are carefully illustrated by Newton. As an example, the first six verses of "Paradise Lost" are quoted, down to the words "Sing heav'nly Muse". The same passage is cited in p. 40 of the pamphlet, for exactly the same purpose of exemplifying Milton's skill in varying the pauses.

---

815) "...the eternal Repetition of the same Pause is the Reverse of Harmony: Three Feet and three Feet for thousands of Lines together, make exactly the same Musick as the ting, tong, tang of the same Number of Bells in a Country-Church" (p. 74).

816) P. L. I. 1 *n.*

Newton adds instances of every kind of pause possible within the limits of a blank-verse line, starting with the pause after the first syllable and ending with the break before the last. An analogical case is found in p. 36 of "Poet. Transl.", though the arrangement is the reverse of that given by Newton: the position of the pause moves from the end of the verse towards the beginning, the last verse quoted having it after the first foot.

Newton apparently takes quite an unusual interest in the pause following the first syllable of a blank-verse line. He generally finds it used after a verb, in order "to mark the action more strongly [817]). This he supposes to be regularly the case with Homer's pauses after the first foot, whereas Milton is shown to use the break also where a line begins with a noun or an adjective [818]). His own examples are mainly of pauses after verbs [819]). He seems to be following the lead of "Poet. Transl." for there it is discussed more than once, and in at least one case Newton undeniably becomes a mere copyist. Newton's note on P. L. XI. 489 is in part an accurate repetition of the substance of a remark on p. 45 of "Poet. Transl." though the words are altered [820]).

The comprehensive note on P. L. I. 1 treats not only of Milton's pauses but also of the problems of accent and quantity in his verse. Newton finds that Milton's metre "is to be measur'd

---

[817]) P. L. IX. 122 n.

[818]) Ibid.

[819]) Cf. P. L. VII. 548 n., P. L. IV. 351 n.

[820]) Both critics comment there on the passage (P. L. XI. 491—2): "And over them triumphant Death his Dart Shook, but delaid to strike..." Both of them dwell on the effect of the verb "shook" being placed before the isolating pause. In "Poet. Transl." it is described how "This Passage makes the Reader see Death with his Dart in his Hand, shaking it over the Heads of the unhappy Creatures describ'd in the Lazar-house, as plainly as if the whole was painted upon Canvas" (p. 46). Newton seems to echo this: "One thinks one almost sees the dart shaking" (XI. 489 n.). In the pamphlet an experiment is made: „But let this Line be alter'd thus: Over their Heads Death shook his dreadful Dart. How much of the Fire and Spirit of this Passage is lost, will be easily perceiv'd" (p. 46). Newton's imitation of this is very faithful, although his alteration keeps more closely to Milton's text: "If the line was to be alter'd, as thus, And o'er them Death triumphant shook his Dart, much of the fire and spirit would be lost" (Ubi supra). Examples of almost equally faithful borrowings might be found without much difficulty.

by the tone and accent, as well as by the time and quantity". He apparently tries to prove this by quoting some "almost pure Iambics", where, as a matter of fact, length and stress coincide with considerable regularity:

"He call'd so loud, that all the hollow Deep
Of Hell resounded" [821]).

In a number of other examples there is no such coincidence. The ordinary stress and the scansion clash [822]), though the common pronunciation would fit perfectly into the metrical scheme. Newton even scans the verses so as to upset the metre, as in the example of the tribrachus, blindly applying the principle of quantity even though it makes the verse unreadable.

It is not unlikely that the "Poet. Transl." contributed to this confusion. Its author's interpretation of the concept of quantity is not quite clear. He protests against those foreigners, particularly Vossius, who, as he says, assert that "there is no such thing as Measure or Feet, or long or short Syllables in *English* Words" [823]). Nevertheless, he does not regard English verse as purely quantitative. He either thinks that it is capable of combining both stress and quantity, or else he employs the wrong word, using "quantity" in the sense of stress. The examples of perfect Iambics which he gives like Newton, would dispose one in favour of the former possibility, for like those given by Newton they nearly satisfy the requirements of ancient prosody, being also regular from the point of view of accentuated verse (*e. g.* "Divine, Attend, Directs", "The Lord"). In a case like "The Man" the length of the second syllable is questionable though contemporary phonetics would prove that it is much longer than the first, unstressed one. One or two cases of scansion might possibly be due to the critic's adoption of the quantitative principle, *e. g.* "Thus to his Son au-dī-bly spake" (p. 50 of "Poet. Transl.": "For so it must be read and not after the common manner") or "Thro' the in-fī-nite Host" (*ibid.*). Yet the author's description of what

---

[821]) P. L. I. 314 & c.

[822]) Cf. *ibid.* the example of the "Anapaest or foot of two short and one long syllable ᴗ ᴗ — ...

Mȳrĭāds though bright! If he whom mutual league"... or of the "Tribrachus or foot of three short syllables ᴗ ᴗ ᴗ ...

Tŏ mănў a row of pipes the sound-board breathes"...

[823]) p. 69.

he regards as a long syllable might equally well apply to mere stress. He says of the examples "The Lord, The Man, The Rock" that "...the last Syllable strikes the Ear more than the first, or, in other Words, the last is longer than the first, which is all that makes an Iambic *Latin* Foot". The impression that the sounds "strike the ear" is even more typical of stress than of quantity, which is mere duration, though in the classical metrical tradition it is apparently *combined* with stress.

The treatment in Newton's notes of contraction and elision is inconsistent. Milton's "contractions" are defined as two syllables "contracted into one or pronounc'd as two short ones" (V. 482 *n.* — here said with regard to the word "spirits"). The only conclusion that may be drawn more or less safely is that two syllables are supposed to act as one with respect to the metrical scheme. It remains a problem whether the actual pronunciation is merely considered to be more rapid and brief than usual or the vowel to be dropped altogether. Newton's treatment of elision would incline one to assume the latter, for he conjectures that Milton like "Shakespear and others of our old poets ... in imitation of the Greeks and Latins often cuts off the vowel at the end of a word, when the next word begins with a vowel" [824]). The vowel according to him seems to be retained only in the spelling [825]) : "he does not like the Greeks wholly drop the vowel, but still retains it in writing like the Latins" [826]).

Alliteration and descriptive effects of various kinds are repeatedly discussed by Newton, the "ridiculous degree of affectation" to which the former device is said to have been carried by the "Moderns" being contrasted with Milton's sparing use of it [827]). Here again the "Poet. Transl." are followed, as in VII. 470 *n.* where the same Miltonic and Virgilian instances are quoted. In general, in his notes on metre, Newton shows little logic, as in his conception of quantity, and very little independence, even his main principle, that of the variety of the pauses, being obviously borrowed in nearly all its details.

---

[824]) P. L. I. 38 *n.*
[825]) But cf. P. L. VI. 189 *n.* where a case of contraction is apparently pronounced without omitting the supernumerary vowel (cf. above).
[826]) *Ibid.*
[827]) P. L. IX. 901.

10. THE PERIOD BETWEEN NEWTON'S AND THOMAS WARTON'S EDITIONS (1749—1785).

The publication of Newton's edition was an event of considerable importance and seems to have discouraged Milton scholars from undertaking anything on a similar scale, at least for a while. Of the commentary on "Paradise Lost" by Callander of Craigforth which was more comprehensive than the popularizing publications fashionable at that time, only the first book was published, the rest being deposited with the Society of Scottish Antiquaries [828]). Its design is different from that of Newton's edition. According to the advertisement, its chief object is to illustrate Milton's mythological allusions and to quote classical parallels to his poem. The suggestion has been made that the work is, to a great extent, a plagiarism from Hume's commentary [829]). The copious parallels given by the accuser prove, in the opininon of the present writer, that Callander did not scruple to borrow without acknowledgment, but the same, as is shown in our appendix, is true of Newton. A minute comparison might discover further debts to earlier Miltonic research. It is clear, for instance, that Callander owes much to Addison. The note on the exordium of the poem is a fair example of the influence of the "Spectator" articles on many of the more theoretical notes in the volume. Both Callander and Addison — the latter towards the beginning of his first article on "Paradise Lost" — describe Milton's classicist practice of plunging into *medias res* and afterwards relating the

---

[828] MILTON'S PARADISE LOST, BOOK I. — *ΚΑΛΟΝ ΑΚΟΥΕΜΕΝ ΕΣΤΙΝ ΑΟΙΔΟΥ ΤΟΙΟΥΔΕ ΟΙΟΣ ΟΔΕ ΕΣΤΙ, ΘΕΟΙΣ ΕΝΑΛΙΓΚΙΟΣ ΑΥΔΗΝ.* HOM. GLASGOW: PRINTED AND SOLD BY ROBERT AND ANDREW FOULIS PRINTERS TO THE UNIVERSITY. M.DCC.L.

4°: pp. [4] + 167.

The author is, according to the DNB, the Scottish antiquary John Callander of Craigforth, Stirlingshire, fellow of the Society of Antiquaries of Scotland. He presented the Society with various MSS., among others with 9 volumes of notes on Milton, whereof only those contained in the above-mentioned publication were ever brought out.

[829] A contributor to "Blackwood's Magazine" (IV. 658—62) compared the two commentaries, whereupon the Society of Scottish Antiquaries appointed a committee to settle the problem. The result was that only a comparatively small proportion of Callander's notes were found to be borrowed from Hume but his obligations to be insufficiently acknowledged (cf. DNB).

earlier events by way of episodes. Both adduce the same classical examples and mention, in almost identical words, Horace's remark on the ridiculous effect which might have been produced had Homer started his account of the Trojan war with a description of Leda's offspring. Similar parallels are frequent.

Callander's knowledge of historical and mythological works is very considerable and his notes abound in learned references. However, he hardly succeeds in interpreting the spirit and artistic significance of the material collected by him, though his method is logical and orderly. Only in some chance notes are traces of the commentator's critical views to be found.

Callander's theoretical views show a classicism hardly less extreme than Newton's, though the former critic is probably more cultured and intelligent, as indicated by the very fluency and subtlety of his style. The classical theorists of poetry are Callander's chief authorities; Aristotle and Quinctilian are not infrequently mentioned by him [830]). Classical precedents are overrated and sometimes become the writer's main criteria [831]), whereas romantic subjects are often depreciated [832]). All this, no less than the objections to deviation from history [833]), reminds one of Newton, although the unhistorical mention of the name of Busiris as the Pharaoh who was drowned in the Red Sea is excused, possibly in imitition of Pearce, for the reason that Milton presumably did not mean it to be fictitious and may have borrowed it from historians, e. g. from Sir Walter Raleigh [834]). This, as a mere apology for the poet, does not greatly affect the fundamental point of view. Digressions from reality and history are regarded as excusable under certain conditions though still in themselves faulty. Accuracy in representing historical facts or ancient mythology is, on the contrary, valued [835]), and Callander makes a careful study of the actual circumstances connected with the names and events mentioned by Milton [836]). Particular value seems to be attached to accuracy in scriptural matters, and the

---

[830]) *E. g.* ll. 48, 282 *nn.*
[831]) Cf. ll. 198, 229 *nn.*
[832]) Cf. p. 123.
[833]) Cf. p. 123.
[834]) I. 307 *n.*
[835]) See ll. 438, 449 *nn.*
[836]) Cf. pp. 52—53 on the description of the Northern invasions.

alteration of a biblical name is regarded as admissible only because the name is derived from an apocryphal book [837]).

Imagery connected with contemporary subjects is sometimes praised, but apparently only where it is true to fact, as *e.*, *g.* in the astronomical simile describing the studies of the "Tuscan Artist" in Valdarno [838]). The exact correspondence of similes to the subjects they illustrate receives much attention and appreciation, *e. g.* in I. 302 *n.* where emphasis is laid upon the greater variety and elaboration of Milton as compared with the classics.

Callander's careful analysis is scholarly and delicate. Sometimes his inquiries into the actual background of Milton's fiction lead to the discovery of details which may have been present to the poet's mind and influenced the artistic character of his work. Callander's investigation of the scenery of the Red Sea enables him to point to the suggestive pale greenish colour of its sedge, a feature harmonizing with the "withered glory" of the angels [839]). The value of this observation depends to a great extent on the sensitiveness to visual effects shown repeatedly by the critic, *e. g.* in the remark on the typical Miltonic "sudden blaze" [840]), which is found to surpass the corresponding effects of illumination in Homer, Lucretius and Virgil owing to its use of contrast.

Callander's scholarly cast of mind appears in his references to technicalities of classical poetry and to their echoes in Milton. Thus, the commentator points out the resemblance of Milton's mention of the places where he supposes his muse to reside, to the πολυωνυμία of the classics [841]). More ingenuity is sometimes shown in the examination of allusions to classical *realia*. The likening of Satan's shield in P. L. I. 288 to the moon with its mountains and rivers is compared to the classical manner of raising figures on shields — a practice which, as Callander shows, is mentioned by Milton. himself in P. L. VI. 83—84 ("Shields Various, with boastful Argument portraid"). This analogy, not

---

[837]) See p. 155.
[838]) I. 290 *n.*
[839]) I. 306 *n.*
[840]) I. 665 *n.*
[841]) I. 10 *n.*

previously noticed, undoubtedly diversifies the impression produced by the poet's imagery. However, Callander's tendency to encyclopædic completeness produces merely a more or less detailed account of classical instances of the above habit instead of an analysis of Milton's artistry.

Older English poetry is not drawn upon very frequently but some of its peculiarities are discussed. The invention of fantastic names by Spenser is referred to in connection with the Miltonic proper name "Pandæmonium" [842]. Callander knows that Spenser named his heroes according to their characters, forming their names "indifferently from any language, that best suited his purpose. Our poet has imitated him in this liberty". Shakespeare [843] and Chaucer [844] are mentioned repeatedly, while mediæval matters are investigated with much erudition [845]. The great number of authorities on the dark ages quoted by Callander proves his interest in this period though he shows no understanding of the atmosphere of Milton's mediæval allusions. He confines himself to a parade of his own wide reading, instead of studying the sources used by Milton and their effect on his poetry.

Callander's culture and erudition make the work pleasant reading though it contributes little to the understanding of Milton's artistic intentions. It is undertaken on a large scale, differing in this respect from the popularizing editions of that period. A typical instance of this latter class is the edition of "Paradise Lost" by John Marchant [846].

---

[842] Cf. p. 159.
[843] Cf. ll. 241, 266 *nn*.
[844] *E. g.* p. 160.
[845] Cf. p. 160 on mediæval ways of combat, & c.
[846] MILTON'S PARADISE LOST. A POEM, IN TWELVE BOOKS. WITH NOTES, Etymological, Critical, Classical, and Explanatory. Collected from Dr. *Bentley;* Dr. *Pearce,* the present Bishop of *Bangor; Richardson* and Son; *Addison; Paterson; Newton,* and other Authors; intended as a Key to this Divine POEM; whereby Persons unacquainted with the Learned Languages, and Polite Literature, will be introduced into a familiar Acquaintance with the various Beauties and Excellencies of this Master piece [*sic*] of Heroic POETRY. DEDICATED to the KING, *By* JOHN MAR-CHANT, *Gent. Author of the Exposition of the Old and New Testament, & c.* LONDON: Printed by R. WALKER, in the *Little Old Bailey.* MDCCLI. Two volumes, 12-mo. Vol. I: pp. 428. Vol. II: pp. 429—746. — Contains Fenton's life of Milton. With 14 plates.

Marchant's edition is almost entirely based on Newton, from whom most of its notes are taken, the main exceptions being a number of remarks by Paterson and some by the editor himself. Though the work is dedicated to the king and contains some obvious flattery, the editor finds it possible to defend the author's political views, ascribing the supposed hostility to the poet during the first years after the publication of the poem to partiality caused by his republicanism — an attitude which, as he thinks, would have been inevitable even if Milton had "wrote with the Pen of an Angel" [847]).

The praise bestowed on the poem is enthusiastic and refers mainly to its moral intent and learning, "the Nobleness of its Plan, and the rich Treasure of Erudition it contains" [848]). The reputation of the work is regarded as "so prodigiously increased, that it's now the Standard of Heroic Poetry; and he who professes he has no Taste for MILTON, is justly deemed to have no Taste for Polite Literature" [849]). But Marchant regards the poem as more than a mere literary achievement. Anyone who dared to alter the work "even in the minutest Iota, he has been attack'd with as much Vigour and Warmth, as if he had robb'd a Church, or endeavour'd to alter or abolish the establish'd Religion of his Country" [850]), as Marchant describes. This is perhaps the highest praise that could be given to a literary work, were these eulogies not dogmatic, unfounded upon analysis.

The popularizing character of Marchant's edition agrees with his view of Addison's "Critique" that it is too learned [851]). Marchant apparently aims at conciseness, the manner of the Richardsons is found to be too "verbose", though their "curious and uncommon Thoughts" are acknowledged to be valuable. That the editor's aims went beyond mere learning, is clearly indicated by his censure of Paterson who is denied to "enter into the Spirit of our Author" or to "lay down any Rule to direct the Judgment in gathering the Flowers that so profusely grow in this fragrant and ever-blooming Garden." Newton's edition is praised as a

---

[847]) Cf. the dedicatory matter.
[848]) Cf. the preface.
[849]) *Ibid.*
[850]) *Ibid.*
[851]) *Ibid.*

"judicious compilation" but Marchant's own is evidently meant for a different public, for he emphasizes his intention of bringing it out at a cheaper price.

Attacks on Newton's heavy, learned quotations [852]) show that Marchant preferred to work with a lighter apparatus. He does not, however, add any very illuminating or lively remarks on artistic features. The few observations made by himself, though not unsound, are of no particular value. Newton's and Bentley's short-sightedness in condemning Milton's early foreshadowing of an episode later described at greater length, as "wrong Conduct, and want of Oeconomy" [853]), is not imitated by Marchant. He understands that slight preliminary sketches may be of use, and shows convincingly that Milton was in the habit of drawing such sketches [854]). Yet these isolated remarks are too slight to enable one to trace the editor's views on poetry in general and that of Milton in particular. The most prominent feature is his unqualified and indiscriminative praise of the poem, showing the height to which Milton's reputation had attained.

The next independent commentary on Milton's poetry is that by W. Massey [855]). The contemporary reviews are not at all consistent in their views on this publication. The "Critical Review" of 1762 [856]) finds the notes "executed with care and judgment" and probably "of great service to the readers and admirers of Milton", though it is emphasized that this applies "especially to the young and illiterate, who are incapable of relishing many of his [= Milton's] beauties from their ignorance of ancient and modern history". Another reviewer (in the "Monthly Review", vol. 25, pp. 497—8, 1761) finds almost exclusively negative features in the book, deriding its truisms and ex-

---

[852]) *E. g.* P. L. IV. 158 *n.*
[853]) Cf. P. L. II. 1023 *n.* in Newton's edition.
[854]) II. 1021 *n.*
[855]) REMARKS UPON MILTON'S PARADISE LOST. HISTORICAL, GEOGRAPHICAL, PHILOLOGICAL, CRITICAL AND EXPLANATORY. By W. MASSEY. HIC AMOR, HOC STUDIUM. Ovid. LONDON: Printed for G. KEITH, at the *Bible and Crown*, in *Grace-church Street*. MDCCLXI.
12-mo: pp. XXV + 276.
William Massey (1691—1764?) was a miscellaneous writer who translated Ovid and others (cf. DNB).
[856]) Vol. XIII. p. 433.

cessive display of learning and calling attention to the absurd
inconsistency of first declaring the gardens of the Hesperides to
be mere fable and conjecture and then speculating as to the real
character of the golden apples in the gardens, which, as Massey
thinks, were oranges [857]).

These deficiencies, as well as a good many more, must be
admitted, and yet there remains much in the commentary that is
valuable. There are, it is true, unmistakeable traces in it of the
old prejudice that an epic based on divine revelation is more
reliable and therefore more valuable than one founded on mere
fiction [858]). "Paradise Lost" is regarded as superior to the epics
of Homer and Virgil because it rests "on a more certain and interesting Argument", their basis "being extremely fabulous" whereas
Milton's goes back to heavenly inspiration. Nevertheless the right
of poetry to use fiction is acknowledged in other places, as if the
critic was hesitating between two principles. Certain improbabili-
ties are excused as having "to be understood in the Sense of an
imaginative Poet, rather than of a philosophic Reasoner" [859]).
Massey even goes so far as to praise the "imaginary Beings"
invented by Spenser, as productions of a remarkable "creative
Genius" [860]). Massey's artistic instincts apparently induce him
to trespass against the principle by which he acknowledges only
the representation of reality, wherever some example of beautiful
fiction pleases him in an unusual degree. Travellers' stories which
are evidently regarded by him as quite incredible are praised as
"ornaments to poetry" [861]). A totally fictitious and fantastic
passage like that on the Limbo of Vanity, which, moreover, was
condemned by Newton as falling short of the dignity of epic
poetry [862]), is admired by Massey for its abundant imagery, its
"Pindaric Copiousness of Invention", *i. e.* its purely imaginative,
artistic excellence.

This harmonizes with the commentator's great fondness for
Spenser, who to him is the prototype of a spontaneous poetic mind.
Shakespeare is forgotten and Spenser "of all our *English* Poets"

---

[857]) Cf. III. 568 *n*.
[858]) IX. 14 *n*.
[859]) VIII. 615 *n*.
[860]) II. 960 *n*.
[861]) IV. 161 *n*.
[862]) III. 447 *n*.

found to excel in "a natural *Genius* and *lively Invention*" [863]).
His "fruitful Imagination for lively Description" is found to
surpass that of any other poet whom Milton might have imitated [864]). It is evident that Massey's sympathies ran counter to the
formalistic attitude of classicism. Though he does not appear to
have any definite theory of poetry, any imaginative stimuli seem
to affect him strongly, for example those of suggestive vagueness
and haziness, as in the indefinite expressions used by Milton to
describe the vastness of Chaos and original night. Massey finds
"something astonishingly descriptive" in the expression,

"the void profound
Of unessential Night",

pointing out the exciting impression it produces: "Every Word
expresses a horrible Uncertainty, that, wide-gaping, was to receive
the *infernal Monarch*..." The "Stretch of Imagination" shown
by Milton in connecting "the Ideas of *void, profound, unessential,*
and *Night*", whereof "the Assemblage is enough to terrify the
Thoughts of any Creature less than Devil" [865]), attracts him by
its mysterious effect.

The whole attitude is decidedly in advance of Newton's as
regards the commentator's sensitiveness to imaginative qualities.
Inconsistencies and blunders are studied but sometimes excused
if found to be due to "Warmth of Imagination" [866]). A bold,
stirring style stimulates the critic even though he may find it to
clash with his ideals. Sometimes the contrast between the
principles acknowledged intellectually and the qualities enjoyed
instinctively is striking. Some features he condemns though he
is unable to deny the delight he derives from them. There are
"some *daring* Expressions in the best of Poets" which "may be
justly found Fault with" yet "give us more Pleasure perhaps than
if they had been unexceptionable" [867]). These are evidently the
stirrings of a new sense of poetry which had developed in him in
spite of the inability of his theoretical insight to keep pace with it.

---

[863]) XI. 481 *n.*
[864]) III. 640 *n.*
[865]) II. 438 *n.*
[866]) II. 874 *n.*
[867]) I. 63 *n.*

Massey's references to older literature are mainly confined to Chaucer [868]), Spenser [869]), Sandys's Ovid [870]) and Sir Richard Blackmore [871]). He seems to have studied Hickes [872]), yet some of his linguistic instances are grotesque and lead to a complete misunderstanding of Milton's imagery. Thus, it is quite intelligible that Massey sees "a catachrestical Liberty" in Milton's use of the expression "sail-broad vans" for the angel's wings in P. L. II. 927, for he is ignorant of the Italian expression "vanni" meaning "wings", seeing only two possibilities: (1) that the word means "Fanns, that they winnow Corn with, in some Counties of England", or (2) "the Sails of a Wind-mill, which are also termed *Vanes*" [873]). The heroical associations connected with "brand" in its traditional acceptation: "a sword" seem to be foreign to Massey who seems to regard it as a mere metaphorical use of the Saxon expression employed in the sense of "a Piece of Stick, of burning Wood, or a red-hot Iron", failing to note that the traces of this meaning must be relatively feeble in a word which has been used for centuries in a different signification. Massey apparently associates Milton's "flaming brand" in XII. 643 *n.* with the more realistic acceptation, lowering the dignity of the passage. Thus the conclusion drawn by Massey that the supposed audacity of Milton, that "bold Adventurer in adapting old Words to new Meanings", is so extreme that it "would hardly be tolerated in any other Writer", becomes intelligible, considering the critic's inability to appreciate the exact value of his author's expressions. His déficient knowledge of older literature and language would disqualify him from commenting on Milton, particularly if his obsolete theoretical views are taken into account, were it not for his instincts, which go with the new movements in poetry, enabling him to throw light on the importance of the purely imaginative elements in the poet's works.

The same number of the "Critical Review" which acknowledged the "care and judgment" of Massey's performance attacks

---

[868]) Cf. I. 12 *n.*, VII. 457 *n.*, I. 307 *n.*, & c. & c.
[869]) Cf. above.
[870]) *E. g.* I. 728 *n.*
[871]) *E. g.* I. 17, II. 874 *nn.*
[872]) Cf. I. 673 *n.*
[873]) II. 927 *n.*

another commentary, that edited by "the Rev. Mr. Dodd", as good "for none but the very young, ignorant, and illiterate" [874]), and the "Monthly Review" of the same year [875]) derides it even more contemptuously, exclaiming that it "May do well enough for children! Alas! poor Milton! Who knows but thou mayest yet be transformed into a Spelling-book?" The publication to which these observations refer may be said to deserve this ridicule. It differs from most other commentaries in explaining difficult words and concepts not in the order of Milton's text but arranging them alphabetically. The explanations are extremely obvious and hardly add anything new to what had been said before Dodd. Slipshod explanations, e. g. that of the word „Meteor" as "Any bodies in the air or sky that are of a flux and transitory nature" or of "Roseate" as "Rosy, full of roses" [876]) are not very rare. Sometimes the picturesque definitions of earlier annotators are copied word for word, e. g. that of the colouring of the opal (cf. under "opal") where Hume's and Richardson's expressions as found in Newton's edition [877]) are very faithfully repeated [878]). Much of the book is mere encyclopædic information of a primitive kind [879]). The value of the commentary is quite negligible. The preface shows that Dodd is not the author of the notes but had only accepted the offer to write them and afterwards commended the enterprise to a gentleman who has executed his task, as Dodd says, "with good Judgment and Propriety".

Very little is to be said in favour of Wesley's annotated

---

[874]) 1762, vol. XIII, pp. 433—434.

[875]) Vol. 26, p. 478.

[876]) Though the only case of this word in Milton's poetry, "roseate dews" in P. L. V. 646, evidently cannot have the latter meaning.

[877]) P. L. II. 1049 n.

[878]) A FAMILIAR EXPLANATION OF THE POETICAL WORKS OF MILTON. To which is prefixed Mr. ADDISON'S CRITICISM on PARADISE LOST. With a PREFACE By The Rev. Mr. DODD. LONDON: Printed for J. and R. Tonson, in the Strand; and J. NEWBERY, in St. Paul's Church-Yard. MDCCLXII.

12-mo: pp. VII + 144 + [94].

The Rev. Dodd is apparently William Dodd, LL. D., Chaplain to the king, forger and author of the blank-verse poem "Thoughts in Prison" (1777), editor of "Beauties of Shakespeare" (1752).

[879]) E. g. the note on "Diamond".

edition of "Paradise Lost" [880]) which endeavours in a very crude manner to popularize Milton in his capacity as a religious poet. This edition is intended for the simplest readers, for those who are of only a "common Education". For their benefit, Wesley has added "short and easy Notes, intelligible to any uneducated Person, of a tolerably good Understanding" [881]). All those lines which Wesley "despaired of explaining to the unlearned, without using abundance of words", *i. e.* most of the mythological allusions and learned similes, are ruthlessly dropped, whereas the accumulations of biblical names to be found now and then in the work are retained, evidently as being intelligible even to the commonest reader. The result is very similar to that of the excisions of Bentley, who objected on principle to the passages which Wesley omits for practical reasons. The notes are generally explanatory of very elementary matters, and little is to be seen of the editor's personal views. His theological bias is, however, unmistakable and makes it possible that Satan's description of the power of the mind to make "a Heav'n of Hell, a Hell of Heav'n" [882]) is ridiculed as "a fit Rant for a Stoic of a Devil". The excisions are made deftly enough, so as relatively seldom to make alterations of the text itself indispensable, though now and then some expressions have had to be changed for metrical considerations, after the intermediate verses had been dropped.

The posthumous edition of the first six books of "Paradise Lost" by Buchanan [883]) is a work of an entirely scholastic

---

[880]) AN EXTRACT FROM MILTON'S PARADISE LOST. With NOTES LONDON: PRINTED IN THE YEAR MDCCXCI.
12-mo: pp. 335.
The prefatory address "To the Reader" is signed "John Wesley".
[881]) Cf. Preface.
[882]) I. 255 *n.*
[883]) THE FIRST SIX BOOKS OF MILTON'S PARADISE LOST, Rendered into GRAMMATICAL Construction; the Words of the TEXT being arranged, at the bottom of each Page, in the same natural Order with the Conceptions of the mind; and the *Ellipsis* properly supplied, without any Alteration in the Diction of the Poem. WITH NOTES Grammatical, Geographical, Historical, Critical, and Explanatory. To which are prefixed REMARKS on ELLIPSIS and TRANSPOSITION, exhibiting an easy Method of construing and reading with Judgment, either Prose or verse. DESIGNED For the USE of our most eminent Schools, and of private Gentlemen and Ladies; and also of Foreigners of Distinction, who would

character and does not aim at elucidating the original meaning of Milton's text. It is meant "for young readers chiefly", particularly for "our youth of distinction" [884]), its object being to make young people, but also ladies in general, "for whose interest the author professes a very great regard", "tolerable masters of ellipsis and transpositions" [885]), the two main difficulties in Milton's language, as the editor supposes. The title-page of the edition shows Buchanan's method with sufficient clearness. The paraphrases at the bottom of each page normalize the style, though not, as the title suggests, "without any Alteration in the Diction of the Poem". The editor apparently does not understand that Milton's ellipses and peculiar word-order constitute two of the main characteristics of his language and cannot be abolished without affecting the personal idiosyncrasy of his style. A regular, ordinary manner of expression is thought to be preferable, especially as regards the word-order, violent transpositions in prose being found "disgusting" and inconsistent with the style of the "purest writers" [886]). "Irregularities" are condemned as mere carelessness on the part of the writers, even when they are to be observed in the language of the best eighteenth century authors, which might suggest that the divergence from ordinary usage may be deliberate. Thus, Buchanan misunderstands Milton's use of the old preterite form "wert" [887]). He thinks it a subjunctive and deplores the impropriety of the use "of *were* for *was*" ... "in several of our best writers besides Milton, *viz.* Pope, Dryden, Swift, Addison, Prior, Atterbury, & c. who must have been led into such inaccuracies merely from inadvertency" [888]).

Many of the notes that are of any interest are adaptations or even positive plagiarisms. Massey particularly seems to have

---

read this admirable POEM with Unstanding [*sic*] and Taste. By the late JAMES BUCHANAN, Author of the BRITISH GRAMMAR, a Regular ENGLISH SYNTAX, & c. The Manuscript was left with Dr JAMES ROBERTSON, Professor of Hebrew, who has published it for the benefit of Mr BUCHANAN'S WIDOW. EDINBURGH: Printed for A. KINCAID and W. CREECH, and J. BALFOUR. MDCCLXXIII.

8^0: pp. [4] + 444.

[884]) Cf. preface.
[885]) *Ibid.*
[886]) Cf. preface.
[887]) III. 9 *n.*
[888]) *Ibid.*

been drawn upon very frequently. His characteristically appreciative pronouncement on the Paradise of Fools is repeated almost
word for word [889]). The "mixture of pride, envy, contempt, and
resentment" found in Satan's behaviour at the beginning of
book IV, as well as even the emphatic tone of the repetition of the
pronoun "thy" in P. L. IV. 32 are described with the identical
expressions in both commentaries [890]). Even the derivation of
the angel's "vans" from "the sails of a wind-mill, which are called
Vanes" is found here too, as it was in Massey's corresponding
note [891]). The cited examples are chosen from a much larger
number.

The whole period from the edition of Newton to that of
Warton may be characterized as one of popularization, as the
above should have proved. Warton's important edition of Milton's
minor poems marks the beginning of a new era, that of a more
profound study of Milton's sources and his literary and historical
background as well as of a far subtler artistic analysis of his
poetry. Moreover, the classicist attitude which prevailed in most
of the publications discussed in the present chapter, in Warton's
edition gives way to newer and freer tendencies, and the dogmatism
to be found so frequently up to then is replaced by a psychological
method concentrating more closely upon the character of the
poet and the æsthetic effect upon the reader.

---

[889]) Cf. III. 447 *n.*
[890]) Cf. notes to this passage.
[891]) II. 927 *n.* in both books.

11. THOMAS WARTON'S EDITION OF THE MINOR POEMS.

POEMS UPON SEVERAL OCCASIONS, ENGLISH, ITALIAN, AND LATIN, WITH TRANSLATIONS, BY JOHN MILTON. VIZ. LYCIDAS, L'ALLEGRO, IL PENSEROSO, ARCADES, COMUS, ODES, SONNETS, MISCELLANIES, ENGLISH PSALMS, ELEGIARUM LIBER, EPIGRAMMATUM LIBER, SYLVARUM LIBER. WITH NOTES CRITICAL AND EXPLANATORY, AND OTHER ILLUSTRATIONS, BY THOMAS WARTON, FELLOW OF TRINITY COLLEGE AND LATE PROFESSOR OF POETRY AT OXFORD. LONDON, PRINTED FOR JAMES DODSLEY IN PALL-MALL. MDCCLXXXV.

8⁰, pp. XXVIII + 620. *Contents:* p. [I], title; pp. III—XXIV, preface; pp. XXV—XXVIII, table of contents; pp. 1—590, text of poems with notes (including extensive final remarks on "Lycidas", "L'Allegro", "Il Penseroso", "Ad Joannem Rousium"; preliminary remarks on "Comus", p. 112 *et seq.*, dealing with Ludlow Castle, the Egerton family, & c.; p. 126 & c., on some sources of "Comus"; pp. 591—593, appendix to the notes on "Comus", treating mainly of Milton's possible imitation of George Peele; pp. 594—605 & c., corrections and supplemental observations; pp. 606—618, various readings from the Camb. MS.; pp. 618—620, list of editions.

The title-page of the second edition differs after the editor's name, where it reads as follows: "...B. D. LATE FELLOW OF TRINITY COLLEGE, PROFESSOR OF POETRY, AND CAMDEN PROFESSOR OF HISTORY, AT OXFORD. THE SECOND EDITION, WITH MANY ALTERATIONS, AND LARGE ADDITIONS. [motto] LONDON, PRINTED FOR G. G. J. AND J. ROBINSON, PATER-NOSTER ROW. MDCCXCI.

8⁰; pp. XLVI + 608. *Contents:* p. [I], title; pp. III—XXVI, preface; pp. XXVII—XLII, the nuncupative will of Milton, with the editor's notes, and other documents; pp. XLIII—XLVI, list of contents; pp. 1—574, text of the poems with notes and explanatory matter ("Comus" in this edition preceded by a series of special articles on "Ludlow Castle", "John Earl of Bridgewater and his family", "Henry Lawes" and the "Origin of Comus", pp. 123—136; pp. 403—407 contains an "Appendix to notes on the English poems" including some of Robert Baron's imitations of Milton); pp. 575—577, appendix to the notes on

"Comus", mainly on Milton's literary debts to George Peele;
pp. 578—590, the Trinity College MS. readings; pp. 591—605,
appendix containing remarks on the Greek verses of Milton by
Charles Burney; pp. 606—608, list of editions.

Warton's edition [892]) is evidently intended as a weapon
against the one-sided, artificial style of his period, against "Wit and
rhyme, sentiment and satire, polished numbers, sparkling couplets,
and pointed periods", features which he finds to have "kept
undisturbed possession in our poetry", excluding from it "fiction
and fancy", "picturesque description, and romantic imagery" [893]).

[892]) Warton's is no variorum edition such as Newton's. "It was no
part of my plan to add to my own the Notes of my predecessors" (p. XXII,
ed. 1785). A few "Notes by Mr. Bowle, the learned and ingenious publisher
of Don Quixote, extracted from his interleaved copy of Milton's second
edition of these poems" and some remarks by Warton's brother Joseph
Warton are all the contributions acknowledged by the editor in the first
edition. In the second edition, a number of remarks by Hurd should be
noted. Bowle does hardly anything but adducing parallels from older
English literature and from writers of the Latin countries, mediæval as well
as of the time of the Renaissance, but his erudition is remarkable. Joseph
Warton's notes, which are not very numerous, show his critical views more
clearly. A considerable sense of imaginative excellence is combined in him
with conventional prejudices. He notices a "natural little circumstance"
of great suggestiveness such as "the minute drops from off the eaves" in
Il P. 130, and the exquisite strain of "Lycidas", "L'Allegro" and "Il Penseroso' is thought by him sufficient to make Milton's name immortal. The
picturesqueness and wildness of the imagery in "Comus" are pointed out,
but no less its sentiment and moral (Co. 496 n.). Some of his notes are
nevertheless rather valuable from an artistic point of view, e. g. the one
containing a selection of Milton's compound epithets (Co. 233 n.). He
defends Milton's use of the alternation of Iambic and Trochaic verses, though
he does not define the character or reasons of their pleasing impression.
His knowledge of Italian literature is displayed in notes on Tasso's life and
loves (p. 491) and on the Italian sonnet (Son. I. n., p. 336), that of late
Latin poetry in a couple of observations (El. I. 92 n., Pass. 26 n.) but nothing
like the penetrating analyses of his brother is given.

The mixture of conventional views with a vivid sense of imaginative
beauty reminds one of the article on the "Blemishes of Paradise Lost" in
"The Adventurer" of 1754 (N. 101) ascribed to Joseph Warton (cf. e. g.
Todd's bibliography in his edition of Milton). Moderation and intellectualism
prevent the critic there from a full appreciation of his poet. The modesty
of Adam and Eve leaving Paradise is particularly praised, the disorderly
splendour of Milton's early poetry regarded as satisfactory only to those
who exercise no faculty but fancy and refrain from thinking.

[893]) Cf. p. III, op. cit.

These latter, and even some weightier qualities, are, in his opinion, typical of Milton's early poetry, and he opposes the judgment of Sir Henry Wotton, who, in the letter usually prefixed to "Comus", praises the "Doric mellifluence" of the lyrical parts of the masque. Warton sees more than this in the work, appreciating "its graver and more majestic tones", as well as the "solemnity and variety of its peculiar vein of original invention" [894], *i. e.* exactly those features which most of all distinguish Milton's poetry from the usual easy, polished verse of the 18th century.

Warton describes and deplores the neglect into which these poems had fallen. He is right in the assumption that their peculiar excellence had not been generally appreciated partly at least because they had not yet found a really congenial interpreter. It was Warton's destiny to help to establish a more or less adequate valuation of Milton's early works. The method by which he proposes to do this is in part the same as that of his predecessors, if his own definition is to be trusted. He describes it as his object "to explain our author's allusions, to illustrate or to vindicate his beauties, to point out his imitations both of others and of himself, to elucidate his obsolete diction, and by the abduction and juxtaposition of parallels universally gleaned both from his poetry and prose, to ascertain his favorite words, and to shew the peculiarities of his phraseology" [895]. There is hardly anything in this scheme that is new except the stress laid on the study of Milton's peculiarities of language. Pearce already had diligently studied these, as has been shown, but Warton did this, like most other things, on a much larger scale and with a far greater competence. His plan as stated here, however, does not show sufficiently his contribution to Milton scholarship. This must be discovered mainly from his critical practice.

The critical analyses in Warton's edition are more minute and keener than those in any of the earlier Milton commentaries. Warton's brilliant erudition, particularly in the department of older English literature [896], but also in that of other countries

---

[894] Cf. p. IV.

[895] Cf. p. XIX.

[896] Warton is perfectly conscious of the importance of his wide reading in old English literature for the elucidation of the *artistic* aspect of Milton's poetry. He knows that Milton's "style, expression, and more extensive combinations of diction, together with many of his thoughts, are...

and periods, *e. g.* of Italy and France, and notably of classical
antiquity, as is shown by his notes on Milton's Latin poems, as
well as his liberal, cultured taste and his acute intellect enabled
him to attain to a far more adequate conception both of Milton's
poetry itself and of its literary background, than earlier criticism
had reached. The very remarkable thoroughness of his knowledge
of Milton's own works helped him greatly. He had at his disposal
a large number of illustrations from Milton and other authors
for nearly everything he wished to exemplify. He may, in this
respect, be regarded as the very reverse of Addison, who
probably did more for the elucidation of Milton's artistic qualities than most critics before Warton, if Dr. Johnson be left out
of account. Addison's method was typically ratiocinative, the
illustrations were relatively few, and were taken almost exclusively from Milton himself and from the classics. His
exemplifications from Milton are seldom of quite the same
interest as Warton's, and he impresses one as generalizing
somewhat vaguely, not diversifying and enlivening his remarks
by characteristic and vivid details. He had no such immense
materials as Warton's at his command and was therefore totally
incapable of building up a critical structure which should embrace
not only Milton's poetry itself and its relations to his personal
life but also the historical groundwork, the various contemporary
and other allusions, the whole literary and social frame of his
writings. His successors did much to approach this ideal.
Particularly Peck and Newton with his collaborators contributed
a great deal to the study of the setting of Milton's poetry,
ransacking old archives and miscellaneous publications and
manuscripts on questions relating to him. However, their
labours only skimmed the surface of the welter of material
waiting for investigation. The "Gothic" libraries of England,
which, it is true, attracted Peck in an unusual degree, remained

---

to be traced in other English poets, who were either his contemporaries or
predecessors, and of whom many are now not commonly known" (p. XX).
He is aware that the neglect of the old black-letter publications, which was
one of Newton's faults, led to the overlooking or misinterpreting of many
subtleties: "and thus the force of many strikingly poetical passages has
been weakened or unperceived, because their origin was unknown, unexplored,
or misunderstood" (*ibid.*). Milton to him is "an old English poet", at least
in his early productions.

none the less unscrutinized except for a few chance excursions into their riches. Warton's earlier activities, on the contrary, eminently qualified him for this task. His studies in Spenser, and his extensive inquiries into the history of English poetry, though they resulted in a work not quite systematic enough to be called a real history in the modern sense, undoubtedly showed an exceptional knowledge of his field of research and made him unusually fit for all kinds of historical illustration. Moreover, the sympathy with the spirit of Milton's poetry evinced by him in his own lyrical pieces together with his considerable descriptive powers furnished him with the weapons needed for the management of this erudite apparatus.

Newton's edition of Milton's Minor Poems, though meritorious enough as a first attempt, suffered from the editor's lack of the temper of passionate literary antiquarianism, besides being relatively superficial and prejudiced in its critical part. Peck, who had this temper, and did not lack a sense of historical atmosphere, was not nearly intelligent and systematic enough in the collection and utilization of his materials, and Callander, though he seems to have been a zealous amateur in antiquarian research, did not succeed in applying his considerable erudition to the task of interpreting Milton's art. Warton, on the contrary, combined most of the good qualities of those scholars with a far higher intellectual level, possessing, besides, a knowledge of English literature and social history of a thoroughness never even approached by the two former commentators. Furthermore, neither of these were genuine men of letters, whereas Warton's powers as a writer were considerable. There is nothing in him of Peck's helplessness or of the somewhat anæmic academic manner of Callander. This enables him to present his many-sided and sometimes not very entertaining material in an attractive form, commenting and interpreting instead of piling quotation on quotation. He is no very eager student of the intricacies of Milton's philosophy, but the balance is restored by his remarkable understanding of the artistic and personal elements in Milton's writings.

As the result of Warton's method, we have a large picturesque survey of Milton's early poetry and its setting, necessarily rather disconnected as it must be traced from foot-notes, but vivid enough even in this shape. Warton possesses the genuine commentator's gift of fixing his attention so intently on little items as to reach the heart of the matter and see the connection of the details with larger issues. This cannot be done without a considerable capacity for logical analysis, and an intense imagination. The Richardsons, at all events the elder, possessed the latter faculty, but their logical powers lacked discipline and training. Their deficient method rendered unreliable the conclusions they drew from the perceptions of their notable sense of concrete detail; it also impaired the value of the suggestions of their impulsive instinct for emotional values. Warton may here and there trespass on accuracy but he still remains the very type of a scholar, though, of course, liable to human failings. Moreover, his wide literary erudition enabled him to judge of poetry with a very wholesome impartiality, without being shackled to the standards prescribed by the official taste of his time.

A. WARTON'S STUDY OF THE SETTING OF MILTON'S POETRY.

A detailed account of Warton's erudition as shown in his commentary would lead us too far afield. It may suffice to cast a glance at the main spheres of his research and to describe his manner of approaching them.

He shows the greatest care in collecting data on the *personal* in Milton's writings. No one before him had taken the trouble to peruse a similar amount of documents on Milton's life and on the miscellaneous contemporary allusions in his poetry. In consequence, his introductory notes to some of Milton's poems are of the size, and contain more than the ordinary substance, of small independent articles, for example that on the Greek poem "In Effigiei Ejus Sculptorem" which describes the extant portraits of Milton [897]), or those on "Comus" [898]) and on the letter by Sir Henry Wotton prefixed to the play, & c. The information supplied by Warton often goes beyond the limits of what is necessary for the understanding of Milton's works. At times he appears merely to avail himself of a chance of communi-

---

[897]) Cf. pp. 544—546 of Warton's first edition.
[898]) Cf. pp. 112—114 *ibid.*

cating his valuable miscellaneous discoveries to the public. Particular value should be attributed to the notes in which biographical facts are used for elucidating characteristic features of Milton's art or the interplay between the personal or more or less casual and the strictly literary elements in it — a method which never before in Milton scholarship had been made use of to the same extent. The reflection of the poet's everyday habits in his works is *e. g.* pointed out in a note describing in some detail the connection between Milton's early rising and his fondness for treating of "the beauties of the morning, which he so frequently contemplated with delight, and has therefore so repeatedly described, in all their various appearances", delineating them "with the lively pencil of a lover" [899]). The illustrations of this statement from Milton's early and late poetry, and also from his prose, which, as is shown by numerous references, Warton knew particularly well, are convincing and vivid, proving the poet's unusual predilection for this theme. A number of remarks show interesting correlations between the elements of fiction and real life in his works. The intrusion of personal allusions into the texture of Milton's fictitious plot and their disturbing influence on the progress of the dramatic action is treated in Co. 494 *n.* Warton suggests that Milton's impulsive eulogies on Henry Lawes threaten to interfere with the natural development of the play, so that its movement slows down without any satisfactory reason. The brothers, instead of proceeding resolutely to save their sister, who is in the power of Comus, while away their time "in a needless encomium, and in idle inquiries how the shepherd could possibly find out this solitary part of the forest". Dunster differs from this way of explaining the effect of the digression [900]) but Warton has the merits of starting the inquiry into the problem and of suggesting a plausible interpretation. Ambiguous hints which refer at the same time to fictitious and to real characters are studied with some care, *e. g.* in Co. 244 *n.* where several cases of this kind are discussed. The allusion to the voice "of my most honour'd Lady" [901]), *i. e.* evidently of the actress of the rôle, which is found in the description of the strains that "might create

---

[899]) Lyc. 27 *n.*
[900]) Cf. Todd's ed., Co. 494 *n.*
[901]) Cf. l. 564.

a soul Under the ribs of Death", is pointed out, with the remark that "the real and assumed characters of the speaker are blended". Warton's study of these small but typical traits helps the reader to realize the circumstances of the actual performance as Milton imagined it, and thus to attain to a better understanding of the author's point of view.

His investigation of social and historical matters and of the whole environment of Milton's early poetry is even more adventurously many-sided than Peck's though its thoroughness and neatness are on quite a different level. Peck, as was observed, examined poetry, popular ballads, dances, games, customs, superstitions, even culinary curiosities, & c. & c. Warton studied all these and many other matters [902]), expanding Peck's stray hints into detailed inquiries. The arts and gardening, town architecture and rural life, details of court-life and chivalry are described with zeal and devotion. It seems as if the atmosphere of Warton's own academic surroundings at Oxford with all the traditions of the university, which are frequently referred to in his notes, had particularly inspired him and enabled him to reproduce the style of the olden time [903]).

Oxford and its neighbourhood afforded him ample opportunity for studying typical monuments of ancient architecture. This is important, as similar surroundings are reflected in Elizabethan poetry and in the early verse of Milton. Warton was free to develop a taste for painting and interior decoration and valuable antiquarian objects of great artistic distinction. The vividness of his representation of the poet's time and of the time preceding it gains therefore very considerably. He appears to have a thorough knowledge of the hanging of halls and state-apartments with tapestry as well as of the poetical treatment of this subject in older English literature [904]). Shakespeare, "Britannia's Pastorals", Cowley, Drayton, Beaumont and Fletcher, and — which is

---

[902]) Drinks and drinking customs of the past are studied by him more than once. Much material is collected on the various shades of meaning of the word "wassailers" (Co. 178 n.). Even the exact recipe of the "Spicy Nut-brown Ale" in "L'Allegro" (L'A. 100 n.) is given ("ale, nutmeg, sugar, toast, and toasted crabs or apples") and various allusions to this "delectable beverage" are traced (*ibid.*).

[903]) Cf. Co. 707, 719, & c., & c.

[904]) Co. 322 n.

noteworthy, as no one before him had studied this part of Milton's poetry with sufficient care — also the author's own Latin pieces, which are often drawn upon in his remarks [905]), constitute his sources for the illustration of a small point such as this. The superabundance of quotations might impress one as tedious, were these not selected with a keen literary sense. Old paintings and engravings — objects which were easily accessible at Oxford — are used by Warton very skilfully to explain obscure points in Milton's poetry. Bowle seems to have been his model here, for in Il P. 12 n. Warton quotes an observation of his concerning the influence of Dürer's "Melancholia" on Milton's conception of melancholy and contemplation whereas on the next page a note by Warton himself compares a different passage of the same poem with another work of art, a representation of the "Starr'd *Ethiope* Queen" Cassiopea. It is "an old Gothic print of the constellations" found "in early editions of the Astronomers, where this queen is represented with a black body marked with white stars" [906]). Verity's comprehensive commentary does not mention the point at all. This is regrettable, as it seems to throw a rather vivid light on the symbolic use of blackness made here by Milton, and the emphasis laid upon it throughout the first part of his poem. Its conspicuousness in the print discovered by Warton may very easily have been the germ of the peculiar visual effect aimed at by the poet in describing the beauty of the dark-complexioned sister of Prince Memnon who becomes even more

---

[905]) Warton's preface (p. XIII) emphasizes that in his edition Milton's Latin poems are for the first time "accompanied with a series of Notes of proportionably equal extent with those attached to the English text". Milton's Latin verse is compared with the poetry of Ovid, being found "more clear, intelligible, and flowing; less desultory, less familiar, and less embarrassed with a frequent recurrence of periods." Ovid is found to want dignity and to be too conversational, whereas Milton, whose dignified style is emphasized by this contrast, is supposed to lack "the simplicity of Lucretius, Virgil, and Tibullus", preferring "prolixity of paragraph and length of sentence" (p. XV). Nevertheless, he is described as superior to the "false and extravagant thoughts" of Cowley's Latin compositions (p. XVIII), because of his being "a more just thinker, and therefore a more just writer", as well as being "more deeply tinctured with the excellencies of antient literature" (*ibid.*). The emphasis laid on the classicist features in Milton ought to be taken notice of, for similar traits will be dealt with in a different connection in the next section of the present chapter.

[906]) Il P. 19 n.

imposing if imagined as residing among the stars, as in the old picture. Other old illustrated black-letter editions are studied by Warton for various purposes, e. g. in order to explain Milton's conception of the art of gardening [907]). Never before had these by-ways of literature apparently dear to Milton, and familiar only to consummate scholars and antiquarians, been explored by a student of the poet with a care and understanding approaching Warton's.

Much attention is given to the study of the Elizabethan drama as well as of the stage-craft of that period. Warton's essay on the sources of "Comus" shows this with particular definiteness [908]). The conditions of the Elizabethan stage are examined in connection with "L'Allegro" and "Il Penseroso", as well as in the notes to "Comus", where, naturally enough, the masque mainly is studied. Warton handles these matters with the confident grasp of the specialist, finding numerous ways of approach to the solution of the problems suggested by Milton's text. The figure of Hymen "In Saffron robe, with Taper clear" [909]) is traced back to the "masques, pageantries, spectacles, and revelries" of the Elizabethans, Echo in Milton's song addressed to "Sweet Echo, sweetest nymph" in "Comus" is derived from the goddess Echo as occurring in the stage performances of that time [910]). A very bold and not quite improbable conjecture showing the zeal with which Warton examined the slightest indications of allusions of this kind is his supposition that the "sweet musick" breathing "Above, about, or underneath" to Il Penseroso, sent by "som spirit to mortals good" or by the genius of the woods, is a reminiscence of the secret music of hidden nymphs in the masques as conducted by Inigo Jones [911]). It is evident that the machinery of the stage of that period, so far as explored at Warton's time, was vividly present to his mind.

In view of the pastoral style of much of Milton's juvenile poetry, it is a fact of some importance that Warton evinces a far more considerable knowledge of country life than earlier Milton

---

[907]) Il P. 50 n.
[908]) Cf. p. 591 et seq.
[909]) L'A. 125 n.
[910]) Co. 243 n.
[911]) Il P. 151 n.

scholars, not excepting Peck. The surroundings of Oxford afforded him much opportunity for studying rural conditions. Most of his notes on this subject are spiced with literary reminiscences and references to learned works, showing that he had made a special study of the life of the democratic part of society, just as he had acquired a detailed knowledge of the atmosphere in which the higher classes lived. A comparison with the corresponding note of Peck shows the far greater reliability and erudition of Warton in the examination of the prototypes of the "jocond rebeck" [912]). Peck seems originally to have been Warton's model, but the casual remark of Peck is expanded into a considerable special investigation of the problem. First-hand mediæval documents are used, including even "the old French writers", to which Du Cange, Steevens's Shakespeare studies and other learned authorities are added. An important stimulating influence in these inquiries is Warton's fondness for the genial spirit of old pre-puritan England, in which he resembles Peck. He is violently opposed to the one-sided solemnity and rigour which characterize Milton's later works. The poet's disapproval of festivities and holidays in S. A. 1418 *et seq.* is interpreted as "a concealed attack on the ritual of the church of England" [913]), a tendency odious to the conservative critic who, on his own part, devotes much space to a description of the mirth and various diversions of the people as well as to their serious and humorous legends and superstitions [914]).

Nature also is among his favourite themes. Small but poetically important details, such as the description of the „rathe primrose" that dies forsaken [915]) are explained according to Warton's own observations. He disputes Jortin's explanation, which ascribes the lonely decay of the flower to its grief at being put out of countenance by later and more gorgeous blossoms. Warton knows that the "true reason" is its growing "in the shade, uncherished or unseen by the sun, which was supposed to be in love with some sorts of flowers". His vivid description of those features of "Lycidas" regarded by him as real natural painting

[912]) L'A. 94 *n.*
[913]) L'A. 131 *n.*
[914]) Cf. *e. g.* L'A. 103 *n.*
[915]) Lyc. 142 *n.*

and no mere "bucolic cant" 916) — the day-break with "the faint appearance of the upland lawns under the first gleams of light", or the sunset with the "buzzing of the chaffer", and the fresh dews which the approaching night sheds on the flocks — seem to indicate a diligent first-hand study of nature.

A further result of Warton's interest in the country seems to be his familiarity with special local idioms and terms, a class of expressions which forms an important part of Milton's pastoral style, as, for instance, with the expressions used in various parts of England to denote peculiarities of rural scenery. Warton ridicules Peck's simple-minded definition of "dingle" as meaning boughs hanging "dingle-dangle" over the edge of a dell 917). He makes various additions to Newton's and Thyer's communications on these matters, which in a chance way referred to provincial language, as Thyer had had opportunity of studying the speech of the surroundings of Manchester 918). A good example is Warton's treatment of "bourn" 919), in connection with which he traces the meanings of the word in the hilly parts of England as well as in the "waste and open countries", taking care to add copious literary illustrations and to study the history of the expression in works of scholars such as Du Cange and Furetière.

A department in which very little work had been done previous to Warton, is the examination of the connection of Milton's poetry with local traditions and history. An excellent instance showing at once Warton's wide knowledge of the latter and his skill of utilizing this knowledge for literary interpretation is his inquiry into the allusion to the apparition on St. Michael's Mount in Lyc. 159 & c. It is true that the note embodies without any acknowledgement the results of Meadowcourt's studies of the same passage. The latter had already done some valuable work, identifying part of the geographical and legendary names and availing himself of the aid of Camden's erudition to ascertain the meaning of the reference to "Namanco's and Bayona's hold". The exact identification of these names is the merit of Todd, but Camden had already stated in a passage not specified by Meadowcourt

916) Lyc. 193 n.
917) Co. 312 n.
918) Cf. Co. 312 n.
919) Co. 313 n.

that the mount is the only part of England pointing directly towards Spain [920]). However, neither Meadowcourt nor Newton attempt to explain the allusion to the "great vision". Here Warton shows his knowledge and acumen. The material added by him is more helpful for the understanding of the passage than that which he has bc. rowed. Carew's "Survey of Cornwall", Caxton's "Golden Legend", William of Worcester's "Itinerarium" and particularly local documents and traditions are made use of to establish the fact that Milton intends the vision to be that of St. Michael which according to a popular belief appears on the mountain. The epithet "guarded" is stated to refer to a fortress formerly situated there, the word "mount" to be used as the "peculiar appropriated appellation" of the promontory. These inquiries, which also show an intimate knowledge of the scenery and betray Warton's endeavour to arrive at a full realization of the visual impression present to the poet's mind while he wrote, culminate in the conclusion that the "Angel" mentioned in v. 163 is not the spirit of Lycidas looking down from heaven, as Thyer thought [921]), but the archangel himself. This is supported by the circumstance that the invocation in v. 163 is apparently designed to contrast with the preceding description of the apparition looking towards the sea. The antithesis would be very considerably impaired if the references were to different persons. Warton points this out, besides mentioning a number of additional arguments, and his conjecture is strongly defended by recent editors such as Verity [922]). Thorough research and trained logical thinking combine here to explain this passage, which gains much in impressiveness by the substitution of the great imposing vision of the angel for the gentle spirit of "young Lycidas".

B. WARTON'S CRITICAL VIEWS AND METHODS.

Warton's great miscellaneous learning, his antiquarian instinct and his knowledge of the atmosphere of town and country, of aristocracy and peasantry, only helped him to collect the material which his gift of representation and his trained sense of literary analysis had to shape and utilize. He was out of sympathy

[920]) Cf. Lyc. 160 n., ed. Newton.
[921]) Cf. note in Newton's ed.
[922]) Cf. his ed. of Lyc., Notes.

with certain features of Milton's poetry. The puritanic and republican tendencies in Milton's poetry he found to be harmful to some of its best qualities. The "splendours of society", the *studious cloysters pale*, and the *high embowed* roof", the "storied windows richly dight", the *"pealing organ* and the *full-voiced* quire" are regarded by him as "totally inconsistent" with the "very repugnant and unpoetical principles" afterwards adopted by Milton [923]). "The delights arising from these objects were to be sacrificed to the cold and philosophical spirit of calvinism, which furnished no pleasures to the imagination" [924]). Warton is extremely conservative, and Milton's tendency "to subvert monarchy, to destroy subordination, and to level all distinctions of rank" [925]) offends his sense of loyalty to existing institutions. The most extreme high-church tendencies of to-day would possibly have been after his mind, for he finds papacy a "very poetical" religion [926]).

All this might have been expected to make it somewhat difficult for him to attain to an unbiassed appreciation of "Paradise Lost" and Milton's later works. His early poetry, in which imagination and bright, varied description are so prominent, could be very well appreciated by such a temper — without doubt infinitely better than by the dogmatic classicist Newton. Warton becomes its main interpreter, one of the heralds of the cause of imagination, in a far higher degree than Richardson or Thyer had been, though it must be remembered in justice to Thyer that his original notes were lost and that there is extant only a set of fragments set down in great haste.

Yet Warton's literary horizon is sufficiently wide to make it possible for him to understand some aspects of Milton's poetry almost radically opposed to the trend of thought just described. He values certain features which are conspicuous in Milton's later "puritanic" period but occur only very rarely in the works of his youth and early manhood. More than that — he rates them above everything else in Milton's early poetry. The ideal of sublime simplicity favoured alike by such divergent personalities as Bentley and Thyer is indirectly acknowledged by Warton to be the highest

[923]) Cf. Il P., final note.
[924]) *Ibid.*
[925]) *Ibid.*
[926]) This attitude is reflected in Warton's pronouncements on Milton's prose, *e. g.* in the final note to the Latin poems of Milton.

literary doctrine to be discovered in Milton. The manner of the
poet's greatest works seems to have impressed him sufficiently
deeply to neutralize his other literary sympathies, though they
were as genuine, and suited his character as perfectly, as the
tendency mentioned above. The last verses of the poem "At a
Solemn Music" elicit the verdict that possibly there are "no finer
lines in Milton, less obscured by conceit, less embarrassed by
affected expressions, and less weakened by pompous epithets" [927]).
He praises this "perspicuous and simple style" in which there "are
conveyed some of the noblest ideas of a most sublime philosophy,
heightened by metaphors and allusions suitable to the subject".
It is, however, to be noted that Warton does not insist on incul-
cating this philosophy. He does not recommend the obtrusively
pedagogic style eulogized by Newton and even by Thyer.

Warton finds many traces of this grand manner in Milton's
early poetry. The reproach referred to by him that the poet
"never learned the art of doing little things with grace" is met by
the retort that "If by *little* things we are to understand *short* poems,
Milton had the art of giving them another sort of excellence" [928])
— the excellence of sublimity, as is evident from the same note.
It resembles the sublimity ascribed by Bentley to the flights of
Milton's imagination through the universe [929]). It is identical
with the "great reach of imagination" which is admired by
Warton in his description of a huge archetype of Man, "stalking
in some remote unknown region of the earth, and lifting his head
so high as to be dreaded by the gods" [930]). The "great and lofty
imagery" which Milton manages to raise from a "trifling and
unimportant circumstance" in the sixth elegy [931]), the "high strain
of philosophy, delivered in as high strains of eloquence and poetry"
in Co. 584 *et seq.* fall under the same category and find full
acknowledgement. That mere moralizing and volubility did not
satisfy Warton, is, however, obvious from his treatment of the
learned dialogue of the two brothers in "Comus" which, in spite
of the "flowers of eloquence" that adorned it, is regarded as "little
more than a solitary declamation in blank verse", greatly resembl-

[927]) Sol. Mus. 17 *n.*
[928]) Cf. Passion, introductory note.
[929]) Cf. above, chapter on Bentley.
[930]) Id. Plat. 3 *n.*
[931]) Cf. El. VI, final note.

ing the immature "manner of our author's Latin Prolusions at Cambridge, where philosophy is inforced by pagan fable and poetical allusion" [932]). The impressive, masculine grandeur of really "cosmic" passages, such as the poet's "sublime mode of describing the study of natural philosophy" by a symbolic relation of how he passed through the elements after beholding "each blissful Deity" "at Heav'n's door", is, on the contrary, dwelt upon with much enthusiasm [933]), and Warton sees promise of "Paradise Lost" in the interplanetary roamings described immediately before these verses. It seems evident that he deemed the manner of Milton's great epic superior to that of his early attempts, though the picturesque style of "Comus" is regarded by him as falling just short of the perfection of the poet's masterpiece [934]). Yet even in discussing "Comus" he lays particular stress on its classicist features [935]), on its simplicity and on the "principles and form of rational composition" to which he finds the old English masque there reduced for the first time [936]). It is true that in the same note the "sublime sentiment", the "fanciful imagery of the richest vein", the "ornamental expression" characterizing the work are admitted and praised.

However, his valuation of these is extended to them only within certain bounds. The dislike of the "affected expressions" and "pompous epithets" mentioned in the above-quoted criticism on the poem "At a Solemn Music" evidently made Warton disinclined to approve of the Italian style. In this he concurs with so great an admirer of imaginative excellence as Thyer. His attitude appears very clearly in the judgement he passes on Milton's Italian sonnets, in which he praises those features which are the reverse of the usual Italian manner, the "natural severity of mind" appearing there and the "remarkable air of gravity and dignity" which it lends even to the poet's love-verses [937]). "They are free from the metaphysics of Petrarch, and more in the manner of Dante", is his definition of their relation to the classical poets of Italy. The word "metaphysics", which may have been used

---

[932]) Co. 458 n.
[933]) V. Ex. 40 n.
[934]) Cf. Comus, final note.
[935]) Cf. also Warton's preface on Milton's Latin poetry, see above.
[936]) Comus, final note.
[937]) Cf. p. 338.

here in allusion to the English metaphysicists, seems to indicate the grounds of his objection to the Italians. The reference apparently is to the logical distortions, the eccentric flights of thought that distinguished the school of Donne and Cowley [938]). This tendency impresses one as a lingering trace of the spirit of *rationalism* which Warton, on the whole, seems to have been able to overcome. He appears to distinguish between a mere exaggerated richness of description, which, as shown above, may appeal to his sensitive mind, and the lack of clear, straightforward logic. The "forced thoughts" the occurrence of which at the end of sonnet V [939]) is considered "intolerable", disturb him more than the somewhat "unnatural" profusion of imagery in Co. 932 *et seq.* [940]) which he finds it possible to forgive as being meant to represent not "truth and reality" but poetry. In certain cases, his dislike of a seemingly arbitrary, unjustified strangeness in the angle of vision seems to blind him to the *emotional* value of this peculiarity, as appears from his comparison of a passage from Milton with one from Pope. There seems to be a touch of incongruity in the action described in the following sentence which Warton quotes from Milton's book on Reformation: "God, when we least deserved, sent out a *gentle gale*, and message of peace, from the *wings* of those his Cherubims that FAN his mercy-seat" [941]). The "gentle gale, and message of peace", fanned from the wings of the angels, is certainly a more elaborate and less common image than the "perfumes" in the verse by Pope adduced to show the superiority of a style which is "natural, rational, and highly poetical without extravagance":

"The wings of Seraphs shed divine perfumes".

The word "rational" ought to be noted. Yet it seems as if the very commonness of Pope's phrase would impair its poetic value. Milton's "puerile Italian conceit", as Warton calls it, appears to be charged with genuine emotion and is therefore more impressive than Pope's conventional line. Warton's hostile attitude may in part have been prompted by religious and political considerations, which would explain the violence of his tone. He regards Milton's

---

[938]) Cf. Warton's preface pp. XV—XVIII on Cowley. Cowley's "false and extravagant thoughts" are Warton's main reason for attacking him there.

[939]) Sonnet V, final note.

[940]) Co. 932 *n.*

[941]) D. F. J. 57 *n.*

sentence with apparent contempt as a combination of "the enthusiasm of puritanical devotion" with "the mystic visions of monastic quietism". There is certainly some enthusiasm in it, but hardly in any bad sense, and the "mystic visions" are closely connected with the atmosphere of inspiration and poetry which Warton seemed to recognize in Roman Catholicism, as was shown above. The critic apparently considers it the extravagance of a Puritan indulging in the follies of a fanatic Romanism. He is far more intelligible when he calls Lyly's "Euphues" a "book full of affected phraseology" [942]), contrasting it with Milton's "superior genius" which is said to raise him "above the level of the fashionable rhymers" [943]).

This occasional tendency towards rationalism which, generally speaking, is not obtrusive, does not destroy Warton's genuine appreciation of rich and ornate imagery nor does it prevent him from analysing it with great eagerness and understanding, so long as a certain moderation is observed and as sound commonsense does not appear too palpably to be trespassed against. The "brilliancy of romance" distinguishing Milton's Ligea from the Ligea of Ovid, is not condemned [944]). The critic's skilful study of fine pictorial effects in the luxurious manner of the Elizabethans and perhaps even some overvaluation of artificial magnificence are shown in his treatment of Milton's metaphor of the "sea-girt isles" that like "rich and various gems" inlay "the unadorned bosom of the deep" [945]). He compares this with Shakespeare's metaphorical description of England as "This precious stone set in the silver sea" [946]) where the "silver sea" strikes him as a "petty conceit" and the "conception of a jeweller". He seems to forget the vividness with which the epithet "silver" renders the impression of the sparkling surface of the sea. Milton's simile is even more elaborate and artificial, and gives no help in visualizing the scene described. However, it has a decorative merit of its own, despite its lack of verisimilitude, and Warton points out the artistic refinement achieved by contrasting the "rich inlay" of the islands

---

[942]) V. Ex. 18 *n.*
[943]) *Ibid.*
[944]) Co. 880 *n.*
[945]) Co. 22 *n.*
[946]) Rich. II, ii. 1.

with the "simple ground" of the sea, "else unadorned" [947]), a device not to be found in Shakespeare's phrase.

This keen appreciation of the effect of sensuous perception enables Warton to do justice to the not uncommon Elizabethan method of likening the impressions of one sense to those of another or of positively identifying them. This practice may have resulted from the extreme sensitiveness to physical impressions observable in the writers of that age and recurring from time to time at periods of great general sensibility, *e. g.* in the poetry of Coleridge, Keats and Shelley, as well as in that of the French symbolists and their precursors, for instance Baudelaire, Rimbaud, Mallarmé. Warton notices it in "Comus" [948]) and quotes some typical parallels from Ben Jonson's "Vision of Delight" and from Bacon's essays. All these cases compare sound to odour or *vice versa.* The annotator is apparently anxious to ascertain the exact nature of the sensorial impressions used by Milton, for he studies the MS. draft of the masque, calling attention to the epithet originally used instead of "rich distill'd" as applied to perfumes. It was "slow-distilled", a word indicating, as Warton says, "the gradual increase and diffusion of odours in the process of distilling perfumes". This is found to correspond with the structure of the musical air composed by Lawes for the song of Echo, "which", according to Warton, "begins with the softest strains". This deft analysis of the most complex interplays of sensory effects would have been impossible without a highly developed sensibility on the critic's part.

Warton's skill in the observation of characteristic inobtrusive details helps him in the study of Milton's *epithets.* He is conscious of their importance, knowing like the Richardsons that a slight individualizing touch may alter the whole character of a passage [949]). The Richardsons noticed this only with regard to

---

[947]) *Ibid.*

[948]) Cf. ll. 555—8.

[949]) An example where Warton notices a slight change of the point of view which none the less alters the whole impression is Il P. 85 *n.* He deals with the verses: "Or let my Lamp at midnight hour, Be seen in som high lonely Towr". The simple sense of these verses is, according to Warton, turned into "a picture... which strikes the imagination" by the sole addition of "the extraneous circumstance *be seen*". It would only mean "Let me study at midnight by a lamp in a lofty tower" but for this additional

pictorial details. Warton does so in a more general way in dealing with Milton's Latin verse: "Me tenet urbs reflua quam Thamesis alluit unda" [950]). The epithet "reflua" is found to rescue the verse from the commonplace. The "peculiar circumstance of the reflux of the tide" makes "new, poetical, and appropriated" what otherwise would have been "a general and a trite allusion" [951]).

Warton is keenly bent on establishing the literary ancestry of Milton's epithets, apparently recognizing that the sources of an expression largely determine its associations. He is particularly successful in tracing epithets and phrases borrowed from the romances of chivalry, as in the case of Milton's invocation of Euphrosyne in "L'Allegro": "thou Goddes fair and free". The note to this line shows the frequent occurrence of this combination of adjectives in works of a romantic charaster, and especially of "free" as a common epithet for a lady. This archaic flavour, if, as seems likely, it was intended by Milton, must have been meant to contribute to that peculiar atmosphere of classical mythology mixed with mediæval romance which strikes one immediately in the twin poems [952]). A similar study is made of many other expressions from similar sources, e. g. of the combination "hall or bower" which is quoted from Spenser, Chaucer, & c. [953]), or of "temple and tower" [954]), a phrase lending an air of romantic richness to a poem combining mediæval notions of knightly honour with allusions to the glory of classical poetry.

Various refinements in Milton's use of words had been studied by Hume who examined with particular zeal the ambiguity of many of Milton's Latinisms and Græcisms where the old coexisted with the modern meaning. Similarly, Warton notices some curious instances of the ambiguous combination of literal and metaphorical senses of words. In Il P. 40 *n.* the epithet "rapt"

---

feature. Warton appears to be right, for the idea of an observer watching the lonely scholar from outside adds a touch of dramatic tension to the situation.

[950]) El. I. 9 *n.*

[951]) *Ibid.*

[952]) Cf. *e. g.* the parallel case of "bucksom, blith, and debonair" in L'A. 24, resembling Spenser's use of the word "debonair" as applied to ladies and knights.

[953]) Co. 45 *n.*

[954]) Sonnet VIII, l. 11 *n.*

is traced in the poetry of the Elizabethans and almost throughout Milton's poetical works, and Warton discovers a number of passages where the meanings "snatched away" and "enraptured" seem to be intended simultaneously [955]).

The keen appreciation of poetic artistry and workmanship shown by this and many similar observations points to the independent literary activity of the critic [956]). Himself a trained craftsman in the composition of verse, Warton is able to enjoy technical and purely æsthetic features with an acuteness which is beyond the reach of the mere scholar, even when highly cultured. The superior subtlety of Warton's observations is apparent from the relative frequency with which cases of ambiguous associations of ideas are analysed, (e. g. the above-mentioned blending of the literal and metaphorical meanings of words, of the characters of Milton's *dramatis personæ* with those of the actors, of the perceptions of different senses) — a tendency differing radically from the 18th century ideal of simplicity. Both the ability to appreciate æsthetic values as such, conceived apart from moral dogmas, and the penetration which, refusing to accept appearances, considers the various implications of seemingly simple phenoména, are shown in the more comprehensive studies of the individual poems generally affixed by way of summaries to Warton's comments on separate passages. To these qualities is added a vivid sense of the author's personality, of the moods giving rise to his works.

All these elements seem to have influenced Warton's understanding of the concept of "theme" or "substance" in poetry. To him, it is not mainly by its execution of a professed intention that a work must be judged. The fundamental mood, the poet's manner of approach to his subject, his various ways of relieving his mind from the burden of poetical inspiration are, as it seems, regarded as more important than the announced theme. This may

---

[955]) P. L. XI. 706, P. L. VIII. 23, possibly also P. R. II. 40, and some examples from Pope, the "Faery Queen", Berni and "Orlando Innamorato".

[956]) Milton's versification, however, seems to present serious difficulties to Warton's understanding. He dislikes its redundant syllables, particularly those in the blank verse of "Comus" and, notwithstanding Milton's "singular skill in music", charges him with having had "a very bad ear" — a judgement which proves how even a sensitive mind may commit the most striking blunders in matters of æsthetic perception.

quite possibly be used as a conscious or unconscious pretext for the treatment of quite different matters. Further, literary inspiration, the glow of the imagination, seem, in his opinion, to outweigh an absence of sincerity or at any rate of emotional warmth in the treatment of the proposed subject even in such a conspicuous case as Milton's expressions of sorrow for Edward King, the hero of "Lycidas". This is the very reverse of the attitude which demanded solemn instruction and moral feelings from the higher type of poetry. Warton, on the contrary, in the present case tends towards an extreme æstheticism. The impassioned artistry of the work he seems to consider a sufficient substitute for less esoteric emotions. The literary passion becomes of equal value with commoner passions [957]. Warton admits the possible lack of real affliction in the elegy and the artificial nature of its imagery, but the "peculiar and irresistible" charm of the poem is found to pervade even its conventional symbolism and scenery. Warton's summary of the matter is that "in this piece there is perhaps more poetry than sorrow. But let us read it for its poetry" [958].

Much of the same penetration is found in Warton's criticism of "L'Allegro" and "Il Penseroso". Here, however, his ways of approach are not purely æsthetic. In trying to discover the personal feelings behind these poems Warton detects traits which appear to be more fundamental in his author's mind than the aesthetic attitude which he finds in "Lycidas". Warton here proves his competence to probe deeply into human consciousness. In his analysis of the two poems he tends to explain every detail from the point of view of the poet's personality which lurks behind the serene disguise of "L'Allegro" while appearing no less in the dreams and speculations of his more thoughtful companion. The author's character affords the connecting link serving to combine and explain the varying individual features of these poems. This is the main difference of Warton's method from the methods of many of his predecessors, particularly from that of Newton, who treated the diverse characteristics of Milton's works separately, far too seldom regarding them as one organic whole. Warton shows definitely that the title of "L'Allegro" ought to

---

[957] Cf. Lyc., final note.
[958] Ibid.

deceive no one and that the complicated problem of the melancholy pleasures of the hero of the poem is easily solved if L'Allegro and Il Penseroso are assumed to be the same person, namely the author, Milton himself: "Both poems are the result of the same feelings, and the same habits of thought" 959). "It was impossible for the author of IL PENSEROSO to be more cheerful, or to paint levity" 960). These statements are supported by a careful analysis of the expression which this mood has found in the external details of "L'Allegro". It is pointed out that the personifications of laughter and jollity are never exemplified and that quips and cranks and wanton wiles are named only in general terms. The landscape, though it has flocks and flowery meadows, everywhere betrays the author's turn of mind, wearing "a shade of pensiveness" on its "russet laws [sic], fallows gray, and barren mountains, overhung with labouring clouds". "Even his most brilliant imagery is mellowed with the sober hues of philosophic meditation" 961). Warton, under the impression of this scenery, even asserts that "There is specifically no mirth in contemplating a fine landscape" 962). It is perhaps not quite certain whether this was a permanent doctrine with him or a passing remark but it is in conformity with that ideal of solemn, profoundly emotional beauty which under the influence of such poets as Young and Gray had taken hold of the literature of the period.

Here his demand for serious, sublime poetry, which was dealt with before, again asserts itself. It was shown that Warton's delight in purely artistic qualities was able to reconcile him to the absence of intense human sympathies and passions. Yet exclusively æsthetic poetry is most obviously not his highest ideal. The very note which finds poetry and feigned, or tepid, sorrow to be compatible, dwells on the relieving effect of the "graces of sentiment" in "Lycidas". Yet the sentiment discovered in "L'Allegro" and "Il Penseroso" is deeper. There is no violence in it. It is so subdued that Warton feels entitled to speak of the "sober hues of philosophic meditation" 963), but it is evident that he does not mean the "cold and philosophical" spirit of Calvinism

---

959) Il P., final note.
960) Ibid.
961) Ibid.
962) Ibid.
963) Il P., final note.

which is denounced in this note. There is much emotion behind its sobriety. It is "a train of solemn and romantic, perhaps melancholy, reflection" 964). This is the mood regarded by Warton as inspiring "the colours of higher poetry", which he found to be inconsistent with levity 965). The very highest type of poetry acknowledged by him, that of sublime simplicity as found in the lines "At a Solemn Music" shares with the present its gravity, though it exceeds it in terse intensity. Warton shows by these and various similar observations that he was equally well qualified for studying the emotional and the formal aspects of poetry and that the scope of his criticism, extending from classicism to Elizabethan exuberance, from popular humour to solemn seriousness, and from æstheticism to the enjoyment of genuine, deep feeling, as well as the delicate, flexible art of his analyses enabled him to approach the shifting moods of Milton's lyrics with a competence never matched before.

This same faculty for getting at the core of his author's personality enables Warton to see the unity and inner coherence of features which might otherwise appear whimsical and irregular. This is important in his handling of a "wild" and grotesque style. Apparent incongruities can be explained as being ruled by some inner principle, though this generally remains unintelligible until the author's mood is considered. This is the clue to them and can be discovered only by a sensitive temper.

Warton's perpetual sifting of chaotic historical and literary materials had forced him to strain his sensitiveness to the utmost. He was accustomed to the task of concentrating on minutiæ and of picking out the grains of psychological information from heaps of chaff. Eloquent details seem to have been sufficient to compensate him for the dullness and incoherence of the whole. He could appreciate works the main charm of which depended on occasional flashes of poetry and invention. His description of his impression of Burton's "Anatomy of Melancholy" shows this gift, a gift indispensable to the literary antiquarian. He apparently looked mainly for the curious personal touches in that work. Peck appears to have valued the book highly, but to have found it difficult to sum up his opinion 966). Warton evinces this ability

---

964) *Ibid.*
965) *Ibid.*
966) Cf. above.

in a considerable degree. His criticism proves, at the same time, that he could regard singularity and quaintness as desirable literary qualities, in spite of his praise of 18th century neatness in some of the observations discussed above.

His opinion of this "very elaborate work" is that "the writer's variety of learning, his quotations from scarce and curious books, his pedantry sparkling with rude wit and shapeless elegance, miscellaneous matter, intermixture of agreeable tales and illustrations, and perhaps, above all, the singularities of his feeling cloathed [sic] in an uncommon quaintness of style, have contributed to render it, even to modern readers, a valuable repository of amusement and information" 967). Almost every detail shows that Warton had formed a definite idea of the author's personality, of the disorderly but rich and original mind felt to live among the somewhat amorphous profusion of material presented in the book.

A critic able to detect the unity of atmosphere in the extreme irregularity and eccentricity of Burton's work was hardly likely to be deterred by Milton's peculiarities. Warton did not approve of them all, as was pointed out, but he rarely condemned them wholesale, trying, as a rule, to find their real significance. To do this was much easier in the case of Milton than in that of Burton, since the former's artistic intentions were beyond doubt incomparably more definite, while his terseness and power of expression conveyed his emotions in a highly suggestive way, making a misunderstanding of his meaning much more difficult. The apparent disorder in some of his works could be more easily reduced to its leading principle. The expressive nature of his extravagances of style and imagery, their correspondence with the general mood, usually prevented Warton from taking up a condemnatory attitude. This seems to be true of his analysis of "Lycidas". It has to be admitted that he does not approve of its mixture of "religious disputes with pagan and pastoral ideas", merely excusing it as "irregularities and incongruities" not to be tried by modern criticism because the poem was composed at a time when "our poetry was not yet purged from its Gothic combinations" 968). The "legitimate notions of discrimination and propriety" in the 18th century sense are recommended but not very

967) Il P., final note.
968) Lyc., final note.

urgently [969]). The element of "agreeable wildness" pointed out by Thyer [970]) evidently impresses Warton as one of the main attractions of the elegy. He dwells on the "unexpected touches of picturesque beauty", the "novelties of original genius" striking one among the varying and shifting matter of the poem [971]), and the superabundance of classical imagery censured by Johnson as college pedantry [972]) is defended by him because of the vividness, the "fancy and poetical description" it introduces [973]). The anachronistic device of "transferring the classical seats of the Muses to Britain" and substituting "places of the most romantic kind, inhabited by Druids, and consecrated by the visions of the British bards" is called a sign of "great force and felicity of fancy", and contrasted with Pope's "cold and unpoetical" though "very correct" pastorals. The rough, gigantic, weird scenery of the elegy, all its "wild imagery", is described at some length and with an impressiveness showing the critic's sensitiveness to its peculiar glamour. The "tombs of the Druids, dispersed over the solitary mountains of Denbighshire, the shaggy summits of Mona, and the wizard waters of Deva" attract him by their wildness [974]). He appears to grasp the effect of mysterious breadth and suggestiveness caused by the introduction of "the old British traditions and fabulous histories" [975]). All these features contrast very sharply with the smoothness and narrowness of common 18th century classicism.

Warton succeeds in finding a theoretical basis for his attitude. In a note on the baroque description of heathen deities in the "Nativity Ode" [976]) he defines the "wildness" of the passage as "most interesting to the fancy". Here the mainspring of all literary experience is touched upon. It is intimated that the value of the description depends on the impression produced on the reader's mind. As Warton studies the author's mental attitude, so he repeatedly treats of the mental state of the reader or spectator on receiving artistic or literary impressions. This leads to

[969]) *Ibid.*
[970]) Cf. above, section on Thyer in chapter on Newton's Milton.
[971]) Lyc., final note.
[972]) Cf. Life of Milton, on "Lycidas".
[973]) Lyc., final note.
[974]) Lyc. 55 *n.*
[975]) *Ibid.*
[976]) N. O. 205 *n.*

the ultimate recognition of the imagination as the main agent in poetry.

Thyer already stated clearly enough that the most important aspect of a literary work is its effect upon the reader [977]) — far more than the completeness or elaboration of the details of the text. The author has to stimulate the mind, not to suffocate its activity by an overwhelming abundance of detail. The logical conclusion to be drawn is that the slightest and vaguest literary stimulus is sufficient, provided it fulfils its object of calling forth a certain mood in the reader. Vagueness and incompleteness may even be desirable in so far as they force him to continue independently in the direction indicated by the author. These truths, as will be shown, are recognized and in part clearly formulated by Warton.

He describes in a vividly written note how the impressions received by Milton in his youth contributed to the development of the imaginative element in him [978]). It is apparently the very vagueness and suggestiveness of the dim interior of Gothic churches which are supposed to have left their traces in his mind. Warton depicts the original cathedral of St. Paul, this "most stately and venerable pattern of the Gothic style", situated in the close neighbourhood of St. Paul's school where Milton was educated. The "solemnities of the antient [sic] ecclesiastical architecture, its vaults, shrines, iles, pillars, and painted glass, rendered yet more aweful | !] by the accompaniment of the choral service" are thought to have impressed him "with an early reverence" and are compared with the present church by Sir Christopher Wren, the "Grecian proportions" of which may "gratify the judgment" with their "Truth and propriety" but "do not affect the imagination".

These views correspond with the description which the poet himself gives of the effect produced on him by the "dim religious light" [979]) of a church. Some other notes by Warton treat more clearly of analogical impressions, giving definite theoretical formulations of them. A typical case is his treatment of the incomplete representation of certain details of landscape [980]) in connection with its effect on the spectator. Milton describes

[977]) Cf. above, section on Thyer.
[978]) Il P. 157 n.
[979]) Il P. 160.
[980]) L'A. 77 n.

"Towers and Battlements... Boosom'd high in tufted Trees".
Warton's opinion is that these "symptoms of an old palace,
especially when thus disposed, have a greater effect, than a discovery of larger parts, and even a full display of the whole edifice", for
"Where only a little is seen, more is left to the imagination" 981).
The combination of "the spreading tops of a tall grove" with the
"embosomed battlements" "interests the fancy" and just enough
is given "to compose a picturesque association" 982). This, to
Warton's mind, is one of the main attractions of the architecture
of "our Gothic ancestors" as opposed to that of modern country
seats which "are seldom so deeply ambushed" and disclose their
beauty at once, instead of exciting expectation "by concealment,
by gradual approaches, and by interrupted appearances" 983).

There is only one step from this appreciation of suggestive
incompleteness to the conscious theoretical recognition of the
stimulating effect of a vagueness resembling the manner of Ossian.
The latter method may be even more effective as it gives more
scope to the imagination. Warton deprecates the tendency always
to look for a definite meaning in a poetic passage. The author may
have meant to be indistinct, as in the case of the vague personification of horror in P. L. IV. 989 984), which the commentator finds
fully justified, in opposition to Newton, who identifies its abstract
quality with a definite concrete object, assuming that horror is here
literally "made the plume of his [= Satan's] helmet". Warton
regards this almost as a profanation of Milton's poetry: "...we
detract from the sublimity of the passage in endeavouring to explain it, and to give a distinct signification". The less definite
conception of the expression gives it a peculiar, significant effect,
"a nameless terrible grace, resulting from a mixture of ideas, and
a confusion of imagery". This is the very principle which explains
the effect of Coleridge's masterpieces. "The Ancient Mariner",
"Christabel" and "Kubla Khan" are the best evidence in favour
of Warton's statement. Confusion itself is regarded as a laudable
æsthetic quality. It would be difficult to acknowledge further
the rights of the imagination as opposed to classical perspicuity
and definiteness.

981) *Ibid.*
982) *Ibid.*
983) *Ibid.*
984) Cf. V. Nov. 148 *n.*

12. THE COMMENTARIES BETWEEN WARTON AND TODD (1785—1798).

A. MINOR PUBLICATIONS.

It was mentioned in the introduction to the present treatise [985]) how enthusiastically some critics received Warton's edition. This welcome was not quite unanimous. The pamphlet we have to treat of [986]) attacks Warton's Milton from the point of view of staunch literary conservatism. Warton's "Spleen, Prejudice, or Party-Spirit" are condemned. The pamphleteer professes to be no Calvinist himself [987]) but he sneers at the Church of England and censures Warton for his hostility to Calvinism [988]). This tendency agrees with the critic's anti-romantic trend, in accordance with the spirit of the religion he defends. Warton's predilection for popular poetry and "the English *blacke Letter* Classics" are ridiculed, "the present age" being accused of manifesting "an uncommon Relish for all such Reading as was never read" [989]). These writers are considered "very well" for children: *"Young Ravens must have Food".* Shakespeare is, however, exempted from this condemnatory verdict. The critic finds that he "can hardly be published too often" [990]).

Much attention is given to the looseness of the editor's method, particularly to his excessive quotations [991]).

Some attacks on Pope and Newton in Warton's edition are rigorously censured [992]), but the remarks made by the writer on Bishop Parker [993]) are so hostile that his right of criticizing

---

[985]) Cf. p. 18.

[986]) A LETTER TO THE REV. MR. T. WARTON, ON HIS LATE EDITION OF MILTON'S JUVENILE POEMS. LONDON: Printed for C. BATHURST, in Fleet-street. MDCCLXXXV.
[Price One Shilling.]
8°: pp. [2] + 41. Anonymous.

[987]) Cf. p. 38.

[988]) Cf. pp. 37—38.

[989]) Cf. p. 40.

[990]) *Ibid.*

[991]) Pp. 16 *et seq.*

[992]) Pp. 21—23.

[993]) P. 32.

the comparatively reserved strictures of Warton seems very
questionable. Yet some of the retorts in the pamphlet show its
author's positive qualities in a more favourable light than this.
Occasionally he shows some imaginative insight, *e. g.* in his
explanation of "amber stream" in P. R. III. 288 994). According
to Warton, this word means clearness, when applied to water, and
a bright yellow, when used of hair. His critic finds that "A clear
transparent Stream, rolling over a fine yellow Sand, suggests the
Idea of Amber", a hint which would seem to agree with the situation described by Milton. Now and then, the writer shows some
knowledge of philology, *e. g.* in his discussion of the original
meaning of "kirtle" 995), and Warton's descriptions of country
life are criticized and supplemented by him 996). All this does not
mean that the critic disapproves of Warton's work as a whole.
The very beginning of the pamphlet welcomes the edition, stating,
however, that the writer's principal aim is to study its defects.
His inability to do justice to the most conspicuous feature of Warton's labours, his rehabilitation of older English literature, proves, nevertheless, that the opponent was not particularly well
qualified for his task.

David Steel's "Elements of Punctuation" 997) contain some
notes on Miltonic passages. Most of these elaborate the punctuation without contributing to the elucidation of the text. In certain
cases, emendations are proposed which show some sense of artistic
effects, as *e. g.* the suggestion to regard "however small" P. L. V.
257 as referring to "no cloud or ... Starr" P. L. V. 257—8
instead of connecting it with "Earth and the Gard'n of God"
P. L. V. 260. Steel vishes to intensify the visual effect of the scene
and asks whether it would not "give a stronger idea of the amazing
clearness of the prospect, to say, *no cloud or star,* however small,

---

994) P. 17, cf. Warton Co. 863 *n.*
995) Cf. p. 7.
996) Cf. p. 9, see Warton p. 169.
997) ELEMENTS OF PUNCTUATION: CONTAINING REMARKS
ON AN "ESSAY ON PUNCTUATION"; AND CRITICAL OBSERVA-
TIONS ON SOME PASSAGES IN MILTON. By DAVID STEEL, junior.
[*Motto from Horace.*] LONDON: Printed for the Author; and sold by
Mess. G. G. J. and J. Robinson, Pater-noster Row [+ 4 more names].
MDCC.LXXXVI.
8⁰: pp. XV + 175. — Pp. 121—129 contain "CRITICAL OBSERVA-
TIONS ON MILTON".

interpos'd to obstruct his sight?" A comma after "small" in
P. L. V. 258 would be sufficient to achieve this effect. But the
instances where Steel adds anything essential to the analyses of
his predecessors are rare.

The edition of Gillies [998]) contains little beside biblical parallels. The few explanatory notes subjoined by him are insignificant. He seems to be anxious to disprove that Milton might have
suggested the possibility of any sordid thought in Mammon before the rebellion of the angels [999]) and objects to Newton's hint
that Milton avoided religious rites in his family [1000]). An attempt
towards a more adequate understanding of the characters of the
poem is made in VI. 568 *n.* where the puns of Satan and the other
devils are described as "proud malignant scoffing", which seems
to agree with the gloomy temper of the fallen angels. But these
are merely chance observations. The main aim of this edition is,
according to its preface, "to show *this only,* that Paradise Lost
owes its chief excellence to the Holy Scriptures". Hence Gillies's
careful study of scriptural parallelisms.

B.   CAPEL ·LOFFT'S EDITION OF "PARADISE LOST".

> PARADISE LOST. A POEM IN TWELVE BOOKS. THE
> AUTHOR JOHN MILTON. Printed from the FIRST and
> SECOND Editions collated. THE ORIGINAL SYSTEM OF
> ORTHOGRAPHY RESTORED; THE PUNCTUATION COR-
> RECTED AND EXTENDED. WITH VARIOUS READINGS:
> AND NOTES; CHIEFLY RHYTHMICAL. By CAPEL LOFFT.
> "Ego" (hîc quidem locî) " *sic scribendum Quicque judico quo-*

---

[998]) Milton's Paradise Lost ILLUSTRATED WITH TEXTS OF
SCRIPTURE, by JOHN GILLIES, D. D. ONE OF THE MINISTERS IN
GLASGOW. [Motto from P. L. III. 26 & c.] LONDON: PRINTED FOR
J. F. AND C. RIVINGTON, L. DAVIS, B. WHITE AND SON, T. LONG-
MAN... [altogether 22 names]... MDCCLXXXVIII.

12⁰: pp. [2] + XXIV + 384 + [22]. *Contents:* p. [1], title; p. I,
dedctn; pp. III—IV, preface; pp. V—XIX, Fenton's life with postscript;
pp. XX—XXIII, laudatory verses on P. L.; p. XXIV, The Verse; p. 1—384,
text of P. L. with notes; pp. [1—22], index.

The second edition, 12⁰, 1793, is slightly different. Both this and the
third edition, 12⁰, 1804, have lists of Milton's imitations of the classics at
the end of each book. The names of the publishers in the imprints differ.

[999]) I. 679 *n.*
[1000]) IV. 720 *n.*

*modo sonet. Hic enim usus est Litterarum, ut custodiant voces,
et velut* Depositum *reddant legentibus. Itaque id exprimere
debent quod* dicturi *sumus."* QUINTIL. 1. 7. *Worthy of sacred
Silence to be heard! In nobilissimo Poemate* MILTONUS: *cujus
celebritas crescit indies; cum* MILTONUS *non sit tam hominis
nomen quàm Ingenii et Libertatis.* Wakefield SILV. CRIT. II.
§ 101. BURY ST. EDMUND'S: PRINTED AND SOLD by
J. RACKHAM. AND SOLD ALSO by J. STOCKDALE,
PICCADILLY; J. PHILLIPS, GEORGE YARD, LOMBARD-
STREET; T. C. RICKMAN, UPPER MARYBONE-STREET,
LONDON; W. STEVENSON, NORWICH; AND W. H. LUNN,
CAMBRIDGE. MDCCXCII.

4⁰: pp. [4] + LXIV [numeration wrong: numbers XLIX—
LIX used twice, so that actually = pp. LXXIV] + sign. B—D⁴,
E⁴. *Contents:* p. [1], title; p. [3], advertisement; p. [4], errata
& c.; pp. I—LXII, prefatory matter; p. LXIII, half-title to bk.
I of P. L.; signn. B—E₄r, text of bk. I with notes.
THE FIRST AND SECOND BOOKS OF PARADISE LOST.
THE AUTHOR JOHN MILTON. Printed from the FIRST and
SECOND Editions collated. THE ORIGINAL SYSTEM OF
ORTHOGRAPHY RESTORED; THE PUNCTUATION COR-
RECTED AND EXTENDED. WITH THE VARIOUS READ-
INGS: AND NOTES; CHIEFLY RHYTHMICAL. BY CAPEL
LOFFT, BURY ST. EDMUND'S: PRINTED AND SOLD BY
J. RACKHAM, STATIONER. AND SOLD ALSO BY J .STOCK-
DALE, PICCADILLY; J. PHILLIPS, GEORGE-YARD, LOM-
BARD-STREET; T. C. RICKMAN, UPPER MARYBONE-
STREET, LONDON; W. STEVENSON, NORWICH; AND W. H.
LUNN, CAMBRIDGE. MDCCXCIII.

4⁰. As before, but added: advertisement to ed. II., with
special numeration [pp. I—IV], text of bk. II (signn. F—L₂v),
with notes, a portrait and a facsimile from the Trin. Coll. MS.

Capel Lofft's edition, or what has been published of it, contains few notes, but the preliminary matter announces what he
intended to do.

The title-page already indicates the main aspects under which
he proposes to investigate the poem. Milton's rhythm, orthography
and punctuation, as well as the various readings of his text, are
mentioned there and apparently constitute the principal subjects
of his study. Elsewhere he writes of subjoining "a copious *Index;*
a *Table* illustrative of MILTON's Use and Application of Scripture; an Extract from the *Criticisms* of JOHNSON; and perhaps
the critical Essay of ADDISON; and some, possibly, of the most
remarkable of the modern TESTIMONIES", but no life of the

poet, for want of space [1001]). The introductory part of the book contains a considerable amount of bibliographical and textual information which cannot be dealt with in detail here, as it falls outside the scope of the present thesis. A minute account of the authentic editions [1002]), a table of all the editions known to Lofft, a bibliographical description of two of the earliest posthumous ones, *viz.* those of 1688 and 1707, and various miscellaneous matter prove the editors care and thoroughness.

However, Lofft's studies in Milton's spellings, punctuation, rhythm, and, in connection with these, notably also in his intonation, remain the principal part of his introductory matter. He examines these features from a phonetic point of view, investigating the artistic effects produced by their aid. The authentic editions are scrutinized in order to understand the poet's phonetic intentions. The editor's method of approaching his subject is systematic, and his knowledge of phonetics that of a specialist, or at least of a remarkably well-informed amateur. He acknowledges his indebtedness in these matters to various scholars, *e. g.* in his study of Milton's punctuation, to his uncle, the Shakespeare editor Edward Capel [1003]), in points of orthography to J. Walker, the author of the "Rhetorical Grammar" [1004]), the elder Richardson [1005]), & c.

Lofft's remarks on Milton's *orthography* mean to show that the poet purported both to mark "the usual pronunciation with more certainty and consistency from the common mode" and to suggest a pronunciation more acceptable to the ear than the usual one — one that is "more dignified, or more impressively solemn [1006]).

A conspicuous defect of Lofft's disquisitions is his excessive tendency to theorize, often without adducing any sufficient evidence. His interpretation of his materials strikes one as rather arbitrary, though his ideas considered apart from the data of Milton's text are ingenious enough. Only two instances are given of the poet's supposed method of doubling the consonants in order

---

[1001]) Cf. p. XXVII.
[1002]) Cf. p. II & *seq.* and p. LIII & *seq.*
[1003]) Cf. Lofft, p. XV.
[1004]) Cf. p. VIII.
[1005]) Cf. p. I.
[1006]) Cf. p. VII.

to indicate that the preceding vowel is short, but neither of these examples ("solid, metal") is very convincing [1007].. Both the double and the single spellings of the consonants are found in Milton's poetry in these cases, "solid" even being generally spelt with a single *l*. The same carelessness appears in Lofft's statements as to the spellings of "ball" and "hill". According to him, Milton uses a single *l* in these words. As a matter of fact, the double spelling predominates in "ball", and "hill" is generally written in the contemporary fashion. This unreliable basis is used by Lofft for a superstructure of theories. In his view, the single spelling of *l* in "ball" is due to the desire to avoid the clash of the double consonant with "the long and open power of the vowel" [1008]). In "hill", the same method of spelling is ascribed to the circumstance that "the vowel, short in its own power, has no need of doubling the consonant to show it to be short" [1009]). This is evidently inconsistent with the assumption that the double spelling of the consonants in the cases mentioned above indicates a short vowel, for even there the vowels are "short in their own power", no matter how the consonants are spelt. The manner of expression is vague, to say the least.

Conjectural spellings based on theories as to the pronunciation of Milton's verse that sometimes are of a rather questionable character, occur repeatedly. An example is the distinction drawn by Lofft between the phonetic value of *y* and *ie* ["*Y* in termination is very similar to the short *i*; when the vowel rests a little longer upon it, *ie* will express its power better", p. X]. The observation that a vowel is weakened (or, according to Lofft, shortened) when following a strongly stressed syllable [1010]), is in accord with contemporary phonetics, but there are hardly any traces of Milton having attempted any discrimination of this sort, at any rate not among the instances adduced by Lofft. Parallel spellings such as "massy" and "massie", "luxury" and "luxurie", "cloudy" and "cloudie", "happy" and "happie", "every" and "everie" are frequent in "Paradise Lost", as a glance at the concordance would prove, and it would probably be very difficult to find in them

---

[1007]) Cf. p. X.
[1008]) Cf. p. IX.
[1009]) *Ibid.*
[1010]) Cf. p X.

any indications of differences in the pronunciation of the ending. Lofft's spelling of these words is independent of Milton.

In spite of these and other failures, Lofft succeeds in bringing out the phonetic character of some of Milton's spellings. This was already the elder Richardson's aim [1011]). Etymological preconceptions blinded the more narrow-minded Newton to this important aspect of Milton's orthography [1012]). In his distinction between emphatic and non-emphatic forms [1013]), Lofft seems to be guided by Richardson and J. Walker, the author of the "Rhetorical Grammar" [1014]). The category of "softened" or "mollified" forms observed by Newton and Peck [1015]) is dealt with in connection with such cases as "perfet" for "perfect", "counterfet" for "counterfeit", & c. (p. IX). The phonetic intention in a spelling such as "wrauth" for "wrath", where it is unmistakable, is indicated with sufficient precision, and Aubrey's testimony, which is not mentioned by Lofft, corroborates the assumption that Milton may have felt induced to double the r in order to indicate "a more forcible and animated utterance" [1016]) (cf. warr II. 41 & c., farr II. 98 & c., scarr II. 4C1, demurr II. 431). Though the idea of bringing home Milton's care in conveying phonetic effects by orthographic means is not new, Lofft is the first to carry it out on a large scale, and even his less convincing conjectures in this department are often stimulating, as most of the examples dealt with in the preceding paragraph may show.

The boldest part of Lofft's enterprise is his attempt to mark Milton's *"ambiguities* of *Accent, Emphasis,* or *Cadence"* (which evidently means *intonation, stress* and *rhythm*; Lofft distinguishes between acute, grave and compound or circumflex accent, *e. g.* p. XV, and cadence and rhythm are identified, *ibid.*). His admiration for the "majestic flow of numbers" in "Paradise Lost", which he considers "analogous to a grand *Concerto* Composition for

---

[1011]) Cf. above, chapter on Richardson.

[1012]) Cf. chapter on Newton.

[1013]) *E. g.* "thir" and "their", "he" and "hee", & c., cf. p. L.

[1014]) Cf. p. VIII.

[1015]) Cf. above, on Newton and Peck.

[1016]) Cf. Aubrey, Bodleian MS., fol 63v: "He pronounced ye letter R very hard"...

the favourite instrument of *Milton,* the ORGAN", causes him to adopt a new, more varied system of punctuation. He wishes to help "the understanding, the ear, and the heart" towards an appreciation of the full effect of Milton's verse [1017]), evidently "so as to approximate, as much as might be, to the Design of the Author" [1018]). But this is done in a somewhat arbitrary manner. Partly owing to the influence of his uncle Edward Capel, his punctuation becomes so minute that no security remains of its corresponding with Milton's actual intentions. Not only the ordinary stops are given, though Lofft professes to confine himself to them as far as possible [1019]). Quite new marks are introduced in order to convey the subtler effects of Milton's verse as Lofft himself interprets them. What his punctuation expresses, is mainly his personal way of reading Milton.

Some of the most conspicuous marks used by Lofft are: 1) dots to denote "an agitated Pause; from the Influence of some powerful Emotion", 2) "double breaks" for indicating "longer and more disconnected" pauses and "a less regular Continuance of the succeeding Passage" caused rather by "Perplexity and Perturbation, as of Shame and Remorse", than by "the high and vehement Emotions", 3) so-called "suspensive pauses" used to mark sometimes "the *merely Rhythmical* Cadence", sometimes "the Cadence, as relative to the Sentiment and Expression; but usually both" and comparable to "the *Pesick,* enumerated amongst the *tonic* Accents of the Hebrew Poetry", but also in certain cases "to the ᾿Αγωγη, or *Ductus Rhythmicus* of the Antients"; 4) marks for ironical turns of language, as well as a considerable number of other symbols [1020]). It is noteworthy that in most of these marks the *emotional* values of rhythm, stress and intonation are taken into account.

Sometimes Lofft pays attention to the hints actually given by Milton concerning these features, though more often he seems to be following his own imagination. He takes into consideration the remarks which now and then precede the speeches of Milton's characters to describe their rhythm. Thus,

---

[1017]) *Ibid.*
[1018]) Cf. p. XXVI.
[1019]) Cf. p. XV.
[1020]) Cf. p. XXXII.

according to him, "in the first Book, the *bold* Words previously
ascribed to the first Speech, the quickness of Reply to the second,
the *Despair* (in the parenthetic *Epiphonema*) to the third, give
the general Movement almost as distinctly as indicated at the
head of a Piece of Music" [1021]). The last part of this sentence
shows, however, the confidence with which Lofft drew inferences
from the vague hints he found.

Lofft's judicious method of basing his conjectures on a study
of the peculiarities of the English language instead of adopting
conventional notions derived from classical scholarship, prevents
him from interpreting the apostrophe ['] as an indication of
the complete omission of a vowel. He apparently describes the
impression of his own ear in calling it "The mark of greatest
Acceleration, when placed over a vowel: rarely of *Apocope* or
Elision: which is not suited to the genius of our Language" [1022]).
His careful study of the connection between form and emotion
appears from a remark on Bentley's treatment of Milton's metre.
Bentley tries to avoid all redundant syllables [1023]), to which Lofft
objects, finding such cases of metrical redundancies frequent in
Milton in passages so "full of Passion and Agitation" as the one
under consideration [1024]).

Lofft's adherence to the principle of investigating Milton's
literary practice by the aid of authentic data ought to have been
more strict to lead to satisfactory results. His critical self-control
is much inferior to his ingenuity and his interest in artistic effects.
Nevertheless, his experiment is remarkable as an attempt at
applying new scientific standards to the study of Milton's art.

C. CHARLES DUNSTER'S EDITION OF "PARADISE REGAINED".

PARADISE REGAINED, A POEM, IN FOUR BOOKS, BY
JOHN MILTON. A NEW EDITION, WITH NOTES OF
VARIOUS AUTHORS, By CHARLES DUNSTER, M. A.
[*Motto from Plato*]. London: PRINTED FOR T. CADELL,
JUN. AND W. DAVIES, (SUCCESSORS TO MR. CADELL,)
IN THE STRAND. 1795.

[1021]) Cf. p. XIV.
[1022]) Cf. p. XXXII.
[1023]) Cf. chap. 3, sec. B.
[1024]) P. L. I. 91.

4⁰: pp. [4] + IV + [4] + 280. *Contents:* p. [1], title;
p. [3], dedctn to the Earl of Egremont; pp. I—IV, preface;
p. [1], half-title to book I; p. [3], argument of bk I (like the
arguments to the other books, by Dunster); pp. 1—270, text of
the poem with notes and retrospective summaries added to each
book; pp. 271—280, "Corrections and Supplemental Notes".

The second edition appeared probably in 1800 (= B. Mus.
Cat.), though the title-page does not indicate the date: PA-
RADISE REGAINED A POEM BY JOHN MILTON, with
NOTES, of various Authors, BY CHARLES DUNSTER, M. A.
[illustration] LONDON Printed by Geo. Stafford, Crane Court
Fleet Street; and Sold by R. H. Evans, Pall Mall; T. Payne,
Mews Gate; J. Robson, Bond Street; J. Nicholls, Red Lion
Passage Fleet Street. — Archer DUBLIN; and Layng EDIN-
BURGH.

The size and most of the contents the same as in the first
edition. Added: a full-page illustration from Salvator Rosa,
a map of the places mentioned by Milton, a dedicatory poem (page
unnumbered) and some introductory matter (pp. III—VI; the
numeration wrong, for numbers III and IV here for the second
time). The additional prefatory matter includes a comparison
of a scene in the poem with the picture of S. Rosa and speculations on the circumstances of the composition of the epic.

Warton seems to have left the mark of his method on much
that is found in Dunster's edition. The latter's preface, which,
though acknowledging the merits of Newton's edition of "Paradise
Lost", speaks slightingly of his „Paradise Regained", on the
contrary, bestows the highest praise on Warton's "eminence in
every branch of criticism", which "so particularly qualified him
for the office" of editing "Paradise Regained" and "Samson
Agonistes" in accordance with a plan frustrated only by the
critic's death. According to a further remark in Dunster's
prefatory matter, Joseph Warton had been willing to lend him
his deceased brother's interleaved copy of "Paradise Regained"
but was unable to find it. There are distinct traces of Dunster
being influenced by Warton's method. He adopts Warton's practice
of adducing copious parallels from Milton's own works, referring
to the arguments in favour of this method found in "the excellent
OBSERVATIONS ON THE FAERY QUEEN" by Warton, *i. e.*
to its value as showing the poet's favourite images, as making
it possible to trace his different ways of putting similar ideas,
and as leading to the elucidation of the meaning of difficult

passages and words [1025]). Similarly, the relative frequency and manysidedness of Dunster's illustrations from other authors seems to indicate that the attention which Warton paid to this branch of his studies has stimulated the industry of his successor. However, the differences between the tastes of the two critics are conspicuous. Dunster's inclinations seem to suit the task of editing "Paradise Regained" better than that of dealing with his early poems. He is indeed interested in Milton's English predecessors, as many notes in his edition as well as his inquiries into the relationship between Milton and Joshua Sylvester [1026]) and his contributions to Todd's later edition of Milton's poetry distinctly prove. Nevertheless, he could not be compared to Warton in this respect. His first-hand knowledge of the literature of various languages, especially of Italian [1027]) and Neo-Latin [1028]) writers, is exploited less consistently than his thorough familiarity with scriptural and classical lore. His erudition in this latter field is exactly what was needed for the explanation of the main difficulties in "Paradise Regained". Particularly his minute observations on historical, geographical, social and other problems of a non-literary character show his competence in these remoter departments of scholarship. A good example of his care in these matters is found in his treatment of the problem from what mountain Milton supposes Christ and the Tempter to be looking down in P. R. III. 253. Dunster's interest in biblical questions [1029]) and a certain religious tendency [1030]) qualify him for the study of the sacred

---

[1025]) Cf. pp. III and IV of the preface.

[1026]) On Milton and J. Sylvester: CONSIDERATIONS ON MILTON'S EARLY READING, AND THE PRIMA STAMINA OF HIS PARADISE LOST; TOGETHER WITH EXTRACTS FROM A POET OF THE SIXTEENTH CENTURY. IN A LETTER TO WILLIAM FALCONER, M. D. FROM CHARLES DUNSTER, M. A. PRINTED BY AND FOR JOHN NICHOLS, RED-LION PASSAGE, FLEET-STREET, LONDON; AND SOLD BY R. H. EVANS... 1800.

8°: p. [4] + 249.

[1027]) Cf. I. 13 supplem. note, I. 474, 500 nn. II. 289, 295 nn., & c.

[1028]) P. R. I. 83 n., I. 209 n., & c.

[1029]) Cf. P. R. I. 306 n., II. 17 n., II. 20 n., & c.

[1030]) His preface describes the spirit of the two epics with some religious fervour: "... the two poems mutually coincide with, and admirably

aspects of Milton's epic. His literary leanings, which **are** considerably influenced by the classicism of his period, though they show distinct traces of the influence of the freer movements of the latter part of the century, harmonize with the intellectual, academic trend that becomes stronger in Milton's later poems. For all that, his imagination is vivid enough to make him susceptible to the artistic excellence of many passages of the poem the rescue of which "from neglect and oblivion" [1031]) is, as he declares, his object.

Warton's influence may have caused Dunster to give due consideration to the biographical and personal aspects of "Paradise Regained". A careful, intimate description of the house at Chalfont where he supposes Milton to have written the epic is one of the best examples of Dunster's care to give an idea of the environment in which the poet composed his work [1032]). The whole problem of the composition of the poem is dealt with from a point of view combining *artistic* and *psychological* with *biographical* considerations, with an acuteness reminiscent of Warton. Dunster's argument is that Milton must have composed the whole of the work at Chalfont. Besides studying the biographical documents, he takes into account Milton's character as shown in a letter to Diodati of Sept. 2. 1637 "where he describes his own temper to be marked with an eagerness to finish whatever he had begun". Furthermore, he bases his calculations on the *artistic* character of the poem, particularly, in a manner typical of him, as has to be shown below, on its *structure:* "There is... such a high degree of unity, connection, and integral perfection in the whole of his second poem, as indicates it to have been the *uninterrupted* work of one season, and, as I would suppose, the exclusive occupation of his divine genius during his residence in Buckinghamshire". He calculates the exact amount of work falling upon each day of that period, carefully weighing the degree of inspiration perceptible in the different passages of the poem: "To have composed the whole of the poem in that time, would require him to produce only about

illustrate, each other; while they comprehend the *whole* of an argument the most interesting that can be to human beings, — to *fallen* and *redeemed* creatures" (p. IV.).

[1031]) Pref. p. II.
[1032]) Cf. p. IV, 2nd ed.

ten lines a day; and many parts are given so perfectly *con amore*, that I am confident, upon those occasions, he proceeded *at a very different rate*" 1033). These conclusions may be bold but the argumentation is by no means devoid of logic and the manner of approach is entirely psychological and artistic, while being based on a study of the hard facts of Milton's life. We have tried to show that this was, to a great extent, also Warton's method. It is not unlikely that the latter may have influenced Dunster in this respect. This refined method could be managed only by a keen intellect, a faculty which Dunster evidently possessed.

The main characteristics of Dunster's critical temper are calm, deliberate calculation and balanced, sensitive culture. They appear in his fundamental views on the artistic character of the poem. His conception differs considerably from that of his predecessors, Newton and Thyer 1034). One of the main problems dealt with in their estimates of the work was that of the respective intensity of Milton's imaginative faculty as manifested in "Paradise Lost" and "Paradise Regained". Newton found it decidedly on the decline in the latter work. He even thought, as has been pointed out, that Milton's knowledge of this circumstance caused him deliberately to avoid any comparison with the descriptive excellence of "Paradise Lost". Thyer, on the contrary, held that Milton's imagination struggled with the fetters imposed by the narrow, inconvenient plot and broke forth wherever the subject allowed it. He regards the argumentative manner as a handicap on the poet which is mainly due to the theme of the work.

Dunster assumes neither a decline in Milton's poetic powers nor a struggle between those two styles, but a deliberate handling of these opposite methods, the one being used to set off the other. Thyer tended to ascribe his own impulsive manner to the poet, whereas Newton did not seem to feel the great imaginative beauties of many parts of the work. Dunster does not deny the artistic excellences of the descriptive passages but also tries to follow the *combinative* logic in the author's technique, tracing the use he makes of the interplay of various poetic methods. Milton is supposed to have enjoyed the opportunities for

---

1033) *Ibid.*
1034) Cf. above, chap. 9, sec. A.

"introducing... admirable descriptions", being aware of "the great effect which the *argumentative cast* of the poem would give to that which is purely descriptive" [1035]). Dunster may over-emphasize the deliberateness of Milton's method of composition. Thyer's opinion is supported by various critics. M. Denis Saurat ascertains even in "Paradise Lost" the contrast between the "stiff conventionalism" of most parts of it, and the sudden explosions of the revolting imagination to be found every now and then [1036]). Both he himself and, as shown by his quotation, Walter Savage Landor see the same divergences in "Paradise Regained" [1037]). Nevertheless, the emphasis laid on Milton's conscious workmanship is valuable as a stimulus towards the study of this aspect of the poet's art [1038]).

How much deliberation in Milton's method of producing the effects of vividness and reality Dunster assumed, is shown by various notes. A good example is found in a somewhat later note, one incorporated in Todd's edition, but illuminating in this connection, and therefore to be discussed here. It deals with P. R. IV. 549. The treatment of the temptation in the gospel of St. Luke is compared with that in Milton's pœm. In St. Luke's gospel, Christ, according to Dunster, sees mere visions, which in Milton are transformed into reality. Dunster finds this necessary, because, as he says, "no succession of visionary scenes, however exquisitely described", could have effected a sufficient contrast to the argumentative parts. There seems to appear in this statement a certaiń overvaluation of the mere assumption of reality, but the remark certainly shows that Dunster was perfecly conscious of the *practical* importance of the imaginative element in poetry.

His *theoretical* views on the part played by the imagination indicate, however, that he had only a superficial notion of its actual import. He does not seem to regard it as inherent in the poetical attitude but rather as added to the real essence of the latter as a kind of external decoration. Such at least is his opinion with regard to sacred poetry, in which the imaginative

---

[1035]) Cf. IV. 238 *n.*
[1036]) Saurat's "Milton", p. 220.
[1037]) *Ibid.* p. 235.
[1038]) Dunster's observations at the end of each book show this tendency very clearly.

touch is considered by him a mere means of attracting the reader's attention, in order to secure a public for the religious teachings which, in his opinion, are the main object of this poetic species 1039). The note containing these ideals also states his theory of poetry. Prose, according to him, needs no ornaments but "purity and perspicuity" whereas poetry is "elevated and ornamented language". The only means of such decoration expressly mentioned by him are "metrical arrangement" and "mythological references and allusions and classical imitations" — none of these, except possibly the first, indispensable constituents of poetry. They are essentially the requisites, rather, of a certain traditional literary manner, *viz.* the classicist style. The fact that he regards them as inconsistent with the character of religious poetry, a poetic kind which he seems to value particularly highly, and that he admits them in this species only for entirely extraneous considerations, shows that he does not very firmly believe in the value of these features himself. He finds it unsuitable for a divine poem to be written in anything but what he regards as "the chastest style", the only alternative he sees being the introduction of "false ornament" — as if there were no possibility of using "ornament" sincerely and as a result of emotion. The only justification for the use of these spurious embellishments is, in his view, the propagandist object already mentioned: "... the great reason of exhibiting any serious truths, and especially the more interesting facts of religious history, through the medium of poetry, is thereby more powerfully to attract the attention" 1040). "Poetry, to please, must continue to be pleasing" 1041). This is why Milton "sprinkled his *Paradise Lost* with flowers of Classick Poetry, and the fictions of Greek and Roman Mythology" 1042). Poetry here becomes entirely subservient to religion, as in Meadowcourt's theories 1043). The reactionary character of this attitude becomes particularly obvious if compared with Warton's advanced views. However, Warton did not formulate the theoretical basis of his criticism with sufficient distinctness. It is only to be guessed

---

1039) P. R. II. 188*n.*
1040) *Ibid.*
1041) *Ibid.*
1042) *Ibid.*
1043) Cf. section on Meadowcourt.

at, at least in his edition of Milton; and Dunster from intellectual inertia seems to have fallen back on the current views of his age. His capacity of perceiving subtle effects of descriptive beauty and of enjoying them does not seem to have been affected by his almost anti-imaginative tenets. Little touches of fine imagery impress him far more deeply than they did Newton. An instance is P. R. 499 *n.* Newton finds the *brevity* of the representation of night scenery in this passage an indicatiom of the poet's sense of his present inferiority to the perfection of similar passages in "Paradise Lost". Dunster, on the contrary, bases his different judgement on quality and not on quantity. He considers this description as a "small but exquisite *sketch*, which so immediately shews the *hand of the master*, that his larger and more finished pieces can hardly be rated higher" [1044]).

Dunster's grasp of the structural element appears also in his treatment of Milton's characters. He sometimes studies their conduct in connection with the development of the action, pointing out the structural effects produced by their behaviour [1045]). He succeeds sometimes in showing the important effect on structure of the *irrational* impulses of Milton's *dramatis personæ*. Thyer similarly saw the shifting, struggling emotions of the characters of Milton's poems, but he concentrated on *isolated moments* [1046]). Dunster may be a less acute observer of a given frame of mind, but he is more skilled in seeing its *connection with the rest*. An illustration of his method is found in the note to P. R. IV. 166, written to refute Newton's rash condemnation of Satan's "awkward and preposterous demand" that Christ should worship him, though the gifts which he had offered to tempt the Saviour had already been "rejected.... unclogged with any terms at all".

Newton sees merely the seeming absurdity of the point, apparently assuming that Satan's actions must needs be logical and consistent. Dunster, on the contrary, tries to analyse the possible reasons of the incongruity of Satan's action, both from the point of view of his character and from that of the structural intentions of Milton. He studies the Tempter's behaviour from

---

[1044]) P. R. I. 499 *n.*
[1045]) See the retrospective surveys at the end of each book.
[1046]) Cf. above, chap. 9, sec. A.

the very beginning of the poem, explaining it in the present case as an unexpected impulse of emotion prepared by the whole previous course of the work and at the same time very helpful to Milton's artistic plan. Satan's careful, sane attitude is said to have been eventually turned into irresponsible rage through his successive failures. He is thrown "completely... off his guard", betraying his purpose by revealing, "with the most intemperate indiscretion, those *abominable terms*, which, could it have been possible for his temptations to have succeeded, we may imagine were intended in the end to have been proposed to our Lord". This tends to make Satan's step intelligible as a revelation of his character. Dunster also tries to show that it was inevitable for the sake of the structure of the poem, for if Satan had stated his conditions simultaneously with his offer of the gifts, the "pushing the question immediately to the point" would have "precluded the gradually progressive temptations", thus spoiling Milton's plan. This hypothesis and the tentative explanation of the arising difficulties by the plausible assumption of the emotional inconsistency of Satan's actions prove, firstly, a less rigid and narrow conception of character, and, secondly, a keener insight into the possibilities of poetic construction than were to be found in Newton's remarks.

Dunster deals less with Milton's *style* and *language* than Warton or Newton did. Occasionally he traces classical features of expression, sometimes adding quite substantially to the observations of earlier commentators: in ascertaining, for example, the occurrence in Greek poetry of expressions corresponding to phrases of the type of P. R. I. 94: "on the utmost edge Of hazard" [1047]) or in studying peculiar Latin acceptations of common words, as in P. R. IV. 235 *n.* At times he also calls attention to Elizabethan features of style [1048]). But such remarks are not very frequent, and Dunster does not go very deeply into this aspect of the matter. Some stray observations show which artistic features seem to have struck him in Milton's style. Dunster's classical training is reflected in these notes and leads him to a high valuation of Milton's concise, energetic manner of expression, notwithstanding the obscurity which

[1047]) See P. R. I. 94 *n.;* cf. also P. L. I. 276, VI. 108.
[1048]) Cf. *e. g.* P. R. III. 217 *n.*

occasionally results through excessive condensation. In this appreciative judgement he is notably at one with the elder Richardson [1049]), though it is of interest to note that the latter can hardly have been influenced by the style of classical antiquity whereas by Dunster the classics are expressly mentioned. Dunster contrasts Milton's taste with that of the thoughtless crowd who are puzzled by energy and compactness [1050]). His assumption is that much of this tendency is of Latin origin [1051]): "Milton sometimes, from a wish to compress, latinises, so as to confuse and obscure his language considerably" [1052]). Despite these drawbacks, the remarkable qualities accompanying them are readily acknowledged. Dunster quotes "what Cicero has said of the ancient orators: *Grandes erant verbis, crebri sententiis, compressione rerum breves, et ob eam ipsam causam interdum subobscuri*" [1053]). The contrasts which this affords to Calton's shallow strictures on Milton's elliptic style is noteworthy. Thorough scholarship and a vigorous taste combine to rectify the blunders of less penetrating minds.

It is to be noted that Dunster successfully analyses Newton's fundamental error of reading Milton's verse according to the prescriptions of classical prosodians [1054]). His main authority in metrical questions is Blair, whom he quotes, amongst other things, on the problem of supernumerary syllables. These, according to that quotation, do not disappear but are only slurred, so as "to bring the verse, with respect to its effect upon the ear, within the usual bounds" [1055]). Dunster seems to be more conservative than this on the question of elision, holding the view that a final *y* disappears before a vowel [1056]).

As a whole, Dunster's edition indicates that he was a man of considerable culture and acuteness whose poetic sensibility enabled him to appreciate the subtleties of his author. His keen

---

1049) Cf. chap. 5.
1050) P. R. I. 439 *n*.
1051) Prof. Masson in his ed. of Milton 1893, vol. III, p. 192 ascribes some of this trend to the elliptic rapidity of Elizabethan speech.
1052) P. R. I. 137 *n*.
1053) *Ibid.*
1054) P. R. I. 302 *n*.
1055) *Ibid.*
1056) *Ibid.*

combinative faculty makes him a good judge of problems of structure. Moralism and intellectualism are probably the main defects of his literary theories, particularly of his treatment of what he regards as the ornamental element in poetry. These handicaps are, however, hardly felt in his critical practice. He accomplished for "Paradise Regained", though not in the same degree, what Warton had done for the Minor Poems, *viz.* he supplied the illustrative material needed for the understanding of a very considerable part of its more difficult allusions, and a number of illuminating remarks on artistic points. In thoroughness and critical sensitiveness, he far surpasses Newton and most of his collaborators. What one rather misses, is an endeavour equal to that of Warton to explain Milton from *contemporary* sources. Dunster, as has been shown, was perfectly well acquainted with the biographical method of interpretation. If he did not practise it more, the reason was probably in part his keen interest in the facts of ancient history, geography and letters, which claim so much of his attention.

13. HENRY JOHN TODD'S EDITIONS OF MILTON.
A. "COMUS" (1798).

COMUS, A MASK PRESENTED AT LUDLOW CASTLE 1634, BEFORE THE EARL OF BRIDGEWATER, THEN PRESIDENT OF WALES: BY JOHN MILTON. WITH NOTES CRITICAL AND EXPLANATORY BY VARIOUS COMMENTATORS, AND WITH PRELIMINARY ILLUSTRATIONS; TO WHICH IS ADDED A COPY OF THE MASK FROM A MANUSCRIPT BELONGING TO HIS GRACE THE DUKE OF BRIDGEWATER: BY HENRY JOHN TODD, M. A. CHAPLAIN TO THE RIGHT HON. THE EARL OF FIFE AND THE LORD VISCOUNT KILMOREY, AND MINOR CANON OF CANTERBURY. "THE HARP OF ORPHEUS WAS NOT MORE CHARMING." MILTON'S TRACTATE OF EDUCATION. CANTERBURY, Printed by and for W. Bristow on the Parade: For Messrs. Rivingtons St. Paul's Churchyard, and ... Clarke New Bond-street, London; Messrs. Fletcher and Co. Oxford; and J. Deighton Cambridge. MDCCXCVIII.

8⁰: pp. XXI + [1] + 62 + [2] + 199. *Contents:* p. I, half-title; p. III, title; p. V, dedictn to the Rev. F. H. Egerton; pp. VII—XX, preface; p. XXI, list of contents; p. [1], half-title to preliminary matter; pp. 1—2, Lawes's dedctn; pp. 3—8, Wotton's letter; pp. 9—18, account of Ludlow Castle; pp. 19—35, account of the Earl of Bridgewater and his family; pp. 35—49, on Henry Lawes; pp. 50—62, on the origin of "Comus"; p. [1], half-title to text and appendixes; p. [2], list of persons; pp. 1—144, text of "Comus", with notes; pp. 144—150, opinions of various critics; p. 151, half-title to Appendix No. 1; pp. 153—162, original various readings from the Trinity College MS. [= Appendix No. 1]; p. 163, half-title to Appendix No. 2; pp. 165—192, account, and copy, of the Ashridge MS. [= Appendix No. 2]; pp. 193—199, account of editions of "Comus".

a. The Preface.

Most of the main principles of Todd's edition of "Comus", which is the first instalment of his large edition of Milton's works, are stated or implied in his preface. It is evident that Warton [1057]), most of whose material concerning "Comus" is reprinted in this edition, as well as the majority of the other annotators and editors of Milton, have been carefully studied by Todd. His method shows that he has tried to keep pace with the development of research and criticism.

The tendency to found his edition on the authentic texts (which he praises as one of the main features of Newton's "well executed" and Warton's "admirable" editions) seems to have become a matter of course with him [1058]). A more conspicuous, because not quite so commonly found, characteristic, apparent from his preface, is his methodical way of studying Milton's spellings and, to a certain extent, his vocabulary also. In the first of these two departments, he seems to have been influenced by Capel Lofft [1059]). Warton's influence is manifest in the attention paid by Todd to his careful treatment of old words in Milton which "had been gradually and silently refined" by earlier editors [1060]). To Todd, these unusual expressions and spellings are "venerable anomalies or imitations" [1061]). He finds the poet's special words "more significant, or more suited to his purpose" than the ordinary vocabulary [1062]). Both in his treatment of Milton's vocabulary and of his spellings, Todd sides with the ideals of individuality and originality championed by Warton and Lofft.

In the preface, Todd adduces a considerable number of Miltonic spellings regarded by him as used deliberately to denote peculiarities of pronunciation. Thus, by carefully comparing a number of cases of the omission of vowels in Milton, he shows that this sometimes is a matter of pronunciation, not of spelling only.

[1057]) See also ed. of the Poetical Works of Milton, 1801, vol. I. preface, sg. Asv: "The chief purpose of the new notes, is, in humble imitation of Mr. Warton, 'to explain the allusions of Milton; to illustrate or to vindicate his beauties; to point out his imitations both of others, and of himself; to elucidate his obsolete diction; and, by the adduction and juxtaposition of parallels universally gleaned both from his poetry and prose, to ascertain his favourite words, and to show the peculiarities of his phraseology' ".

[1058]) Cf. preface, p. VII.

[1059]) The footnote to p. XII refers to Capel Lofft's "great learning and ingenuity". Roth Lofft (cf. above) and Todd (p. VIII) draw upon J. Walker's "Rhetorical Grammar".

[1060]) Cf. pref. p. VII.

[1061]) Cf. p. VIII.

[1062]) *Ibid.*

Newton reads "medicínal" in S. A. 627 ("Or medicinal liquor can assuage"), stressing the penultimate, as he says in his footnote. Milton's own text has "medicinal" and the only further instance of this word in his poetry, in Co. 636, is spelt "med'cinal", which makes it not improbable that this omission is intentional, and that the verse has four feet instead of five, like several other lines in the neighbourhood of this passage. On the other hand, some of the examples quoted seem to indicate that the *retention* of vowels in writing is not quite accidental, either. Such spellings as "prosperous", "hovering", & c. are supposed by the editor to indicate „three short, but distinct, syllables" 1063). This is certainly true of some cases, *e. g.* of P. L. XI. 364: "Prosperous or adverse: so shalt thou lead", as is proved by the metre. The ending *t* in some "perfect adjectives", *e. g.* in "thatch't" 1064), "dark't" 1065), "hutch't" 1066) is described as phonetic, which it is virtually, if not in design. Various further spellings are discussed from the same phonetic point of veiw. The contributions to Richardson's and Lofft's efforts in the same department are not inconsiderable.

An observation which seems to be new and appears to be due to a careful study of the characteristics of older poetry, is the remark that the spelling sometimes differs from the ordinary usage in rhyming words 1067), *e. g.* in "woom" Co. 131 (rhymes with "gloom"), in "clime" Co. 1020 instead of "climb" (rhymes with "chime"), in "chere" Co. 955, & c. Todd compares this practice with similar cases in Spenser 1068).

The remarks on the *vocabulary* of "Comus" refer mainly to the rustic air of Milton's archaisms, and may very easily have been influenced by the example of Peck, who called attention to this feature of the poet's style 1069). Due notice is taken of Milton's Italianisms 1070). Though most of the above observations merely develop the ideas of earlier critics, Todd's careful treatment of facts as well as his solid knowledge of his material make

---

1063) Cf. p. IX.
1064) Co. 318.
1065) L. 730.
1066) L. 719.
1067) Cf. p. XI.
1068) Cf. FQ. I. X. 57, Shep. Cal. July, the end. & c.
1069) Cf. above, chapter on Peck.
1070) Cf. p. XI.

these remarks valuable. An illustration of his careful method is also afforded by the pains he takes to check the statements of his predecessors as to Milton's coinages of new words. Todd is able to show that several of these supposed coinages can be traced back to earlier literature [1071]).

In the notes, much of the material found in Newton's and Warton's editions (that of the former has been drawn upon with some reserve) as well as in various other publications, such as Headley's "Select Specimens of Ancient English Poetry", Steevens's Shakespeare, Dunster's "Paradise Regained", & c. is said to have been used [1072]), some of it in an abridged form. Special attention is called to the parallels of thought and expression in "Fancy's sweetest children", Spenser, Shakespeare and Milton, and Milton's vocabulary is said to have been traced in his poetry and (which is especially mentioned) also in his prose. These aims are not new. A typical feature of Todd's method, which is also pointed out in the preface, is his device of adding extracts from the opinions of various critics on the poem, evidently in order to make his edition as complete a survey of the work done on "Comus" as possible [1073]). The same desire for completeness induced Todd to treat of the translations of the masque, of its fame, its theatrical performances, to include Warton's accounts of the background of the work as well as of its origin, his collation of the Trinity MS., a copy of the MS. of the Duke of Bridgewater in the Ashridge Library, a considerable amount of information on the place of the first production of the masque and on the persons concerned with it [1074]), & c. The Ashridge Library is said to have become accessible through the courtesy of the Rev. Francis Henry Egerton, a member of the family to whom the edition is dedicated [1075]). This thoroughness reminds one of Warton, and the fact that the study of the circumstances accompanying the composition and first performance of the poem is presented as the direct continuation of the work of Warton in this department (which is also reprinted), is only one of the

---

[1071]) Cf. p. XIII—XIV.
[1072]) Cf. pp. XII—XIII.
[1073]) Cf. preface p. XIII.
[1074]) Cf. pp. XV—XX.
[1075]) Cf. p. XIX.

symptoms of the editor's great indebtedness to the labours of
his most prominent predecessor.

β. The Preliminary Matter and the Notes.

The patience and labour, with which the preliminary articles
on Ludlow Castle, the Earl of Bridgewater and his family, Henry
Lawes and the sources of "Comus" as well as the bibliographical
sections have been composed, surpass even the arduous efforts of
Thomas Warton. Todd's additions to Warton's essay on the
origin of the masque mainly confine themselves to a summary
of the research in this department done after Warton's
edition [1076]).

The main body of the notes is from Warton's edition, to
which Todd's own very considerable contributions are added.
Among the new material, Headley's notes contain parallels from
seventeenth century poets. Steevens's contributions concern
themselves with parallelisms from Shakespeare and old
romances [1077]). On the whole, the new material is slight, with
the exception of that collected independently by Todd. Lord
Monboddo's notes, which deal mainly with the language and are
worthy of separate discussion [1078]), are treated more conveniently in connection with his observations on the other works of
Milton [1079]).

Todd's own notes betray the same keen interest in the background of Milton's masque. The ways of long ago are illustrated
by him from publications then little known [1080]). The erudition
and the copious collection of material remind one of Warton,
though Todd in this department as usual shows little of Warton's
sensibility and literary skill.

Todd's knowledge of Milton's own works enables him to quote
with evident ease both from his poetry and prose [1081]). His fa-

---

[1076]) Cf. pp. 56—62.
[1077]) Cf. 565 n., on "Syr Eglamour of Artoys".
[1078]) Cf. preface, p. XIX.
[1079]) Cf. below, p. 329.
[1080]) Cf. his explanation of the meaning of "the measure" (144 n.)
by the aid of Barret's "Alvearie" (see also 168 n.) or his references to
Munster's "Cosmographia", ed. 1656, and Alexander de Alexandro in 207 n.
[1081]) Cf. 377, 602, 121, 623 nn. & c.

miliarity with older English literature is notable. In the notes to
the first 300 lines, the following names and works are mentioned,
among many others: Donne's Poems [1082]), Ben Jonson's "Fortun-
ate Isles", "Neptune's Triumph", & c. [1083]), Drayton's "Polyolbion" [1084]), "The Muse's Looking-Glass" by Randolph [1085]), "The
History of King Leir and his Three Daughters" [1086]), Cartwright's
"Ordinary" [1087]), Crashaw's "Sacred Poems", various plays by
Shakespeare, & c. Among the foreign authors referred to, Italian
names are conspicuous. *Classical* allusions are somewhat less
frequent. The secular character of the masque makes it understandable that biblical references are rare.

There is the same tendency to accumulate parallelisms in these
notes as in Warton's, but it is a sign of Todd's caution and care
that he usually refrains from asserting any actual borrowings on
Milton's part. A characteristic example is found in Co. 140 *n.*
where Milton is compared with Spenser, Sylvester, Fairfax, P.
Fletcher, & c., but only as using "an expression of which our elder
poets appear to have been fond".

Considerable pains are taken to illustrate Milton's peculiarities
of *style* and language, sometimes skilfully, sometimes not. Todd's
knowledge of the old language is his greatest asset here (see *e. g.*
155 *n.* where Shakespeare, Sylvester and 16th century anthologies
are used to adduce parallels to the phrase "to blear the eye"). The
somewhat haphazard character of Todd's selection of his material
is shown *e. g.* by 178 *n.* where linguistic speculations as to the
Oriental origin of the word "wassail" are given some space, though
the commentator deals also with more reliable conjectures. Todd's
comparisons of Milton's imagery with that of the poetry of his
time [1088]) are elaborate, but not very thoughtful. As in Warton,
phrases of romance are studied, *e. g.* in 972 *n.* where "hard assays"
is shown to be found in Fairfax, Chaucer, in old romances. in
several of Milton's own works, & c.

The present account, which does not pretend to be exhaustive,

---

[1082]) 3 *n.*
[1083]) 3, 28, 77, 275 *nn.* & *c.*
[1084]) 24 *n.*
[1085]) 195 *n.*
[1086]) 189 *n.*
[1087]) 195 *n.*
[1088]) Cf. 542, 544 *nn.*

may have given an idea of the considerable display of learning
and industry in this edition, as well as of the lack of an adequa:
analytical or literary capacity on the editor's part, which often
makes of the notes a somewhat barren accumulation of material.

B. TODD'S EDITION OF THE POETICAL WORKS.

THE POETICAL WORKS OF JOHN MILTON. IN SIX
VOLUMES. WITH THE PRINCIPAL NOTES OF VARIOUS
COMMENTATORS. TO WHICH ARE ADDED ILLUSTRA-
TIONS, WITH SOME ACCOUNT OF THE LIFE OF MILTON.
BY THE REV. HENRY JOHN TODD, M. A. [Two mottoes]
LONDON: Printed for J. Johnson, W. J. and J. Richardson,
R. Baldwin ..... By Bye and Law, St. John's-Square, Clerken-
well. M. DCCC. I.

8⁰; vol. I: pp. [24] + CCXV + 303; vol. II: pp. [IV] + 504;
vol III: pp. [IV] + 494; vol. IV: pp. XIX + 511; vol. V: pp.
[III] + 511; vol. VI: pp. [III] + 458.

Contents: Vol. I: p. [1], title; p. [3], dedication to the
Duke of Bridgewater; pp. [5—18], preface; pp. [19—24], list of
contents; pp. I—CLX, life of Milton; pp. CLXI—CLXXXIX,
Milton's will, with notes; pp. CXC—CCXIII, bibliographical
lists; pp. CCXIV—CCXV, appendix to the life; pp. 1—23,
commendatory verses on Milton; pp. 24—194, Addison's Critique;
pp. 195—247, Dr. Johnson's remarks on the versification of
Milton, with additions and comments; pp. 248—303, an inquiry
into the origin of Paradise Lost.

Vol. II: p. [I], title; p. [III], contents; pp. 1—504, bks. I—VI
of P. L., with notes.

Vol. III: p. [I], title; p. [III], contents; pp. 1—468, P. L.
VII—XII, with notes; pp. 469—487, opinions of various critics
on P. L.; pp. 489—494, Trinity College MS. drafts of P. L.

Vol. IV: p. [I], title; pp. III—XIX, preliminary matter on
P. R., mainly by Dunster; pp. 1—329, "Paradise Regained",
with notes; pp. 329—335, critical opinions on P. R.; pp. 337—357,
preliminary matter on "Samson Agonistes", including Johnson's
and Cumberland's criticisms; pp. 359—494, S. A., with notes;
pp. 494—499, critical opinions on S. A.; pp. 501—511, Trinity
College MS. dramatic drafts.

Vol. V: p. [I], title; p. [III], contents; pp. 1—511, Lycidas, L'Allegro, Il Penseroso, Arcades, Comus, Sonnets, with a
number of introductory articles, collections of critical pronouncements, footnotes, various readings from the Trinity and
Bridgewater MSS., appendixes on supposed poems of Milton,
and miscellanea, the matter of Warton's edition being incorporated almost bodily, as well as that of Todd's edition of "Comus".

Vol. VI: p. [I], title; p. [III], contents; pp. 1—397, the rest of Milton's English, Latin, and Greek poems, with notes, various readings from the MSS., and introductory and final comments, including most of the matter of Warton's edition, with Burney's remarks on Milton's Greek verses; pp. 399—440, appendixes on Baron's imitations of Milton, Lauder's interpolations, corrections and additions; pp. 441—458, glossarial index.

Note: With a portrait of Milton and one of Queen Christina of Sweden.

THE POETICAL WORKS OF JOHN MILTON, WITH NOTES OF VARIOUS AUTHORS. TO WHICH ARE ADDED ILLUSTRATIONS, AND SOME ACCOUNT OF THE LIFE AND WRITINGS OF MILTON, BY THE REV. HENRY J. TODD, M. A. F. S. A. RECTOR OF ALLHALLOWS, LOMBARD-STREET, & c. THE SECOND EDITION, WITH CONSIDERABLE ADDITIONS, AND WITH A VERBAL INDEX TO THE WHOLE OF MILTON'S POETRY. IN SEVEN VOLUMES. VOL. I. LONDON: Printed for J. Johnson; R. Baldwin; Otridge and Son; Nichols and Son; F. C. and J. Rivington ...... By Law and Gilbert, St. John's-Square, Clerkenwell. 1809.

8⁰: vol. I: pp. [5] + XV + 217 + [4] + [416]; vol. II: pp. [8] + XIX + 462; vol. III: pp. [8] + 473; vol. IV: pp. [8] + 395; vol. V: pp. [8] + XIX + 503; vol. VI: pp. [8] + 503; vol. VII: pp. [7] + 414 + [26].

Note: Three plates. The main addition is a bulky Verbal Index.

THE POETICAL WORKS OF JOHN MILTON. WITH NOTES OF VARIOUS AUTHORS. THE THIRD EDITION, WITH OTHER ILLUSTRATIONS; AND WITH SOME ACCOUNT OF THE LIFE AND WRITINGS OF MILTON, DERIVED PRINCIPALLY FROM Documents in his Majesty's State-Paper Office, NOW FIRST PUBLISHED. BY THE REV. H. J. TODD, M. A. F. S. A. & R. S. L. CHAPLAIN IN ORDINARY TO HIS MAJESTY, AND RECTOR OF SETTRINGTON, COUNTY OF YORK. IN SIX VOLUMES. VOL. I. LONDON: PRINTED FOR C. AND J. RIVINGTON; J. CUTNELL; J. NUNN; J. AND W. T. CLARKE; LONGMAN AND CO ..... 1826.

8⁰: vol. I: pp. XXX + 370 + LXVII; vol. II: pp. [4] + CXXXVI + 535; vol. III: pp. [4] + 527; vol. IV: pp. [6] + XIX + 501; vol. V: pp. [5] + 517; vol. VI: pp. [4] + 433 + [26].

With one facsimile and 3 full-page illustrations. The life "greatly augmented with original documents illustrating the private and publick character of Milton, which have long been

hidden among literary curiosities, and till now have never been
published" (pref., p. V). Verbal index omitted.

THE POETICAL WORKS OF JOHN MILTON. WITH NOTES
OF VARIOUS AUTHORS; AND WITH SOME ACCOUNT OF
THE LIFE AND WRITINGS OF MILTON, DERIVED PRIN-
CIPALLY FROM ORIGINAL DOCUMENTS IN HER MA-
JESTY'S STATE-PAPER OFFICE. BY THE REV. HENRY
JOHN TODD, M. A. CHAPLAIN IN ORDINARY TO HER
MAJESTY, AND ARCHDEACON OF CLEVELAND. Fourth
Edition. IN FOUR VOLUMES. VOL. I. LONDON: RIVING-
TONS; LONGMAN AND CO.; T. CADELL; J. BOHN ......
1842.

8⁰: vol. I: pp. XVI [not seen] + 523; vol. II: pp. [4] + 589;
vol. III: pp. XXIII + 431; vol. IV: pp. VIII + 560. Facsimile
and illustrations as formerly.

The "Advertisement to the Fourth Edition" (vol. I. pp.
V—VIII) states that Todd has made no use of the latest commentaries, having "no right to take advantage" of them. Hence
the edition has essentially remained the same, except for some
very slight additions. The editor defends himself against recent
attacks and criticizes J. Prendeville's aversion to the "curious
though idle" learning of the "Gothick library". In this connection
T. extols Milton's excellent fusion of "Gothick" extravagances
with "the dignity of Homer".

Todd's edition has retained much of its value up to the present day, as one of the most important collections of material relating to Milton's poetry.

Its plan in many respects resembles that of the edition of
"Comus". It is a typical *variorum* edition, aiming at an approximately complete survey of the views of earlier critics. This appears
from its copious collection of footnotes, which, though apparently
based on the most important earlier editions 1089), has been supplemented from earlier and later Milton scholars, leading up to the
close of the century. Many extracts are given from miscellaneous
works occasionally dealing with Milton. A number of critics have
contributed fresh notes. To some of the larger works, selections
of the statements of notable critics are subjoined. Introductory

1089) The minor poems retain most of the apparatus of Warton's
edition, to which much old and new material is added; most of the notes
included in Newton's "Paradise Lost" and "Samson Agonistes" are reprinted; for "Paradise Regained", Dunster is the main source.

articles deal with Milton's works in general or with special
questions relating to them. Thus, "Paradise Lost" is preceded by
the traditional "Spectator" papers, and a collection of "Observations on the Versification of Milton, by Dr. Johnson, and others",
as it is called in the later editions, or "Dr. Johnson's Remarks on
Milton's Versification, with remarks by the editor", as the first
and second editions call it [1090]), as well as by a study of its
sources [1091]). The Rev. Henry Boyd's "Observations on the
Characters of the Fallen Angels" are subjoined as an appendix
in the second edition [1092]). The "Preliminary Observations on
Samson Agonistes" [1093]) consist of Johnson's adverse criticism
from "The Rambler" [1094]) and of the reply by Cumberland [1095]).
The apparatus added to some of the other works is very similar.
The study of the contemporary background of Milton's poetry
is continued in footnotes as well as in the introductory matter to
some works, e. g. to "Arcades", "Lycidas", & c. All the above
and some further material makes of the edition a kind of critical
Milton encyclopædia. The life of Milton, which tries to give
a reliable account according to the authentic sources; bibliographical lists; reprints of Milton's dramatic schemes in the
Cambridge MS. and lists of the various readings; indexes, & c.,
mostly done with signal care, increase the value of this edition,
which is a summary of the research in Milton's poetry of more
than a century, as Newton's edition summed up the labours of a
period of more than fifty years.

a. Todd's Contributors.

The preface gives an account of the new contributions to the
commentary. Malcolm Laing, Esq. is reported to have favoured
Todd with an interleaved copy of "Paradise Lost" with memoranda
and a few completed notes by Callander [1096]). The Wartons, both
Thomas and Joseph, are represented — in the second edition and

---

1090) Cf. pp. 195 & c. of vol. I, ed. 1801.
1091) Cf. p. 248 of vol. I, ed. 1801.
1092) Cf. pp. 257 ff. of vol. II.
1093) Cf. p. 345 of vol. IV, ed. I.
1094) Vol. III. No. 139 and No. 140.
1095) From "The Observer", vol. IV. No. III.
1096) Cf. p. IV of vol. I, ed. II; abs. in first ed.

after — by some observations given to Todd by the Rev. John
Warton [1097]). Dunster has given for selection a great number of
notes, from among which "many an ingenious and solid remark"
distinguished by "taste and learning" has been reprinted in the
second edition [1098]). Copies of "Paradise Lost" and of the minor
poems with remarks by Bowle; observations by "the late Joseph
Cooper Walker, Esq. the author of the very elegant Historical
Memoir on Italian Tragedy" [1099]); notes by Benjamin Stillingfleet,
who, according to a letter of his to the father of Dr. Dampier,
late Bishop of Ely, intended to edit Milton but was prevented by
Newton's edition of "Paradise Lost" [1100]); remarks by Isaac
Reed and James Bindley [1101]); are among the new material added
to Todd's commentary. Published sources, such as "the compositions of Lord Monboddo, Dr. Beattie, and Dr. Blair,... the late
commentaries on Shakespeare, ... Mr. Headley's Select Specimens
of Ancient English Poetry,... the acute observations of
Dr. Johnson and Mr. Hayley" and others are similarly named in
Todd's preface as having helped to enlarge his annotations [1102]).
Beside these, the notes by Greenwood and Hurd have to be
especially mentioned, though a complete list of Todd's sources
would include a considerable number of further names, many of
which are represented only by a few brief remarks and hardly
deserve any special treatment.

Among the above contributions, those of Dunster, Bowle,
Stillingfleet and Lord Monboddo have here been singled out for
special examination, partly owing to their numerousness, and
partly because of their marked character. The rest are mostly
of a somewhat chance kind and hardly enable one to form any
definite impression of their method, though the material amassed
in those *membra disjecta* is often very valuable.

1. *Dunster.*

The notes contributed by Dunster contain many interesting
literary illustrations, particularly from the classics, but also from

1097) Cf. p. VI of vol. I, ed. II.
1098) Cf. p. VI of vol. I.
1099) Ed. I, vol. I, sg. A6r.
1100) *Ibid.*
1101) *Ubi supra,* sg. A7r.
1102) Ed. I, vol. I, sg. A5r.

older English literature, from the Italians, & c., as well as a number of observations on style and language. However, their main importance rests probably on Dunster's remarks on the artistic peculiarities of Milton's works, which show much more insight than Todd's own critical analyses, and supplement the idea of Dunster's views afforded by his notes to "Paradise Regained".

His last remark on "Paradise Lost" (included among the selection of critical views on the poem as a whole, subjoined at the end of the work) which deals with its plan, shows what Dunster values in the poem. He does not deny the importance of its imaginative beauty, but he dwells more on features of a more purely intellectual kind. Compression and terseness are the qualities which he mainly emphasizes (as in his notes on the style of "Paradise Regained"), though he likes them to be combined with vivid description. The intellectual feat of compressing a large mass of material in a few pages seems, however, to impress him more than brilliant and picturesque detail, however well executed.

These features appear in his treatment of the problem discussed by Addison [1103]), whether the narrative form of the history of mankind in book XII of the epic is inferior to the representation of the same events as a succession of visions in book XI. Addison compared the former manner to mere writing and the latter to colours [1104]). Dunster mainly tries to show that the structural device of using the brief form of narrative, which only sketches out the story, is a more rational way of handling the enormous mass of events in the last book than their treatment as visions, which would imply giving much lengthy, description without making it possible to avoid adding a good deal of explanatory material and thus impairing the vividness of the whole. This preference for the last book of the poem may be partly due to artistic considerations. Dunster finds the "bold sketches and brief delineations" of this book to "equal in effect the larger and more finished productions of the pencil", speaking of the "admirable comprehensive brevity" of the former. One feels inclined to ascribe this tendency to the classical influences

---

[1103]) The Spectator No. 369.
[1104]) *Ubi supra.*

on Dunster, which have been traced in his treatment of "Paradise Regained" [1105]).

If Dunster in spite of this preference of the style of the last book to that of the rest still agrees with the opinion of most critics that the earlier parts are superior to the last, he attributes this superiority to the *subject* of the former. To prove this, he analyses the *structure*, as usual, in order to show the relation of the last to the previous books. The action, as he finds, passes from hell to heaven and from heaven to the terrestrial paradise, whence it goes to the actual earth, the habitation of mankind. A decrease in the poetic magnificence of the poem would have been avoidable only by a change of the subject, *viz.* by refraining from a description of the world after the fall. This he finds inadmissible, but for non-artistic reasons. He emphasizes the value of the instructive tendency of Milton's poem. Milton, according to him, abandoned the higher spheres of paradise in order to instruct mankind, which could be done efficaciously only by addressing it on its own ground. In Dunster's opinion, "A poem, however wonderfully pregnant with the *delectare*, will be wanting in its most essential parts, if it does not close with the *monere*, or materially involve it" [1106]). This reminds one of the tendency shown in Dunster's edition of "Paradise Regained", to regard poetic imagery as a mere extraneous addition to the instructive essence of poetry [1107]). However, the present note does not go so far. It values both the moral and the artistic aspects. This view is summed up in the image of "Milton, even while 'rapt above the pole' he meditated his vast design", being "fully aware that he was 'standing upon the earth', and writing to the inhabitants of it for their instruction as well as their delight" [1108]).

Dunster's sensitiveness, which goes hand in hand with good solid commonsense, and his attentive study of Elizabethan literature, enable him to appreciate the spirituality, which in the Elizabethans alternates with naturalism, broad humour and high-flown, even incongruous, conceits. Newton compares Milton's

[1105]) Cf. above.
[1106]) *Ibid.*
[1107]) Cf. above, p. 308.
[1108]) *Ubi supra.*

description of "Celestial voices" that sing in "the midnight air" to Lucretius [1109]). Dunster, on the contrary, sees "ideas... of a higher order" in Milton, finding in this passage the same "spiritual music" and "fine natural beauty" as in the description of the magical voices in "The Tempest" (A. III. s. 2. "The isle is full of voices" & c.).

It has been shown that Dunster values vigour more than fluency and smoothness [1110]). This is corroborated by some typical remarks in Todd's edition. Newton praised Milton's strict adherence to Scripture *despite* its spoiling the harmony of the verse [1111]). Dunster finds these very discords a positive beauty; Milton was studious to avoid an excessive smoothness "from a sort of reverential awe and chastened fear of appearing to attempt decoration of language, where it cannot serve to elevate the ideas, and therefore is peculiarly unappropriate and unseemly" [1112]). Similarly, the value of irregularity is seen in a note on the impressive disorder of some passages, which is found to correspond with that "turbulent rapidity" with which associations of various kinds crowd in upon an excited mind [1113]).

These are perhaps the main features of Dunster's contributions to Todd's edition. Dunster's predilection for the intellectual element in poetry, which does not prevent him from keenly appreciating imaginative vividness, as well as his valuation of instructive tendencies and of religion, are found here again. Subtleties of Milton's plan and excellences of detail are both expounded with much keen insight, which is only occasionally obscured by the somewhat inadequate doctrines that connect Dunster with the more narrow-minded classicists of the earlier part of the eighteenth century [1114]).

2. *Bowle.*

Bowle's notes, which comment very scantily on the facts they present, show the annotator's wide reading in older English and Romance literature as well as in the miscellaneous non-

[1109]) P. L. IV. 682 *n.*
[1110]) Cf. above, p. 312.
[1111]) P. L. X. 175 *n.*
[1112]) Note ibid.
[1113]) Cf. P. L. IX. 965 *n.*
[1114]) Cf. above, p. 308.

literary publications of the past. "Huon de Bordeaux" [1115]), Boiardo [1116]), Amadis de Grecia [1117]), La Sylva de Medrano [1118]), Froissart [1119]), Purchas [1120]), Gascoigne [1121]), Sackville [1122]), & c. are drawn upon, beside various more popular and obvious sources of information. P. L. VI. 325 *n.* is an example of his erudite method. Descriptions of the descending of swords are quoted from different French, Italian and Spanish romances, no comments being added. Old miscellaneous publications are *e. g.* referred to in P. L. III. 478 n. where the belief, that to be clothed in a friar's habit was an infallible road to heaven, is illustrated from "Pasquine in a Traunce" 1584, Weaver's "Discourse of Funeral Monuments" 1621, Buchanan's "Franciscans" and Dante's "Inferno".

3. *Stillingfleet.*

Stillingfleet's speciality in Milton annotation appears to be the study of classical parallels, though there are also some parallelisms from later authors, *e. g.* from Philippe de Commines [1123]), Spenser [1124]), Tasso [1125]). Some acute remarks are made on the connection between style and mood, as in P. L. V. 28 *n.* where the breaks in Eve's narrative V. 28 *et seq.* are explained by her inability to recollect her thoughts immediately after awaking. This is also in accordance with the subject of her narration which is visionary and somewhat vague.

Stillingfleet makes some attempts to explain Milton's philosophy, *e. g.* in P. L. III. 108 *n.* where he deals with the poet's pronouncement that "reason also is choice". He studies the effect of material irregularities, finding them to take away monotony and approving the close adherence to scriptural passages

---

[1115]) P. L. I. 665 *n.*
[1116]) VI. 317 *n.*
[1117]) X. 575 *n.*
[1118]) VIII. 47 *n.*
[1119]) XI. 250 *n.*
[1120]) II. 716 *n.*
[1121]) IV. 603 *n.*
[1122]) I. 619 *n.*
[1123]) P. L. VII. 322 *n.*
[1124]) P. L. III. 533 *n.*
[1125]) P. L. I. 56 *n.*

which is made possible by disregarding the requirements of regular verse [1126]). All this shows some reading, attention, and insight into character, though too little material is given to make it possible to venture on any detailed characterization of the commentator.

4. Lord Monboddo.

The notes of Lord Monboddo nearly all deal with direct or indirect traces of the classics in Milton and show the annotator's classical mode of thought and taste. Much attention is given to syntactic features.

Monboddo praises a simple style unadorned by any metaphorical or figurative words, finding great beauty in unassuming, balanced perfection — in "the justness of the thought, in the propriety of the expression, in the art of the composition and in the variety of the versification" [1127]). He is convinced, it is true, that this literary manner "will appear flat and insipid to those who admire the present fashionable style, far removed from the simplicity of the ancients" [1128]). However, a blunt, everyday style is regarded by him as equally "flat and insipid" [1129]), unusual, terse elliptic expression being found to be suitable to the "very high style of classical gallantry" which he recommends [1130]). His ideal appears to be the polished, precise, expressive but reserved style of the ancients which is as far removed from bluntness as from bombast.

Supposed or real Græcisms or Latinisms form the subject of a number of his notes. He prefers to see in P. L. III. 344 et seq. "an anomalous construction" imitated from Homer (viz. a sentence without a verb) instead of the more normal and intelligible "ablative absolute" as which this passage is more generally interpreted [1131]). Most of his syntactic notes deal with ellipses, e. g. P. L. VIII. 645 n. where "it is necessary" is supposed to have been omitted on the model of the Greek [1132]).

[1126]) P. L. III. 703.
[1127]) Cf. P. L. II. 106 n.
[1128]) Co. 704 n.
[1129]) Co. 270 n.
[1130]) Ibid.
[1131]) P. L. III. 345 n.
[1132]) Cf. also P. L. VII. 38 n., X. 157 n.

β. Todd's Literary Views.

Though Todd's edition includes much critical material on Milton's poetic works, there is relatively little matter for an inquiry into the editor's own literary views and theories. Todd generally prefers giving mere statements of facts or quoting the opinions of others to advancing any views of his own. In this respect he adheres to the method adopted in his "Comus". His life of Milton follows the same practice. A sketch of some of his tenets can, however, be given.

He is undoubtedly influenced by the new currents of taste and the widening scope of literature, but he does not seem to have thoroughly revised his critical views in order to adapt them to the standards of his age. He still appears to value tame, orderly, decorous expression in the usual eighteenth century manner. "Elegance" is one of the artistic qualities apparently especially esteemed by him. He admires the "remarkable elegance" of Crashaw's metaphor: "The primrose's pale cheek" (M.M. 4 n.) and that of Collins's expression: "he ....Shook thousand odours from his dewy wings" [1133]. The "elegant imitations" of Miltonic expressions by Pope and Gray are accorded the same ready approval [1134]. "Propriety" remains one of his foremost requirements even in notes added subsequently in some of his later editions. Thus Knight's "Principles of Taste", ed. 1805, pp. 122—123, is attacked because of its strictures on the lack of "the rapturous glow of enthusiastick passion" in the passage describing Adam's wooing of Eve in "Paradise Lost", bk. IX. [1135]. Todd fails to bring forward any artistic arguments in defence of Milton, but is surprised at the critic's neglect of his author's endeavour "not to excite an improper idea" [1136].

The editor's final remark on "Comus" is a good example of his moralizing and pedagogic tendencies. Though he does not disregard the imaginative excellence of the masque, at least equal stress is laid on its instructive and moral sides. The play is said to exhibit "the true sources" both of "poetical delight and moral

---

[1133]) P. L. V. 286 n.
[1134]) P. L. IX. 193 n.
[1135]) P. L. IX. 1029 n., here cited according to Todd's fourth edition.
[1136]) Ibid.

instruction" and to advance "virtuous sentiments". Similarly, "Paradise Regained" is recommended for the gratification which it gives to "taste and virtue" by the "fine sentiments which it breathes; the pure morality which it inculcates; and the striking imagery, with which it is frequently embellished" [1137]).

Todd does not seem to have any prejudices against the fusion of the styles of classicism and romance. On the contrary, the imitations "both of the classical and the romantick Muses" in "Paradise Regained" are praised [1138]). Sometimes objection is raised to a mixture of classical and scriptural imagery, as in the final note on "Lycidas", but Todd is impartial enough to reprint the substance of a letter to himself by Mrs. Anna Seward who calls attention to the free, playful spirit of the piece which she finds to harmonize with the inconsistent character of its mythological and religious elements. And in a passage in his life of the poet, Todd dwells with special approval on the wide range of Milton's prose which includes "romantick, and classical, and scriptural allusions", marking him along with Jeremy Taylor and Bishop Hall as a leading master of "the diversified arrangement and application of bright and majestic sentiments, of the most powerful and commanding words" [1139]).

These last quotations already show that Todd was not destitute of the capacity for appreciating Milton's traditionally recognized "grand style" as well as the bright, rich element of romance in his works which some of the admirers of his sublime manner seemed to underrate. The surprising amount of Elizabethan and mediæval parallels found in Todd's notes unmistakably proves his interest in these matters, which is reflected in his critical pronouncements. Newton's rash condemnation of Milton's early reading of romances disagrees with these tendencies [1140]). The poet's imagination is found by Todd to have been enlarged by "the striking embellishments and graces of romantick fiction" which are added to his "Own unborrowed imagery" [1141]). Todd values "romantic" picturesqueness. About the end of his account of Ludlow Castle, he describes the "delightful and romantick"

[1137]) Cf. the final observation on "Paradise Regained".
[1138]) *Ibid.*
[1139]) Vol. I. of ed. IV, p. 146.
[1140]) Cf. P. L. I. 580 *n.*
[1141]) *Ibid.*

situation of this seat of nobility, its position on a rock, its "walls of immense height and thickness", its "round and square towers", & c. That Todd sometimes was capable of seeing the attraction of the extremer features of the "grand" variety of Milton's style, appears from his notes on the "inimitable strength" of Milton's "fine expression" in P. L. II. 846: "Death Grinnd horrible a gastly smile", or on the picture of battle in P. L. VI. 848, which is found to remind one of "the bold and tremendous painting of Æschylus" in Prom. Vinct. v. 356 [1142]). On the other hand, extravagances and what Todd regards as "bombast" are censured, as in the case of some eccentric metaphors in the English translations of Du Bartas and apparently also in Milton's earliest poetic attempts [1143]). It is evident that these latter features of style clash very violently with the ideal of "elegance" alluded to before. The last verses of "Paradise Lost" are praised for their "beautiful simplicity" [1144]), which agrees far better with the above ideal.

As this brief summary should have made clear, Todd still clings to some of the most typical features of the classicist tradition, though not fanatically. He has assimilated only some of the lessons of Warton and others, but his ideals of moralism, didacticism and decorum do not prevent him from appreciating a wider scope of style and sentiment.

γ. *Todd's Treatment of Milton's Language, Style and Metre.*

Todd's treatment of Milton's style and language does not abound in original ideas or keen analyses. His thoroughness in correcting earlier misstatements is a leading feature of his notes on these matters, exactly as in his edition of "Comus". His familiarity with old English writers enables him to show the occurrence in their works of a number of expressions supposed by other critics to have been invented by Milton or derived by him from foreign languages. P. L. II. 900 *n.* points out that "embryon", a word described by Addison as being of Milton's own coinage [1145]),

---

[1142]) P. L. VI. 755 *n.*
[1143]) Cf. Ps. CXIV. II. *n.*
[1144]) Cf. Todd's second note on P. L. XII. 648 *n.*
[1145]) Cf. The Spectator, No. 285.

had actually been used by Sylvester, Donne, Massinger and Browne. Similar remarks are found in P. L. I. 752 *n.*, IV. 50 *n.*, IX. 330 *n.*, X. 426 *n.*, S. A. 345 *n.*, *& c.*

Todd collects some interesting material concerning Milton's peculiarities of word-formation. Thus S. A. 442 *n.* shows Milton's fondness for the prefix *dis-* and points out a number of cases, some of which actually seem to be peculiar to Milton or appear to have been rare before him, if the data of the NED are to be relied upon. Of *disexercise, disespouse, disgospel,* only their use by Milton is registered in the NED, whereas to *disinure*, to *disglorify* are cited only once before Milton. In S. A. 453 *n.* Milton's relatively frequent use of derivations from *idol* is shown, and the forms referred to in this note are found in the NED only once or twice with a date previous to their occurrence in Milton, in the sense in which Milton used them.

Some attention is given to *phonetic* points, and their illustration is sometimes copious and skilful [1146]. Unusual obsolete accents are studied with the same or greater care than in Newton's edition [1147], the attempt being sometimes made to undertake a closer study of the shifting of the old stresses to their present position, *e. g.* in P. L. II. 301 *n.* where the changes of the accentuation of "aspect" are traced in seventeenth century texts. Neither Richardson [1148] nor Bowle, who both treat of Milton's form "ammiral", had convincingly shown where the poet might have derived it from. Todd points out the existence of this word in the same sense and with an *m* or *mm* instead of *dm* in various early English translations of French, Italian and Portuguese poets [1149]. These are only some chance instances of Todd's care in these questions. Old language, especially old phraseology, is traced with notable industry, though without much subtlety of analysis [1150].

Little new light is thrown on more complicated features of style. Cases of successions of similar forms used in order to achieve a strong cumulative effect repeatedly attract Todd's

---

1146) Cf. P. L. II. 132, V. 482, 798, VIII. 12, 155 *nn.*

1147) Cf. above, p. 239.

1148) Cf. above, p. 124.

1149) Cf. P. L. I. 294 *n.*

1150) Cf. P. L. I. 48 *n.*, where Ariosto, Spenser, P. Fletcher, Drummond and others are studied; I. 202 *n.*; II. 302 *n.*; X. 718 *n.*; S. A. 326 *n.*

attention. Thus, the frequent introduction of series of negative adjectives beginning with *un-* is compared with the similar practices of Spenser and Fairfax, an example of the early derision of this habit being quoted, apparently in order to illustrate the commonness of this artifice [1151]). This reference to the attitude of Milton's contemporaries shows the same interest in the background of his poetry as so many of Warton's remarks. Similar cumulative devices discussed by Todd are the use of series of successive participles [1152]) and the frequent repetition of the invocatory particle "o" [1153]).

Todd's syntactic remarks are of a somewhat casual kind and add relatively little to earlier research. He is sufficiently familiar with the poet's style to acknowledge the authenticity of occasional irregularities and ellipses. Newton recommends the emendation of P. L. IX. 673: "while each part, Motion, each act", into: "whole, while each Motion, each act", inserting "whole" and omitting "part" in order to obtain a regular recurrence of "each" before the nouns, as Bentley demands. Todd defends the genuine reading by a considerable display of classical scholarship, excusing its irregularity as a feature common in Milton and hardly apt to obscure the sense of the passage.

Milton's imagery is seldom analysed [1154]). Parallelisms from earlier writers or from Milton's own works are frequently adduced but generally bare facts are stated without any, or with very little, comment upon them. Some of these comparisons are vivid and suggestive, as *e. g.* that of the descriptions of red liquor sparkling in the sun in S. A. 543, Co. 613 and Prov. XXIII. 31 [1155]). However, the analysis here is confined to the pointing out of verbal similarities. Similarly, echoes of the biblical image of the scorpion which is offered to one's father are traced in various

---

[1151]) P. L. II. 185 *n.*

[1152]) Cf. S. A. 365 *n.*

[1153]) Cf. P. L. X. 860 *n.*

[1154]) It is hardly to be wondered at, under the circumstances, that Todd has little to say about Milton's characters. His comparisons of Milton's treatment of them with the way in which other authors handle their characters are of some interest owing to the commentator's erudition rather than because the traits he takes notice of are very subtle or intriguing' (cf. *e. g.* P. L. IX. 529, 875 *nn.*).

[1155]) Cf. S. A. 543 *n.*

Miltonic passages, without any comment except that the poet "has been peculiarly happy in the use of this imagery" [1156]). These are more or less typical examples.

Todd's opinions on Milton's verse may be traced most easily in his preliminary "Observations on the Versification of Milton, by Dr. Johnson and others", where his own views are stated explicitly and implicitly. As this article shows, Todd has perused a very considerable number of authorities, apparently surpassing all earlier commentators in this respect. Johnson's onesidedness and limitations are constantly checked by references to more advanced critics or by Todd's own comments. Tyrwhitt's "Essay on the Language and Versification of Chaucer", Foster's "Essay on Accent" (2nd ed.), Mitford's "Essay upon the Harmony of Language", Sheridan's "Lectures on the Art of Reading", & c., Samuel Say's "Remarks on the Numbers of Paradise Lost", Dr. Pemberton's "Observations on Poetry", Webb's "Observations on Poetry and Musick", the Richardsons, Lord Monboddo, Rich. Payne Knight's "An Analytical Inquiry into the Principles of Taste" [1157]) and others are made use of in this connection.

Todd quotes these and other writers to rectify Johnson's errors and further down gives an account of their main contributions to the investigation of Milton's metre. In this connection he makes some remarks which reflect his own views. In opposition to Johnson, he defends Milton's art of adapting the sound to the sense, but the idea is not new [1158]) and most of his examples are borrowed. What he says of the value of spondees in unexpected places, particularly after pyrrhics, is, however, presented as his own opinion and is of some interest [1159]). He mentions the emphasis which is given to the words thus accentuated, especially after two unstressed syllables, e. g. in P. L. IV. 719 ("On him who had stole Jove's authentic fire") where "stole Jove's" becomes emphatic because of the force of the stresses after the unstressed words "who had" [1160]). Similarly, in Co. 37 ("Lies through the

---

[1156]) S. A. 350 *n.;* similar cases cf. S. A. 184 *n.;* P. R. I. 94 *n.*
[1157]) Referred to vol. II, p. 205 of ed. II.
[1158]) Cf. even Hume, *e. g.* above, p. 39.
[1159]) Cf. ed. II, vol. II, pp. 199—200.
[1160]) Todd quotes an emendation by Dr. Pemberton ("On him, who Jove's authentick fire had stole") and shows that there the force of expression is lost.

perplex't paths of this drear Wood"), the stressed syllables in "the perplex't paths" are those which are logically important. Todd quotes a number of further instances of a similarly happy use of spondees.

· In connection with these cases, he assumes that, in Milton, "supreme" may have the stress on the last syllable when a stressed syllable follows, because (as Todd says) a spondee is "more digni- fied and impressive", and because in some cases the metrical result of this pronunciation would be a pyrrhic followed by a spondee, as in the above instances. He makes the proposal to read: "...whom the Suprēme King" in P. L. I. 735 and: "That He, the Suprēme Good" in Co. 217, though he admits that at Milton's time "supreme" could also be read with the stress on the first syllable. His argumentation seems plausible if taken by itself, as he is able to show that his manner of reading the word does not disagree with Milton's metrical practice, at any rate in the instances quoted by him. However, it partly clashes with the observations of later scholars, e. g. A. Schmidt [1161]), who have pointed out that the stress seems in Milton and Shakespeare regularly to recede to the first syllable in disyllabic adjectives standing before a noun which begins with a stressed syllable [1162]).

The above cases suffice to show Todd's ability to connect metrical with logical considerations. They display some freedom from conventionality, illustrating the value of so-called "irregular- ity" where it serves to enhance the impressiveness of the verse. Some other remarks of his show a similar capacity to combine the study of rhythm with the observation of matters of mood and character. Thus, Johnson condemns the "volubility and levity" of Milton's expression of "an action tardy and reluctant" in Moloch's speech in P. L. II. 76 *et seq.* [1163]). Todd calls attention to the character of Moloch, "the *most impetuous* Spirit that fought in Heaven" whose rash and desperate sentiments he finds reflected in the quick rhythm chosen by the poet [1164]).

[1161]) Cf. Shakespeare Lexicon, Appendix.

[1162]) Dr. Bridges is of a different opinion and shows the possibility of a development towards the "irregularity" assumed by Todd. Cf. Milton's Prosody, ed. 1921, pp. 71 *et seq.*

[1163]) Cf. ed. I, vol. I. p. 239.

[1164]) Cf. footnote, *ibid.*

On the whole, Todd's metrical remarks show considerable insight. His attentive study of prosodical theory seems to have borne fruit. His footnotes to Milton's preface on "the Verse" of "Paradise Lost", which are copiously provided with historical material, similarly prove the editor's erudition, though they mainly sum up earlier work instead of stating Todd's own opinions.

δ. Todd on Milton's Sources and on the General Allusions in his Works.

The best work done by Todd in the purely literary department of his edition, is probably his investigation of Milton's sources. It is based on a thorough study of the efforts of his predecessors and shows a very remarkable erudition.

His essay on the origin of "Comus" contained little independent speculation and criticism. A similar inquiry into the sources of "Paradise Lost" (beside which are found a number of less thorough attempts of the same sort on some of the other works) is more critical and independent, though it also mainly deals with the work of earlier scholars. However, it supplies some valuable new material and weighs and criticizes the earlier examinations of the question [1165]). The material is arranged in a historical order, beginning with the first hints known to Todd as to any literary debts on the part of Milton. Todd tries to describe the history of the reception of the theories concerning the poet's literary indebtedness (cf. his treatment of Voltaire's opinion that Milton had been influenced by Andreini, p. 248 & c. ubi supra). One-sided views, such as that of Dunster that Sylvester's Du Bartas was the main reason why Milton wrote "Paradise Lost", are examined in connection with the evidence known to Todd of other possible early influences on the poet [1166]). An interesting remark which apparently had induced Todd to undertake further investigations, is Archbishop Laurence's observation that Milton may have made use of rabbinical words [1167]). Todd's illustrations from Moses Bar Cepha may have been collected upon

---

[1165]) Cf. ed. I., vol. I. pp. 248 *ff*.
[1166]) Cf. p. 293, *ubi supra.*
[1167]) Cf. p. 268 of vol. I, ed. IV.

this suggestion [1168]), though this writer had already been drawn upon in Hume's notes [1169]). Todd, like Newton and others [1170]), dwells on the independent character of Milton's imitations, acknowledging the great skill with which he interweaves elements from various sources [1171]). However, his notes on similarities between Milton and earlier writers very seldom analyse the exact character of these relations. Most of them merely ascertain parallels.

Todd's parallelisms from the classics, which show considerable knowledge, nevertheless do not deviate very much from the main roads of ancient literature. There similarly seems to be little that opens up new paths in his references to biblical matters, though he is able plausibly to explain some allusions that formerly had been misunderstood. Thus an adjective ("death-like") had been substituted for Milton's reading "death like [sleep]". Todd defends the original text, seeing in it an allusion to certain scriptural passages (particularly to I. Cor. XV. 51) and explaining its justification in the context. More attention than to biblical lore is paid to older English literature. Anglo-Saxon writers [1172]) and pre-Elizabethan authors are mentioned occasionally, but greater stress is laid on the literature of the end of the sixteenth and of the seventeenth centuries. In this latter department a very considerable amount of material has been amassed which is by no means confined to the best-known writers of that period. The names mentioned in the notes to the first two books of "Paradise Lost" include, amongst others, the following: Lodge's "Looking Glasse for London" [1173]), Goffe's "Amurath" [1174]), the "Mirror for Magistrates" [1175]), Dr. Holdisworth's "An Answer without a Question" [1176]), "The Cobler's Prophecie" [1177]), Chamberlayne's

---

[1168]) Cf. pp. 268, 269, *ubi supra.*
[1169]) Cf. Hume I. 34 *n.*
[1170]) Cf. above, on Newton, p. 229.
[1171]) Cf. p. 284 of vol. I, ed. 1801.
[1172]) Cf. *e. g.* P. L. IV. 20 *n.* on the venerable Bede.
[1173]) P. L. I. 181 *n.*
[1174]) P. L. I. 576 *n.*
[1175]) P. L. I. 742 *n.*
[1176]) P. L. II. 229 *n.*
[1177]) P. L. II. 132 *n.*

"Pharonnida" [1178]), & c. French romances [1179]), Spanish [1180]), and particularly Italian, authors are conspicuous among the Romance sources used. Of the Italians, Dante occurs with special frequency. Only Richardson seems to have had the same predilection for parallels from the "Divine Comedy" as Todd [1181]). The lurid imagery of Dante's Hell and Purgatory, which may have lingered in Milton's mind, is naturally enough quoted from fairly frequently [1182]). It is of more interest to note that the description of paradise in P. L. IV is found to resemble a number of passages of canto XXVIII of Dante's "Purgatory" [1183]). Similarly, parallels are drawn between Dante's "Paradise" and the representation of the angelic choirs in "Paradise Regained" [1184]). Todd does not explain these parallelisms, but, in his usual way, merely points out similarities, so that the problem of the extent and character of Dante's influence on Milton is not solved.

Beside these literary investigations, the scope of which is only slightly sketched in the above, inquiries into various fields of history, social and cultural life, & c., are found throughout Todd's own contributions. They are often based on obscure contemporary sources. That Todd owes something to Peck in this respect, appears e. 'g. from P. L. I. 711 n. where possible allusions to the Elizabethan stage are admittedly traced in continuation of Peck's hints. Jewish customs [1185]), traditions of chivalry [1186]), Elizabethan pastimes and sports [1187]), early gardening [1188]), & c. are dealt with in some detail, some of these notes referring to, and quoting from, dozens of books, many of which are obsolete. Thus, in S. A. 1323 n. Prynne's "Histrio-mastix", Stubbe's "Anatomie of Abuses", the "Tragicall Comedie of Damon and Pithias", Dekker's "Gul's Hornebooke", Cavendish's "Memoirs of Wolsey",

---

[1178]) P. L. I. 673 n.
[1179]) Cf. P. L. I. 580, III. 135 nn.
[1180]) Cf. S. A. 1736, 1740 nn.
[1181]) Cf. above, p. 105.
[1182]) Cf. e. g. P. L. I. 94, 181, 193, 196 nn.
[1183]) Cf. IV. 135, 153, 229, 264 nn.
[1184]) Cf. P. R. I. 169 n.
[1185]) S. A. 1020, 1730 nn.
[1186]) S. A. 1226, 1736 nn.
[1187]) Cf. S. A. 1323 n.
[1188]) Il P. 50 n. — the continuation and elaboration of a note by T. Warton.

various editors of Milton and Shakespeare, Milton's own prose & c. are examined for the illustration of the names of various kinds of actors, jugglers & c. enumerated in S. A. 1323 *et seq.*

As may be seen from the above, Todd is a very industrious follower of the line of research pursued by Warton. While he added much to the material of his subject he contributed little to its method, and must be classed rather among the useful than the great editors. What is unexpectedly seldom to be found, is the discovery and application of new leading principles in matters of literary interpretation.

CONCLUSION.

It might be profitable to add a few words emphasizing what the present writer regards as the main conclusions to be drawn from the matter presented in this book. The miscellaneous character of the material dealt with may have slightly obscured the logical structure of the whole.

The principal tendency directing the activities of Milton commentators during the period in question is the drift from a rather primitive dogmatism towards a close critical scrutiny of authentic facts. This is evident throughout the whole field of Milton research. The text, so badly treated by Bentley, is conscientiously compared by his successors with the original editions and MSS. Milton's spellings are gradually found to reveal the author's own phonetic intentions instead of being taken for a mere medley of odd deviations from the accepted norms. The peculiarities of the poet's language come to be regarded not as mere irregularities which have to be corrected as in Bentley's edition but as important clues to Milton's individual taste and style, and their connection with the language of Milton's predecessors and contemporaries is carefully examined. The petrified prosodical principles of classical scholarship, often applied to English verse without any feeling for the peculiarities of the mother-tongue, are little by little abandoned for a more flexible method. The apparent incongruities of Milton's versification are shown to express valuable shades of sense and emotion, and critics get accustomed to listening to the perceptions of their own ear instead of trusting to ready-made metrical dogma (cf. esp. the Richardsons, but at times even Bentley).

The same trend prevails in the handling of certain even more fundamental problems of a less technical type. The belief in classical and biblical authority, obscured by no doubts in Hume, and in many respects at its height in Bentley, is superseded by a more critical mentality. Bentley, who professes the tenets of a rationalist, narrow-minded classicism, declares everything not in keeping with these to be spurious and non-Miltonic. But the fanatic bluntness of his onesided yet trenchant comments is met by an equally consistent but broad-minded and critical attitude. The refined technique developed by classical scholarship is applied to a conscientious inquiry into the actual facts of the case. Since this inevitably involves some study of Bentley's doctrines, which happen to be the typical doctrines of that age, the very foundations of classicism are subjected to a damaging scrutiny. The Richardsons, who embrace the cause of individual genius, evince more enthusiasm than critical discipline, but their dogma, that of the independence of genius, induces them to study with unflagging care the idiosyncrasies of Milton's poetry, as far as their imperfect scholarship permits. Eccentricities of taste are not merely excused but even eulogized where they do not occur. Other commentators, *e. g.* Peck, though holding rather hazy theoretical principles, accumulate valuable authentic material, serving to show the setting as well as to elucidate the precise character of Milton's poetry. Bishop Newton's honest endeavour to find a reliable basis for his critical comments partly fails owing to certain shortcomings of his intellectual and emotional equipment. Clerical and classicist prejudices handicap his mind. In spite of his not inconsiderable learning, he misses the organic unity of Milton's work. Among his collaborators, Thyer excels in poetic sensitiveness. He succeeds in taking a closer view of the artistic character of Milton's poetry. Part of the reason for this is to be found in his relative freedom from theoretical preconceptions as well as in his practice of carefully observing his own literary impressions, even though they might clash with his theories. His typically 18th century definition of poetry as a means of instruction and easy pleasure does not prevent him from perceiving poetic qualities inconsistent with this formula. His adequate descriptions and analyses of these perceptions prove him to be a considerable critic.

The culmination and turning-point of Milton annotation during the period discussed is Warton's edition. His method is more consistently psychological, his erudition incomparably greater than Thyer's. Owing to his learning, which is particularly remarkable in the department of older English literature, and to his unusual poetic responsiveness, the tendency to see the author's point of view finds a fuller realization than in the case of any previous commentator. His grasp of the facts of Milton's personal life as well as of the setting of his poetry is exceptional. Hence his intimate understanding of the atmosphere of Milton's verse. He sees with surprising distinctness the significance of the non-classicist features in the poet's early manner.

His way of using the author's personality as a starting-point for his analyses enables him to do full justice to the compli-cated moods reflected in L'A l l e g r o and Il P e n s e r o s o. Mil-ton's poetry becomes much more intelligible by being regarded as a mirror of his mind — a mind whose mazes could hardly be disentangled without a competent knowledge of the mentality prevailing during the period which moulded the poet's early sensibility. Thus, not only the treatment of textual, biographical, historical or philological puzzles and literary sources but also the examination of the poet's mind and of the atmosphere of his works undergoes a radical reform in accordance with the general tend-ency towards a reliable, authentic basis of investigation. The inward and outward factors of Milton's poetic activities are stud-ied with unprecedented competence.

It is only natural that this development should have brought as a corollary a more adequate understanding of poetry in general. Milton's poetical practice was too many-sided and original to fit into the narrow frame of 18th century literary doctrinairianism. The critics felt it to be of exceptional value, and once its principles had been grasped, the exclusive authority of conventional doctrine became seriously endangered. Nowhere is this more obvious than in Warton's commentary — not even in the annotations of the Richardsons. The notes in Warton's edition point out unexpected poetic subtleties, which lead out of the world of reason and pro-portion into one abounding in strange, suggestive complexities of thought and emotion. The new subversive truths thus discovered prepare the way for the Revival of the Imagination.

Warton's successors add much that is useful and new, and surpass him in various special departments of their own, but they contribute few essential principles. Lofft knows more about phonetics, Dunster about matters of literary structure, Todd amasses an imposing amount of new historical, biographical and literary facts relating to the setting of Milton's poetry. All this, however, may hardly be regarded as much more than supplementary work. Todd's important edition once more proves the triumph of Warton's method — the method of careful, impartial analysis based on conscientiously collected, thoroughly sifted material and guided by that novel feature of the scholarship of those times, the sense of historic perspective.

APPENDIX I.

ON UNACKNOWLEDGED SIMILARITIES TO EARLIER COMMENTARIES IN NEWTON'S NOTES ON BOOK II OF "PARADISE LOST".

A.

SELECTION OF UNACKNOWLEDGED SIMILARITIES.

3 *n.*: The debt to Pearce seems to be much greater than Newton acknowledges. His remark that "the gorgeous east" is not mentioned in opposition to "Ormus and Ind" but because the choicest pearls and gold & *c.* are found in it, and the next but one sentence, stating that these pearls and gold are said to be showered upon the eastern kings because in those countries the principal share of property belongs to the rulers, are in part almost literally identical with Pearce's observations.

The reference to the classical use of "barbaricus" in connection with matters of luxury and splendour is found in Hume and Pearce. In Richardson's corresponding note, the idea that the "pearl and gold" are called barbaric because the Greeks and Romans thought all other nations barbarous, is stated in almost exactly the same words.

21 *n.*: Newton's distinction between the spelling of his own time, which he finds to be phonetic ("We spell it as we pronounce it *atchiev'd*") and Milton's etymological spelling "achiev'd" is new, but Hume already mentions both spellings as well as the derivation of "achiev'd" from the French ("Achiev'd, or Atchiev'd, of *Achever*, Fr. . . . . . . ").

47 *n.*: Hume, who is followed by Richardson, already identifies "He reck'd not" with "He made no account of", "to reck" with "to reckon", "thereafter" with "accordingly".

89 *n.*: Hume explains "exerceo" as meaning "to vex and trouble as well as to employ and busie". Newton uses literally the same expressions, only substituting "to practice and employ" for "to employ and busie".

138 *n.*: With some slight modifications the same as Bentley's note on II. 136.

151 *n.*: The defence of Milton's reading "[Devoid of . . .] motion" against Bentley's proposal to read "action" is the same as in Pearce. Both annotators argue that the power of motion *ipso facto* includes a power to act.

174 *n.*: Newton explains that by "his" in "His red right hand" "seems to have been meant *God*'s, who is mention'd so often in the course of the debate, that he might very well be understood without being nam'd".

3*

The Richardsons state much the same idea, but in a far terser form: "His; they knew who he meant without naming him. God's Hand...." (II. 174 *n.*).

220 *n.*: Newton's interpretation of "light" as an adjective synonymous with "easy" corresponds with Pearce's suggestion that Milton does not want to denote "the highest degree, but only something that, in comparison of what they suffer'd, might be call'd *mild* and *light*".

274 *n.*: The similarity in the drift of Mammon's and Belial's speeches is pointed out by Bentley (II. 274 *n.*). That Belial's idea is carried farther by Mammon, is shown in the corresponding note of the Richardsons.

294 *n.*: The varying pronunciation of names of the type Michael, Raphael (sometimes pronounced as disyllables, sometimes as trisyllables) which is pointed out here, was taken notice of by Bentley and Pearce (cf. above, chapter on Pearce p. 91).

305 *n.*: The retort to Bentley that "Majestick though in ruin" refers to "his face" and not to "Princely counsel" is the same as in Pearce's note.

309 *n.*: There is some similarity to this in the descriptive parts of Hume's picture of the heat and somnolence of noon in "great Continents". The parallel with Bentley is even more conspicuous. See Bentley: "For it was not the *Air*, that made the Silence and Stillness, but the *Hour*; when in hot Countries, the Sun shining fierce, both Men and Animals retire to Shade and Rest". Newton writes: "...*noon-time*, when in hot countries there is hardly a breath of wind stirring, and men and beasts, by reason of the intense heat, retire to shade and rest". Even the typical turn of phrase at the end has been repeated.

367 *n.*: Both Hume and Newton derive "puny" from "puis né" and intimate that Milton may have intended to suggest something of the French meaning of the word (Hume: "*Puisné*, born since, created long since us, Angelick Beings boasting Eternity"... Newton: "*puis né*, born since, created long after us").

434 *n.*: The reference to the promiscuous use of "convexum" and "concavum" in ancient poetry and some of the classical material adduced to illustrate this use are given by Hume.

512 *n.*: Newton: "A *globe* signifies here a battalion in circle surrounding him"... Richardson (II. 512 *n.*): "The Antients have call'd the Circle of Soldiers round the *Suggestum* from whence the Emperor Harrangu'd them a Globe".

513 *n.*: On "horrent". Richardson: "This Word sometimes means *Terrible*; but Here, as Rightly and much more Poetically *Bristled*; their Spears seem'd as the Bristles of an Enrag'd Wild Boar". Newton sees the possibility of a combination of the two senses but his note seems to contain verbal echoes of the above: "*Horrens* includes the idea both of terrible and prickly, set up like the bristles of a wild boar".

517 *n.*: Newton: "*Alchemy* is in short what is corruptly pronounc'd *Ockamy*, that is any mixed metal". Bentley's corresponding note begins: "There is a cheap Kitchin mix'd Metal for *Spoons, & c.* vulgarly call'd *Ockamie*, perhaps corruptly from Alchymie".

528 *n.*: Pearce's exposition of the situation is repeated almost word for word at the beginning of the note.

539 *n.*: Hume (II. 555 *n.*) dwells on the contrast between the reasoning and singing angels and the corresponding difference in their situations. Richardson's note on the present passage describes the author's different ways of representing the contemplative and the active spirits. Newton takes notice of these points. However, he adds new features and develops the whole into a skilful demonstration of the copious use here made of the device of contrast.

568 *n.*: Pearce already, like Newton, shows that the first editions have "obdured", not "obdurate", and refers to the occurrence of the former in P. L. VI. 785.

708 *n.*: The quotations from Virgil and Tasso, the identification of Ophiuchus with Anguitenens, the reference to the frequent mentions in poetry of the fearful effects of comets, eclipses, & c. are all found in Hume.

758 *n.*: Hume already suggests the parallel between Sin springing out of Satan's head and Wisdom or Minerva out of the head of Jupiter. The Richardsons mention Lucian's description of the ravishment of Minerva by Vulcan soon after her birth.

809 *n.*: Hume and Newton mention the same parallels but Newton tries to describe the difference between the attitude of the heathen deities in Homer and Virgil and that of the fallen angels, whereas Hume fails to make any attempt at such an analysis.

842 *n.*: Hume's note already contains the references to the old meaning of "búxom" and to the Spenserian passage alluded to by Newton (F. Q. I. XI. 37). Newton's additional exemplification of the word from Spenser's prose seems, however, to prove a comparatively intimate independent knowledge of the poet.

894 *n.*: The comparison of Milton's cosmology with that of the ancients — not in itself a strikingly original idea — is found in Hume, though in a more diffuse form. The reference to Orpheus in Newton's note corresponds with the quotation from Orpheus in Hume's remark. The exposition of Milton's own system of cosmology resembles that of the Richardsons, who in part mention the same Miltonic passages (II. 892 *n.*). The main new feature in Newton is his terser and more disciplined style.

927 *n.*: Hume calls attention to the usage of interchanging, in metaphorical speech, expressions for sailing and flying, and gives the same Virgilian illustrations as Newton. The Spenserian parallelism is found in Peck's note on this passage.

933 *n.*: The probable derivation of "pennon" from Lat. "penna" is shown in Hume's note.

941 *n.*: Newton indicates the similarities between the descriptions of Spenser's old dragon and Milton's Satan, referring to F. Q. I. XI. 8 — a passage which is in the closest neighbourhood of those alluded to in Peck's note on II. 927 (*viz.* F. Q. I. XI. 10 and 18), one of which is quoted by Newton (cf. above, on II. 927 *n.*). It may be conjectured that Peck's remark caused Newton to undertake further inquiries into the Spenserian passage.

965 *n.*: The references to Lucan, F. Q. IV. 2. 47 and I. 5. 22, Statius and Tasso are all found in Hume, those to F. Q. IV. 2. 47 and Lucan in Bentley also. The Richardsons hint in a rather general way that by "the dreaded name Of Demogorgon" Demogorgon himself is meant [it "very Poetically says *He* was there"]. Newton cites definite evidence to prove that such was the meaning of this periphrasis in classical literature — *i. e.* he shows that this is no chance individual way of expression but a traditional habit of style.

1017 *n.*: Hume already connects Milton's "justling Rocks" with the Greek Symplegades. His explanation is substantially the same as in Newton though the wording very closely resembles that of the Richardsons, who state the same idea as Hume.

Richardson: „they were so near to One Another that they seemed at a Distance to be but One, and Near to Open and give way, and then Close again, chiefly when the Ship vary'd its Course This way and That as Usual..."

Newton: "...they were so near, that at a distance they seemed to open and shut again, and justle one another, as the ship varied its course this way and that as usual".

The main difference is in the greater smoothness of Newton's style.

1053 *n.*: Pearce already suggests that "this pendent world" is the universe: "The sense is, This *pendant World* (seen far off v. 1047.) seem'd to be no bigger than a *Star of smallest magnitude*; nay not so large; it seem'd no bigger than such a *Star* appears to be, when it is *close by the Moon*; the superior Light of which makes any *Star* that happens to be very near her Disc, to seem exceedingly small and almost to disappear." See Newton's verbal repetitions of the preceding: ... "and *beheld far off* it [= this pendent world] appear'd in comparison with the empyreal Heaven no bigger than a *star of smallest magnitude*; nay not so large, it appear'd no bigger than such a star appears to be when it is *close by the moon*, the superior light whereof makes any star that happens to be near her disk, to seem exceedingly small and almost to disappear."

B.

The following list of literary parallels referred to both by Newton and Hume but not acknowledged by Newton to have been taken from the latter gives, first, the references to Newton, second, those to the parallelisms alluded to, and, third, those to the notes by Hume containing these parallels (Hu. = Hume).

II. 3: Æn. II. 504 — cf. Hu. II. 4 *n.*

II. 11: Coloss. I. 16 — cf. Hu. II. 11 *n.*

II. 227: quotation from Virgil ["Ignobile otium"] — cf. Hu. II. 227 *n.*

II. 254: quot. from. Persius — cf. Hu. II. 254 *n.*

II. 352: references to Virgil and Homer (in the case of Homer, to the same turn of speech though not to the same passage) — cf. corresponding note by Hume.

II. 432: quot. from Virgil — cf. Hu. II. 434 *n.*
II. 435: references to Virgil — cf. Hu. II. 435 *n.*
II. 489: the same Homeric features discussed as in Hu. II. 490 *n.*
'I. 513: quotations from Virgil — cf. Hu. II. 514 *n.*
II. 528: references to Virgilian descriptions of sports as in Hume, though only partly to the identical passages (cf. Hu. 532, 555 *nn.*).
II. 542: refer. to Ovid's "Metamorphoses" — cf. Hu. II. 543 *n.*
II. 577: Æn. VI. 438 — cf. Hu. II. 577 *n.*
Æn. VI. 107 — cf. Hu. II. 578 *n.*
Æn. VI. 550 — cf. Hu. II. 579 *n.*
Odyss. X. 513 — cf. Hu. II. 579 *n.*
Æn. VI. 714, IX. 355 — cf. Hu. II. 583 *n.*
II. 595: Virg. Georg. I. 93 — cf. Hu. II. 595 *n.*
Eccles. ch. 43 v. 20, 21 — cf. Hu. II. 595 *n.*
II. 628: Æn. VI. 287 — cf. Hu. II. 628 *n.*
II. 692: Revel. XII. 3, 4 — cf. Hu. II. 692 *n.*
II. 708: Æn. X. 272 — cf. Hu. II. 711 *n.*
II. 809: Æn. III. 375, IV. 614 — cf. Hu. II. 809 *n.*
II. 842: F. Q. I. 11, 37 — cf. Hu. II. 842 *n.*
II. 881: Æn. VI. 573 — cf. Hu. II. 881 *n.*
II. 894: Orpheus's Hymn to Night — cf. Hu. II. 894 *n.*
II. 904: Æn. IV. 42 — cf. Hu. II. 904 *n.*
II. 927: Æn. I. 300 — cf. Hu. II. 927 *n.*
II. 943: Lucan, Phars. III. 280 — Hu. II. 945 *n.*
II: 964: Lucan, Phars. VI. 744, Statius's Thebaid IV. 514, Tasso's Ger. Lib. XIII. 10, F. Q. I. V. 22, IV. II. 47 — cf. Hu. II. 965 *n.*
II. 965: Æn. VI. 273, & c. — cf. Hu. II. 967 *n.*

APPENDIX II.

The following prospectus of Newton's Milton was communicated to the author by Mr. H. E. B. Brett-Smith after the completion of the thesis. Its size is exactly that of Newton's first edition:

PROPOSALS
FOR
PRINTING *by* SUBSCRIPTION
a NEW EDITION *of*
MILTON'S PARADISE LOST.
With NOTES of VARIOUS AUTHORS.
By THOMAS NEWTON, D. D.
Rector of St. *Mary-le-bow, London.*

CONDITIONS.

I. THE Text will be correctly printed according to *Milton*'s own Editions, from which few Variations will be made, and those only such as shall be judged absolutely necessary.

II. To the Text will be subjoin'd large Notes Critical and Explanatory, not only the best of those which have been already publish'd, but likewise many others compiled by the Editor, or communicated by several learned Men.

III. A new Life of *Milton* will be prefix'd, and copious Indexes be added in the conclusion.

IV. There will be a new Set of Copper Plates, design'd by Mr. *Hayman,* and engrav'd by the best Masters.

V. This Work will make two handsome Volumes in *Quarto,* Royal Paper, and will be printed in the same Character as the Specimen annex'd.

VI. Every Subscriber to pay a Guinea at the time of subscribing, and half a Guinea upon the Delivery of the Books in Sheets.

VII. The Subscribers [*sic*] Names shall be printed.

VIII. The Subscription will be closed in *May,* at which time the Work shall be put to the Press, and be deliver'd to the Subscribers some time the Winter following.

Subscriptions are taken in by *J.* and *R. Tonson* and *S. Draper* in the *Strand,* where some of the Prints may be seen.

If any Gentleman has any Notes or Observations to communicate, the Favour will be thankfully acknowledg'd.

Note: p. 3 of Newton's first edition is subjoined as a specimen.

APPENDIX III.

SELECT LIST OF SOURCES.

This list does not claim to be complete. It includes a selection of what appeared to be helpful for the present thesis. As some knowledge of the personalities of the writers dealt with is often indispensable for a proper understanding of their critical attitudes, some general books and articles relating to them have been mentioned. With regard to materials concerning the commentaries themselves, greater completeness has been aimed at, but it has not been the object of the present writer to register every casual reference. As to periodical sources, no exhaustive inquiries were undertaken, but what has been mentioned should be in some way illuminating. Ordinary works of reference, such as the *Dictionary of National Biography*, the *Encyclopædia Britannica*, *Chambers and Thomson's Biographical Dictionary of Eminent Scotsmen*, *Chalmers's Biographical Dictionary*, *Baker's Biographica Dramatica*, *Nichols's Literary Anecdotes* and *Illustrations of Literature*, *Lowndes's Bibliographical Manual*, are mentioned only in special cases. The present list has to be regarded as a supplement to the data given in the text or in the foot-notes. This is why these data have here been mentioned only where the context seemed to make this particularly desirable. Of books and articles dealing with the whole range of the present subject, or with large parts of it, though only in a cursory way, special mention has to be made of the following: "STUDIES IN THE MILTON TRADITION BY JOHN WALTER GOOD [UNIVERSITY OF ILLINOIS STUDIES IN LANGUAGE AND LITERATURE VOL. I, NOS. 3. AND 4 AUGUST-NOVEMBER, 1915..... PUBLISHED BY THE UNIVERSITY OF ILLINOIS...]" 8⁰, pp. 310; "THE INFLUENCE OF MILTON ON ENGLISH POETRY BY RAYMOND DEXTER HAVENS OF THE UNIVERSITY OF ROCHESTER [device] CAMBRIDGE HARVARD UNIVERSITY PRESS LONDON: HUMPHREY MILFORD OXFORD UNIVERSITY PRESS 1922", 8⁰, pp. XII + 722; and Prof. Edward Dowden's essay on "Milton in the Eighteenth Century (1701—1750)", pp. 275—293 of the "Proceedings of the British Academy 1907—1908". The last edition of Dr. Bridges's study of Milton's prosody (Oxford 1921, 8⁰) has been very helpful. Professor R. P. Cowl's "Theory of Poetry in England" (Macmillan, 1914, 8⁰) suggested new tracks of reading.

Hume: See especially the prefaces to Newton's and Warton's editions of Milton; Blackwood's Magazine IV. p. 658 & c., containing some characterization of Hume's commentary in connection with an attack on

J. Callander of Craigforth's alleged plagiarisms from Hume; and, in
revision of, and partly as a retort to, the above article, a report on the
unpublished part of Callander's commentary in "Archaeologica Scotica:
or Transactions of the Society of Antiquaries of Scotland", vol. III, p. 83 & c.

Bentley: See contemporary sources mentioned in the second and
third chapters; Prof. Mackail's Warton Lecture (cf. above p. 50); J. H.
Monk's Life of Bentley, I and II editions, 1830 and 1833, cf. indexes to
these; R. C. Jebb's Bentley, English Men of Letters series, I ed. 1882;
Jacob Maehly, Richard Bentley, 1868; Biographia Britannica, I ed. 1748,
vol. II, p. 739 & c., esp. pp. 743—744, where the evidence as to Bentley's
early preoccupation with Milton annotation is queried; see also II ed. vol.
II, pp. 224 & c., esp. 244—245 (in ed. I probably by the Rev. Hinton,
acc. to p. VIII of the preface to vol. II of ed. II, whereas ed. II. vol. II. pp.
244 *et seq.* are apparently by the editor, A. Kippis, judging from the
signature K.); "Biographia Borealis; or Lives of Distinguished Northerns,
by Hartley Coleridge....LONDON....1833", 8⁰, (pp. 65 *et seq.* on Bentley,
p. 172 on his Milton); Thomas De Quincey's essay on Bentley, published as a
review of Monk's Life, ed. I, in Blackwood's Edinburgh Magazine, vol.
XXVIII, p. 437 *et seq.*, p. 644 *et seq.*, 1830, and accessible in De Quincey's
Works, *e. g.* Edinburgh 1862, vol. VI, pp. 35—180; Henry James Nicoll, Great
Scholars. Edinburgh 1880, 8⁰ (pp. 73 & c. on Bentley's Milton). "Richard
Bentley, D. D. A Bibliography of his Works and of All the Literature Called
Forth by his Acts or his Writings by A. I. Bartholomew, M. A., of Peterhouse,
Cambridge, With an Introduction and Chronological Table by J. W. Clark....
Cambridge.... 1908" [8⁰] enumerates some more critical articles & c. but
the rest seems less illuminating on the subject of the present treatise.

Pearce. See section of chap. III relating to him; especially Monk's
Bentley, cf. index; his life in: "A COMMENTARY, WITH NOTES, ON
THE FOUR EVANGELISTS AND THE ACTS OF THE APOSTLES,
....BY ZACHARY PEARCE, D. D. LATE LORD BISHOP OF ROCH-
ESTER. TO THE WHOLE IS PREFIXED, SOME ACCOUNT OF HIS
LORDSHIP'S MANUSCRIPTS, BY JOHN DERBY, A. M.......Vol. I.
LONDON... MDCCLXXVII" [4⁰]; Welch's Alumni Westmonasterienses,
pp. 253—255 (ed. 1852, as everywhere in this list).

The Richardsons. See the prefatory matter to their commentary;
Horace Walpole, Anecdotes of Painting in England, ed. 1888, vol. II. pp.
275—6 (Nichols's Literary Anecdotes, vol. II, 38 *et seq.* borrows from
Walpole); Samuel Redgrave's Dictionary of Artists of the English School,
ed. 1878; De Quincey in Tait's Edinburgh Magazine, vol. VI, p. 9, on
Richardson's portrait of Milton.

Peck. The principal account in Nichols's Illustrations of Literature,
I. 507.

J. Paterson, "Raymond de St. Maur", & c. See authorities in the
corresponding chapter.

T. Newton. Autobiography in vol. I, pp. 7—136 of: "THE WORKS
OF THE RIGHT REVEREND THOMAS NEWTON, D. D. Late LORD
BISHOP of BRISTOL, And DEAN of St. PAUL'S, LONDON. WITH
SOME ACCOUNT OF HIS LIFE, AND ANECDOTES of several of his

FRIENDS, WRITTEN BY HIMSELF. IN THREE VOLUMES...
LONDON... MDCCLXXXII", 4⁰. See esp. pp. 50 and 52 on his Milton.
Cf. also Welch's Alumni Westmonasterienses, pp. 285—7, and Boswell's
Johnson, ed. Birkbeck Hill, IV. 285—6, on Newton's lack of originality.
   Newton's Collaborators. See prefaces to Newton's own editions, as
well as to those of Todd and other Milton editors. An account of Meadow-
court's country life is found in pp. 246 & c. of the 2nd vol. of: "LETTERS
BY SEVERAL EMINENT PERSONS DECEASED. INCLUDING THE
CORRESPONDENCE OF JOHN HUGHES, ESQ...AND SEVERAL OF
HIS FRIENDS... LONDON... MDCCLXXII", 8⁰. Jortin's Milton notes are
dealt with in John Disney's "Memoirs of the Life and Writings of John
Jortin, D. D." 1792, 8⁰, pp. 25—27, and in W. Trollope's Life of Jortin,
ed. 1846, p. XXVIII of vol. I, but neither of these lives gives more than
an account of the opinions of others, mainly of those of Newton and Warton
in the prefaces to their editions. On Thyer's notes see mainly Newton's own
prefaces. The sources mentioned by the DNB. give some idea of his
character and activities. On William Benson see Nichols's Literary Anecdotes, cf. Index (Lit. An. II. 139, foot-note definitely ascribes to him the
"Letters on Poetical Translation"). On Warburton's Milton notes see p.
367 of: "THE LIFE OF WILLIAM WARBURTON, D. D. LORD BISHOP
OF GLOUCESTER FROM 1760 TO 1779: WITH REMARKS ON HIS
WORKS. BY THE REV. JOHN SELBY WATSON, M. A. ... LONDON
... 1863", 8⁰. A good general outline of Warburton's life and works is
found in pp. 119—176 of Mark Pattison's Essays, ed. Nettleship, Oxford
1889, 8⁰, vol. II. Pp. 202—3 of J. Savage's edition of "The History of
Taunton, in the County of Somerset", by Joshua Toulmin, D. D., contain
an account of J. Upton's life and writings.
   Period between Newton and Warton. Cf. above, authorities on Hume.
The report of the Society of Antiquaries of Scotland mentioned there
defends Callander's honesty and refers to Newton's similar failure to
acknowledge his literary debts. Letters by Callander are found in
"LETTERS FROM THOMAS PERCY, D. D. AFTERWARDS BISHOP
OF DROMORE, JOHN CALLANDER OF CRAIGFORTH, ESQ. DAVID
HERD, AND OTHERS, TO GEORGE PATON. EDINBURGH...
MDCCCXXX", 8⁰. The Johnson bibliography of W. P. Courtney and Prof.
D. Nichol Smith (ed. 1925, p. 136) mentions some attacks by Callander on
Johnson's Lives of the Poets. Periodical sources on some of the other
commentators of this period are referred to in the text of our chapter on
this period.
   Thomas Warton and his Collaborators. A copious bibliography is
given in: "THOMAS WARTON A BIOGRAPHICAL AND CRITICAL
STUDY BY CLARISSA RINAKER UNIVERSITY OF ILLINOIS"
("UNIVERSITY OF ILLINOIS STUDIES IN LANGUAGE AND LITER-
ATURE vol. II FEBRUARY, 1916 No. 1")) which is also valuable for
its critical analyses. There is much bibliographical material in: "THE
THREE WARTONS A Choice of their Verse EDITED WITH A NOTE
AND A SELECT BIBLIOGRAPHY BY ERIC PARTRIDGE LONDON
THE SCHOLARTIS PRESS... 1927". See also "The Critical Review"

354

of May 1785 (p. 321 *et seq.*, 421 *et seq.*), "The Monthly Review" vol. 79, pp. 4, 97, 342 (an appreciative review of the ed. of 1785; but Warton's hatred of Puritanism is censured and many details are queried), vol. 10 of the second series, p. 24 (on ed. 1791), "The Gentleman's Magazine" vol. LV, p. 416, where Warton's excessive habit of quotation, his remarks on Milton's "bad ear" & *c.* are criticized; p. 513 *ibid.* where Warton is defended against the author of the "Letter" to him, and vol. LVI p. 210 & *c.* containing a critical examination of Warton's condemnatory verdict on Milton's prose. "The Critical Review", vol. LX, pp. 159—160, censures the "Letter" as trifling and partial, whereas the "Monthly Review", vol. LXXIX, p. 380, advises Warton to consider every word of that publication.

Of recent general estimates, three Warton lectures deserve attention: "THOMAS WARTON BY W. P. KER. FELLOW OF THE ACADEMY" (pp. 349—359 of "PROCEEDINGS OF THE BRITISH ACADEMY 1909—1910"); "Two Pioneers of Romanticism: Joseph and Thomas Warton by Edmund Gosse, C. B., LL. D." ... [From the Proceedings of the British Academy, Vol. VII], 8⁰, pp. 19. See also quite particularly: "WARTON'S HISTORY OF ENGLISH POETRY by DAVID NICHOL SMITH Merton Professor of English Literature in the University of Oxford WARTON LECTURE ON ENGLISH POETRY BRITISH ACADEMY 1920 *Price 1s. 6d. net* FROM THE PROCEEDINGS OF THE BRITISH ACADEMY. VOLUME XV LONDON: HUMPHREY MILFORD AMEN HOUSE, E. C."

For an adequate understanding of Joseph Warton's critical views, including his views on Milton, his "Essay on the Genius and Writings of Pope", 1756, 8⁰, should be studied, beside the remarks in "The Adventurer" (see above p. 263 *n.*).

Further remarks on Milton by Hurd are found in pp. 289, 303, & *c.* (cf. index), and an observation on Pearce's notes in p. 288, of the Rev. Francis Kilvert's "Memoirs of the Life and Writings of the Right Rev. Richard Hurd, D. D., Lord Bishop of Worcester ... London ... 1860", 8⁰.

The Commentators between Warton and Todd. On the "Letter to the Rev. Mr. T. Warton", see preceding section. There is relatively little material on the other commentators. It is quite understandable that the slight contributions of D. Steel and Gillies should not have caused much discussion. Pp. 52, 348 of "THE NEW SUFFOLK GARLAND ... COLLECTED, COMPILED, AND EDITED BY JOHN GLYDE, JUN. ... IPSWICH ... 1866", 8⁰, give some idea of Lofft's life and character [1189]). On his edition cf. "Critical Review" 1793, p. 12—14 of vol. VII of 2nd series. On Dunster see mainly Nichols's Literary Anecdotes vol. IX, p. 236; this is the main source of The Gent. Mag. LXXXVI, pt. I, p. 472 (published a year later, in 1816; Lit. Anecd. vol. IX in 1815). Gent. Mag. 1796, Jan., pp. 47—48 gives a reasonable review of Dunster's edition, comparing his method and erudition with Warton's. Read also: "CONSIDERATIONS ON MILTON'S EARLY READING, AND THE PRIMA STAMINA OF HIS PARADISE

[1189]) See also Henry Crabb Robinson's "Diary, Reminiscences, and Correspondence", ed. 1872, 8⁰, 2 vols, cf. index to this publication.

LOST; TOGETHER WITH EXTRACTS FROM A POET OF THE SIX-
TEENTH CENTURY, IN A LETTER TO WILLIAM FALCONER, M.
D. FROM CHARLES DUNSTER, M. A. PRINTED BY AND FOR JOHN
NICHOLS, RED-LION PASSAGE, FLEET-STREET, LONDON; AND
SOLD BY R. H. EVANS..... 1800".
Todd and his edition. On Todd, see Gent. Mag. 1846 I. 322—324.
There also a characterization of his literary work describing him as
laborious and "in some sense, a learned man", but not poetical, and in his
life of Milton, so dry and dull as if he had been writing "the Life of
Milton's father, the scrivener". Illustr. of Lit. VI, p. 620, foot-note, is more
appreciative of Todd's literary pursuits, cf. also Illustr. of Lit. VII, pp. 54,
58, 59 and Lit. Anecdotes II. 53. On Todd's "Comus", cf. Gent. Mag.,
LXVIII, p. 703. See Gent. Mag. 1801, vol. LXXI, p. 1185—87, on his large
Milton edition. The Literary Gazette, 1846, pp. 88—89, which also gives
a short biographical account of Todd, praises his erudition and describes
him as "an invaluable living reference" to his contemporaries.

For data on B. Stillingfleet, see Gent. Mag. XLVI, pp. 162—4 and
XLVII, 440. Most of the material given there, and considerably more, is
incorporated in Lit. Anecdotes II, pp. 336—339. Boswell's Johnson, IV. 108
of Birkbeck Hill's edition, describes the rôle played by Stillingfleet in
literary society, and pp. 84—94 of "LITERARY LIFE AND SELECT
WORKS OF BENJAMIN STILLINGFLEET, SEVERAL OF WHICH
HAVE NEVER BEEN PUBLISHED BEFORE. ILLUSTRATED WITH
PLATES. VOL. I. LITERARY LIFE. LONDON ... 1811" (8⁰, pp.
256) deal with his Milton notes. These have been preserved in the British
Museum (1346 m. 16) in a copy of Bentley's Milton. Particularly the preface
is interesting as showing the way in which Stillingfleet proposed to deal
with Milton's language (he studies his idiomatic expressions, and recognizes
the enlivening effect of many licences) and metre (he has advanced beyond
the stage of Newton, as he acknowledges the pre-eminence of stress in
Milton's metrical system).

Some good remarks on Lord Monboddo's personality and writings are
found in the Hon. Alex. Fraser Tytler of Woodhouselee's "Memoirs of the
Life and Writings of the Honourable Henry Home of Kames", Edinburgh
1814, 8⁰, p. 250, and pp. 409—23 of vol. I of the „Memoirs of the Life, Writings, and Correspondence of William Smellie", ed. 1811, 8⁰, in 2 vols.

INDEX.

Note: This index does not include the appendixes.

sons 129; spirit, need of insight into, emphasized by Marchant 259.
Authorship, of Milton Restor'd and Bentley Depos'd 78 & seq., of The State of Innocence 175 & seq.
Auzout 85.
Bacon, Francis, 285.
Baker's Biographia Dramatica 182, 183.
Baptistes by George Buchanan 12, 140, 145.
Barcephas, Moses, 24.
Baron, Robert, 266.
Barret's Alvearie 318 n.
Basil, St., 25.
Baudelaire, Charles, 285.
Beaumont, Francis, 63.
Beaumont and Fletcher 207, 225, 274.
Beautiful simplicity valued by Todd 332.
Beauty, in landscapes, melancholy as an integral element of, Warton on, 289; emotional, 289; of discords, Dunster on, 327.
Benson, Auditor, 138.
Bentley 5, 9—10, 11, 15, 43, 48, 49, 50—99, 100, 107, 122, 128, 129, 130, 147, 147 n., 159, 185, 186, 194, 197, 202, 203, 205, 209, 211, 220, 225, 232, 240, 244, 247, 248, 249, 257, 264, 280, 281, 303, 334, 341, 342.
Bentley's Milton by J. W. Mackail 50 & seq. (cf. Mackail).
Bible (passim; esp. the following references to it), authority ascribed by Hume to, 29 & seq.; classical literature supposed by Hume to be based on, 30—31; Bentley's principle of adherence to, infraction of, 89; Pearce's knowledge of language of English, 91, 92; classics as derived from, Paterson and The State of Innocence on, 185; Newton expects poetry to conform to, 233; deviations from, condemned by Callander 256.
Biblical, sources of PL. studied by

Hume 8; erudition, Hume's, 24; learning, Bentley's, weak points in, 78; expressions, Peck's ignorance of, 161; knowledge, Newton's classical and, his chief assets 223; parallels, Gillies's, 297; learning, Dunster's copious application of his, 305; style, Dunster's respect for, 327; references in Todd 319.
Bindley, James, 324.
Biographical, documentation in Peck's notes 163; facts, Thyer sees connection between, and Milton's poetry 209; method applied by Newton 226—227, by Warton 270, 272—273, by Dunster 306; method combined by Dunster with artistic and psychological considerations 306—307.
Blackmore, Sir Richard, 262.
Blackwall, Anthony, author of Introduction to the Classics, 152 & seq.
Blackwood's Magazine on Callander 254.
Blank-verse, Milton's, the Richardsons on flexibility and intricacy of, 128.
Blemishes of Paradise Lost 268.
Bluntness of style, Monboddo opposed to, 329.
Boccaccio 7 n., 63.
Boiardo 214, 287 n., 328.
Boldness of Milton's style, Peck unaware of, 161.
Bona fides, Bentley's, and Mackail 52 & seq., 70 & seq., 74, 75.
Book of Wisdom 133.
Bowle 263, 275, 324, 327, 328, 333.
Boyd, The Rev. Henry, 323.
Boyle's Critical Dictionary 171.
Bridges, Dr. Robert, 66, 336 n.
Bridgewater, Duke of, 317, 320, Earl of, 315, 318.
Britannia's Pastorals 274.
Broken style, Bentley on, 62.
Buchanan, George, 12, 138, 140.

ley's appreciation of vigorous ruggedness of metre 66; theory of verse misapplied by Bentley 68; scholarship, weak points in Bentley's, 78; literature, Pearce's solid knowledge of, 90; allusions in Milton, Pearce on, 90; writers, authority attributed by Pearce to, 90; idioms examined by Hume and Pearce 91; pronunciation of proper names, Pearce on, 91; dramatic chorus, Pearce examining influence of style of, on Milton 91; scholarship, the elder Richardson's lack of, 101, and his son's competence in, 102, 123; idioms studied by the Richardsons 107; style, the Richardsons on Milton's wise utilization of the advantages of a, 110—111; grace, majesty and simplicity, and preferableness of classical languages for poetry, the Richardsons on, 111; flavour of Milton's language, the same on, 111; style and Christianity combining to make Milton incomparable, acc. to the same 111; literature, superiority of, the same on, 112; syntax in Milton, the same on, 125; models of Milton's verse examined by the same 129; idioms and shades of meaning studied by Peck 156; models, Peck on Milton's, 170; writers, Peck does not overrate the authority of, 170; literature, regarded by Paterson as based on Bible 170, and as inferior to Milton 186; editors: Paterson's commentary to rival the work of, 186, and Newton's edition imitating them 202; scholarship, Jortin's, 219; and biblical reading Newton's main assets 223; authority, Newton's excessive respect for, 228 & seq., 234; tradition, Newton's explanation of the value of, 229; drama and SA., Newton on, 237; preferred by Newton to modern

languages 239; allusions, uncommonness objected to by Newton except in, 240; writers, Callander's overvaluation of authority of, 255; traits in Milton, Callander on, 256; realia, Callander dealing with, 256; literature, Thomas Warton's familiarity with, 270; features mixed with elements of mediæval Romance, Warton on, 286; training reflected in Lofft's method 303; learning, Dunster's, 305; allusions and metre regarded by Dunster as mere decorations of poetry 309; idioms, Dunster on, 311; prosody, Dunster on Newton's misapplication of principles of, 312; references in Todd 319; parallelisms in Stillingfleet's notes 328; traits in Milton, Monboddo on, 329; idioms in Milton, Monboddo on 329.

Classicist, tendencies in Newton 15—16; standards, Bentley's rigorous, 54, their definition 55, their positive features 72; prejudices, Pearce's, 90; tendencies, Peck's, superimposed on Dryden's views regarding poetry 143; Meadowcourt as a, 221; regularity of metre, Sympson's dissatisfaction with, 223; Newton as a, 233, 245; tendencies in Callander 255; spirit opposed by Massey 261; superficiality disliked by Warton 263; moderation, Warton's occasional taste for, 282; perfection, Warton on lack of stimulus in cold, 293; tendencies, Dunster's, 306, 308—309, 325; style and romance, Todd on, 331.

Classification, rigorous, opposed by the Richardsons 110; Peck takes into account Milton's liberal views with regard to literary, 147; Newton's interest in, 236.

Claudian 35, 228.
The Cobler's Prophecie 338.
Colbatch, Dr., 79.

early English commentaries 7, read by Peck 12, 171, Todd dealing with, 20, effeminacy of, condemned by Hume 37, Bentley's references to, 63, the Richardsons dealing with, 104, 105, 107, 130—131, Thyer's knowledge of, 207, 208, 209 *n.*, 212, prolixity of, Thyer's objections to, 213—214, Newton's reading in, 225, fantastic style of, censured by Newton 234, Joseph Warton's knowledge of, 268, Thomas Warton's familiarity with, 270, affectation and pomp of, disliked by T. Warton 282, Dunster interested in, 305, 325, Todd's references to, 319, 333, 339, Bowle's and Stillingfleet's allusions to, 328; 2) sonnet, disciplined manner of, praised by Newton 234; 3) commentaries referred to by Speght 7; 4) expressions derived from the, in Milton: Hume 38—39, the Richardsons 123, Thyer 209.

Italianate smoothness, censured by Bentley 60 & *seq.*

Itinerarium, William of Worcester's, 279.

Jacobean period 34.

Jerome, St., 25.

Johnson, Dr. Samuel, 72, 128, 163, 270, 292, 298, 320, 323, 335, 336.

Jones, Inigo, 276.

Jones, The Rev. Morgan, 176.

Jonson, Ben, 151, 168, 223, 225, 234, 285, 319.

Jortin 205, 207, 219, 220, 277.

Josephus 29, 226.

J. T. 74.

Juvenal 163.

Keats, John, 285.

Kennet, Bishop, 93.

Ker, Prof. W. P., 143.

King, Edward, 288.

King Lear 166.

Kircher, Athanasius, 90, 91 *n.*

Knight, Richard Payne, An Ana-

lytical Inquiry into the Principles of Taste 330, 335.

Kubla Khan 294.

Kynaston, Sir Francis, 8.

Laing, Malcolm, 323.

L'Allegro 103, 145, 164, 170, 210, 212, 233, 268, 274, 276.

Landor, Walter Savage, 308.

Landscapes, Warton on melancholy as an integral element of beauty in, 289.

Laocoon, Lessing's, 86.

La Sylva de Medrano 328.

Latin = cf. Classical.

Latin, Dunster regards Milton's terseness as derived from the, 312.

Latin Poems, Milton's, 18, 103, 103 *n.*, 148, 207, 270, 275, 275 *n.*

Latinity, the Richardsons praising Milton's "pure L." 122.

Lauder 321.

Laurence, Archbishop, 337.

Lawes, Henry, 266, 273, 285, 313, 318.

Learned, expressions, Bentley's partiality for, 93; character of Milton's poetry making indispensable the study of his sources, acc. to the Richardsons 104.

Learning, range of, Hume's, 23, 24, 25, 26, 29, Bentley's, 63, Pearce's, 89, 90—91, the Richardsons', 101——102, 104—105, Peck's, 140, 165 & *seq.*, Paterson's, 176, 177, Thyer's, 208—209, Jortin's, 219, Meadowcourt's, 220, Newton's, 224 & *seq.*, Callander's, 257, Massey's 262, Jos. Warton's, 268 *n.*, T. Warton's, 269 & *seq.*, Lofft's, 299, Dunster's, 305, 324—325, Todd's, 318—319, 331, 334—335, Bowle's, 327—328, Stillingfleet's, 328; considered by the Richardsons less useful than critical intuition 106; and subject of PL. regarded by Paterson as its principal features 186; Milton's, overemphasized by Paterson 195, pre-

371

dropped by Hume with regard to Satan 44; views in Paterson & c. 185.

Morality, Thyer opposes Shaftesbury's description of, and reason as the principal qualities of Milton's poetry 212.

Moses Bar Cepha 337.

Mother Hubbard's Tale by Spenser 63.

Muiopotmos, Spenser's, 63.

Munster's Cosmographia 318 n.

Music, painting and poetry, the Richardsons on, 114; Peck on Milton's knowledge of, influencing his versification 163 & seq.

Mutschmann, H., 25.

Mystery and suggestion 292.

Mysticism combined with Puritanism, Warton on, 284.

Mythology (see Folklore), Hume fond of, 36; Callander's knowledge of, 255.

Names, proper, Spenser's, chosen to suit his characters 257.

National, subjects of Selden's annotations 8; setting of Milton's poetry, Peck on, 12.

Nativity Ode 63, 145, 292.

Nature, primitive, tendency of the Richardsons towards, 117; Jortin on, 219, 277; Warton's delight in, and knowledge of, 277 & seq.

Neologisms, Milton's, 39, 65, 155, 188, 240—241, 333.

New Memoirs of the Life and Poetical Works of Mr. John Milton by Francis Peck: 139 & seq., cf. also Peck.

Newton, Sir Isaac, 72, 166.

Newton, Bishop Thomas, 5, 9, 13, 14—16, 19, 20, 22 n., 25, 56, 96, 121, 129, 137, 157 n., 161, 171, 199 & seq., 254, 257 n., 258, 259, 260, 261, 270, 270 n., 278, 279, 281, 288, 295, 301, 304, 307, 309, 311, 312, 316, 322 n., 324, 327, 331, 334, 338, 342.

New Version of the Paradise Lost 183.

Night Thoughts, Young's, 190.

Non-literary aims of Selden's notes to Polyolbion 7.

Nonnus 219.

Observations on the Faery Queen by T. Warton 304.

Odyssey, Pope's, 192.

Of Verbal Criticism 76 n.

Onslow, Speaker, 138, 139, 204.

Oppian 125.

Organic whole, Warton's treatment of Milton's works as one, 289, 290.

Origenes 170.

Originality, the Richardsons on, and imagination 110; id. on, as opposed to authority 110; Warburton on, 218; Newton's lack of, 223; his respect for Milton's, 228; Todd's ideal of, 315; of opinion, lack of, in Todd 319, 332, 340.

Orpheus 25, 29.

Osborne, Thomas, 181.

Ossian 294.

Othello 104.

Ovid 46, 90, 186, 212, 231, 250, 259 n., 262, 275.

Owen, Galyn, 176.

Oxford, Gentleman of, (= George Smith Green) 183.

Oxford, Gentleman of, (= Semicolon) 77—81.

Oxford, Gentleman of, supposed author of The State of Innocence, 173 & seq.

Painter's point of view in the artistic analyses of the Richardsons 119; portrait p.'s attitude of the same 121.

Painting, the Richardsons on, music and poetry 114; and poetry, Dryden and Peck on, 143; ancient, studied by Warton 275.

Pallavicino 171.

Paracelsus 26.

Paradise Lost passim.

tence structure, their, 124; probability in PL., the Richardsons on,
137; features of style, Peck on, 160;
valuation of poetry, Thyer's, 214;
inquisitiveness, Newton usually
lacks, yet gives a p. explanation
of the value of classical tradition
229; method, Warton's, 18, 287
& seq., combined by Dunster with
æsthetic and biographical methods
306—307; and artistic considerations applied by Dunster to chronological problems 306; treatment
of style in Stillingfleet's notes,
rudiments of, 328.
Punctuation, Hume's misreading of
Milton's, 47; Bentley's treatment
of Milton's, 97, 98; Pearce on
Milton's, 97; Hawkey tries to restore Milton's original, 197; David
Steel on Milton's, 296; Lofft on,
298, 301, 302; Lofft's system of,
too elaborate and arbitrary 302.
Puns, Hume's dislike of, 40; Richardson's and Sir W. Raleigh's defence
of, 40.
Purchas, Samuel, 328.
Puritanism, of Milton's later poetry,
Warton opposed to, 277, 280; combined with mysticism, Warton on,
284; Warton's antagonism to,
attacked in Letter to Warton
295.
Pythagoras 185.
Pythagoreans 25.
Quantitative standards in Newton's
appreciation of poetry 310.
Quantity in verse, Newton's misapplication of principle of, 252.
Quinctilian 255.
Quotation (cf. Illustration), excessive, in Warton's edition attacked
in Letter to Warton 295.
Rabbinical, literature, 20, 24, 171;
expressions 30, in Milton, Todd
on, 337.
Raleigh, Sir Walter, the Elizabethan
29, 176, 255.

Raleigh, Sir Walter, Professor at
Oxford 40.
Randolph, Thomas, 319.
Raphael 111, 135.
Rapidity, of speech, and character,
the Richardsons on, 127.
Ratiocinative method of Addison's
essays 270.
Rationalism, Bentley's, 55, 72; Bentley's simplification and regulariza-
tion of Milton's syntax due to
his, 56 & seq.; often identifiable
with solid but misapplied commonsense 72; traces of, in Warton 283.
Reader's imagination, Richardson's
demand of stimulus for the, 109.
Realism, and humour appreciated
by the Richardsons 117—118; absurd, indulged in by them 135.
Reason, Thyer opposes Shaftesbury's description of, and morality as the principal qualities of
Milton's poetry 212.
Reason of Church Government 90,
131, 148.
Reed, Isaac, 324.
Relativity, of value of words recognized by Pearce 94; of characterization, Newton's occasional insight
into, 247—248.
Religion, and poetry, the Richardsons
on, 111; Thyer on poetry as a
vehicle of, 211; Dunster on imagination as means of advertizing,
308—309.
Religious, poet, Milton valued by
Hume as a, 31, 110; prejudices in
dealing with Milton's characters,
Hume's, 44; feeling, Hume's,
enables him to appreciate PL. 47;
considerations of the Richardsons
105; character of PL., their praise
of, 110, 111; poem, PL. as a, praised by Paterson 195; tendencies
in Milton, unorthodox, Thyer on,
213; prejudices: Warburton's, 216
& seq., Newton's, 227, 233, Heylin's, 228; views, Newton's, occa-

sionally liberal 228; conservatism, Warton's, 280; bias, Gillies's, 297; tendency, Dunster's, 305; poetry, Dunster on, 308—309, and on desirability of writing it in an austere style 309.

Remarks upon Milton's Paradise Lost... by W. Massey 259 & seq.

Renaissance, literary commentaries of the, influencing English scholarship 5.

Reni, Guido, 135.

Repetition, Hume opposed to Milton's, of whole lines 43; Bentley dislikes, 59 & seq.; Pearce on, combined with gradation 88; the same on variation in, 88; Peck on, 156, 159; Paterson on, 194; Newton's excessive dislike of, 232.

Republicanism, Warton opposed to Milton's, 280.

Retardation by emphasizing details 244.

Review of the Text of Milton's Paradise Lost by Pearce, cf. Pearce.

Rhetorical Grammar by J. Walker 19, 299, 301, 315 n.

Rhetorical tendency of Bentley's style 61.

Rhymes, condemned by Bentley 66; Peck on Milton's, 163 & seq.; id. opposed to Dryden's depreciation of Milton's, 163.

Rhythm, the Richardsons on, 144; they feel the connection between meaning and, 126; Peck on flexibility of, in Il P. and L'A. 164; Lofft on Milton's, 298, 302.

Richardson, Jonathan, Father and Son, 11, 12, 19, 40, 40 n., 43, 46, 100—138, 143, 144, 145, 146, 147, 148, 185, 194, 205, 207, 208 n., 228, 241, 257 n., 272, 280, 285, 299, 301, 313, 316, 333, 335, 339, 341, 342, 343, 344.

Riley 103.

Rimbaud 285.

Ritual, Warton fond of ancient ecclesiastical, 280.

Rivinus 171.

Robertson, Dr. James, 265.

Romance, Hume's style showing elements of, 28, 29, 36; condemned by Hume as fiction 36; Bentley's condemnation of, 71; Pearce's sympathy with vague suggestiveness and, 83; the Richardsons theoretically opposed to, 104, 112; Peck interested in, 166; Meadowcourt opposed to, 221; Newton objects to, 232, and to the style of, 240; mixture of mediæval, with classical features, Warton on, 286; and classicist style, mixture of, Todd on, 331.

Romantic Revival adumbrated in Milton annotation 10.

Romanticism, Walter Pater's definition of, 37; English, a period of unusual sensitiveness to physical impressions 285.

Rosa, Salvator, 304.

Rowland, Henry, author of Mona antiqua restaurata 167.

Rules, the Richardsons' dislike of fixed, 110; Thyer on, handicapping and excess dulling the mind 214.

Run-on lines, the Richardsons on, 128.

Rural — cf. Country-side.

Ruskin, John, 190.

Sackville, Thomas, 328.

St. Maur, Raymond de, i. e. Nicolas Francois Dupré de St. Maur, supposed and real, 13, 173 & seq., 204.

Samson Agonistes — cf. 'esp. 12, 16, 63, 74, 145, 146—147, 151, 216, 223, 226, 236, 277, 323.

Sandys's Ovid 260.

Sandys's Travels 26, 89.

Sannazaro 105.

Saurat, Denis, 64, 308.

Say, Samuel, 335.

Schmidt, Alexander, 336.

163 & *seq.*; Calton's liberality in matters of (admits hypercatalectic verses), opposed to Newton's conservatism in metrical problems 222; Sympson appreciates the variety of Milton's, contrasting it with classicist monotony 223; Newton on Milton's, 249—253; Warton does not understand the technique of Milton's, 287 *n.*; Lofft on, of PL. 301—308, Dunster on technique of, and classical allusions as mere decorations of poetry 309; Milton's, Dunster on, 312; Dunster shows Newton's misapplication of classical principles in dealing with Milton's, 312; of Comus, Todd on, 316; Stillingfleet on, 329; Todd's erudition in matters of, 335, his treatment of Milton's, 336.

Vida, Marco Girolamo, 105.

Vigour, Hume on Milton's passionate, restrained, 35; Bentley sides with, as opposed to sweet smoothness 60 & *seq.*, 65; austere, passionate, admired by Bentley 62; of Milton's manner emphasized by the Richardsons 108; in poetry valued by the same 113; Peck prefers false elegance to, 162; Milton's grim, Newton demands the conventional grand manner instead of, 232; preferred by Dunster to smoothness 327.

Virgil 23, 29, 30, 31, 32, 33, 34, 35, 41, 42, 45, 66, 83, 94, 103, 110, 111, 121, 125 *n.*, 127, 148, 170, 186, 217, 228, 229, 230, 231, 232, 250, 253, 256, 260.

Vision of Delight by Ben Jonson 285.

Visual effects, observed by Callander 256, David Steel on, 296.

Visualization, of Milton's scenes by Pearce 86; Pearce on need of, as opposed to vague generalization 86; the same on gradation of, 86; Pearce's, of nature more acute than Bentley's 98; the Richardson's, of Milton's scenes 119 & *seq.*; careful, helps them to explain Milton's language 125.

Vocabulary (cf. Classical, Italian, Hebrew, Rabbinical, Anglo-Saxon, Technical, Archaic, Neologisms, Dialect, Word-formation), Hume on Milton's, 38 & *seq.*; influence of literary associations on value of Milton's, 41 & *seq.*; shifting value of elements of, felt by Pearce 94; Milton's (the Richardsons) 123, (Peck) 154, (Paterson) 187 & *seq.*, (Newton) 240 & *seq.*, (Dodd) 263, (Warton) 278, (Letter to Warton) 296, (Dunster) 311, (Todd) 315, 316 & *seq.*, 333.

Voltaire, 145, 337.

Volubility, Warton condemns mere moralizing, 281.

Vossius, Isaac, 26, 252.

Vowels, Todd on retention and omission of, in Milton's spellings 315—316.

Walker, J., author of Rhetorical Grammar 19, 299, 301, 315 *n.*

Walker, Joseph Cooper, 324.

Walsh, Pope's letter to, 250.

Warburton, Bishop, 16, 145, 204, 205, 207, 215, 216—219, 234.

Warton, the Rev. John, 324.

Warton, Thomas, 5, 6, 12, 17—18, 19, 20, 161, 166, 169, 212, 214, 219, 224, 227 *n.*, 254, 266, 267—296, 303, 306, 307, 309, 311, 315, 317, 318, 323, 332, 334, 342—345.

Weaver's Discourse of Funeral Monuments 328.

Webb's Observations on Poetry and Musick 335.

Wesley, John, 17, 263—264.

William of Worcester 279.

Winckelmann 101 *n.*

Wolsey, Cavendish's Memoirs of, 339.

ERRATA.

P.	32		l.	30	Deites	read	Deities
„	53		„	17	as as	„	as a
„	54		„	34	brillant	„	brilliant
„	62		„	35	showed	„	shown
„	67		„	18	pronouced	„	pronounced
„	90		„	9	Gouvernment	„	Government
„	101		„	34	Wtnkelmann	„	Winckelmann
„	114		„	23	strinctly	„	strictly
„	152		„	4	tripp- ings	„	trip- pings
„	153		„	37	word-order.	„	word-order,
„	232		„	12	lessons	„	lessens
„	238		„	20	Miltons's	„	Milton's
„	255		„	23	imitition	„	imitation
„	277		„	17	pre-puritan	„	pre-Puritan
„	286		„	15	charaster	„	character
„	296		„	28	vishes	„	wishes
„	308		„	20	pœm	„	poem
„	350		„	8	a NEW EDITION	„	A NEW EDITION
„	368	2d col.	„	21	Lauder 321	„	Lauder 208, 321
„	378	1st col.	„	46	158—159	„	156—159